CHALLENGE OF EUROPE 1992

JOHN A. QUELCH
Harvard Business School

ROBERT D. BUZZELL
Harvard Business School

ERIC R. SALAMA
Henley Centre

 **Addison-Wesley Publishing Company**

READING, MASSACHUSETTS • MENLO PARK, CALIFORNIA
NEW YORK • DON MILLS, ONTARIO • WOKINGHAM, ENGLAND
AMSTERDAM • BONN • SYDNEY • SINGAPORE • TOKYO
MADRID • SAN JUAN

Library of Congress Cataloging-in-Publication Data

Quelch, John A.
   The marketing challenge of Europe 1992 / by John A. Quelch, Robert D. Buzzell, Eric R. Salama.
      p.   cm.
   Rev. ed. of: The marketing challenge of 1992, © 1990.
   Includes index.
   ISBN 0-201-56400-9
   1. Marketing—European Economic Community countries—Case studies.
   2. Corporations, Foreign—European Economic Community countries.
   3. Europe—Economic integration.   4. Europe 1992.   I. Buzzell, Robert D.
   (Robert Dow), 1933–   . II. Salama, Eric. III. Quelch, John A.
   Marketing challenge of 1992.   IV. Title.
   HF5415.12.E82Q45   1991
   337.1'42—dc20   90-37880
                                                                        CIP

BCDEFGHIJ–DO–943210

Preface

"1992" is the target date for achieving a truly unified market within the European Community. The original Common Market, formed by six nations in 1957, will not only have grown to include twelve member states, but will be free of almost all the remaining barriers to open internal trade. Most product standards will be harmonized, and the costly delays of goods in transit at border crossings will be eliminated. Regulations affecting services, such as banking and insurance, will also be harmonized.

The 1992 program of trade reforms has been designed to improve the efficiency of EC industries, stimulate economic growth, and thus make the EC economy more competitive in global markets. In designing the specific proposals that make up the program, the EC Commission relied on extensive economic and technical studies that were carried out by outside consultants and academic experts as well as the Commission's own staff. These studies show, for example, that completion of the integrated EC market may lead to an increase of as much as 7% in gross domestic product; a reduction of 5% in prices; and the creation of 5 million new jobs. But these benefits will only be realized, as one authority on European trade has put it, if "governments, business, and the other economic participants make full use of the opportunities presented."[1]

The 1992 reforms will create significant opportunities *and* threats for companies both within and outside the EC. The completion of the program will "change the rules of the competitive game" in the EC marketplace. To take advantage of the opportunities and guard against the threats, managers must reconsider all aspects of their strategies, including R&D, manufacturing, distribution, and marketing. While all of these strategic dimensions are important, we believe that effective marketing will be especially critical to competitive success in the post-1992 EC arena. The economic studies that have been prepared for the EC Commission largely ignore, or take for granted, the marketing processes by which many of the benefits of 1992 must be achieved. These processes include such things as the conception and development of new products

---

[1] Michael Calingaert, *The 1992 Challenge from Europe* (Washington, D.C.: National Planning Association, 1989), p. xiii.

suited to the "Euromarket"; rationalization of distribution systems; and the development of new advertising and promotion programs.

The marketing challenges of 1992 are explored in this book via five text chapters and nine case studies. In the text chapters we explore the nature of the 1992 reforms and their implications for marketing management. The case studies illustrate in much greater detail how companies in a variety of industries will be affected.

We hope that this study will be useful to practicing managers who are concerned about the implications of the 1992 program for their firms, and to government officials responsible for regulating competitive practices in the "New EC." The study is also intended to provide a basis for discussion in classes and seminars at business schools and management education programs.

We were fortunate to be able to assemble a truly multinational team to contribute materials for this book. Fifteen academics, management consultants and corporate executives from eleven countries in Europe, North America, Latin America, and Asia collaborated in this effort to provide a diversity of company, industry, and national perspectives on the impact of the EC 1992 program.

The Harvard Business School Division of Research supports much of the original development work represented in the materials included here. Our thanks to the Division and to Dean McArthur. Other research reported in this book was funded by the Henley Centre for Forecasting Ltd. and by five other academic institutions — H.E.C.–I.S.A. in France, Helsinki University of Technology in Finland, Keio Business School in Japan, Lovanium International Management Center in Belgium, and the Universidad Adolfo Ibanez in Chile.

Mary Fischer and Peter Hoenigsberg of Addison-Wesley worked closely with us in the planning and preparation of this volume. We appreciate their enthusiasm and their efforts to bring this book to market as quickly as possible. Our thanks also to Laurie Fitzgerald and Phyllis Sexton for their help in typing the manuscript, to Cynthia Mutti for her assistance in editing, and to Thelma Prince for her customary professionalism in proofreading.

While many people have helped us, we remain responsible for any errors or other shortcomings in this book. We nevertheless hope that both managers and students will find value in the information and insights presented here as they consider how to respond to the marketing challenges posed by the 1992 market integration program.

Boston	J.A.Q.
Boston	R.D.B.
London	E.R.S.

Contributors

ROBERT D. BUZZELL, Sebastian S. Kresge Professor of Business Administration, Graduate School of Business Administration, Harvard University, Boston, Massachusetts.

JEAN-FRANCIS HARRIS, Senior Associate, The MAC Group, Paris, France.

JONATHAN HIBBARD, PH.D. Candidate in Marketing, Graduate School of Management, Northwestern University, Evanston, Illinois.

TAMMY BUNN HILLER, PH.D. Candidate in Organization Behavior, Graduate School of Business Administration, University of North Carolina, Chapel Hill, North Carolina.

KYOICHI IKEO, Associate Professor, Graduate School of Business Administration, Keio University, Japan.

ERICH JOACHIMSTHALER, Associate Professor, IESE, Barcelona, Spain.

THOMAS KOLLOMEIER, D.B.A. Candidate in Marketing, IESE, Barcelona, Spain.

JEAN-JACQUES LAMBIN, Professor of Business Administration, Louvain University, and Dean of the Lovanium International Management Center, Belgium.

ILKKA LIPASTI, Research Associate, Helsinki University of Technology, Helsinki, Finland.

JON I. MARTINEZ, Assistant Professor of Marketing and International Management and Director of the Research Division, Universidad Adolfo Ibanez, Chile.

JOSE LUIS NUENO, D.B.A. Candidate in Marketing, Graduate School of Business Administration, Harvard University, Boston, Massachusetts.

JOHN C. PATTISON, Senior Vice President, Canadian Imperial Bank of Commerce, Toronto, Canada.

JOHN A. QUELCH, Professor of Business Administration, Graduate School of Business Administration, Harvard University, Boston, Massachusetts.

ERIC SALAMA, Associate Director, The Henley Centre for Forecasting Ltd., London, United Kingdom.

AIMEE STERN, Research Assistant, Graduate School of Business Admitistration, Harvard University, Boston, Massachusetts

ANDRE TORDJMAN, Associate Professor of Marketing, L'Ecole des Hautes Etudes Commerciales and Institut Superieur des Affaires, Jouy-en-Josas, France.

Contents

PART 1

Overview

CHAPTER 1

The Road to Market Integration

In Western Europe there are now only small countries — those that know it and those that don't know it yet.

> Theo Lefevre
> Prime Minister of Belgium, 1963.

Europe stands at the crossroads. We either go ahead — with resolution and determination — or we drop back into mediocrity.

> European Commission White Paper
> on the Completion of the Internal Market, 1985.

To anyone familiar with the history of the European Community (EC)[1] the transformation that has occurred over the past two years has been truly remarkable. The idea of unifying European markets by removing the remaining nontariff barriers to trade within the Community has caught the imagination of political decision makers and the business community. To a Community whose greatest problems were often the absence of a common objective, an unwillingness to cooperate, and a rhetoric that bore little relation to reality, the "1992" program has acted as a catalyst for thought and change.

At a political level, agreement has already been reached in areas where progress had been stalled for years, including politically sensitive areas such as freedom of movement for capital. Wider considerations such as the future of Europe, its role in the world, and the ability of its companies to compete on world markets are on the agenda in a way that they have not been for over 30 years. Sterile political arguments over the size of contributions to the EC budget and the cost of the Common Agricultural Policy have been replaced by debates over the nature of the Europe that should emerge in the 1990s. National governments

---

[1]The European Community (EC) refers to the bodies and institutions established by treaties in 1957 and 1951, specifically the European Economic Community and the European Coal and Steel Community. The European Commission is the executive arm of the European Economic Community. Its terms of reference were set out in the Treaty of Rome in 1957.

are not united in their objectives, but practical progress has been made and the nature of the political debate has shifted.

At a business level, companies are analyzing the impact that the proposals would have, reassessing the attractiveness to them of the European market, and determining their strategies accordingly. A sense of panic and opportunity has gripped companies across Europe. Companies outside Europe fear the creation of a "Fortress Europe" and the exclusion of foreign firms from a revitalized market. Questions about the appropriate organizational structure, where to locate, from whom to source, variations in consumer attitudes across Europe, and the desirability and ability to execute a common marketing program throughout Europe are no longer limited to a set of multinationals. These issues are being considered by small- and medium-sized companies as well.

REASONS FOR THE PROPOSALS AND THE POTENTIAL BENEFITS

The creation of the Economic Community in 1957 brought together countries that 15 years earlier had been fighting a world war. The EC was designed to ensure their permanent reconciliation. Much as Jean Monnet, the Community's founding father, had anticipated, the unification of Europe was coming in a thousand little steps. European-inspired legislation was common and extended into numerous areas. Removing the remaining nontariff barriers to trade was a natural extension of a process that began with the signing of the Treaty of Rome in 1957.

While the rationale for the EC's creation in 1957 was political, the impetus for the European Commission's proposals contained in the 1985 White Paper lay in Europe's poor economic performance. The recession initiated by the second oil shock of 1979 was one from which the United States and Japan emerged far more creditably than did European countries. Looking at a range of economic criteria, the EC underperformed relative to both the United States and Japan. During the early 1980s and compared with their American and Japanese counterparts, European economies grew less, created far fewer jobs, suffered higher inflation, and saw both investment and productivity grow by lesser amounts. European companies retained their share of intra-EC trade but were losing over 1% market share each year in external markets. The evidence for Europe's relative economic decline was overwhelming.

Even more worrisome was Europe's performance at a sector level, for this revealed a deep-seated structural weakness. As *Exhibit 1.1*

EXHIBIT 1.1 Changes in export market shares (%)

	1973–1968	1979–1973	1985–1979
Industry, total			
Europe 10[a]	−1.83%	+0.24%	−1.44%
United States	−3.63	−0.17	+0.73
Japan	+1.61	+0.85	+5.37
Strong demand			
Europe 10[a]	−3.43	−0.56	−2.54
United States	−4.96	+0.57	+1.24
Japan	+2.21	+0.70	+7.14
Moderate demand			
Europe 10[a]	−1.19	−0.29	−2.42
United States	−4.61	−0.99	+0.21
Japan	+2.85	+1.64	+5.66
Weak demand			
Europe 10[a]	−1.67	+1.70	+1.93
United States	−1.55	−0.09	−1.05
Japan	−0.71	−0.40	+1.85

Source: European Commission.
Note: Share of exports of a certain country or zone in total exports of all OECD countries (at current prices), including intra-EC trade.
[a]Europe 10 does not include Greece and Portugal and excludes intra-EC trade.

shows, the EC's share of export markets had been steadily declining. The decline during the first half of the 1980s was all the more distressing given that it occurred at a time when Europe's competitiveness had been boosted by a 35% fall in its effective exchange rate. More important than Europe's overall loss of share was the distribution of that loss. European companies maintained their market share of slow-growing markets but lost share in those markets that had been expanding most rapidly. For example, between 1979 and 1985, European companies:

Lost shares of 4.4% in electrical goods, 4.3% in cars, 2.3% in office machinery; and
Gained shares of 5.5% in leather and footwear goods, 4.9% in wood and furniture, and 3.9% in textiles and clothing.

In other words and in complete contrast to Japan, Europe was failing in the industries of the future, in key areas such as information technology, electrical and office equipment, and telecommunications. Interestingly and importantly in view of the proposals yet to come, Europe's performance was best in those areas where research and development was relatively unimportant and where economies of scale could often be realized (at least in production terms) at the national market level (for example, food, drink, tobacco, textiles, clothing, and building materials). This gave credence to the view that it was the inability to exploit production-led economies of scale in the higher technology sectors that was responsible for the poor performance of European companies. Community-wide technology programs were initiated (see *Appendix A*), but their overall value was small and more structural changes were required.

Acknowledging Europe's poor economic performance and the threats from the United States and Japan was not new. After all, it had been central to the argument put forward by Jean-Jacques Servan-Schrieber as far back as 1967 in his best selling book, *The American Challenge*.[2] In it he warned of a takeover of the European market by giant American multinationals and called for Europe-wide companies to concentrate on high-technology industries within the context of a common industrial policy.

What was novel about the early 1980s was the identification of non-tariff barriers to trade and the fragmentation of European markets as a cause of that poor economic performance. For years companies operating in Europe had faced a series of individual country rules, which had left the market fragmented and discouraged many from looking to markets outside their own national boundaries. Banks and insurance companies had to set up an office in each country in order to sell financial services to their consumers; food manufacturers and retailers faced a bewildering variation in standards and regulations relating to the ingredients that they could use and the way in which they could use them; telecommunications companies found their way into foreign markets blocked by discretionary public procurement rules; and pharmaceutical companies found themselves having to establish plants throughout Europe, most of them working below capacity, to ensure that their drugs were designated as reimbursable by national health services.

Academics and industrialists began to identify these barriers as significant. A report written by Albert and Ball and presented to the European Parliament in 1983 sought to identify the factors contributing to Europe's economic stagnation.[3] The report laid most of the blame on well-documented economic factors — wage rigidity, low company profits, a lack of investment, a reliance on external energy sources, the ab-

---

[2]J. J. Servan-Shrieber, *The American Challenge* (New York: Avon, 1969).

[3]M. Albert and R. J. Ball, *Towards European Economic Recovery,* European Parliament Working Document, August 31, 1983.

sence of monetary and exchange-rate stability in an increasingly interdependent world, and the unwillingness of governments to coordinate their economic policies, as evidenced in the Mitterand government's failed experiment in "go-it-alone" growth.

The report also criticized what it termed "non-Europe." It cited examples of differences in television and telephone standards, the difficulties in merging video recorder producers as a way of competing with the Japanese, and the duplication of research into high-speed trains, and it estimated their overall cost at over 2% of gross domestic product (GDP). The report called for common technical standards and an opening up of public sector contracts to competition from EC firms. The academics' cause was boosted by a series of calls in the early 1980s by leading industrialists for standardization and an end to national government discrimination.

Other factors were important in promoting the idea of a unified market — notably the sense that individuals were by no means enjoying the benefits envisaged at the EC's outset. They faced inconveniences (e.g., passport control, changing currencies, not enjoying as wide a choice of goods and services) which were in some way incompatible with the idea of a European Community. Outrageous stories about individuals being held up at frontiers and being unable to cross frontiers with their musical instruments or their electrical equipment stuck in the mind. As Jacques Delors, president of the Commission, put it in January 1985:

> We would like to see the people of Europe . . . enjoying the daily experience of a tangible Europe, a real Community where travel, communication and trade are possible without any hindrance.[4]

The economic imperative remained the overwhelming imperative, however, and formed the basis of the Commission's own White Paper on the completion of the Internal Market. As Lord Cockfield, architect of the 1992 program, stated later:

> We have been losing ground compared with our major competitors in world markets. This comes out very clearly if you look at the major indicators of economic progress. . . . The fragmentation of the European Market into twelve penny packets is not the only reason for this indifferent performance. But it is one of the major reasons. It means that we impose on ourselves quite unnecessary costs in complying with frontiers and frontier controls; we deny ourselves the economies of scale that would flow from being able to manufacture and market on the basis of a market of 320 million consumers.[5]

---

[4]Jacques Delors to European Parliament, January 14, 1985.

[5]Speech by Lord Cockfield to the Confederation of British Industry, March 3, 1988.

EXHIBIT 1.2 Comparative demographic and economic data for the 12 EC member countries

	Population (millions, 1987)	GDP[a] ($ billions, 1987)	GDP per head ($, 1987)	Exports to EC ($ billions, 1988)	Exports to non-EC ($ billions, 1988)
Belgium	10	$ 117	$11,802	$ 68.3	$ 23.6
Denmark	5	69	13,329	13.4	13.7
France	56	712	12,803	99.7	62.0
Germany	61	815	13,323	176.0	147.3
Greece	10	64	6,363	4.4	2.2
Italy	57	703	12,254	73.9	55.2
Ireland	4	27	7,541	13.9	4.8
Luxembourg	0.5	6	14,705	77.0[b]	26.1[b]
Netherlands	15	180	12,252		
Portugal	10	61	6,297	7.7	3.0
Spain	39	337	8,681	26.4	13.8
United Kingdom	57	703	12,340	73.0	72.0
Total EC	325	3794	11,729	633.7	423.7
United States	244	4473	18,338	75.9	244.5
Japan	122	1610	13,182	47.2	217.8

Source: Organization for Economic Cooperation and Development.
[a]GDP calculated at OECD purchasing power parity rates.
[b]Luxembourg figures are included with Belgium.

The economic rationale was clear. European companies were able to compete successfully in low-tech sectors where economies of scale could be exploited in a national context. But because of nontariff barriers that fragmented the market, European companies were unable to reap the advantages available to their American and Japanese counterparts in other sectors. For the sectors where exploitation of economies of scale demanded a large market, success could only come by making available to companies a unified market as big, in terms of size and population, as those of the United States and Japan. As *Exhibit 1.2* makes clear, a unified Europe could offer such a market.

A quantification of the benefits that such unification could bring was provided by the Cecchini Report,[6] commissioned by the EC and pub-

---

[6]Cecchini Report, *The Cost of Non-Europe,* European Commission, 1988.

lished in 1988, three years after the 1992 program was first launched. The abolition of frontier controls, opening up of public procurement contracts, liberalization of financial services, and supply-side effects resulting from the actions taken by firms facing increased competition would, according to the report, lower costs and prices, stimulate investment, and improve competitiveness. *Exhibit 1.3* illustrates the means by which such effects were to be realized.

Removal of some barriers — for example, frontier controls — would result in immediate cost falls and a subsequent mix of higher profits and lower prices. The removal of some of the other barriers — public procurement rules, for example — would open up the market to greater competition. Increased competition would improve efficiency and provide the impetus for industry restructuring and a fuller exploitation of the potential economies of scale available at a Europe-wide level. Subsequently, lower prices would boost demand and allow further exploitation of scale economies, while improved competitiveness would boost market share and lead to an improvement in the EC's overall trade balance. The overall effect once all of the mechanisms had worked through would be to raise growth by 5%, reduce prices by 6%, create 1.8 million new jobs, and improve the external balance by 1%.

Two elements are crucial to an understanding of the process. First, it is essentially a supply-side-led gain. The improvements in performance would result from a response by companies reacting to changes in costs and increased competition. The increase in demand that is assumed to occur is important but is contingent on prices falling as a result of both lower immediate costs and the subsequent effects of greater competition, restructuring, and the exploitation of economies of scale. The supply-led nature of the changes is not always appreciated. A survey of CEOs revealed that 50% of them thought that the greatest benefits of 1992 would be either higher growth in the EC or being able to exploit a larger home market.[7] Neither is inevitable.

The second crucial element is that few of the gains are immediate or direct. One could think of the sources of the potential gains falling into five categories, only the first of which could be thought of as immediate or not contingent on subsequent company action:

1. Lower costs due to the elimination of frontier controls and the simplification of administrative procedures.
2. Lower costs and improved efficiency due to increased competition.

[7]"1992 Harmonisation: A Survey of Chief Executives," Booz, Allen and Hamilton, 1988.

EXHIBIT 1.3 Microeconomic effects triggered by EC market integration

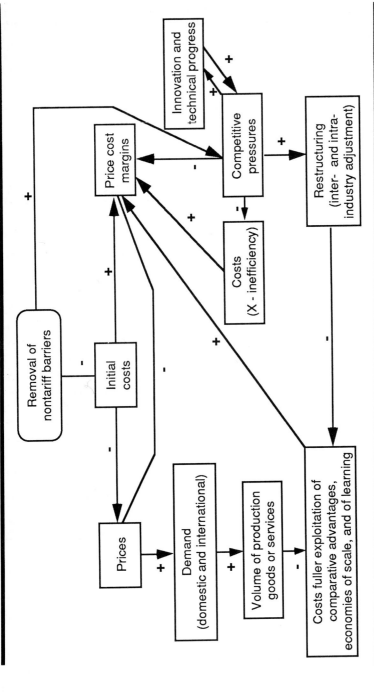

Source: European Commission.

Note: + = increase; − = decrease.

EXHIBIT 1.4 Potential gains in economic welfare

	ECU (billions)	GDP (%)
Removal of trade barriers	8–9	0.2–0.3%
Removal of trade barriers that hinder market entrants and restrict competition	57–71	2.0–2.4
Gains from exploiting economies of scale, including long-run gains through restructuring	max 61	max 2.1
Efficiency gains through intensified competition	max 46	max 1.6
Total for sample	127–187	4.3–6.4
Total for EC at 1988 prices	174–258	4.3–6.4%

Source: Cecchini Report, *The Cost of Non-Europe*, European Commission, 1988.

3. Lower costs due to improved exploitation of economies of scale.
4. Reallocation of resources and new patterns of competition, leading to a truer exploitation of comparative advantage.
5. Increased innovation and dynamism as a result of liberalization, freer competition, increased cross-border business, and so forth.

The bulk of the gains are assumed to result from the removal of the barriers providing a dynamic impetus (see *Exhibits 1.4* and *1.5*).

While the rationale for the EC's proposals was clearly economic, the political impetus that lay behind the widespread acceptance of the program cannot be ignored. Europe found itself during the early 1980s faced with a United States president whom it distrusted. Additionally, relations within the Atlantic Alliance were strained over a range of is-

EXHIBIT 1.5 Macroeconomic consequences of integration

	Customs formalities	Public procurement	Financial services	Supply side	Total
GDP (%)	0.4	0.5	1.5	2.1	4.5
Consumer prices (%)	−1.0	−1.4	−1.4	−2.3	−6.1
Employment (000)	200	350	400	850	1800
External balance (% of GDP)	0.2	0.1	0.3	0.4	1.0

Source: Cecchini Report, *The Cost of Non-Europe*, European Commission, 1988.

sues: arms control, the deployment of Cruise and Pershing missiles, the development of the Strategic Defense Initiative, the Siberian gas pipeline, and the imposition of martial law in Poland. There was also a growing feeling of impotence over its inability to make its voice heard on issues such as South Africa and the Middle East.

Europe was far from united in its attitude toward many of these questions. Political and defense cooperation in Europe was complicated by historical factors, a wide divergence in the perceptions of national interests, Ireland's neutrality, and the lukewarm positions of France and Greece toward NATO. Europe was still a long way away from the "European pillar" envisaged by John F. Kennedy in the early 1960s. Aside from the defense questions, there were and continue to be differences in perceptions of national interests, not least as a result of Germany's special position in Europe and what Mrs. Thatcher believed to be her "special relationship" with the United States generally and former President Ronald Reagan in particular.

Nevertheless, the belief that a distinct European interest existed and should be nurtured grew. In economic terms this sentiment surfaced toward the end of 1985, with the resignation of a senior British cabinet minister over the government's unwillingness to intervene in favor of the European option, when rival bids were being made by Sikorsky of the United States and a Franco-Italian-British consortium for Westland, an ailing U.K. helicopter manufacturer. Debate over national interests versus European interests intensified during the 1989 European elections, ostensibly over the Delors Committee's recommendations on monetary and economic union,[8] though in truth more as a result of having to come to an understanding over how Europe should develop.

There was a simpler and more pragmatic reason behind the conversion to the importance of the Internal Market. European ministers found it hard to agree about anything else. They had markedly different attitudes toward the Common Agricultural Policy, spending on regional and social funds, social policies such as worker information and participation, and most important, economic priorities. Coordinating economic policies or research and development work was something that was hard to contemplate — though a degree of coordination has implicitly taken place through the full membership of all countries except for the United Kingdom in the European Monetary System, which limited the degree of volatility in cross-EC exchange rates. Amidst this disunity

---

[8]Committee for the Study of Economic and Monetary Union, chaired by Jacques Delors, Brussels, Belgium, 1989.

appeared the idea of the Internal Market — a visionary idea that conformed to the EC's founding ideals and whose logic was such that governments would find it hard to object to.

Important in this respect was the acquiescence of the political Left in Europe. Although the 1992 program was framed as and inspired by a free market philosophy, the European ideal was one that united both the Right and Left in Europe. With the exception of the United Kingdom, the Left saw the unification of Europe as a positive step in the pursuit of social democracy. In part this was a reaction to the policies being pursued at the time by the center-right governments that dominated Europe during the mid-1980s. Cooperation on a European scale was seen as a way of circumventing the policies of people such as Mrs. Thatcher and Chancellor Kohl. But it was more than simply a tactic. The dream of a unified Europe struck a chord with many Europeans. Some on the Left viewed unification as important a creed as the primacy of the market was to those on the Right. The Left and the trade unions may not have been able to shape the way in which the Internal Market developed, but their support more than facilitated the adoption of the program at a time when political opposition to it may have killed it.

It was not a coincidence that the 1992 program, when first published, attracted little attention in the Commission or among national governments or businesses. There were more pressing concerns — the terms of Spain and Portugal's accession to the Community and the long-standing problems over the level of contributions to the EC budget. It was only after these issues had been resolved in 1986 and 1987 that the EC found itself turning to the idea of the Internal Market as the next goal to be pursued. Indeed, it is interesting to note that the primacy of the Internal Market as *the* objective to be pursued did not emerge in speeches and statements by Commission leaders until well into 1987, almost two years after the original program was published.

The importance of the bureaucracy (in the form of the Commission) in promoting the program, keeping it alive, and extending its scope should not be underestimated. A long-term goal was attractive to the talented people staffing the Commission. It was certainly more attractive than having to spend all night drafting communiqués about farm prices. The Commission contained powerful figures in the persons of Jacques Delors, Peter Sutherland, and Lord Cockfield, whose determination, single mindedness, and willingness to use their Treaty powers to the full were crucial in elevating the program to center stage. Indeed, by 1988 the Commission was wholly preoccupied with the Internal Market, to the virtual exclusion of everything else.

WHAT IS THE INTERNAL MARKET?

According to the Single European Act,[9] the Internal Market, which would evolve progressively during the period ending December 31, 1992, was to be

> *an area without internal frontiers in which the free movement of goods, persons, services and capital is ensured.*

The closest the EC has come to defining this "area without internal frontiers" is in the White Paper that it published in 1985.[10] According to the White Paper, the goals called for "the creation of a growing unified market that utilizes to the full the resources available to it" — hardly an inspiring vision or a blueprint for action. The White Paper contained 300 measures, which, in the opinion of the Commission, "are directly necessary to achieve a single integrated market embracing the 320 million people of the enlarged Community." The White Paper also set out a detailed timetable for submission of the proposals, national government agreement to them, and their introduction into law.

Significantly, the Internal Market referred to in the White Paper was all-encompassing. It covered goods as well as persons, services, and capital. Indeed, what was impressive about the White Paper was that it was comprehensive and went beyond the idea of freedom of movement for goods, notably in its coverage of financial services and the freedom of movement of individuals.

In some ways the Internal Market envisaged an "Americanization" of Europe, in that a company could produce a good in one member state and sell and market it throughout the EC. In important respects, though, it went beyond attempting to replicate the United States — notably in seeking to approximate taxation and remove the barriers to trade in financial services, which in the United States are enshrined in the Glass-Steagall and other Acts. In other respects it was less ambitious. Until the publication of the Delors Committee Report in 1989, little was said about the creation of common monetary and economic instruments.

There were disagreements over the need for some of the proposals contained in the White Paper. Each country was unhappy about those

---

[9]"Single European Act," *Bulletin of the European Communities*, Supplement, February 1986.

[10]*Completing the Internal Market*, White Paper from the Commission to the European Council, June 1985.

proposals that were seen as an infringement of sovereignty or that would cause economic or political disruption. Even more fundamental was a dispute that existed over whether the Commission's proposals as set out in the White Paper were the sole steps needed to create a unified market or whether a true Internal Market required a more far-reaching approximation of the business environment.

Beyond the simple rhetoric, there was no agreement as to what the Internal Market should entail. There were conflicting views over the priorities that were to be pursued as well as the features that should characterize a unified European market. There were differences over the need for and desirability of individual measures such as a common currency, a European central bank, a minimum withholding tax on foreign resident investments, and the extent to which worker rights to information and consultation should be made statutory. None of these issues had been discussed in the 1985 White Paper but rather emerged as discussion over the nature of the Community evolved. There were also differences in outlook — for example, over the extent to which the benefits of the Internal Market should be reserved for European-based companies and the extent to which the consumer's interest in competition should be sacrificed to a wider need for large European companies capable of competing in global markets.

Put simply, who was the 1992 program designed to help — European producers or European consumers? The former would point toward protectionism by those less than supremely confident in their own industries; the latter, to open competition. The absence of a strong U.S.-style consumer movement has left Europe traditionally orientated toward serving the interests of the producers. Should this be reflected in the 1992 program? This was not an academic question but one that would need to be answered in virtually all of the Commission's proposals, notably those involving public procurement and merger policy.

That such differences exist should come as no surprise. Despite the progress that has been made, there has not been a sudden infusion of altruism into the Community's decision-making process. Company and national self-interests are still the key driving forces. Variations in objectives and priorities simply reflect the fact that the EC is composed of 12 sovereign states and thousands of companies with markedly different perceptions of their self-interests. These differences in priorities and perceptions and the way in which they are reconciled (if they are) will determine the shape of the European market in the 1990s and beyond. We will return to some of the key differences later, but for now we concentrate on the core of the 1992 program — that contained in the White Paper.

TRADE BARRIERS AND THE IMPACT OF THEIR REMOVAL

Three types of trade barriers, with examples of each, were identified by the Commission in the White Paper:

1. Physical
     Frontier controls
     Veterinary and plant health controls
     Control of individuals including customs posts
2. Technical
     Standards and regulations
     Discretionary public procurement
     Restrictions on the movement of individuals and the professions
     Restrictions on financial services
     Restrictions on transportation services
     Restrictions on new technologies
     Capital controls
     Differences in company law, intellectual and industrial property
       law, and taxation law
3. Fiscal
     Differences in value-added tax (VAT) rates and the goods to which
       they apply
     Differences in rates of excise duties and the goods to which they
       apply

Exhibit 1.6 is a simplified illustration of the relationship between markets and barriers. While it does not provide an exhaustive list of the barriers identified by the Commission by sector, it does give a flavor of the areas being tackled by the Commission.

The barriers to trade were symbolic as well as practical. Much of the value in their removal lay in making companies and individuals *think* European. The proposed removal of frontier controls was perhaps the best example of this. The desire to remove the frontier controls was partly a result of the costs they imposed on businesses, as anyone who has watched the miles of trucks lined up waiting in the passes leading into and out of Italy will appreciate. More important, frontier controls were the most visible sign of a divided Europe. Their cost went far beyond the cost of the time involved waiting at the frontiers. It extended into inhibiting individuals and companies from thinking about Europe as a single market. Similarly, the ability to live and work in another EC state would arguably have more value at a symbolic level than it would in promoting greater economic efficiency.

This symbolism was also evident in the most controversial of the proposals — those on taxation. The proposals called for the approxi-

EXHIBIT 1.6 Examples of barriers to trade identified by the EC

Products	Services	Persons and labor	Capital
Frontier controls and administrative barriers	National regulations	Frontier controls	Exchange controls
National standards and regulations	Discretionary public procurement	Residency requirements	Nontransferability of securities
Differing rates of indirect taxation	Licensing and cross-border restrictions for banks and insurance	National qualifications and diplomas	
Discretionary public procurement	Quotas on road haulage		
State aids and subsidies	Price, market share, and access restrictions in air transport		
National patents	Restrictions on capital movements		
Monopolistic practices			

mation of value-added taxes into two bands — a standard 14–20% band and a reduced band for essential goods such as foodstuffs and pharmaceuticals of 4–9% — and the setting of a single rate of excise duties for goods such as alcohol and tobacco. The proposals were resisted by all of the member states except for the Benelux countries, both for the highly visible economic effect that they would have and because of the fear of allowing the Commission to encroach on the subject of taxation, which remained at the core of the idea of national sovereignty.

Additionally, most economists would agree that differences in rates of indirect taxation do not discriminate between domestic and foreign firms and that consequently they are not a barrier to trade. Sales taxes vary across the United States with a minimum disruption to trade. The rate at which indirect taxation is levied in the EC on a good or service depends on where that good or service is consumed, not on where it was produced. To give an example, a slice of bacon sold in Denmark will currently incur 22% VAT irrespective of whether it was produced domestically or imported from the United Kingdom where bacon attracts no VAT whatsoever. If the ex-factory price (including transport and distribution costs) of the Danish and U.K. bacon is identical, so will be the price to the consumer in Denmark. The different rates of VAT do not directly discriminate against either the Danish or the U.K. producer.

Yet despite the political unpopularity and the economic arguments over indirect tax rates, the Commission went to great lengths to stress their centrality to the whole process. Indeed, Lord Cockfield went as far as to say:

> *Fiscal approximation is an essential and integral element in the Programme. No way can one complete the internal market unless there is a substantial measure of approximation of indirect taxes.*[11]

The real reason behind the Commission's insistence that indirect tax rates be approximated lay in its desire to remove frontier controls and its worry that governments might resist the proposal if a degree of price convergence did not take place across Europe. The Commission was worried that if consumers were able to cross frontiers freely, without inspection, it might result in cross-border shopping for selected goods on a grand scale. And if that was a serious prospect, it would inhibit national governments from removing all frontier controls.

Significantly, evidence emerged in early 1989 that frontier controls would be abolished, at least in a selection of core countries, through implementation of the Schengen Agreement.[12] This revelation, along with the Commission's desire to avoid further political discord, resulted in the abandonment by the Commission of its original proposals on taxation. They have been replaced by proposals that would largely preserve current VAT and excise duty rates by setting minimum allowable rates and letting market forces deal with countries that choose to levy VAT at a rate higher than the minimum.

In its desire to open up the European market and promote trade within Europe, the Commission has attached great importance to psychological gestures and symbols. In fact, it may well be that the psychological impact of the Commission's proposals and the hype attached to them will prove as important a factor in some cases as implementation of the proposals themselves. On examining their strategies, many companies will realize that the reason they have not moved into new markets has little to do with the nontariff barriers to trade. It is that they have been unwilling or unable (for internal cultural and organizational reasons) to consider the European market outside their home base. In

---

[11]Speech by Lord Cockfield to the Biscuit, Chocolate, and Confectionery Alliance, London, October 30, 1987.

[12]The Schengen Agreement among France, Germany, and the Benelux countries provides for a border-free area by 1990. Individuals would be allowed free access across borders at selected areas and at certain times. External visitors to the zone would be given three-month visas and allowed the same passage rights during that time.

this sense, the actual proposals for the Internal Market are less important than companies placing a renewed emphasis on foreign EC markets, reorganizing internally, and increasing the degree of competition.

The importance of the hype has been most evident in two areas. The first has been in the case of setting up in countries beyond their domestic markets of retailing, where there have never been any barriers to retailers. The prospect of the 1992 program and the fear of greater manufacturer power have pushed a number of retailers toward internationalization — both in terms of internal and acquisition-led growth across Europe and in terms of Europe-wide buying groups. Second, in the case of the multinational manufacturers, the balance has shifted toward the consideration of Europe-wide marketing policies. The organizational initiatives taken by companies such as Unilever, Ford, and Grand Metropolitan, in setting up European strategy groups and centralizing aspects of their marketing policies (witness the growth of Pan-European advertising campaigns), are powerful testimonies to the power of the shifts in attitude that the 1992 program catalyzed.

Interestingly, and somewhat surprisingly, many of the companies that operated Europe-wide in the mid-1980s were Japanese or American. Companies such as Canon, Fuji, Matsushita, IBM, American Express, and Kellogg operated across Europe to an extent that their European counterparts (in most cases) did not. Indeed, they operated in sectors that were traditionally supposed to be fragmented by nontariff barriers to trade and which affected them as much as they did their European counterparts.

Since some companies managed to penetrate the European market as a whole, there must have been factors other than the nontariff barriers that determined the ability of companies to break out of their fragmented national markets. The cultural disposition of American companies to think about Europe as a single entity to an extent that few indigenous European companies did and the marketing ability of the Japanese to overcome country-specific tastes and preferences were skills that the 1992 hype was designed to encourage among European companies.

Attitudinal effects aside, three factors stand out when analyzing the barriers to trade identified by the Commission.

1. *The barriers differ in nature and severity, cutting across both countries and sectors.* It is impossible to generalize as to the severity of the barriers identified by the Commission or their importance, since this will depend on the nature of the barrier, the country imposing it, and the nature and organization of the individual company. *Exhibit 1.7* shows the results of a survey of EC managers, in which they were asked about the importance of seven broad categories of trade barriers. Not surprisingly,

EXHIBIT 1.7 Management perceptions of the importance of barriers by country

	Belg.	Den.	Ger.	Gr.	Sp.	Fr.	Ire.	It.	Lux.	Neth.	Port.	U.K.	Eur.
Difference in national standards and regulations (technical, safety, environment, etc.)	63	47	49	46	46	49	55	60	60	39	58	48	51
Restrictions on open competition for government procurement	43	19	24	27	33	26	32	63	15	19	62	32	35
Administrative barriers (excessive customs formalities)	64	37	46	77	65	40	58	65	95	48	75	47	51
Physical frontier delays and costs	61	31	38	68	64	32	48	62	55	43	68	35	45
Difference in value-added tax (VAT) and sales taxes	32	20	32	59	45	37	34	47	20	18	40	20	35
Regulations of freight transport that increase transport costs (e.g., quotas)	44	24	32	59	53	28	41	41	35	34	55	30	36
Restriction in the capital market (e.g., exchange controls)	45	23	31	74	47	23	38	58	45	20	53	24	36
Implementation and application of Community law (e.g., too costly and takes too long)	38	24	41	53	47	26	26	47	30	29	52	27	37
Other barriers	11	7	8	1	6	4	5	3	45	79	6	9	9

Source: G. Nerb, Research on the "Cost of Non-Europe," *Basic Findings* Volume 3, 1988.
Note: The coefficient ranks responses from 0 (all companies consider particular barrier to be of little or no importance) to 100 (all companies consider a particular reason to be very important).

given individual countries' patterns of trade and restrictions, the surveyed managers clearly see individual barriers varying in importance.

Administrative and frontier barriers are broadly regarded as important, as are individual country standards and regulations. In the case of the latter, it is interesting to note that companies in some countries — for example, Germany, the United Kingdom, France, and Holland — find these barriers less important than companies elsewhere. A number of likely explanations include the relatively large size of companies in these countries, their consequent ability to overcome variations in standards, and their long-standing experience in dealing with variations in standards resulting from the strictness of standards in their own country and their export experience. Surprisingly, national bias in government procurement is not perceived as one of the severest barriers except in Belgium, Ireland, and Portugal, possibly reflecting the fact that few industries are affected by discretionary public procurement and that the number of companies involved in tendering with governments is small. In comparison, different VAT rates, regulations in freight, capital restrictions, and community law are regarded as relatively unimportant.

Clearly, the picture presented in *Exhibit 1.7* and which applies to industry as a whole will not be replicated in each industry or company. Among other things, there will be variations according to the nature of the industry, the size of the company, and whether or not the company is exporting. The survey found, for example, that companies employing fewer than 50 people attached greater weight to the removal of regulations that increase transport costs than did the entire sample — a reflection of the importance of economies of scale regarding distribution and also, perhaps, of the nature of the products being produced by the smaller companies.

The barriers affect each sector to a greater or lesser extent. For example, discretionary public procurement policies will affect providers of telecommunications equipment but not food manufacturers; delays at frontiers will be of more importance to an exporter of cement than to an exporter of semiconductors; and national standards and regulations will affect producers of medical equipment more than producers of shoes.

To take it a stage further, we can distinguish between barriers that restrict market entry and those that raise costs. The unwillingness of national authorities to consider foreign firms for public contracts, the bilateral market-sharing arrangements that operate on most scheduled air routes, and the set of quotas on road haulage firms are all examples of the former. Companies, by the very fact that they come from another EC country or from outside the EC, are denied the ability to compete. On the other hand, individual country restrictions on the additives that are permitted in foods, the standards and regulations that car components must conform to, and the ability of firms to offer financial services without establishing themselves in the country are all examples of the latter. In these cases companies are not denied the ability to compete, but they are forced to change the product specification or marketing program with which they are seeking to compete, with resulting increases in costs.

There will even be differences in the severity of the barriers within the subset of those that raise costs, depending on both the barrier and the nature of the firm. For example, a regulation exists in 9 out of the 12 member states that stipulates that chocolate cannot be made with vegetable fat. Given the volatility in the price of cocoa, most multinational chocolate producers have tended to introduce vegetable fat whenever they can and consequently make chocolate to two different specifications — one containing vegetable fat and the other containing cocoa fat. Given the relative absence of economies of scale in the production of chocolate bars, it is estimated that for the 5 multinationals that dominate the European chocolate market, the unit cost of production is raised by 0.5% — an inconvenience more than anything else and an equivalent problem for all of them. The costs in terms of the marketing approach that can be adopted, such as being unable to standardize packaging and labeling, are not as easy to quantify.

In contrast, differences in national standards on precision instruments may prove costly to a small firm that does not have the capital to invest in the equipment needed to produce a multitude of products. To that company the barrier does not simply raise costs — it effectively denies market access. A similar phenomenon is evident in the financial service sector. An insurance company seeking to sell a house insurance policy to a Spanish consumer must establish itself in Spain in order to be able to do so. The cost of establishing a presence may in effect act as a barrier to entry.

Given that the barriers vary in this way, clearly the effects of removing them will differ across sectors and products and will depend both on the nature of the company (for example, is it exporting or has it a presence in the target country?) and the country that it is targeting. Consequently, the belief that the process of unification will lead to a convergence in incomes and economic performance across the EC is misplaced. Regional disparities will persist given that not all regions will be affected in the same way.

2. *Removal of the barriers does not confer immediate benefits but simply changes the rules of the environment in which business is working.* A question that is often asked by business is "Who will benefit from the proposals?" The honest answer in most cases must be "we can't be sure." We have already mentioned the Cecchini Report. The costs of a non-Europe

identified by the report included administrative delays, a lack of competition, duplication of research and development, unrealized economies of scale, and a consumer facing higher prices and a commensurate lack of product and service choice.

Yet there is no certainty that implementation of the measures would actually result in benefits of the nature or scale envisaged. Apart from the abolition of frontier controls that would result in an immediate reduction in costs for all firms involved in trading within the Community, few of the measures confer immediate benefits. Most of the benefits arise from dynamic as opposed to static gains. Those benefits depend on firms exploiting the changes. They depend on firms exploiting a larger market to realize economies of scale, increasing capacity utilization for those firms left in business, new entrants increasing competition, and on lower prices boosting consumer demand. More than that, in some sectors they depend on a degree of industry restructuring. A much-quoted example is that of the boiler-making industry in Europe. There are 10 boiler makers in Europe, kept in business by nationalistic public procurement policies and collectively operating at 20% of capacity. Outlawing nationalistic public procurement will not, in itself, lead to the necessary restructuring.

In other words, realization of the benefits depends primarily on a supply-side response. Only after companies and markets have restructured and seen an increase in competition is the demand-side impetus through lower prices and consequently higher consumer spending assumed to operate. The key that starts and drives the process is in the hands of individual companies. In practice, therefore, it is not as easy to identify the competitive companies that are likely to prosper if and when the barriers are removed. The winners will not simply be those that are more competitive, whether that competitiveness is measured in terms of price or nonprice factors, but those that reorient their organizational structure and marketing strategy in line with the new and evolving business environment.

3. *The barriers that are being tackled are in many cases not the ones that inhibit business development.* Evidence for the fragmentation of European markets comes in many forms. In some sectors it is the low levels of intra-EC trade; in others it is a wide divergence in prices across national boundaries; and in still others it is the absence of truly Pan-European companies or brands. To what extent is this fragmentation a result of the barriers to trade identified by the Commission? There exist other barriers to trade that the Commission will not or could not legislate for, such as differences in culture and consumer tastes, different languages, tight distribution networks, national rules relating to retail outlets, and volatility in exchange rates.

We have already mentioned insular managements as a factor contributing to fragmentation. The other chief concern is that of consumers themselves. There is no doubt that consumers differ across Europe. Their income, values, and behavior vary enormously. There is nothing in the 1992 program to ensure a convergence in incomes. Nor is it clear, in the absence of a genuinely European culture, that a convergence in values and attitudes will be anything but very slow. The real question concerns the extent to which companies can or should standardize their product and marketing activities. This issue is addressed in Chapter 3. In the context of this chapter, it should be considered one of the potentially critical impediments to the treatment of Europe as a single market.

Take as an example the food sector. It is not obvious that the large differences that exist in prices across Europe, the low levels of trade, or the small number of companies operating Europe-wide are a result of national standards and regulations. In 1987 the European Court ruled as illegal the German beer purity law specifying that imported beer sold in the country had to be made exclusively with certain ingredients. The beer purity law was widely held to be responsible for the lack of imports. Yet the removal of the law has not resulted in a mass of imports. The fact that there has never been a national brand in Germany, that brands are regional, and that the largest producer has only 3% of the market may tell us something about the importance of consumer tastes and distribution networks in the German market, the problems of branding, and the relative unimportance of the barrier to trade removed by the Court.

This brings us to an interesting way of viewing how the proposed changes would affect individual markets. If we accept that European markets are fragmented — the evidence for which can be seen in large price variations, relatively few Pan-European companies or brands, few competitors for public procurement contracts, and low industrial capacity utilization — we must ask the question, "Why are they fragmented?"

How important are the barriers to trade identified by the Commission relative to:

1. Company attitudes and organizational structures?
2. Other "barriers" (such as distribution systems and local consumer values and tastes) that are not being tackled?

The answers will vary by country, sector, and company. Where the formal barriers to trade are the main cause of the fragmentation, we must then assess the nature of those barriers and the nature and size of the potential economies of scale available through their removal.

What is clear is that with some exceptions (on public procurement, for example), the proposals do no more than change the rules of the game. Their acceptance would not confer immediate gains or losses on any company. The extent to which there are winners and losers and who they are depends on the actions taken by companies in response to an evolving business environment.

CONCLUSION

The impetus for the proposals aimed at creating an Internal Market for goods, services, capital, and people in Europe was provided by Europe's poor economic performance. For many years, EC-based companies were less dynamic than their global competitors and lost market share — notably in the fast-growing sectors in which economies of scale could not be exploited at a national level. However, since the proposals can only be seen in the context of a longer, politically inspired path to integration, which began in the aftermath of World War II, the political repercussions of the moves may prove to be as important as the economic.

The Commission's research, which forecast increased growth of 5% and a 6% fall in prices as a result of the completion of the Market, should not be taken at face value. The major source of any gains lies in the supply-side reaction of companies. Removal of the barriers would not confer immediate benefits on anyone. It would merely change the rules of the game and allow companies to exploit a changed business environment — one in which access to markets is not blocked and where costs are not raised by having to conform to a multitude of individual country standards and regulations.

Identifying the winners and losers that may emerge from the process is a difficult task, because the nature and severity of the barriers differ among countries, sectors, and companies. More important, the fragmentation of European markets has its roots in other factors, too. While national bias in public procurement may have been an important factor in telecommunications, it can be argued that in many consumer markets it has been the attitude and organization of companies which have kept them insular, or the variation in consumer values and tastes which precluded product standardization. In these respects, the symbolic nature of the proposals and the hype they have generated are crucial in making indigenous European companies gear up to market to the European market, in a way that non-EC companies such as Canon, Kellogg, and IBM have for some time.

APPENDIX A: EC-Sponsored Technological Cooperation

During the early 1980s the EC established a number of projects, designed to stimulate scientific and technical cooperation among EC-based companies. Seeing its dependence on foreign IT grow and its external balance of trade in the sector fall, the EC felt that the EC's "industrial and economic independence" and subsequently its "political independence" would be seriously jeopardized if no joint action were taken. The aim was to improve the scientific and technological competitiveness of the Community by targeting specific areas and provide matching funding (i.e., the EC providing funds equal in amount to that provided by industry). Projects required participants from more than one member state.

Two points are worth noting in relation to these initiatives:

1. The amount of funding was generally small and certainly insufficient to do more than marginally accelerate the development of the EC's technological base. In areas where massive funding was being undertaken by the United States and (especially) Japan, the funding was minimal — both in relation to that already undertaken by EC firms and compared to that undertaken among the EC's competitors.
2. Some of the large foreign (especially U.S.) companies based in the EC felt that funding was being denied them as a way of promoting the technological competitiveness of indigenous firms. Although there were elements of the programs that were allocated to U.S. companies, the proportion appeared to be small.

The key projects initiated by the EC were:

BRITE (Basic Research in Industrial Technologies for Europe)
Established in March 1985 with ECU 125 million of EC funds available over 1985–1988.
Program aimed at "precompetitive" research in manufacturing.
First tranche (bond series) involved 95 projects (a further 8 were added later) with 432 participating organizations, 60% of whom were industrial companies, 21% research institutes, and 19% universities.
Key areas of research included laser technology, assembly technology, and CAD/CAM.
Examples of projects included:
The development of polymide compounds to withstand high temperatures for use in aeronautics.
The development of a fully automated assembly and sewing machine for use in the clothing industry.
The development of noise and vibration imaging methods for gas turbines.

ESPRIT (European Strategic Programme for Research and Development in Information Technology)
Established in 1984 with a five-year funding program of ECU 1.5 billion.
Aim was to establish a technological base in the IT sector by concentrating on five areas for action (advanced microelectronics, advanced information processing, software technology, office automation, and computer integrated manufacturing) and paving the way for the introduction of international standards of European origin
By 1986, over 240 industrial partners aside from research institutes and universities were participating in 201 projects.
Examples of the work carried out were:
  The development of a 10K array bipolar chip.
  Cooperation on a Common Software Development System by Bull, GEC, IC, Nixdorf, Olivetti, and Siemens.
  The development by Daimler Benz, Bosch, GIA, and GIT of an enhanced language, Prolog III, designed for use within an expert system that could diagnose failures of car engines.

RACE (Research and Development in Advanced Communication Technology for Europe)
Established in July 1985, with initial EC funding of ECU 25 million over 18 months, later extended to ECU 550 million over 10 years.
Aim was to to prepare the R&D necessary for the subsequent introduction of integrated high-speed telecommunication networks and to make a major contribution to the introduction of Integrated Broadband Communication.

By 1989 the EC was discussing further funding and the extension of the programs into areas such as High Definition TV and standardized microprocessor architecture.
  Smaller and more sector focused projects were:

AIM (Advanced Informatics in Medicine)
DELTA (Development of European Learning Through Technological Advancement)
JESSI (Joint European Semiconductor Silicon Project)

CHAPTER 2

Progress and Prospects

In the previous chapter we stressed the psychological impact of the European Community's proposals in making companies reorient themselves away from their national market toward the European market. However, there can be no doubt that implementation of the proposals is critical to the entire exercise, both in objectively changing the operating environment and in continuing the momentum that has built up behind the idea of a unified market. Moreover, the nature of the environment in which businesses will be operating will be affected by the way wider issues — many of which were not even discussed in the 1985 White Paper — evolve. A debate is underway concerning the nature of the European market that will develop in the 1990s.

This chapter will focus on the progress that can be expected on the White Paper proposals, companies' ability to exploit them, and the way in which issues such as a common currency, protectionism, and a social charter are likely to develop.

NEW PROCEDURES HAVE ACCELERATED THE DECISION MAKING . . .

Progress in implementing the EC proposals has been impressive in the context of EC history but too slow to convince many that the unified market will be in place by the end of 1992. By the end of 1988, the number of proposals to be agreed upon having been whittled down from 300 to 279,[1] agreement had been reached on 108. It is not true to say that only the less controversial directives had been passed. Of particular significance were adoption of the measures to liberalize the market in large

---

[1]After the original White Paper was published, a number of proposals were merged, scrapped, or withdrawn to be amended and resubmitted. These included measures on third country nationals, drug legislation, visa and extradition policy, type and approval for heavy vehicles, location of the European trademark office, and excise duty on cigarettes. Measures that were subsequently added to the original list included ones covering sheep and goat meat, plants, and veterinary products.

risk nonlife insurance; the second banking directive; the freeing of capital movements; transferability of unit trusts; partial liberalization of the air transport sector; the removal of road haulage quotas; increased competition in public works and supply contracts; and the freedom of movement for pressure vessels, toys, and construction materials. Little or no progress had been made on the proposals covering plant and animal health, indirect taxation, and the freedom of movement for the individual.

That progress had occurred at all was due to two innovations — a change in the decision-making process and the adoption of a new approach to standardization. For years decision making within the Council of Ministers was impeded by each individual country's right of veto. It was de Gaulle who in 1965, faced with the prospect of budgetary control of the Common Agricultural Policy by the European Parliament, withdrew his Ministers from all sessions of the Council until a year later when other member states agreed to the Luxembourg compromise. It was a deal that introduced the need for unanimous approval for important proposals and gave legitimacy to the right of individual countries to veto progress in areas that they considered essential. Given the diversity of national interests, the need for unanimity effectively precluded further progress.

The most important feature of the 1986 Single European Act was the provision for majority and qualified (weighted) majority voting in a number of key areas relating to the Internal Market. Except for measures covering taxation, the free movement of individuals, and the rights and interests of employees — where adoption still requires the unanimous approval of member states — it would be possible for progress to be made on the basis of securing the majority of the weighted votes. The weights were distributed in such a way as to make it impossible for coalitions of even two of the four largest countries (France, Germany, Italy, and the United Kingdom) to block progress (see *Appendix A*). In addition, the Act allowed the Council of Ministers to delegate powers to the Commission — effectively preserving the Council's role as the decision-making body but speeding up the process. A graphical representation of how the new decision-making procedure works is included in *Appendix A*.

The other key innovation was the introduction of the concept of mutual recognition of individual country standards and regulations. In the past the EC had spent an inordinate amount of time trying to harmonize standards throughout Europe. The result was time consuming. For example, it took 10 years to adopt a directive on mineral waters and 14 years to adopt one on jams.

At the heart of the new approach was a distinction between goods whose freedom of movement could be secured by a mutual recognition of regulations and goods whose freedom of movement required a degree of harmonization of technical regulations.

The use of the former stems from the important 1978 European Court *Cassis De Dijon* case. In it the Court set out the principle that a product lawfully produced and marketed according to the rules of an individual member state should be allowed free movement throughout the EC, the only exceptions being ones in which national standards were required for genuine health or consumer protection reasons. The Commission's attitude has been to follow this approach and to argue that sales bans cannot be enforced solely because an imported product has been manufactured to different standards. The European Court has already used the principle to strike down a number of individual country restrictions, the most publicized being the beer and sausage purity laws in Germany and the pasta purity laws in Italy. What the new approach does is formalize the principle that has been applied by the Court on numerous occasions.

The Commission's innovation has been to extend the idea of mutual recognition to services and in particular to financial services such as banking and insurance. For example, banks that meet minimum standards, such as capital requirements, should be able to operate throughout the Community subject to a single license granted by the EC country in which they are established. Their right to operate would be determined by their domestic authorities (home country control), though the way in which they advertised and marketed their products would still be subject to the rules that applied in the country whose consumers they were targeting (host country control). Their operation on the basis of a single license would be subject to minimum requirements — analogous to minimum health and safety standards for products.

In parallel with the process of mutual recognition, the EC set up a new approach to the harmonization of technical regulations, in areas where their mutual recognition would be insufficient as a guarantee of freer trade. In areas such as telecommunications, information technology, and various kinds of equipment, the EC has dispensed with the process of setting detailed directives. Instead, it is setting essential requirements and promoting the greater use of European standards conforming to those requirements through the use of the standard-setting bodies, CEN (European Committee for Standardization) and CENELEC (Committee for Electrotechnical Standardization). The requirement, which has existed since 1983, for individual countries to notify the Commission of new standards and regulations that it proposes to adopt and which allows the Commission to freeze their introduction for up to a year if it is thought that they would act as a barrier to trade, was an essential complement to this new approach. What was missing in the new approach, though, was a European system for the mutual recognition of tests and certificates. It is no use having acceptance of standards and regulations if there is no standard approach to prove that goods conform to those specifications. Sectors particularly affected by this deficiency include pharmaceuticals and various types of equipment — for example, medical equipment and automobiles. The Commission was due to publish its proposals in this area late in 1989. No doubt the proposals will attract much disquiet given the variety of ways in which test data can be interpreted.

Despite the innovations that have occurred and which have speeded up the decision-making process, a number of key factors that will hinder the move toward the goal of a unified and economically competitive market remain and almost certainly mean that the process will not be completed by 1992. We can think of these factors as falling into two groups — those that will prevent adoption of some of the measures contained in the White Paper and those that will prevent companies from exploiting the changes that do occur.

. . . BUT A LACK OF POLITICAL WILL HAS SLOWED IT DOWN . . .

The Commission has declared on more than one occasion that the White Paper must be taken and considered in its entirety — that member states cannot think of the measures as an "à la carte" menu from which to pick and choose. In reality this is exactly what the member states have been doing. Given the considerable diversity in the way in which they perceive their national interests, this should come as no surprise. This diversity means that securing the necessary number of votes and building a strong enough coalition for any one proposal is a difficult process.

In this context it is important to stress the limitations of the innovations that have facilitated the progress to date. Despite the introduction of majority voting procedures, securing a widespread political consensus is still important, both in ensuring that countries do not infringe on the measures that have been agreed upon and in securing their continued adherence to the concept of a unified market. Infringements are a part of everyday life, with over 500 formal notifications of infringements occurring every year and some 60–100 cases coming up before the European Court. Prior to the accession of Spain and Portugal, four countries — Belgium, France, Greece, and Italy — committed 70% of all infringements. However, recourse to the European Court is an option that is both time consuming (it may take five years for an opinion from the Court) and shunned by many companies that fear tangling with national authorities. In practice, apart from a limited number of well-publicized cases, freedom of movement in the Community still relies on the goodwill of governments as opposed to the limited compliance powers possessed by the Commission and Court.

More importantly, the process of agreement depends largely on political will, which will only be forthcoming if member states continue to believe that the process is to their benefit. As a senior French civil servant put it recently:

> *French enthusiasm for integration stems from the presumption that France will be able to lead the process and shape it in its interests. If that presumption turns out not to be the case, then we could see some real foot dragging between now and 1992.*[2]

Somewhat extraordinarily and as a result of much publicity, most companies across Europe think that 1992 will be good for them. As *Exhibits 2.1* and *2.2* show, while there is some variation across countries and sectors, the majority believe that the process will be of benefit. But 1992 is not necessarily a positive-sum game. It may be that as time goes on, the process boosts growth and allows all companies to share in the benefits. But one of the fundamental tenets of the idea behind unification is that there is a degree of rationalization that leaves the most efficient and competitive companies with a larger share of the market at the expense of the less efficient ones. John Harvey Jones, former chairman of ICI, has talked about a Europe with half the number of companies in 10 years' time than it has now. European governments are not yet ready to pay the price of rationalization on such a scale in return for the abstract benefits of a more efficient and competitive Europe.

It may well be, for example, that the economics of the situation dictate that the EC cannot support 12 national airlines, but government shareholdings and nationalistic tendencies mean that limited strategic alliances of the sort announced by BA, KLM, and Sabena are more likely to occur than are the takeovers and rationalization experienced in the United States. We have already seen an element of this with France's President Mitterand denouncing corporate raiders as "financial gangsters." The French authorities have been seeking ways of building up sufficient stakes in key companies and of pursuing complicated mutual equity stakes of interlocking French companies to prevent hostile takeovers — trends that have affected the attempts of companies such as 3M

---

[2]"Second Thoughts on 1992," *Time*, January 23, 1989.

EXHIBIT 2.1 Proportion of firms thinking that benefits of the internal market will be positive

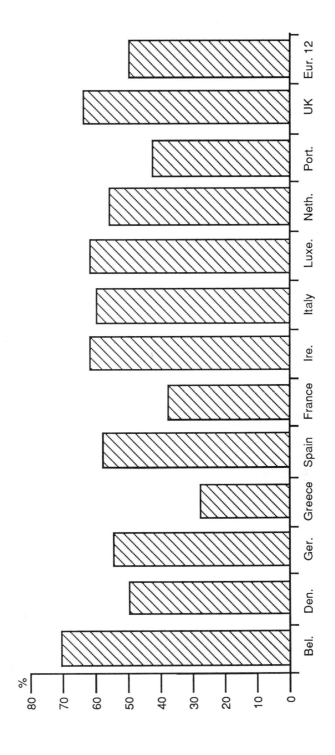

Source: G. Nerb, Research on the "Cost of Non-Europe," *Basic Findings*, Volume 3, 1988.
Note: Excludes "don't knows."

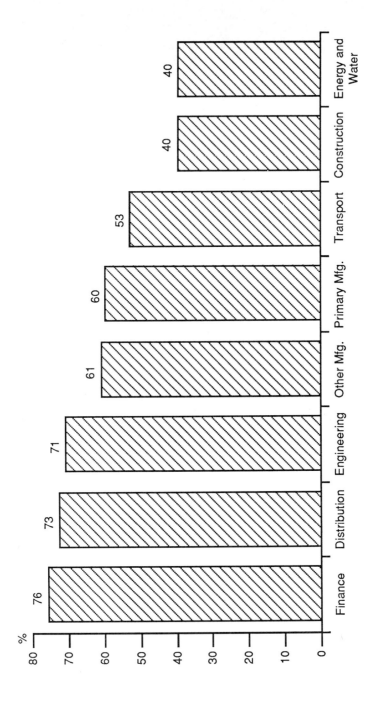

EXHIBIT 2.2 Percentage of respondents who believe harmonization would benefit their firm's growth

Source: Booz, Allen & Hamilton.

34

in succeeding in bids for French companies.[3] The danger is that governments will either prevent the necessary degree of rationalization or that they will lose their enthusiasm for the political process.

In this respect the overall economic climate is of fundamental importance. Anything resembling an economic downturn in Europe in the years leading up to 1992 and beyond would make accepting a degree of rationalization in European industry an even more bitter pill to swallow. Increased capacity as a result of inward investment may worsen the plight of indigenous companies. More generally, the Commission's economic report for 1989 revealed a growing disparity in economic performance. Although countries such as Spain have been benefiting from substantial amounts of inward investment by companies seeking either to establish themselves in the EC or exploit lower wage costs, some of the poorer countries — Greece, Portugal, and Ireland — have yet to be convinced of the benefits of a unified market. To them the Internal Market is less important than securing measures aimed at reducing regional disparities. The idea that the Internal Market would lead to a "golden triangle" — an area of prosperity between London, Hamburg, and Paris — has been feared by many on the periphery of the Community. A realization that it was occurring would do much to dent the prospect of a unified market covering all member states.

The way in which economic realities can dampen the political enthusiasm for unification has already been evident in the case of motor vehicles. Recognition of superior Japanese manufacturing and marketing positions was confirmed by a recent internal Commission report.[4] Fear of the Japanese being in the best position to exploit a unified market has led governments to delay the adoption of Community-wide-type approval for components and has put into question whether a consensus can be achieved over how to deal with individual country quotas on Japanese imports.

Regarding the question of mutual recognition, although progress on the abolition of technical barriers in the form of different standards and regulations is generally going well — over 70% of all the measures already agreed upon have been of this sort — governments are resisting the adoption of the new approach in a number of key areas, many of them related to health and safety.

One of the questions that surrounded the adoption of the mutual

---

[3]"The Chevalier Blanc Heading the Industry Ministry," *International Business Week*, March 13, 1989.

[4]"The Competitiveness of the European Automobile Industry in the Light of 1992," *European Commission Report*, III/4242/88, October 20, 1988.

recognition approach was whether or not it would lead to a fall in standards to the lowest common denominator. To some extent it is this fear and the belief of some member states that their standards are higher than in the rest of the Community which has slowed down progress in areas such as banking, food, and pharmaceuticals. Member states do not wish to see standards of operation developed over years suddenly eroded by having to recognize what are perceived to be inferior practices from elsewhere. This applies as much to rules relating to employment practices and residency requirements as it does to goods and services.

In the case of food, member states have agreed to the broad approach but are unwilling to lose control over critical issues such as the ingredients that can be used in foods and the way in which they are used. In the case of pharmaceuticals, the long history of individual country registration of products is unlikely to end in favor of the mutual recognition of registered products. Agreement on the abolition of all frontier controls is being held up by a lack of trust and confidence in other countries' controls of immigration, drugs, and terrorists. Having labored to produce regulatory provisions in the form of the Financial Services Act, the United Kingdom does not wish to see them circumvented by firms operating elsewhere in the EC and selling to U.K. consumers according to less strict conditions of operation.

The desire to maintain one's own standards will always be in conflict with the concept of a unified market based on a mutual recognition of standards. In some cases it will prevent the adoption of measures; in others it will push countries into infringing against or offsetting agreed-upon measures or in seeking a formal derogation (exemption). Examples of the former may yet include the French government's insistence on a degree of approximation in the withholding tax on investments by foreign residents as a precondition of adherence to the agreement on the removal of capital controls on individuals, out of fear that a lack of such approximation would encourage large-scale capital outflows. An example of the latter was the European Court's decision late in 1988 to uphold the Danish government's insistence that all drinks be sold in returnable bottles for environmental reasons, despite the detrimental effect on trade (imported drinks account for less than 1% of the market).

From the point of view of free trade, there are a number of areas — notably food and pharmaceuticals — where the desire to maintain high standards, coupled with the unwillingness of the Community authorities to be seen as promoters of "standardization to the lowest common denominator," may nullify attempts to create a freer movement of goods. The recent electoral successes of the Greens in France, Germany, and the United Kingdom may well herald the beginning of a renewed emphasis on high consumer standards, notably environmental ones, further hindering attempts to promote a freer movement of goods.

In some areas, the need for unanimity makes progress even harder, as has been the case with taxation, employment, and company-related matters. In the case of the former, member states were unhappy with the proposals — partly because they considered their right to fix tax rates as central to the concept of their national sovereignty and partly for practical reasons. The tax proposals as they stood would have had immediate and visible effects in most of the member states — in some cases resulting in price increases for some goods of over 100% and in other cases resulting in the taxation of food, where none had previously occurred. The need for unanimity ensured that little progress would be achieved.

. . . AND COMPANIES WILL STILL FIND IT HARD TO EXPLOIT THE CHANGES

Quite apart from the factors that will determine the extent to which the various proposals are accepted and adhered to, there is the equally important question of whether firms will be in a position to exploit the changes. Some of the factors inhibiting such exploitation, such as the organizational structure of companies, the continuing divergence in consumer attitudes, culture, and language, will be considered in the next chapter in the context of the marketing implications of 1992. Two factors are worth stressing here — the difficulties in persuading consumers to make use of the changes and the difficulties of rationalizations and mergers.

Persuading consumers is straightforward as it applies to individual consumers, but it also applies to industrial consumers. In the case of technical standards and regulations, distributors and retailers will have been used to goods made to national specifications. The changes may mean that external suppliers can offer their products to them — it does not mean that they will be preferred, even if the cost is lower. After all, standards such as the ones set by the German DIN and British Standards Institute have never had a basis in law. They have always been voluntary and set up to benefit the industry and the consumer, though they are taken into account for insurance purposes. Will German companies buy equipment made to anything but DIN specifications even if they are able to? Maybe, depending on the source and the relative cost. Will French architects use building materials that do not conform to the specifications of those they have been used to? Again the answer is a qualified maybe. The Chloride case in Chapter 7 suggests that these preferences are important and may be slow to change.

The problems in this respect are especially acute in the case of Germany. Exporters to the German market have long been aware of the absolute necessity of conforming to German (voluntary) standards if they are to succeed in penetrating the German market. Examples of the uniqueness of German demand, both in number and strictness, are well documented. To some extent the problem that this causes is mitigated by the fact that standardization is taking place largely on German terms, with German nationals chairing over 40% of all standard-setting committees under the auspices of CEN and CENELEC. Nevertheless, to the extent that German specifications are not incorporated in European-wide standards, the usefulness of the mutual recognition procedure for exporters to the largest market in Europe will be lessened.

A similar though slightly different problem exists in the case of public procurement. Government procurement of goods and services accounts for 15% of the EC's GDP, yet it is estimated that only 2% of the value of those contracts goes to companies outside the home country. It is therefore a crucial area. The new directives specify that contracts should be awarded to the company meeting the nondiscriminatory conditions of the tender at the lowest cost. It would, however, be foolish to think that years of preferential treatment and use of public contracts as a way of achieving sociopolitical objectives will end by the passing of a directive. Governments will seek to use a variety of escape clauses to maximize their freedom of maneuver. They will not always be allowed to do so, as a recent case involving the Irish government's attempt to discriminate against a Spanish maker of contruction pipes showed,[5] but in the absence of strict compliance measures, they will try. Indeed, in many areas, such as health equipment, the opening up of public procurement contracts to outside competition may well have more to do with national attempts to contain rising costs than the need to comply with European directives.

The second difficulty referred to above concerns the ability of firms to merge and rationalize as part of their attempt to maximize the benefits that they perceive to exist. As *Exhibits 2.3* and *2.4* show, 1988 did not see a tidal wave of cross-border mergers and takeovers in all countries. The number and value of cross-border deals were substantially up over previous years, but most of the activity was concentrated on the United Kingdom and United States. The importance of EC-oriented acquisitions

---

[5]*Community v. Ireland*, case 45/87.

EXHIBIT 2.3 Acquisitions of EC and non-EC companies in other countries, 1988

	Acquisitions by EC companies		Acquisitions by Non-EC companies	
	Value ($ million)	Number of acquisitions	Value ($ million)	Number of acquisitions
In France	2,462	94	1,818	35
In Germany	1,543	65	166	36
In Italy	920	40	1,968	22
In Netherlands	845	53	1,811	14
In United Kingdom	3,787	79	13,954	147

Source: KPMG, *Deal Watch*, London, March 1989.

is raised if the analysis is conducted in terms of the number of deals rather than their value. Nevertheless, the attractions of the European market and the supposed need to reorient oneself toward Europe in order to benefit from the changes that 1992 will bring, do not seem to have induced European companies to undertake a restructuring of European industry on the scale which is required.

This point is crucial, given the importance attached to a restructuring of European industry as a way of eliminating inefficiency and promoting competitiveness. Of course, restructuring and gaining market access can take place through such other means as joint ventures and other forms of strategic alliances. The recent tie-ups involving GEC and

EXHIBIT 2.4 Acquisitions of EC and non-EC companies by other countries, 1988

	Acquisitions of EC companies		Acquisitions of Non-EC companies	
	Value ($ million)	Number of acquisitions	Value ($ million)	Number of acquisitions
By France	3,772	70	7,390	73
By Germany	405	37	2,347	62
By Italy	1,164	18	213	11
By Netherlands	602	17	674	35
By United Kingdom	4,411	245	40,119	639

Source: KPMG, *Deal Watch*, London, March 1989.

a range of partners including GE (U.S.) and Siemens have testified to this. However, in some industries the excess capacity identified by the Commission requires an element of rationalization — the boiler-maker example referred to in Chapter 1 being a perfect example.

This apparent lack of activity in Europe has its roots in at least three factors. First are the difficulties that exist in conducting merger and take-over activity resulting from differences in capital markets and from the share structure of many companies. The power of incumbent boards, the restrictions on foreign shareholdings, and the tendency in some countries for the number of shareholders to be fairly concentrated make hostile bids difficult to undertake successfully. These problems vary across countries, with Germany and the Benelux countries being the hardest to penetrate. Indeed, one of the questions raised by Nestlé's takeover of Rowntrees in 1988 was whether such a takeover should be allowed by the U.K. authorities given Nestlé's two-tier structure (now modified), which concentrated voting shares in Swiss hands.

Second is the fact that most governments in Europe, with the possible exception of the United Kingdom, whose policy is somewhat unclear, operate merger policies in which the public interest is not equated with a narrow concept of competition. Political difficulties were evident in both Carlo de Benedetti's (unsuccessful) attempt to gain control of Belgium's Société Générale and in Nestlé's (successful) bid for the U.K.'s Rowntrees company. In other words, national authorities must still satisfy themselves that bids/mergers are in the national interest of the country concerned.

Third are the economic reasons that often push a company into looking for opportunities outside the EC. For example, the fall in the dollar between 1985 and 1988 made U.S. companies appear undervalued and attractive. Also, in the case of U.K. bidders, part of the expense can be written off in the balance sheet as goodwill.

In some cases these factors have not played a role. Restructuring has been prevented by an inability to merge corporate cultures. This was the case in the attempt to merge Banco Central and Banco Espanol de Credito into what would have been Spain's largest bank. The plan was aborted early in 1989 as a result of boardroom wrangles, personality clashes, and differences in approach.

This is not to say that cross-border merger and acquisition activity is impossible — as *Exhibits* 2.3 and 2.4 show, hundreds of such deals have been conducted in Europe in 1988 alone — but that in some key areas and for some key companies, the prospect of hostile as opposed to friendly deals is out of the question, for the time being at least. Consequently, the restructuring of European industry is taking place where the conditions are favorable to both sides. The highly publicized leveraged buy-outs and hostile bids that have characterized U.S. markets in recent years are absent from the European scene (with the possible exception of the United Kingdom) and will continue to be so for the foreseeable future. A range of strategic alliances will have to be explored, a subject discussed in Chapter 3.

The difficulties of conducting merger and acquisition policies in Europe will be helped by the EC's proposals on merger policy and will preclude the kind of problems that Nestlé had with the French government over its takeovers of Rowntree Mackintosh in the United Kingdom and Buitoni in Italy. However, it is not clear what criteria the Commission will apply. Will they favor the interests of the consumer and promote greater competition, or will there be circumstances in which the economic advantages to Europe of a large European company capable of competing on global terms outweigh any anticompetitive element within the EC?

To summarize this section, therefore, we can say that substantial progress has been made in a number of key areas and a momentum has built up around the process that will make further progress inevitable, but national interests will make that progress slow and uneven. The idea of a unified market encompassing 320 million consumers by 1992 is overly optimistic. Instead, the program should be thought of as an evolving process that will see more progress in some areas and in some countries than in others. Importantly, factors remain that will make it difficult for companies to exploit the changes, even when agreed to by a political majority. Conversely, as we stated earlier, the ability to break out of national markets may depend as much on corporate outlook and skills as it does on removal of the barriers identified by the Commission.

WHAT WILL THE EUROPE OF THE 1990s LOOK LIKE?

So far we have identified differences in national interests only insofar as they relate to the proposals contained in the White Paper. Important as they are, they pale in significance beside the wider differences that exist over the nature, features, and role of the European Community as it evolves into the 1990s. Given the degree of variation in national interests, it is not surprising that the 1992 process has prompted a vigorous debate on key questions such as the following:

- What are the relative weights that the EC attaches to the benefits of consumers and manufacturers, given the potentially (in the short term at least) contradictory twin goals of promoting competition and globally efficient companies?

- Should the benefits of the Internal Market be reserved for European companies and what are the implications of such a market on Europe's external relations?
- Should the Internal Market simply consist of a free-trade area or do the objectives necessitate a wider degree of economic and political cooperation and the adoption of other measures affecting companies and individuals?
- Is the 1992 program one that demands liberalization or a degree of common regulation?
- To what extent and in what areas does the Internal Market require a transfer of sovereignty to Brussels?

The importance of the way in which these questions are eventually resolved cannot be underestimated. They are central to the nature of the operating environment that companies marketing to European consumers will be facing in the Europe that evolves in the 1990s. These issues fall into two categories — the extent to which the EC moves beyond the proposals contained in the White Paper and the extent to which Europe turns itself into a fortress.

A FREE TRADE AREA OR SOMETHING MORE THAN THAT?

The questions over the nature and role of the EC have been around as long as the Community existed. Jean Monnet's first speech to the inaugural session of the European Coal and Steel Community back in 1952 revealed both the political impetus behind its foundation, provided by the desire to avoid further wars in Europe, and the explicitly federalist nature of the institution that was envisaged. The opposition (notably from the Gaullists in France) to the sentiments contained in Monnet's speech, to a reduction in the importance of the national interest, and to any aspect of the federalist concept subsequently resulted in both a shelving of the idea of a European Defense Community and a significant dilution in the powers of the European Commission in the European Economic Community that was to emerge in 1957.

In the context of 1992, the focus of the debate has shifted somewhat away from a simplistic analysis of national sovereignty and federalism. National decision making is still central to each government's view of Europe. But there is now a recognition, albeit implicit, that Brussels *has* acquired powers at the expense of national governments and that the Single European Act confirmed and accelerated this trend. European

Commission and Court decisions and their struggles with individual governments over the validity of national standards and regulations, state subsidies to industry, the requirements attached to individual mergers, competition issues, the ability to exempt certain industries from paying VAT, and other discriminatory practices have been commonplace and increasing in recent years.

The general public in some countries may still be under the illusion that all decision-making powers rest with national parliaments. But those involved in government and who witness the extraordinary amount of legislation emanating from Brussels are under no such illusion. National decision makers find this unpalatable and occasionally stand up and declare their sovereignty over all they survey. The reality is different and everyone knows it. The question is no longer whether or not to cede a degree of authority or to promote cooperation, but where to draw the line. The nature of the debates over monetary and economic integration demonstrates that there are major countries within the EC that are willing to contemplate a substantial erosion of sovereignty in pursuit of the Internal Market.

This question takes us to the heart of the current debate over the nature and role of a united Europe. What is the Internal Market to which countries are striving? The answer to this question holds the key to the resolution of the other debates. To answer whether a genuine Internal Market requires action in areas that go well beyond the scope of the White Paper or whether the explicit goal of making Europe more competitive can be achieved without a degree of cooperation in other areas presupposes a unity of views over the goals of the 1992 process. It is a unity that does not cover the twelve EC members.

At the extremes of this debate are Mrs. Thatcher and the Commission, personified by Jacques Delors. Mrs. Thatcher does not subscribe to the wider aims of the Internal Market insofar as they relate to improving the competitiveness and position of Europe as a whole. She views the Internal Market as a free trade area, 1992 as a process of liberalization, and the EC's role solely as facilitating the adoption of the White Paper (or those aspects of it with which she is in agreement) and ensuring that competition is fair. It is a vision based on her own political philosophy of an industrial landscape in which governments play a minimal role, where competition is undistorted by intervention, where Adam Smith's "invisible hand" ensures the greatest benefit for the consumer, and where there is no such thing as an industrial policy based on political or longer-term economic objectives. Hers is a variation on the Darwinian theme of the survival of the fittest in which she firmly believes that the British will emerge as among the fittest.

The absence of an industrial policy is particular to the political Right in the United Kingdom. But the absence of a belief that the United Kingdom is inextricably linked with the rest of a competitive and unified Europe is in large part common across the entire U.K. political spectrum. In Mrs. Thatcher's words:

> *Britain does not dream of some cosy isolated existence on the fringes of the European Community. . . . Our destiny is in Europe, as part of the Community. . . . That is not to say that our future lies only in Europe.*[6]

This view is received sympathetically in most political circles within the United Kingdom, even though tactical political considerations make it appear at times that deeper divisions exist across the U.K. political spectrum. Such a view has its roots in the mentality of an island race and a recent history which, as often as not, centered on events outside Europe.

On the other hand, there are those led by Jacques Delors who view the Internal Market as a way of promoting a Europe, united politically and economically and capable of taking on the Americans and the Japanese. In seeking to promote a range of such issues as a common European currency, harmonization of working conditions, and a reduction in regional disparities, Delors differs from Thatcher in both the end to which he is working and the means that he wants to employ. In stating that

> *there can be no social progress without economic progress; and there can be no economic progress without social cohesion . . .*[7]

Delors reveals both the history of corporatism that has been characteristic of most European countries and the lack of trust in the workings of a free market that has permeated French decision making for years. Underlying Delors' thinking is a genuine desire to see an Internal Market that offers not only an equality of opportunity, but an equality of outcome for the Community's people, as well as a desire to pursue the ideal of a unified Europe, increasingly seen as economically and culturally desirable.

Delors repeatedly juxtaposes removal of the barriers to trade contained in the White Paper with other goals, such as a reduction in regional disparities, harmonization of working conditions, economic and monetary cooperation, and the promotion of European environmental policies. To Delors the Internal Market consists of far more than simply a barrier-free Europe. The "extras" consist of, among others, a common

---

[6]Speech in Bruges, September 20, 1988.
[7]Speech in Cologne, September 23, 1988.

currency, a European Central Bank, harmonization of rules on the treatment of corporate and foreign resident taxation, worker rights and minimum standards of consultation and participation, a European company statute, and a host of common rules covering everything from migrant workers to aspects of the operation of social security systems. Most of these measures are considered necessary to achieve the Internal Market goals of competitiveness and cohesion and are consistent with the wider vision of a united Europe.

A good example is the call for a Central European Bank and a gradual move toward the use of a common currency — issues that have split the Community. Part of the attraction of such proposals lies in a belief that a genuinely Internal Market in which companies can treat foreign markets as they would home ones, requires a common currency — a not surprising view given the kind of volatility that exporters to individual countries within the EC have experienced. Indeed, as the Cecchini Report and other commentators have pointed out, achieving the full benefits of a united Europe requires a degree of coordination in economic policy that has been notably absent. The Delors Committee on monetary and economic union put it this way in early 1989:

> The full implementation and success of the single market by itself requires an increased degree of economic policy coordination even in areas that are not as such part of the internal market programme.[8]

The Delors Report called for a three-stage process in which the EC moved from greater policy coordination through a transfer of responsibility for monetary policy to a European System of Central Banks, a fixing of exchange rates, and the eventual creation of a single currency. The report, which set no timetable for action, represented a compromise between those countries that see economic and monetary union as an evolutionary process which can only follow a long period of economic integration and those that wish to progress toward a degree of federalism. After intense pressure on Mrs. Thatcher, the European Council agreed in June 1989 to begin the first phase within a year. The extent to which subsequent progress is made will dominate discussions within Europe in the coming years.

Considering the other participants in the process, we must therefore distinguish between their underlying attitude to taking the Internal Market into areas not specified by the White Paper and their attitude toward individual proposals. These must be seen in the following light:

---

[8]Committee for the Study of Economic and Monetary Union, chaired by Jacques Delors, Brussels, Belgium, 1989.

EXHIBIT 2.5 Attitudes toward the EC

	Our future is inextricably linked with that of the EC	We should move toward greater economic integration	We should move toward greater foreign policy cooperation	We should protect against non-EC companies	1992 should be a process of liberalization
Belgium	+	+	+	0	+
Denmark	0	−	−	0	−
France	+	+	+	+	−
Germany	+	+	+	−	+
Greece	0	0	−	0	0
Italy	+	+	+	+	−
Ireland	+	+	−	−	+
Luxembourg	+	+	+	−	0
Netherlands	+	+	+	−	−
Portugal	+	+	+	+	+
Spain	+	+	+	+	−
United Kingdom	0	−	−	−	+

Source: Henley Centre, London, 1989.
Note: + = Yes; 0 = Neutral; − = No.

- The effect that such proposals would have on their own country.
- The degree to which their desire to see an Internal Market that works allows them to accept proposals presented as efficacious and necessary.
- Their commitment to the European ideal.

At a political level and as a guide to the underlying perception of the Internal Market, one could imagine a spectrum of countries based on their attitude toward a number of key criteria. *Exhibit 2.5* presents such a matrix. It is inevitably subjective, though based on close observation and discussions with a number of key participants. And to a degree, it is misrepresentative, in that it seeks to reflect underlying attitudes as opposed to simply those of the government of the day.

At one extreme lies the United Kingdom, whose 1992 information campaign called on U.K. companies to exploit the changes that were to come, and which sees the Internal Market as a way of increasing exports to the rest of Europe. At the other extreme lies Luxembourg, whose national TV station signs off by showing scenes from around Europe to the accompaniment of Beethoven's 9th Symphony (the EC's anthem), and which recognizes that its interest is inextricably tied up with that of Europe as a whole. Somewhere in the middle lie the following countries:

- France and Germany, which seek to tailor the 1992 exercise to their interests but also recognize a wider European interest, which at times necessitates compromise.
- Italy, Belgium, Holland, and Ireland, whose pro-unity sentiments are somewhat greater than those of other countries in Europe — Italy because of a history in which dissatisfaction with internal attempts at unification has led to an embodiment of those hopes at a European level and the latter three because of their relative size.
- Portugal and Greece, which fear the exacerbation of regional disparities that freedom of movement could bring and for which measures aimed at reducing regional disparities are especially important.
- Spain, which is gradually moving from the Portuguese camp to the Italian one.
- Denmark, which has traditionally been anti-EC but recognizes the economic importance of membership.

However, as we have pointed out, the practical effect of some of the measures envisaged in Delors' wider Internal Market must also be taken into account. Take, for example, the measures that can be lumped broadly together as "worker rights" — the Social Charter. Not surprisingly, these are opposed by the U.K. government. To quote British Chancellor Nigel Lawson:

> *Having spent ten years gradually removing the dead hand of corporatism in Britain, I have to say that we have no intention of accepting its reintroduction at a European level.*[9]

Implicit opposition to these measures, however, has also come from what might be seen as an unexpected source — Socialist Spain. The reason is simple enough. Spain has benefited more than any other country from an influx of foreign investment, both from Japanese companies seeking low-cost manufacturing plants within the EC as a way of circumventing moves toward protectionism and from companies such as Volkswagen that are expanding their investment in SEAT in Spain as a way of escaping labor costs that are some four times higher in Germany. Any measures that would result in the harmonization of working conditions would nullify to some extent the economic advantages that Spain has over its neighbors. For the same reason the high-cost countries, led by Germany, are at the forefront of promoting the acceptance of measures that would allay their fears of the Internal Market leading to an exodus of manufacturing to low-cost southern European locations.

What this example demonstrates is that assessing the kind of Europe that will emerge in the 1990s is not an easy matter. A series of proposals, many of them in nascent form, will attract coalitions of different member states, depending on the proposal in question. The extent to which further progress is made and is seen to be desirable — that is, Euro-euphoria continues — will largely determine the willingness and ability of individual countries to compromise.

A FORTRESS EUROPE?

One of the most difficult questions for member states to reach agreement on is the question of protectionism. A widespread perception exists outside Europe that the Internal Market inevitably entails a degree of protectionism against non-EC firms. The decision by a large number of Japanese manufacturers and banks such as Fuji Bank, Futjitsu, the Industrial Bank of Japan, Matsushita, Mitsubishi, Toshiba, and Toyota to establish themselves in Europe has some economic rationale to it. In the light of the rise of the yen, it has become cheaper and more profit-

---

[9]Speech to Chatham House, January 25, 1989.

able to move offshore. There is no doubt, however, that much of the move into Europe is prompted by fears that firms not established in the EC will suffer from an inability to gain access to the European market. As a result, direct foreign investments by U.S. and Japanese firms have been increasing rapidly in the past few years.[10] The calls by U.S. Secretary of State for Commerce, Robert Mosbacher, for an American observer seat at the EC decision-making table reveal a fear that left to themselves the Europeans would make decisions that would be damaging to U.S. firms seeking to operate in the European market.

In both the Japanese and American cases, examples have been held up to demonstrate the protectionist nature of the EC: in the case of Japan, a greater use of antidumping duties in a range of areas, including printers, cassettes, video tapes, photocopiers and electrical motors; in the case of the United States, the ban on the importation of meat containing hormones following the ban introduced on all such meat (EC and non-EC produced) at the beginning of 1988. Overt protectionism, however, was not the driving force in many of these cases. It could be argued that with its greater reliance on foreign trade, the EC has more to lose from protectionism than has either the United States or Japan.[11]

To some it was a surprise that the White Paper, while having much to say about the internal barriers within Europe, had little to say about the implications for Europe's external relations. This was, however, no more than a reflection of the deep divisions existing over the nature and objectives of the Internal Market, both among member states and within the Commission itself.

---

[10]Direct foreign investment by U.S. companies in the EC is currently growing at 24% a year to stand at $122.3 billion in 1987, or 40% of all U.S. external direct investment. That of Japanese companies is growing at 90% a year to stand at $6.3 billion in 1987, or 20% of all Japanese external direct investment. So, although commentators have focused on the rate of growth by the Japanese, it is the United States that has the larger stake in the EC. This is perhaps best illustrated by the fact that IBM employs more people in Europe than do all Japanese companies put together.

[11]Nevertheless, figures published by the World Bank (in *Staff Working Papers 789*) show the EC to be relatively more protectionist than either the United States or Japan. Under their definition, the EC subjects 5.7% of all product lines imported from other industrialized countries to some form of nontariff barriers (NTB), compared with 5.5% in Japan and 3.2% in the United States. Similarly, 15.2% of the actual trade flows into the EC from other industrialized countries are subject to an NTB, compared with 9.7% in Japan and 16.5% in the United States. The figures should not be taken as definitive given the substantial difficulties in measuring the real impact of these measures. It should also be noted that the World Bank's definition of nontariff barriers covers quantitative import restrictions, voluntary export restraints, decreed prices, tariff types, and monitoring measures. These do not exist on intra-EC trade and are not the nontariff barriers targeted for abolition by the European Commission in the 1992 program.

The first thing to say is that it is not clear what protectionism means or how it could be brought about at a time when thousands of non-EC firms are already established in the market. Protectionism could entail one of four things:

1. The setting of standards and regulations in such a way as to favor European firms.
2. An unwillingness to grant public procurement contracts to non-EC firms.
3. A series of antidumping duties and local content rules that would push non-EC firms into establishing themselves within the Community as firms sourcing locally in order to secure equal treatment.
4. Rules on reciprocity that would deny non-EC firms access to the market in the absence of "equal access" being granted to EC firms in the other country.

In some cases, such as the setting of standards and regulations, it is the apolitical standard-setting bodies that will be responsible for the results that ensue. CEN and CENELEC are small bodies which rely on representations from industrial concerns. Contrary to some perceptions, they are bodies which are open and easy to access. In such cases it is up to non-EC firms to ensure that they have the necessary organizational structure and public relations advice to allow them to influence the decisions made by CEN and CENELEC. Not being allowed to participate in the standard-setting process does not imply a lack of influence. In other cases the extent to which any one of the above measures is applied will depend in part on a resolution of the differences among member states.

Divisions within the Community over protectionism arise from variations in perceptions over the objectives of the Internal Market and the effect of free competition on industry. As we mentioned earlier, there is a disagreement over whether or not the prime objective of the Internal Market is to help European companies regain a degree of competitiveness over their Japanese and American counterparts. The belief that this is a prime objective tempts some countries, such as France, to seek to ensure that the system is fixed in such a way as to secure that objective. The belief of the United Kingdom and Germany in the merits of free trade, which as much as anything else reflects their own self-confidence in the results of such a system, and in the case of the United Kingdom in the supremacy of the consumer's interest over that of the producer, points in the opposite direction. These divisions are not limited to member states. As the deliberations over the policies toward telecommunications and financial services have shown, the Commission itself is divided over the relative merits of competition versus regulation and consequently over the merits of free trade.

These divisions have been evident. In the automobile sector, for example, there is a substantial difference between France and Italy, which have quotas on Japanese imports of 3% and 3,000 cars, respectively, and the United Kingdom and Germany — the former with an 11% quota and the latter with no quota at all. These differences point to the most important source of the divisions over the free trade issue — the practical effect that greater competition would have.

Industrialists across Europe have warned about the rationalization that they see as part and parcel of the 1992 process. Not surprisingly, those who have enjoyed the greatest protection in the past and who have the most to lose are the ones at the forefront of urging protectionism. Thus the calls have come from the chairmen of Renault, Peugeot, and Fiat, who in the name of a wider European interest have called for the "shelter of strong competition"[12] and time for the European industry to achieve the standards of efficiency and competitiveness enjoyed by the Japanese and South Koreans. The fact that it is the French and Italian multinationals that have faced the least amount of Japanese competition is no coincidence. Nor is their opposition to the help given by the British government to Nissan's production plant in the United Kingdom, which has already begun exporting cars from there to the rest of Europe and which aims to be producing 200,000 U.K.-made cars for sale in Europe — cars whose high local content allows them to evade the quotas currently in operation. The fear of the Japanese exploiting a common market for cars and the inconsistency of a set of divergent national quotas in a frontier-free Europe of the 1990s have consumed the industry and national governments. These are issues that have stalled work aimed at removing the barriers to trade in cars.

The economic and marketing rationales that underlie many of the attitudes toward the participation of non-EC firms in the 1992 program work both ways — in some cases in favor of free trade — as evidenced by the following two examples:

- The decision by the Italian telecommunications equipment firm, Italtel, to choose AT&T as its partner for the future rather than any of the European firms, Siemens, Alcatel, or Ericsson, which had been in the running.
- The opposition of Germany, Luxembourg, and the United Kingdom to any definition of the reciprocity in financial services that would

---

[12]"Renault Chief Urges Protection," *Financial Times*, March 24, 1988.

affect the subsidiaries of non-EC firms operating in the EC or the attractiveness of these countries to the kind of inward investment in financial services that has secured their preeminence in the area.

The EC's definition of reciprocity, notably in respect to banking services has shifted. In the middle of 1988 it was taken to mean "equal access on equal terms." By mid-1989 the Commission line had softened considerably, and it was proposing to take action only where equivalent treatment of EC and domestic institutions was not available or where "it appears that credit institutions of the Community do not enjoy national treatment and the same competitive advantages as domestic credit institutions in a third country," with the latter case being sufficient grounds for action against subsidiaries controlled from the third country in question.[13] What we have, therefore, is a complex situation, with underlying attitudes toward market access being supplemented by individual country considerations on a sector-by-sector basis.

In general, the attitude toward American firms differs from that toward Japanese and Far Eastern firms. For a host of reasons — cultural, historical, economic, and the risks associated with a trade war — action against Japanese firms is seen as far more acceptable than that against U.S. firms. The decision by the Spanish government to favor French and German tenders for its high-speed rail network, despite a tender by Mitsubishi which was reported as being 30% lower, is an example of an action that may become common with respect to Japanese firms. It would be unlikely in the case of an American one.

Interestingly, however, and somewhat ominously, the latest draft directives on public procurement covering the so-called excluded sectors (telecommunications, water, energy, and transport) allow discrimination against contractors or consortia, which source over 50% of the value of the contract from outside the EC. As a sign of the mood in Brussels, this could be thought to represent a hardening of attitudes. In practice, it is likely to have been the only way in which the Commission could have made political progress in this area.

The move toward bilateralism in world affairs, especially in the service areas not covered by the GATT code, and the ability to use anti-dumping duties and local content rules on a largely bilateral basis reinforce the belief that it is Japanese and Far Eastern firms that will suffer most. The belief on their part that they will need to establish themselves in Europe as genuinely European operations in order to avoid protec-

---

[13]"Britain Gives Detail of Banking Directive," *Financial Times*, April 14, 1989.

tionism is not unjustified. In the past the battle has been over anti-dumping duties; in the future it will be over the degree to which components have been sourced locally and R&D conducted within the EC.

It may also be that the United States will be drawn into an EC-Japanese dispute. The decision by the Commission early in 1989 to seek to impose anti-dumping duties on Ricoh photocopiers made in the Japanese company's U.S. plant may be a sign of things to come. In the future, the same treatment may be accorded to semiconductors, cars, and other consumer goods made by Japanese companies in their U.S. plants and exported to Europe in order to evade either quotas or anti-dumping duties.

What has yet to be resolved to the satisfaction of all is the means by which the goal of improving the competitiveness of Europe is to be achieved. An economic recession in Europe or a substantial degree of rationalization would strengthen the hands of those elements who favor a degree of favoritism toward EC firms.

A TWO-TIER EUROPE?

Aside from the issue of protectionism, it is possible to say that there is a group of countries (Benelux, France, Germany, Italy, and increasingly Spain) for which progress beyond the proposals contained in the White Paper into realms of greater cooperation, political and economic, remains an attractive course. This contrasts with the position of the other member states — which incidentally were not among the founder members — which either treat the idea of further integration with disdain (the United Kingdom and Denmark) or whose priorities lie elsewhere (Greece, Ireland, and Portugal). This split is reinforced in the monetary and economic area by the fact that the economic systems, as in the case of indirect tax rates, for example, of the core six are already remarkably similar and require relatively little change to be harmonized.

The core-periphery split opens up the prospect of a two-tier Europe, with a small number of countries progressing in areas such as the abolition of frontier controls, approximation in the rates of taxation, and greater use of a common currency — areas the other countries would find politically and economically difficult or undesirable.

In the absence of a decision by the core to move ahead regardless of the views of the "periphery" countries, there is no doubt that progress in many of the areas under consideration, both those in the White Paper and those considered beyond it, will be slow. It would require a great deal of frustration about the current system and a lack of progress in areas where progress is considered to be advantageous for a core group of countries to think seriously about moving ahead on their own. Significantly, they have already done so in the case of frontier controls, agreement over which was embodied in the Schengen Accord. In addition, Spanish Prime Minister Gonzalez echoed the feeling of many, when in relation to the United Kingdom's attitude toward monetary integration, he made this statement:

> *One should not work to exclude anybody, but nobody can be given the right of veto over the desire of others to advance toward monetary union.*[14]

The ability of a core group of countries to move ahead separately would further depend on agreement on a set of key issues, one of which is their relations with the outside world. Much will also depend on developments elsewhere in Europe.

Completion of the Internal Market has aroused considerable anxiety among the group of European Free Trade Association (EFTA) countries (Austria, Finland, Iceland, Norway, Sweden, and Switzerland). Just as the Americans and Japanese fear a lack of access to the EC market, so do the EFTA countries. The difference is that they have much more to lose, with over 70% of their exports going to the EC. In some respects the position of companies such as Volvo, which has declared that "if we as a Swedish company lose too much from being treated as outside the EC, Volvo must naturally take the consequences and become an EC company,"[15] is akin to that of many of the Japanese car manufacturers.

In the case of the EFTA countries, the implications of 1992 are not simply related to the question of access to the Community. EC developments concerning employment rights, foreign national visas, inward investment, and others will profoundly affect EFTA's economic development. The EFTA countries are not united in their attitude toward the relationship that they ought to be striving for with the EC, the difference in their links with the Soviet Union being a major factor. And while some in EFTA may favor a customs union with the EC, others consider this step either too radical or not radical enough. Nevertheless, fear of the Internal Market has been sufficiently strong for EFTA to call on more than one occasion for a strengthening of links and "a more structural partnership with common decision making and administrative institutions" and "the fullest possible realisation of the movement of goods,

---

[14]*Daily Telegraph,* June 26, 1989.

[15]"Swedish Nervousness on EC Single Market," *Financial Times,* April 6, 1989.

services, capital, and persons."[16] These moves open up the intriguing possibility of a barrier-free Europe consisting of a core that moves toward greater political and economic integration and a periphery consisting of the reluctant six EC countries, together with the six EFTA ones that co-exist in nothing more than a free trade area.

Alongside the developments within EFTA are the potentially more far-reaching ones in Eastern Europe. While it is the process of *perestroika* that has opened up the possibility of greater trade with the Soviet Union and a degree of economic integration with countries such as Hungary, it is the impact of *glasnost* and the opening up of Eastern Europe on the European psyche that will have the more far-reaching effect. Europeans are now less scared of war than they have been at any time since 1945, and the fear of being squeezed between the United States and the Soviet Union is one that is rapidly losing its hold.

We are far from the situation of pre-WWI Europe, which J.M. Keynes described as one in which "France, Germany, Italy, Austria and Holland, Russia and Romania and Poland, throb together, and their structure and civilisation are essentially one";[17] but at the margin we may be moving in that direction. Does such a move negate the political rationale of the EC's unification? Probably not, but it may be perceived to be in some quarters, notably in Germany. Torn between their desire to pursue EC integration and their desire for German reunification, there is little doubt that the vast majority of Germans would opt for the former. But the political effort needed for reunification, especially at a time when the East is showing a human face, may act as a brake on the pace of integration within the EC. It is to counter that fear that the likes of the French are keen to accelerate progress towards monetary union and "tie in" the German state.

CONCLUSION

A remarkable transformation has occurred within Europe during the late 1980s. Talk of Europe's stagnation has been replaced by a new-found confidence and a willingness to progress toward further integration.

The proposals themselves that have been put forward as part of the 1992 program, and which are designed to rejuvenate Europe's economic

---

[16]"EFTA Calls for Integrated West European Economy," *Financial Times*, March 16, 1989.

[17]J. M. Keynes, *The Economic Consequences of the Peace* (London: Macmillan, 1919).

performance, should not be considered in isolation — partly because progress toward their acceptance will be slow and uneven but also because the hype that the process has generated has resulted in significant changes in attitude within the business community. Retailers are internationalizing and manufacturers are considering Pan-European strategies — not because of any objective changes but because they believe that the opportunities and threats demand it.

What is clear is that the impact of 1992 will vary, both by sector and by company. Among other things, it will depend on the nature of the consumer whom the company faces, the importance and nature of the barriers to trade identified by the Commission, the nature and origin of the company itself, the market and competitors the company faces, and the ease with which restructuring, rationalization, and strategic alliances are allowed to take place. More than anything, it will depend on the ability and skill of individual companies to devise appropriate strategies in an increasingly complex environment and to push them through.

Apart from anything else, the nature of the European business environment is evolving. A debate is under way over the nature of the European entity which should emerge in the 1990s. How far should the process of integration proceed and into what areas? Should Europe restrict the amount of foreign competition? Should the process be extended to involve other European countries, to the north, south, and even the east? It is in the face of the uncertainty of impending radical changes in the structure of European society and of the markets in which they operate that companies are having to devise appropriate strategies. And while generalizations may be of help, those strategies will have to vary considerably across companies, sectors, and countries.

APPENDIX A: Decision Making in the EC

MAIN BODIES OF THE EC
European Council of Ministers

The Council, which consists of political representatives from the 12 member states, is the EC's supreme decision-making body. Under the provisions of the Single European Act, most Internal Market decisions (with the exception of those relating to taxation, employment, and the rights of individuals) were to be taken by qualified majority votes, though the right to invoke vital national interests remained intact. Fifty-four votes were necessary to adopt a proposal and the votes were distributed as follows:

Germany, France, Italy, and the United Kingdom	10 each
Spain	8
Belgium, Greece, Netherlands, and Portugal	5 each
Denmark and Ireland	3 each
Luxembourg	2

Most of the Council's work is done on a monthly basis at the ministerial level, although head of government summits are held twice yearly, with the intent of setting wider strategic goals.

European Commission

The Commission is the Community's executive body and sole initiator of legislation. Legislation consists of either regulations (which are legally binding on adoption by the Council) or directives (which the member states have two years to incorporate into their national legislation). Each member country (depending on its size) appoints one or two commissioners to serve a minimum of a four-year term. Each commissioner has primary responsibility for a specific area, such as Regional Policy, Internal Market, or Competition, for which there is a corresponding directorate staffed by career personnel numbering just over 10,000 in total. In addition, the commissioners are served by a small appointed political staff.

Apart from drafting and initiating legislation, the Commission has numerous functions on a day-to-day basis, such as ensuring that legislation is adhered to and administering EC funds, many of which are delegated by the Council.

European Parliament

The Parliament is elected by universal suffrage every 5 years and consists of 518 representatives from the member states. Although the political groupings are nationally focused, once elected, they form alliances within the Parliament and do not act as national blocs. In some cases, for example, the Socialists, campaigning is conducted on the basis of a common European program. Following the elections of June 1989, the largest groupings consisted of Socialists (180), Christian Democrats (123), Liberals (44), Communists (41), Greens (39), British Conservatives (32), and the European Right (21).

Prior to 1987, the Parliament's powers were limited to an ability to dismiss the Commission (as yet unused) and to reject the budget (used frequently between 1984 and 1988). Since the signing of the Single European Act, the Parliament is involved in a cooperative procedure through which it can alter legislation passed by the Council. (See *Exhibit A1* for a diagram of the way in which this works.) Significantly it was used for the first time in early 1989 to force through stronger measures concerning vehicle emissions.

European Court of Justice

The Court consists of 13 judges and is responsible for interpreting EC law and consequently judging whether parties (which may be member states, the Commission, the Council, the Parliament or individual companies) are acting in accordance with that law. Many key developments, such as those promoting mutual recognition, defining the Commission's merger and competition powers, and interpreting EC law as it applied to insurance, have come in the form of Court rulings. Significantly, the Court is overworked, is unable to address more than a small proportion of the cases that come before it, and is lacking in compliance powers. At the end of 1987, over 500 cases were pending.

THE DECISION-MAKING PROCESS

Exhibit A.1 illustrates the way in which proposals are turned into EC law and the role played by each of the three institutions involved. Importantly, this cooperative procedure does not apply in those areas specified by the Single European Act (for example, taxation, employment), where the Council must act by unanimous agreement.

EXHIBIT A.1 Decision making in the EC

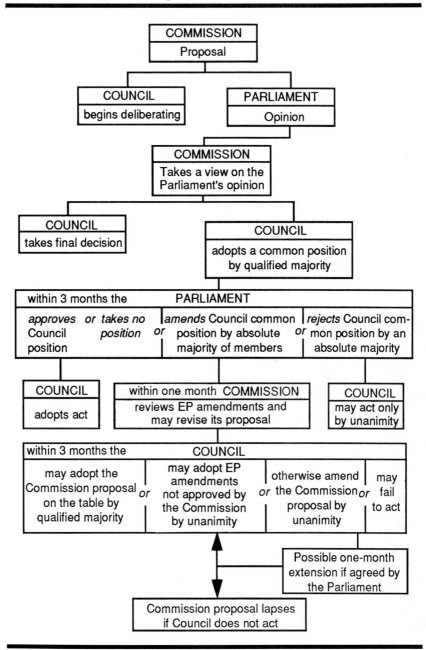

CHAPTER *3*

The Marketing Challenge

The European Community is a giant market of vital importance to U.S. business. In 1987, the EC accounted for 40% of U.S. foreign investment. U.S. direct investment in the EC is 30 times greater than that of Japan. In addition, the EC accounted for 24% of U.S. merchandise exports and 29% of service exports. Sales of goods and services produced within the EC by U.S. companies reached $235 billion in 1987, four times the value of U.S. direct exports.[1] As markets become increasingly global, it is essential that marketing managers understand the implications of the changes that are currently being pursued in the U.S.'s principal export market. After a brief recapitulation of the content of the 1992 program, this chapter examines the implications of the reforms on market structure and industry consolidation, on the design of marketing programs, and on the configuration of marketing organizations.

THE 1992 PROGRAM

Concerns about the ability of EC companies to compete successfully with their American and Japanese counterparts in markets that are increasingly global in scope prompted the European Commission to issue a White Paper in June 1985. This White Paper proposed some 300 reforms that by January 1, 1993 would remove trade barriers such as the following:[2]

- Border controls. Formalities and delays at borders are believed to

---

John A. Quelch and Robert D. Buzzell, "Marketing Moves through EC Crossroads," *Sloan Management Review,* Fall 1989, pp. 63–74, is based on this chapter.

[1]Michael Calingaert, *The 1992 Challenge from Europe* (Washington, D.C.: National Planning Association, 1989), pp. 77–78.

[2]Ibid; and "Completing the Internal Market" (White Paper from the Commission to the European Council, Milan, June 28–29, 1985), COM(85)310, June 14, 1985.

cost $10 billion (2% of EC gross domestic product) plus $5.5 billion in foregone trade each year.[3]

- Divergent technical standards among EC member countries. The costs of nonharmonization have been estimated at $6 billion for telecommunications, $3 billion for building materials, and $1 billion for food products.[4]

- Restrictive public procurement contracts designed to favor national suppliers. Such contracts account for 10% of EC GDP, yet only 2% of them are awarded to firms from other member states.[5] Open public procurement would result in savings of $21 billion.[6]

- Different value-added and excise tax rates among member countries. These cause competitive distortions as customers cross borders to buy lower-taxed products.

- Controls on the free movement of capital and people, including the absence of mutual recognition of each country's professional qualifications.

- National government regulations on financial and transportation services, which result in wide price spreads for similar services across member states.

- Varying national regulations governing mergers and acquisitions, trademark registration, and patent protection.

In May 1988, the Commission published a report that estimated the costs of these barriers and the economic benefits to the EC that would accrue from their removal. The Cecchini Report concluded (with a 30% margin of error) that the EC's GDP would rise 4.5–7.0%, that employment would increase by 2–5 million, that consumer prices would fall by 4.5–6%, and that the EC's external trade balance would increase by 1% of GDP.[7]

Some observers argue that the likely impact of the 1992 program has been exaggerated. They argue that the economic benefits forecasted in the Cecchini Report depend on unreasonable "multiplier" effects and

---

[3]Paolo Cecchini, *The European Challenge 1992* (Aldershot, U.K.: Wildwood House, 1988), p. 8.

[4]Ibid., pp. 25–26.

[5]"Second Report from the Commission to the Council and the European Parliament on the Implementation of the Commission's White Paper on Completing the Internal Market," COM(87)203, May 11, 1987, p. 16.

[6]Cecchini, op. cit., p. 22.

[7]Ibid., pp. 93–97.

are therefore too optimistic; that an economic recession, trade union opposition and/or political pressure to aid economically depressed regions could quickly fuel protectionist sentiment and stanch further progress on the removal of trade barriers; that even if existing trade barriers are removed, they will simply be replaced by more subtle barriers or by more frequent noncompliance with EC directives; and that enthusiasm for the 1992 program will fade — for example, in the United Kingdom — if its success threatens to further the causes of monetary union or European political unity.[8]

We believe, however, that the 1992 reform process has gathered such a momentum that it will now be hard to slow down; that the confidence, ability, and ambition of EC officials to see the program through are growing every day; that the commitment of European business executives and their optimism about the opportunities 1992 presents are both strong; and that the specter of a protectionist "Fortress Europe" is largely intended to maximize intra-EC investment by foreign companies and to persuade Japan to open up its markets.[9] Substantial progress toward common standards has already been made — for example, in such areas as large risk insurance and toy safety. Not every proposed reform will be in place by the end of 1992, but many will. These reforms hold substantial implications for market structure, marketing program design, and marketing organization. These implications are explored in the following sections.

MARKET INTEGRATION AND INDUSTRY CONSOLIDATION

The prospect of an integrated EC marketplace has triggered a wave of consolidation in many industries. Consolidation is going on, or is likely to, at two levels:

- Within companies, manufacturing and distribution activities are being combined into fewer, larger facilities. (For example, in 1989 Ford of Europe was consolidating its manufacturing plants and reducing its work force in anticipation of intensified competition.[10])

---

[8]See, for example, Leigh Bruce, "1992: The Bad News," *International Management*, September 1988, pp. 22–26; and Brooks Tigner, "Fortress Europe," *International Management*, December 1988, pp. 24–30.

[9]Calingaert, op. cit., p. 96.

[10]"Gearing Up for the Race of the 1990s," *Financial Times*, January 25, 1989.

- Industries are becoming more concentrated, and will become more so, primarily via mergers and acquisitions.

Both kinds of consolidation will help EC-based organizations to reduce costs and improve their global competitive positions. Rising industry concentration levels will also affect the nature and intensity of competition in the EC market. In this section, we explore how the process of consolidation is likely to evolve, how far it may go, and how marketing may change as a result.

Mergers and Acquisitions

Even before the passage of the "White Paper" in 1985, companies had started to look for acquisition opportunities in Europe.[11] According to the EC Directorate General on Competition, the number of mergers and acquisitions in the 12 Community countries increased from 117 in fiscal 1983 to around 450 in fiscal 1988. These mergers and acquisitions are occurring in all kinds of industries and involve both EC-based companies and outsiders. For example:

- Deutsche Bank, West Germany's largest bank, acquired Italy's 11th largest bank, Banca d'America e d'Italia.
- BSN, France's largest producer of food and drinks, has bought 8 other European food companies since 1986, including Nabisco's European business.
- Since 1987, U.S.-based Sara Lee has acquired Akzo's consumer products division, Dutch coffee producer Van Neile; and DIM, France's leading pantyhose manufacturer.
- Switzerland's Nestlé has agreed to buy U.K.-based Rowntree (chocolates), and Buitoni, an Italian pasta producer.
- ASEA, a Swedish electrical engineering firm, merged with its major Swiss competitor, Brown Boveri.

Motivations for acquisitions and mergers vary. In some cases, non-EC companies are attempting to buy their way into "insider" status, or to strengthen established positions in the EC, by merging with or acquiring EC companies. In other cases, EC companies are attempting to guard against multinationals dominating their home markets post-1992. In financial services, for instance, major banks and insurance companies

---

[11]Richard I. Kirkland, "Merger Mania Is Sweeping Europe," *Fortune*, December 19, 1988, pp. 157ff.

have merged in Germany (Dresdner Bank and Allianz), the United Kingdom (Lloyds Bank and Abbey Life), and France (Banque National de Paris and Union des Assurances de Paris).[12]

Many mergers between EC companies and/or outsiders with extensive EC operations are motivated by a desire to create a large enough market share in one principal business (or a few related ones) to become a major contender in the Pan-European market. For example, through several recent acquisitions, Thorn EMI has gained leadership in the fragmented Western European commercial and industrial light fittings market. More than 60% of Thorn's light fittings sales are now made outside its home market of the United Kingdom. Becoming the Pan-European market share leader has allowed Thorn to spread its administrative overhead costs and, it is claimed, become Europe's low-cost producer of light fittings.[13] Similarly, BSN's acquisitions in various food and beverage lines are presumably designed to make the company a leader in the post-1992 EC food industry, broadly defined.

Still another objective for mergers and acquisitions, in some industries, is to gain control of distribution. Beginning in 1986, several of the leading producers of distilled spirits scrambled to acquire their distributors or to form joint ventures for the same purpose. Guinness, for example, established joint venture distribution companies with Bacardi in both Germany and Spain and also established a joint venture in France with Moet-Hennessy.

Many acquisitions are fueled by multiple motives. For example, in June 1986, Volkswagen bought the majority stake in SEAT. Volkswagen achieved three objectives with this acquisition: access to the growing Spanish marketplace, access to a pool of low-cost Spanish labor, and (allegedly) the creation of a more Pan-European profile for its automobiles. Some mergers are government-initiated, motivated by an attempt to protect strategic industries from debilitating competition post-1992. An example is the merger of four of the seven largest banks in Spain. The opening of public procurement contracts to nonnational suppliers will also fuel merger activity. Particularly affected will be such industries as construction, now dominated by small- and medium-sized firms, and boiler making, where 15 national companies currently utilizing only 20%

---

[12]"A Marriage of Giants to Defend French Finance," *Business Week,* April 10, 1989, p. 46.

[13]Clay Harris, "A Fitting Tribute for a Road into Europe," *Financial Times,* November 28, 1988.

of their capacity could be reduced to 4 with consequent 20% cost savings.[14]

While the pace of merger activity has quickened in the EC since the early 1980s, we should not exaggerate its importance. As noted in Chapter 2, "merger mania" has thus far consisted much more of talk than of action. Moreover, some of the mergers that press accounts have attributed to the 1992 program have probably been motivated at least equally by other factors. Even when mergers are consummated, some of them may not last. Combinations of company organizations, especially those that have traditionally been strongly national in their orientations, can be expected to produce severe "culture clashes."

Another limitation on the process of consolidation via mergers and acquisitions is the EC's competition policies. Under Articles 85 and 86 of the Treaty of Rome, the EC authorities can block combinations or agreements that are anticompetitive or that constitute "abuse of a dominant position."[15]

Despite these qualifications, it seems clear that there will be an increase in concentration (on a Pan-European basis) in many industries during the 1990s, leading to more intense competition as increasing numbers of companies cross national boundaries to compete against each other. The cartelization that long existed in many European industries is breaking down, and increasingly open competition is impacting companies headquartered both inside and outside the EC.

Strategic Alliances

In addition to mergers, strategic alliances are on the rise in Europe. These alliances take many different forms but are all designed to allow companies to achieve together things they could not do as efficiently individually. These alliances usually involve some combination of:

1. Licensing of technology in a joint venture;
2. A distribution agreement tied to a joint venture; and/or
3. Swapping or sharing products and/or technology between two or more companies.

---

[14]Cecchini, op. cit., p. 22.

[15]Michael Emerson et al., *The Economics of 1992* (Oxford, U.K.: Oxford University Press, 1988), p. 179.

Often, as in the alliance between Banco Santander and Royal Bank of Scotland, companies involved in joint ventures swap reciprocal equity stakes.

Some strategic alliances, usually aimed at cooperative R&D activities, are government initiated. These include such multicompany programs as ESPRIT and JESSI in the electronics field. Other joint ventures are company initiated. For example, Philips and U.S.-based Whirlpool Corporation recently formed a joint venture that will give Whirlpool access to the European home appliance market. The move is also designed to free both funds and management time for Philips, allowing it to concentrate on a few strategic businesses in preparation for 1992. In another joint venture, Philips and Siemens A.G., the West German electronics giant, have formed a $1 billion research project, called MegaSubmicron, to develop semiconductors. These two companies, with a long history of rivalry, now see a need to share the costs and risks of such an enormous undertaking.

Increasing Concentration

Through mergers, acquisitions, and the formation of strategic alliances, many industries are becoming increasingly concentrated. How far is this trend likely to go?

A natural model for the post-1992 structure of EC industries is that of the United States. It is a comparable market in terms of size and economic development but with few of the internal barriers that have impeded concentration in Europe. Following this line of reasoning, a study by Booz, Allen, and Hamilton suggests that substantial increases in concentration are likely. The combined shares of the five leading competitors in the EC passenger car market, for example, are around 60%, compared with 81% for the United States.[16] The disparity is even greater in life insurance (15% versus 44%) and pharmaceuticals (14% versus 28%). Up to some point, increasing concentration may be necessary for EC industries to achieve (or even approach) cost parity with U.S. and Japanese competitors. It seems likely that consolidation will continue *beyond* the level required to attain scale economies, as major firms scramble to strengthen their positions prior to the 1992 deadline.

If the consolidation of EC industries leads to concentration levels similar to those of the United States, the "shakeout" process will be a very painful one indeed. Many small firms will be acquired or forced

---

[16]Martin M. Waldenstrom, "Preparing for 1992: A Time to Buy, A Time to Sell," *Outlook*, March 1989, pp. 55–59.

out of business. In which industries are such shakeouts most likely? Some industries, of course, are already highly concentrated on an EC-wide basis and indeed are already global rather than regional in scope. Examples include aircraft production, computers, petrochemicals, and semiconductor fabrication equipment. These highly scale-dependent industries are not likely to be affected much by market integration. At the other extreme, some industries appear to offer little opportunity for cost reduction through increased scale of output. The EC Commission's studies indicated, for example, that scale economies are of minor significance in the production of footwear, clothing, leather goods, and carpeting.[17] Here again, market integration is not likely to affect industry structure significantly.

Where shakeouts *can* be expected, then, is in industries where significant opportunities for cost reduction or other advantages of large size exist but where attainment of optimal scale has historically been impeded by intra-EC barriers. Some examples are listed in *Exhibit 3.1*, along with the reasons for expecting increased concentration.

In these and some other industries, it seems likely that by the end of the 1990s the leading competitors will be comparable to their U.S. counterparts in terms of size and sales (measured by sales or assets) and EC-wide market shares.

Customer Concentration

If the process of consolidation means increasing concentration among *sellers* in many industries, it also implies greater concentration among *buyers*. This is an obvious point in the case of business-to-business marketing: the shift to fewer, larger publishing companies means fewer, larger customers for paper companies. Increasing buyer concentration seems likely for consumer products, too. While the White Paper contains no specific proposals that deal with retailers or wholesalers, it seems likely that some consolidation will take place at both levels of distribution during the 1990s. In addition, EC-wide cooperative buying groups will increase in importance. Several European retail food chains have already formed collaborative arrangements: one of these, "Euro-groupe," was announced in early 1989. In another grouping, U.K.-based Argyll agreed to cooperate with Ahold (Netherlands) and Casino (France).

Some mergers and acquisitions are likely to occur among retailers

---

[17]*The Economics of 1992*, Commission of the European Communities, European Economy Study No. 35 (Brussels, March 1988), p. 109.

EXHIBIT 3.1 Selected industries in which concentration is likely to increase

Industry	Comments
Banking	Because of historic national regulations, there is excess capacity and significant variations in prices.[a]
Telecommunications, construction products	Differences in standards, along with national preferences in government procurement, have protected suppliers.[b]
Major appliances	Opportunities for scale economies in manufacturing and component supply have not been fully exploited.
Food, beverages, and household nondurables	Potential scale economies in marketing are significant, and broader product scope may be needed to have adequate bargaining power in dealing with large retailers/distributors.[c]
Publishing	There are significant opportunities for scale economies, especially via fuller utilization of computer and telecommunications technologies.
Transportation	There is excess capacity, and costs and prices vary widely among countries.[d]
Business services (consulting, accounting, advertising)	Customers are increasingly multinational firms that prefer a regional approach in the provision of services.

[a]"Banks Face Shakeout as Europe Prepares for Unified Market," *Wall Street Journal*, April 4, 1989, p. 1.
[b]William Dawkins, "Not Enough Staff to Ensure Fair Play," *Financial Times*, November 17, 1988, pp. 9–10.
[c]See European Commission, *Research on the Cost of Non-Europe*, Vol. 12, "The Cost of Non-Europe in the Foodstuffs Industry," by Group MAC (The Commission, 1986).
[d]Henley Centre, *The United Markets of Europe: Transport* (London, 1988).

and wholesalers as a response to the consolidation of their suppliers. This is the pattern that John Kenneth Galbraith observed in the American economy a generation ago — one that he called "countervailing power."[18] To offset the enhanced bargaining power of multinational food producers such as Nestlé, for example, food retailers and restaurant operators will find it necessary to increase their scale of operations.

---

[18]John K. Galbraith, *American Capitalism: The Concept of Countervailing Power* (Boston: Houghton Mifflin, 1956).

For many of them, home market growth opportunities will not be sufficient — hence, the need for cross-border expansion. This is the rationale, for example, for a recent series of acquisitions and joint ventures by GB-Inno, Belgium's largest retailer.[19]

Consolidation among both sellers and buyers in many EC markets will lead to greater emphasis on "major account" approaches to marketing. Just as American marketers are increasingly relying on national account teams to develop and maintain relationships with key customers, so will EC companies come to depend on "EC account" systems. It will be a major challenge for the managers involved in selling to these customers to resist the natural tendency for "major accounts" to devolve into "major discounts." Another result of consolidation in distribution will no doubt be that of smaller accounts banding together to seek the same prices and terms of sale that are given to major accounts.

MARKETING PROGRAMS AND ORGANIZATION

Not surprisingly, changes in the market structure of many industries, along with the 1992 program's efforts to end specific physical, technical, and fiscal barriers, will lead to significant changes in marketing programs and organizations. It is not easy to separate the relative impact of the 1992 program from the effects of other technological, economic, and cultural trends already under way in contributing to these marketing changes. To the marketing manager, however, this issue is academic. The critical challenges are to identify the changes that are likely to occur and to determine how to respond.

Customer Behavior

First a cautionary word about customers. The 1992 reforms focus on supply rather than demand. They will make individual country markets more accessible, not more identical. Most of the well-documented cultural, historical, institutional, physical, and economic differences among the EC countries will survive the 1992 process.[20] For instance, the spread in per capita income between the richest and poorest EC member countries was 138% in 1987. Far from all of the EC population has traveled

---

[19]"GB-Inno Grows Out of Belgium," *Advertising Age,* June 20, 1988, p. 68.
[20]John Kay, "The Lasting Barriers to a United Europe," *Daily Telegraph,* April 27, 1989.

to another country. Such factors are responsible for substantial variation in consumer preferences and product usage behaviors across national boundaries. For example, French consumers prefer top-loading washing machines, British consumers demand front loaders; Germans want high-powered machines, Italians are satisfied with lower-priced, low-powered machines.[21] The 1992 reforms will, however, indirectly and over time promote more commonality in customer behavior across national boundaries. Specifically:

- The publicity surrounding 1992 is itself promoting a more Pan-European outlook primarily among businesspeople and public officials but also among consumers. Receptivity to ideas, products, and services for other EC member countries is likely to increase at the same time that removal of trade barriers promises to make them more readily available.
- Relaxed immigration controls will make it easier for people to live and work outside their home countries. Long-term, increased population mobility — along with increased travel and Pan-European communications — will have a melting pot effect on European consumer behavior. Fashions and trends will cross borders more rapidly.

Standardized market research tools will be needed to monitor changes in consumer attitudes and brand preferences across Europe, to permit cross-border comparisons, and to identify Pan-European consumer segments.[22] As the similarities in consumer behavior across national boundaries increasingly outweigh the differences, geographic segmentation is likely to give way to Pan-European lifestyle segmentation. This will permit segments that were too small to be targeted profitably within a single market to be served on a Pan-European basis. Hence, the variety of consumer needs will be addressed better. At the same time, as marketers focus on the similarities rather than the differences among European consumers, they will market to Europeans as if they were more alike, with the result that eventually European consumers will become more alike. A homogeneous European culture rep-

---

[21]C. Baden Fuller, P. Nicolaides, and J. Stopford, "National or Global? The Study of Company Strategies and the European Market for Major Domestic Appliances," Working Paper No. 28, Centre for Business Strategy, London Business School, June 1987.

[22]Because of the high level of cross-border merger and acquisition activity, companies will also need additional market research to monitor a broader range of actual and potential competitors than in the past.

resenting the lowest common denominator, however, is unlikely to emerge. Similarities in consumer behavior will increase, but respect for national and local cultures will remain strong.

Product Policy

The 1992 program promises to remove many of the more than 100,000 technical barriers that prevent standardized products being sold throughout the EC and impede the free movement of goods. Variations among EC countries in technical standards, health and safety regulations, testing and certification requirements, and trademark registration procedures have developed over the years to protect special interests and strategic industries and to respond to varying consumer concerns in different countries. This approach has imposed a cost on EC competitiveness. For example, the EC countries spent $10 billion to develop 10 telephone switching systems to meet different national standards compared with $1.5 billion in Japan for a single system and $3 billion in the United States for three systems.[23] The situation in the food industry is also instructive. The MAC Group has identified 200 specific barriers to cross-border EC trade in 10 food categories. These barriers include prohibitions or taxes on products with particular ingredients, required content regulations, different packaging and labeling laws, and health certificate requirements on imported products. The removal of such barriers, either through mutual recognition of each EC country's products or through harmonization of different standards, will open the door to more standardized "Euro-products."[24]

As the harmonization of technical standards proceeds, compromises are likely to err on the side of tougher rather than lowest common denominator standards. This approach will favor larger, value-added producers. All manufacturers should ensure that their interests are being represented in the standards-setting process and that their test data will be acceptable, especially if generated outside the EC. Manufacturers should also ensure that their trademarks are properly registered in all EC countries to preempt trademark pirates.

Common technical standards will permit longer and more efficient production runs of standard products. Fewer stockkeeping units will be

---

[23]"Making Europe a Mighty Market," *New York Times,* May 22, 1988.

[24]Group MAC, *The "Cost of Non-Europe" in the Foodstuffs Industry,* Research on the "Cost of Non-Europe" — Basic Findings, Volume 12, Part B (Brussels: Commission of the European Communities, 1988).

needed; sales forecast errors will decrease, permitting more reliable production and logistics planning. The consequent unit cost savings will
either be passed on to the consumer or reinvested in market development or R&D. Of course, the removal of technical barriers will not mitigate existing variations in consumer preferences. Locally adapted
products will still find a market, albeit of diminishing size, particularly
among older and more culture-bound consumers. Flexible manufacturing systems and the incorporation of local adaptations such as package
labels in different languages at the end of otherwise standardized production processes will hold down the costs of customization. However,
the differences in price and perceived value between locally adapted
products and standardized Euro-products will in most cases increase.

Standardized products will not necessarily carry the same brand
name throughout the EC. However, for two reasons, Eurobrands employing a common positioning strategy and package design in all EC
countries will become more common. First, market research is increasingly identifying Pan-European consumer segments, especially among
the young, the affluent, and the mobile with similar needs and life-
styles. Second, much of the merger and acquisition activity in consumer
packaged goods and the hefty premiums being paid for strong national
brand names are fueled by the belief that these brands can be extended
throughout Europe. At the same time, national consumer preferences
require that Eurobranding be an evolutionary process, particularly for
existing products. For example, Nestlé sells Camembert cheese throughout Europe under several national brand names in packages of different
sizes. Recently, Nestlé redesigned the packaging of these cheeses so that
the company brand appears alongside the local brand. Over time, the
Nestlé brand name will be increased in size at the expense of the local
brand name. Within five years, the local brand names will be phased
out.[25] Eurobranding of new products, particularly if they represent new
categories, will be easier than the creation of a Eurobrand from a set of
existing national brands.

In addition to fostering Eurobrands, the 1992 initiatives, along with
the restructuring and increased competitiveness of many industries,
should stimulate new product development. Increased innovation, especially in high-technology industries, is almost as important a goal of
the integration program as cost reduction. Clearly, EC-based companies
will become more innovative in R&D-intensive fields such as electronics;

[25]Cited in Kevin Cote, "1992: Europe Becomes One," *Advertising Age*, July 11, 1988, p. 46.

increased new product activity should follow as a natural result, both in basic components (e.g., integrated circuits) and finished products such as high-definition television.

New products will be more prominent in EC marketing programs for reasons other than increased R&D activities. For one thing, companies entering national markets for the first time, or attempting to expand existing beachhead positions, will place heavy emphasis on new brands, designs, or models as a basis for getting distribution or inducing customers to switch suppliers. A flurry of new product activity seems inevitable during the transition phase of market integration. Beyond this, increased product innovation is likely to persist over the long term because the surviving firms will have a larger potential market — the entire EC — for any single new product or service.

The integration of the EC market will lead to more efficient new product development for three reasons. First, scientists and engineers previously assigned to adapting products to local technical standards and to shepherding new products through 12 separate certification procedures will now be able to devote much more of their time to genuine R&D. Philips estimates the cost of adapting its television sets to meet different technical standards in EC countries at $20 million per year,[26] while the chemical industry spends 15% of R&D costs and Nixdorf 5% of its PABX systems manufacturing costs on technical standard adaptations. Second, single testing and trademark certification for the entire EC will enable new products to reach the market faster, so lost sales associated with testing delays and border-crossing delays will be minimized. A McKinsey study on the consumer electronics industry, for example, estimated that a six-month delay in bringing a new product to market cut life-cycle profits by 30%. Third, the comparative ease of securing Europe-wide certification will motivate marketers to launch more niche products targeted at a similar customer segment across all EC countries that might not have been introduced given the cost and inconvenience of multiple certifications.

The variety of products available in each EC market will increase as a result of the 1992 program. New products will be easier to launch and the removal of national import quotas as well as the forecasted increases in industry competitiveness and consumer demand associated with 1992 will further stimulate their development. Also, the removal of technical

---

[26]Cited by Shawn Tully, "Europe Gets Ready for 1992," *Fortune*, February 1, 1988, pp. 81–84, and by Max L. Turnipseed, "Implications for the Chemical Industry," Europe 1992 Frost & Sullivan Conference, New York, April 17–18, 1989.

barriers and the mutual recognition of products approved for sale in each member country will encourage the broader sale of existing products that have hitherto been excluded for certain EC markets. Imported beers will be sold in Germany, less expensive pasta products will be sold in Italy, and diet soft drinks will be sold in France and Spain. Finally, increased labor mobility will result in large segments of expatriates seeking to buy familiar, domestic products in other member countries. Increased product variety will intensify the battle for shelf space and add to distributor power. Producers will be persuaded, as a result, to allocate proportionately more marketing effort to their primary products at the expense of more marginal items. In addition, manufacturers of mainstream brands that are only distributed in a single market, are not focused in their positioning, and do not therefore enjoy a loyal customer franchise will be especially vulnerable as trade barriers come down.

Pricing Policy

Decreased costs, the opening up of public procurement contracts to broader competition, additional foreign investment in the EC resulting in increased production capacity, more rigorous enforcement of competition policy, and the general intensified competition generated by the 1992 reforms will create a downward pressure on prices in the EC. Increases in primary demand flowing from the 1992 reforms will only partly offset this trend. The European Commission has estimated that the prices of goods and services throughout the EC could decrease by as much as 8.3%.[27] The level of increased price competition will vary across industries. For example:

- Proposed airline deregulation will permit more carriers to compete on the same routes, broader fare zones, and more price competition, especially on heavily trafficked routes. The European Court of Justice has ruled recently that almost all airline pricing pacts violate EC competition policy.
- If financial services firms are permitted to sell across national borders without having to establish offices, average price declines for banking, insurance, and securities ranging from 7% in the United Kingdom to 21% in Spain can be expected.[28]

---

[27]*The Economics of 1992*, Commission of the European Communities, European Economy Study No. 35 (Brussels, March 1988), p. 123.

[28]Henley Centre, *The United Markets of Europe: Financial Services* (London: Henley Centre, 1988), p. 36.

- More efficient border crossings will free up trucking capacity, increase price competition among truckers, and reduce demand for new trucks. Price competition among truck manufacturers and their parts suppliers will intensify as a result.
- Though price spreads on pharmaceuticals of as much as 600% are evident across EC country borders, parallel imports are only 0.5% of sales.[29] Although the Commission is trying to ensure transparency in pricing (whereby governments have to clarify the criteria they use in pricing individual drugs), EC governments want to maintain their current approval power over pharmaceutical prices. Equalization of prices across the EC in this industry is unlikely by 1992, but price spreads will diminish somewhat.

In the short term, price-cutting is likely to be widely used as a means of building EC market share, even before the cost reductions associated with greater scale have been realized. During this phase, price cuts are more likely to be in the form of temporary trade and consumer promotions than reductions in normal or list prices. Intensified sales promotion is especially likely — and, indeed, is already apparent — in industries whose customers are themselves concentrating, such as food and beverages. In the distilled spirits business, for example, large supermarket chains are demanding "listing fees" that make access to distribution prohibitively costly for small brands.

After the most active phase of consolidation has passed, prices will on average be lower than they would have been absent the market integration process. Whether price will play a more important role in competition relative to nonprice elements of the marketing mix, however, is not clear. This is likely to depend in part on the level of competition from non-EC firms, especially those based in Asia, in a given industry. This, in turn, will depend on the policies adopted by the EC toward external trade.

Currently, prices for the same product differ widely from one EC country to the next. These price differences sometimes reflect deliberate manufacturer strategies to vary product positioning based on the stage of market development in each country. They also often reflect varying excise and value-added tax rates, exchange-rate fluctuations, and differences in standard distributor margins from one country to the next. Price differences have spawned cross-border shopping by consumers

---

[29]Henley Centre, *The United Markets of Europe: Pharmaceuticals* (London: Henley Centre, 1988).

and parallel importing by distributors who purchase low-priced product in one country for sale at a higher price in another. Parallel importing is of special concern to manufacturers of low bulk-to-value products for which transportation costs are modest relative to their cost. The disruption to sales forecasts and sales compensation programs caused by parallel importing often adds to production and logistics costs and reduces sales force morale.

If the 1992 program improves the efficiency of border crossings by removing time-consuming customs procedures, parallel importing, which is perfectly legal in the EC, will increase. Cross-border procurement alliances and mergers among distributors will further reduce any manufacturer's ability to charge different prices for the same product among EC countries — though some producers will doubtless still try to force distributors to place separate orders with each of their national sales organizations. On the other hand, efforts to approximate value-added tax and excise rates among EC countries so that the tax rate spread on a specific product is limited to 5% should, if successful, reduce the incentives for cross-border shopping by consumers for all but high-ticket items such as cars. However, easier border crossings will encourage consumer mobility and, in the absence of European monetary union, there will still be exchange-rate fluctuations for consumers to exploit.

In addition, it is important to note that cross-border price variations are often due to different product positioning and distribution strategies on the part of producers and to differences in consumer information and search costs. The 1992 reforms should reduce cross-border price spreads on the same item but will not eliminate them.

What should a manufacturer do in the face of these trends? First, it is essential to understand the price elasticity of consumer demand for each product in each EC country and to identify product substitution effects at different price points. For example, excise rate harmonization would dramatically reduce liquor prices in Ireland, Denmark, and the United Kingdom and dramatically increase them in Italy; assuming the tax break was passed on to consumers, additional production capacity would be needed to meet incremental demand. In the United Kingdom, the price decline would probably be greater for wine than for beer or spirits and lead to some substitution of wine for spirits but not of wine for beer.

Second, manufacturers should try to "mix up" their sales in lower-priced markets by launching higher-margin new products in advance of 1992. The objective here is to persuade current consumers of low-priced items to trade up so that the volume of lower-priced product potentially available for diversion can be reduced.

Third, manufacturers can introduce low-cost, visible differences in brand names and package labels to discourage parallel importing. Richardson-Vicks, for example, sells Oil of Olay in the United Kingdom but Oil of Olaz in Spain. However, such approaches fly in the face of the efficient Pan-European branding that the trends associated with 1992 favor.

Fourth, as suggested previously, manufacturers can try to increase their control of key distribution channels in markets where prices are higher. Firms that enjoy high prices and margins in their domestic markets, which can therefore cross-subsidize aggressive pricing in other EC markets, will be particularly advantaged. German financial service firms, for example, will benefit from industry concentration in their domestic market and from the likely reluctance of most consumers to switch to foreign financial service firms except for products such as credit cards.

Distribution Policy

The efficiency of distribution in the EC should increase as a result of 1992 initiatives to remove customs barriers at borders, quotas on the number of permits issued to road haulers for trips between member countries, and prohibitions on cabotage (collection and delivery of loads within the boundaries of member countries by nonresident haulers). The Council of Ministers has approved a single administrative document for EC border crossings (replacing 100 existing documents in the process)[30] and has ordered an end to quotas on January 1, 1993. Deregulation of cabotage is under discussion.

Road transport accounts for 80% of goods flows across intra-EC borders.[31] Cross-border customs delays range from 11.7 hours on the Belgium-to-Italy route to 1.5 hours on the Netherlands-to-Belgium route. The driver and vehicle time wasted on an 18-hour trip from the United Kingdom to Italy represents 22% of total operating costs. Thirty-five percent of trucks on EC roads return empty from their destinations.[32] True, customs delays often correspond with mandatory driver rest periods, and there is no guarantee that intra-EC trade will expand enough to absorb the road haulage capacity freed up by the reduction in border-

---

[30]*A Letter from Europe*, Delegation of the European Communities, January 25, 1988.

[31]Jacques Pelkmans and Alan Winters, *Europe's Domestic Market*, Royal Institute of International Affairs Chatham House Papers No. 43 (London: Routledge, 1988), p. 51.

[32]Henley Centre, *The United Markets of Europe: Transport* (London: Henley Centre, 1988).

crossing delays. Similarly, the removal of quotas will not mean that all trucks will magically run full. Key constraints are the absence of good information sharing systems among haulers about available cargoes for return trips, the overcapacity in the road haulage industry, and the imbalance of import and export flows between EC countries.

Despite these reservations, an average reduction of 5% in EC road haulage prices is expected. Increasing price competition will favor low-cost producers. The major U.K. and Dutch road haulers are competitively tougher and enjoy lower operating costs thanks to less restrictive national regulations. They are rapidly acquiring road haulers and signing strategic alliances in other EC countries to put together more efficiently operating Pan-European networks. These companies will be well placed to address those multinational firms that wish to procure trucking services on a Pan-European basis.

Faster, more predictable transportation of goods across country borders should enable companies to consolidate warehouses and reduce distribution-related investments in the EC while maintaining, or even improving, customer service. By diversifying into warehouse distribution and packaging, some of the major road haulers are aiding this trend. Inventory holding costs should also decrease since fewer safety stocks will be needed to protect against road haulage delays causing out-of-stocks of raw materials for production, spare parts, or finished goods. Consider, for example, these two examples:

- Philips has to maintain inventories worth 23% of annual sales in Europe compared with only 14% in the United States and Japan. Thanks to the border control and road haulage reforms, Philips expects to save $300 million per year by 1992 by reducing clerical staff, closing warehouses, and cutting inventories.[33]
- Automobile importers may not be needed in each EC country after 1992. Car dealers will become larger, order directly from manufacturers, and hold more inventory on their own lots. By eliminating double handling by importers, the age and condition of vehicles delivered to end consumers should improve. Car manufacturers will save 1.15 billion ECU by reducing channel inventories by one-month's supply.[34]

---

[33]Cited in Tully, op. cit., pp. 81–84.

[34]Ludvigsen Associates Limited, *The EC92 Automobile Sector*, Report to the Commission of the European Communities, 1988.

The cross-border mergers and alliances that are increasingly evident in the road haulage sector reflect a general trend toward consolidation in European distribution. Only one of the top ten EC retailers now has no holdings outside of its domestic market.[35] Specialty retailers like Benetton and Ikea are marching across Europe meeting the needs of similar consumer segments in multiple markets with a common brand name and marketing formula. At the same time, single-market retailers, distributors, and brokers are forming cross-border alliances to consolidate their buying power. Add to these trends the increasing number of products that will be competing for retail shelf space and consumer share of mind in any one country, and it seems likely that distributor power versus manufacturers will increase further. With mutual recognition, many smaller manufacturers will be looking to sell standard products on a private label or OEM business outside their home markets to supplement domestic sales of their branded products; the availability, quality, and price competitiveness of private-label goods are likely to grow as a result.

Cross-border shopping will increase when border-crossing delays are reduced. This will encourage retail expansion in border towns, especially if price differences on goods remain substantial. In addition, there will be pressure for harmonization of retail operating hours; Belgian retailers will press for Sunday opening if Belgians increasingly cross to northern France to shop on Sundays. A domino effect will cause Sunday hours to spread across Europe as retailers seek to stay competitive.

There will be few changes to the aggregate mix of distribution channels as a direct result of the 1992 initiatives. The Commission has, for example, made no move against the French requirement that a pharmacy must be owner-operated — a rule that effectively precludes the emergence of retail drug chains in France. At the same time, certain types of distribution will be significantly affected. Sales through duty-free shops (which have often persuaded consumers to try premium-priced brands) will fall if excise duties are harmonized. On the other hand, Pan-European franchising is likely to increase following the removal of trade barriers. In addition, the end of restrictions requiring financial services firms to have a registered office in each EC country in order to market their products is likely to fuel the growth of direct mail, telemarketing, and other nontraditional distribution channels. Larger

---

[35]See F. Johnston and R. Piper, "Who's Selling What in European Retail," *Marketing Week*, May 20, 1988, pp. 45–51.

and better documented lists, the growing use of credit cards, and the inauguration of Pan-European toll-free numbers are all contributing to the growth of direct marketing.[36]

Communications Policy

Higher levels of industry concentration can be expected to lead to higher levels of spending on marketing communications in both the short run and the long run. During the transitional phase, high levels of spending will obviously be needed to support entries into new markets, beach-head expansions, and new product introductions. In the longer run, higher levels of spending are likely for several reasons: Specifically:

- On average, competitors in a highly concentrated industry have larger gross margins as a percentage of sales. A higher gross margin implies a greater incentive to spend on advertising or personal selling.
- Companies marketing their products throughout the EC will need to rely less on historical personal contacts and more on impersonal means of communication such as advertising.

Technological change and deregulation are reshaping the media landscape in Europe. Independently owned satellite, cable, and broadcast television stations are challenging Europe's state broadcasting monopolies. Today, 10% of European homes can receive satellite television; the penetration level is expected to reach 21% by 1992.[37] The 1985 EC White Paper listed development of a single EC broadcasting area as an objective, and European governments are increasingly deregulating domestic broadcasting companies to permit them to compete more effectively with new satellite and cable services.

The consequences of these trends of most interest to marketers are increased television viewing by consumers and increased availability of advertising: Specifically:

- Additional programming choices will increase the television viewing time of the average European consumer. The quality and language of the programming will determine the level of increase.

---

[36]See Murray Bower, "Direct Marketing in the EEC," *Advertising Age*, March 6, 1989, p. 38.
[37]See "Satellite Broadcasting," *Financial Times Survey*, March 14, 1989, pp. I–VI.

There are opportunities for major marketers such as Procter & Gamble to subsidize the production of programming directed at their target audiences and to engage in other forms of sponsorship and barter syndication. Gillette, for example, already provides sports programming to European television stations in return for advertising time.

■ In most EC countries, television advertising is currently expensive and limited in availability. By 1991, new television stations in Europe will add an estimated 660,000 hours of programming to fill their 18-hour broadcast days. Assuming 6 minutes of advertising per programming hour, there will be by 1992 4 million additional minutes per year available to advertisers compared to 1988.[38] As a result, it will be easier for marketers to secure advertising time to launch new products or to extend existing products to other EC markets on a mass market rather than niche basis. In addition, a buyer's market will permit advertising spots to be purchasable at shorter notice than currently.

Increased availability of advertising plus expanded television viewing by consumers will fuel the growth of European advertising, particularly on television. Advertising spending in Europe is currently growing three times faster than in the United States. Europe is expected to account for 30% of world advertising expenditures within five years, up from 22% in 1988. The recent trend away from advertising toward other "below-the-line" communications expenditures may well be reversed.

An increasing portion of advertising expenditures will be placed in Pan-European media. Pan-European advertising is growing at 50% per year, and media buyers predict that European marketers will eventually spend 25–50% of their media budgets in Pan-European media. The Pan-European approach is being encouraged by the following factors:

■ Satellite television channels are attracting larger audiences and are expected to capture 8% of EC television advertising by 1992. Media spillover across national borders is commonplace. Pan-European print media such as *The Economist* and *Wall Street Journal Europe* are growing in circulation. This trend is not restricted to business publications. Hachette, for example, has launched its *Elle* women's magazine in 14 countries.

---

[38]Cited by Willi Schalk, BBDO Worldwide.

- Media conglomerates such as Bertelsmann, Hachette, Berlusconi, and News Corp. each hold interests in electronic and print media in multiple European countries and can therefore offer attractive discounts on Pan-European media buys.
- Directives have been proposed to unify broadcasting codes throughout the EC. These codes specify the minutes of advertising permitted per hour, the placements of ads during and between programs, the percentage of television programming that must be produced in Europe, and restrictions on alcohol and tobacco advertising. Harmonized rules on these issues will make it easier to develop Pan-European advertising plans.

Three additional factors argue for increasing use of Pan-European campaigns. First, growing media spillover raises the chances of consumers being confused if they see different nationally tailored advertisements for the same brand in different media. Second, higher levels of advertising spending will encourage small- and medium-sized advertisers to use a common campaign throughout Europe to ensure that they break through the clutter of increased advertising. Third, the standardization of audience measurement procedures throughout Europe will further encourage Pan-European campaigns.

Pan-European advertising copy will emphasize visual images over words, will permit voiceovers to be added easily in different languages, will focus on the product or service benefits, and will avoid culture-specific slice-of-life ads. Johnson and Johnson, for example, recently introduced its Silhouette sanitary napkins throughout Europe with symbolic ads that show origami birds that turn from white to blue to convey the message of Silhouette's absorbency.

To coordinate their communication efforts throughout the EC and to tackle the increasingly complex task of media buying, many companies are consolidating their business with two or three advertising agencies, which are often assigned Europe-wide responsibility for particular brands. 3M, for example, recently reduced its agency count in Europe from 60 to 3. Such consolidation increases the client's chances of obtaining the best creative talent and preferential media rates at a time when the advertising agency business itself is consolidating. Agencies are having to tailor their account management teams to multinationals according to whether the balance of power is held by country management, European regional management, or world headquarters. DMB&B, for example, has established a single international unit staffed by 10 experts of different European nationalities to coordinate Pan-European communications campaigns.

Marketing Organization

Since the 1992 program is prompting extensive changes in marketing programming, the fact that companies are also reexamining the appropriateness of their marketing organizations should be no surprise. In general, there is a shift away from the assumption that a product's marketing program should necessarily be adapted to each country's special needs. The new emphasis is on the search for similarities rather than differences across national boundaries so that adaptation costs can be minimized and scale economies maximized. This shift in perspective has important implications for marketing organizations.

The growing significance of Pan-European marketing programs suggests the need for different organization approaches. For example, several companies such as Gillette are expanding the responsibilities of their regional headquarters beyond the financial control function that has been central to their role in most decentralized multinationals. Newly empowered regional managements are now deciding the marketing strategies for Pan-European brands with the benefit of country management inputs; responsibility for developing marketing programs for country-specific brands still resides with the country organizations. Other companies such as Procter & Gamble are also using Eurobrand teams whereby country organizations with special expertise in a particular product category assume a leadership role in working with other country organizations to develop common European marketing strategies for new and existing products.

These organizational innovations signal a power shift from country to region in marketing decision making, at least in Europe, as a result of 1992. The position of vice president for Europe, until recently the nemesis of many executive careers, is increasingly sought after. Task forces to solicit and coordinate business unit plans in response to 1992 are being attached to regional headquarters; Honeywell Europe, for example, has appointed six teams of senior European managers to track and plan responses to subsets of European Commission directives that will impact the company.

The increased importance of European regional headquarters is leading some companies to relocate their offices from London to continental Europe from which they can more easily monitor and influence decision making in Brussels. Any expansion of regional headquarters' role should permit a corresponding reduction in staff overhead in a company's country organizations, as unnecessary duplication of decision making is reduced and scale efficiencies are capitalized on. However, there are exceptions. In Japanese banks, for example, fears about trade retaliation have caused an administrative overhead increase by prompting a rush to establish offices in all the major EC markets as quickly as possible.

For most companies, however, country subsidiary offices will increasingly become sales and service facilities as marketing decisions are more and more centralized. In addition, computer technology will permit paperwork to be handled centrally. Sales forces will be organized increasingly by product line; lower cost and more efficient travel within the EC will enable more specialized salespeople to represent fewer products across larger territories. As more customers take a Pan-European approach to procurement, suppliers will need to bring a new flexibility to their account management organizations to be able to serve a mix of global, regional, and national customers. For example, when Switzerland's Brown Boveri merged with Sweden's ASEA, DEC promptly combined its two account teams and won the bulk of the merged company's computer business.[39]

The shift of authority to the regional level also holds implications for executive development. No longer will multinationals seek to staff each operating unit with local country nationals. Increasingly, promotions will go to executives with experiences in multiple business functions and cultures. Training and career development programs will aim to create a pool of executives with these broader skills.[40] Gradual harmonization of professional qualification requirements within EC countries will facilitate further international career pathing.

These trends are not being fueled solely by 1992. In recent years, the globalization of competition has motivated companies such as N.V. Philips Gloeilampenfabrieken and ASEA Brown Boveri to shift line authority from geography-driven organizations to worldwide business units. Since 1986, Philips, for example, has concentrated on five key technologies (lighting, components, consumer electronics, information technology, and communications), with each product division manager holding worldwide product and profit responsibility.[41] In the case of such giant global companies, 1992 has simply added extra momentum to changes already underway.

---

[39] T. Peterson, "DEC: Making the Most of Vanishing Borders," *Business Week*, December 12, 1988, p. 60.

[40] See Leigh Bruce, "Wanted: More Mongrels in the Corporate Kennel," *International Management*, January 1989, pp. 35–37.

[41] C.J. van der Klugt, "And What About Philips?" Speech to the Strategic Management Society Conference, Amsterdam, October 18, 1988.

CONCLUSION

It is important not to exaggerate the direct impact of the 1992 program. In many ways, it represents but one more step down a 35-year path toward genuine free trade within the EC. In addition, the 1992 reforms do not directly affect consumer demand. Differences in consumer behavior and attitudes across EC borders will doubtless continue. But marketers should note that by 1989 as many as 69% of EC citizens had visited at least one other EC country, and opinion surveys were consistently showing higher percentages of young people identifying with the economic and political aspirations of the EC. The likelihood of Pan-European segments of consumers becoming more prominent seemed stronger than ever as marketers searched more for similarities rather than differences in consumer behavior and attitudes.

Our recommendations to managers regarding the changes they should make in their marketing strategies, programs, and organization structures are summarized in Chapter 14. Suffice to say here that the 1992 program has induced a climate of change and uncertainty that is prompting many companies to reappraise their existing strategies. For example, a recent Confederation of British Industry survey of 200 companies found that three-quarters had undertaken strategic reviews in response to 1992. The new strategic directions that will result from such reappraisals seem certain to redefine the business landscape of Europe over and above the changes directly caused by the 1992 reforms.

PART 2

Competing in the Integrated EC Market

CHAPTER 4

Assessing Market Potential

CIGNA Worldwide and the Insurance Market

EDITORS' INTRODUCTION

CIGNA is an American multinational insurance company with a long-standing presence in Europe. It serves the EC market through independent subsidiaries in the principal EC countries. With saturation of the U.S. insurance market prompting companies to look to overseas markets for higher margins, CIGNA seems well placed, but unfortunately, CIGNA's recent financial performance in Europe has not been satisfactory. Moreover, 60% of CIGNA Europe's business is in large risks that seem most affected by the 1992 program.

CIGNA has appointed a task force to assess the likely impacts of the 1992 market integration program. New EC directives have already been approved that will permit large-risk property and casualty insurance policies to be sold anywhere in the EC by an insurance company with a registered office in only one EC country. Previously, a separate office was needed in each country in which a company wished to write policies.

The directive is expected to increase the range of choices available to insurance customers, to enhance the role of brokers in selecting among them, and to intensify price competition. The sizable differences in insurance premiums for equivalent policies from one EC country to another are expected to erode. The perceived inconvenience and risk that normally inhibit insurance customers from switching carriers will no longer apply, as many customers, sensitive to the increased competition stimulated by the directives, reevaluate the placement of their policies.

CIGNA has to confront the problem of how to make money in an increasingly competitive insurance market. The company must decide what types of policies it will write, what target markets it will serve, and what level of presence it will maintain in each of the 12 EC countries now that it is no longer technically necessary to have a registered office in each country in order to sell insurance there.

CIGNA Worldwide

John A. Quelch and Jonathan Hibbard

On a gray November 1988 day in Frankfurt, Germany, Bruce Howson, president of CIGNA Worldwide, Inc. (CWW), convened a strategy meeting of the company's European country directors and key functional managers to discuss how CWW should respond to the European Community's (EC)[1] plan to remove existing internal barriers and restrictions to the free flow of goods and services in 1992. Howson established a 1992 task force, which would confer immediately after this meeting.

The task force's responsibility would be to define the opportunities, threats, and critical issues posed by the 1992 program. The task force would report its findings to the Philadelphia home-office advisory group by December 15, 1988. *Exhibit 4.1* summarizes the CWW organization and lists the 1992 task force and advisory group members. Under the guidance of Herman Nieuwenhuizen, senior vice president of CWW's European operations, the task force established an overall goal of defining a new Pan-European marketing strategy for this large international insurance provider.

Nieuwenhuizen believed that preparation for 1992 should start with CWW country managers assessing each nation's insurance market and the anticipated impact of the 1992 measures. The managers concentrated on the commercial property, casualty, and marine (P&C) insurance segments, which represented over 85% of the premiums generated by

---

[1]The EC comprised 12 member states: Belgium, Denmark, France, Greece, Ireland, Italy, Luxembourg, the Netherlands, Portugal, Spain, the United Kingdom, and West Germany.

EXHIBIT 4.1 Organization chart for CIGNA Worldwide

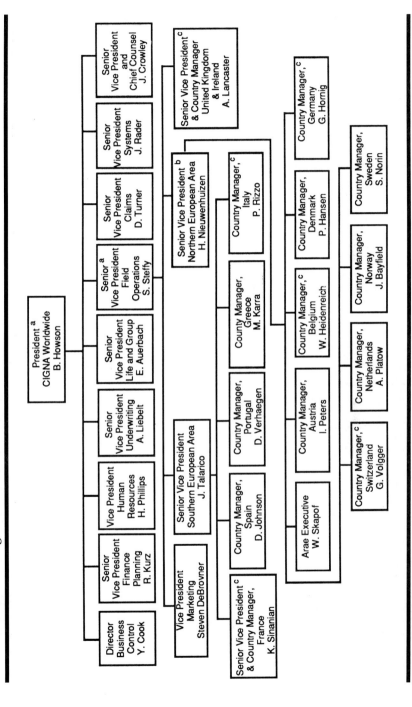

[a] Advisory group member.
[b] Task force chairperson.
[c] Task force member.

CWW in Europe in 1987. The task force would use the country managers' appraisals to develop an overall marketing strategy for CWW's European division.

THE EUROPEAN INSURANCE MARKET

In 1988 the European insurance industry sold life and nonlife insurance products. The European Community (EC) had divided nonlife business into 15 classes, among them health, employee benefits, automobile, marine, and other P&C insurance. P&C insurance included two categories of insurance, one designed for people (car, home, and liability policies) and the other designed for businesses and organizations (aviation, marine liability, workers' compensation, fire, business interruption, and officers' and directors' policies).

In 1986 the EC was the second-largest insurance market in the world, with 22% of the total premiums. *Table A* summarizes total premiums, worldwide premium ranks, premium as a percent of GNP, and insurance per capita, for the members of the EC, the United States, and Japan.

TABLE A   **Selected insurance information for 1986 ($ billions)**

	Total premiums	Worldwide rank	1986 GNP	Premium as % GNP	Insurance per capita
West Germany	$ 60	4	$ 933	6%	$ 978
United Kingdom	46	5	567	8	807
France	36	6	735	5	658
Italy	15	9	624	2	253
Netherlands	11	10	182	6	788
Spain	5	14	239	2	138
Belgium-Luxembourg	5	15	122	4	510
Denmark	4	18	85	5	743
Ireland	2	25	25	8	616
Portugal	1	36	30	3	76
Greece	1	43	41	2	46
EC Community	186	2	3,583	5	468
United States	371	1	4,309	9	1,746
Japan	$170	3	$2,044	8%	$1,399

Source: Swiss Reinsurance Company and EC Commission.

Premium income was not an entirely reliable indicator of size of a nation's insurance market because, in some instances, national governments helped to satisfy insurance requirements through social security benefits. Such benefits were not reported in market estimates of premium income.

MARKET PARTICIPANTS

The major participants in the European insurance industry were insurance carriers, brokers and agents, and customers. In addition, many national governments set premium prices, thereby helping to determine the structure of each country's insurance market.

Insurance Carriers

Insurance carriers sold lines or classes of business, such as life, accident, sickness, and P&C. The insurer's success depended on reducing the risk exposure of the policies it underwrote. Therefore, insurers relied on extensive coinsurance and reinsurance. Coinsurance was an agreement between two or more carriers to participate in a policy directly (either with or without involving a broker or an agent). Reinsurance involved coverage of an entire policy by the carrier who then sold a portion of this coverage to one or more carriers. Both carriers shared the premium income and were responsible for paying their respective percentage of any claim.

Carriers derived their revenues from a combination of direct insurance, coinsurance, and reinsurance. Gross written premiums (GWP) were a carrier's income from underwriting policies. Since most carriers protected themselves by reinsuring portions of their GWPs, their actual revenues were net written premiums (NWP). Because premiums were received in advance of claims, income could be earned on the "float," thereby supplementing underwriting performance. Most industry experts agreed that, while investment income significantly affected the earnings and growth of an insurance carrier, the overall viability of a company depended on its success as an underwriter. However, since the early 1980s, insurance firms had derived the bulk of their corporate profits from investment income because they were willing to accept underwriting losses in order to secure investable funds.

Two standard performance measures were applied to insurance companies writing P&C business: the expense ratio and the loss ratio. Losses due to claims, expected losses from future claims, and associated costs of claims administration were divided by the net earned premium to calculate the loss ratio.[2] The expense ratio included all costs of writing the P&C business. Those expenses were then divided by NWP to calculate the expense ratio. The combined ratio (expense ratio + loss ratio) represented the total cost of underwriting as a percentage of the premiums generated. Typically, when the combined ratio was under 100%, underwriting results were profitable; when the ratio was over 100%, underwriting results were unprofitable. Since a client's "riskiness" partially determined the P&C premium charged, carriers evaluated an insurance risk by scrutinizing many areas of the potential policyholder's operations. Investment income was not included in the 100% calculation.

Insurance Brokers and Agents

Insurance brokers and agents, acting as intermediaries in insurance purchase transactions, represented 80% of the P&C business placed in Europe. Some agents, who worked exclusively for one or two carriers, were not considered insurance professionals; they were not expected to have detailed technical knowledge. By the late 1980s, however, most agents were involved full time in the insurance business, usually representing one carrier's product line.

Unlike agents, brokers were insurance specialists who offered their clients impartial advice in arranging the best insurance terms possible. Brokers often relieved the carriers of such administrative tasks as premium collection and claims handling. As professionals, brokers earned commissions of 15%–20% of the GWP; agents averaged 10%–15% commission. When they evaluated insurance companies, brokers scrutinized the service and price each carrier offered because service considerations sometimes outweighed price differences.

Because they did not have ties to particular carriers, brokers possessed strong leverage over insurers. Brokers could recommend that policies be moved to other carriers at any time. In EC nations in 1992, brokers would be able to sell clients policies without any longer having to hold a license in each EC nation. In the United Kingdom brokers wrote over 70% of the total P&C business, whereas in France, Italy, and Germany they wrote, respectively, 50%, 45%, and 25%. In most of the EC, the larger brokers did not aggressively seek to switch the principal customers of other brokers.

---

[2]Net earned premium was defined as the income realized on a policy from an accounting standpoint. For example, on a 12-month policy commencing January 1988, only 50% of the premium income would have been earned by July 1988.

Industry analysts identified three tiers of brokers. The first tier included international network brokers, such as Marsh & McLennan and Johnson & Higgins. Most European brokerage revenues were concentrated in this top tier. The second tier included large national and regional brokers, while the third tier comprised small local brokers and large insurers with their own exclusive agent networks. Of the top 20 European brokers, 9 were either partially or wholly U.S.-owned and 7 were British.

European brokers generated income from three basic sources: commissions, fixed fees, and investment income. Brokers received commissions on policy premiums they wrote for each carrier. They also received a profit-sharing commission from these insurers at the end of the year. This commission was based on the amount of premium income the broker wrote for a particular carrier, minus the losses the carrier incurred on the broker-written business. Brokers sometimes received negotiated fixed fees from larger clients in lieu of commissions from carriers. Investment income was earned when brokers collected policy premiums from clients. They held this money for 90 days or more before remitting it to the carrier. A typical broker's operating ratios (as a percentage of revenues) were: salaries and benefits (53%), other operating expenses (36%), and interest expense (5%).

Insurance Buyers

Insurance was bought by both companies and individual consumers. In the consumer market individual policies were written, and clients explored many possibilities, either through an intermediary or through their own efforts. In the industrial market both individual and combined policies were written. Combined policies allowed a firm to cover three factories under one policy in certain countries. Most large companies employed risk managers who decided which industrial risks should be covered by individual policies.

CWW segmented its corporate customers according to the value of annual premiums. A major multinational would generate over $5 million in P&C insurance premiums. Large-, medium- and small-sized companies would generate $1 million, $500,000, and $100,000, respectively.

From a customer's perspective, selecting a carrier was based on an insurer's reputation. Most insurers built reputations on the claims service they provided. As one risk manager stated, "The capability of an insurer to provide local claims handling service is critical to my carrier decision, especially with multiple sites and multiple languages in my business."

Once established, the relationship among client, broker, and carrier was fairly stable. The size and complexity of the P&C relationship made it difficult for a client to change carriers. In a typical year analysts estimated that 10% of the total P&C policies in Europe might change hands. Clients sometimes relied on several carriers for different insurance products but usually kept a particular type of coverage with a single carrier. Most experts agreed that service and price were paramount when a company shopped for a carrier or broker.

COMPANY BACKGROUND

CIGNA, Inc., the parent company of CWW, was one of the largest publicly owned financial services companies in the world. Its subsidiaries were leading providers of insurance, health care, employee benefits, and financial services to businesses and individuals worldwide. CIGNA was formed in March 1982, by the merger of Connecticut General Life Insurance Company and INA Corp. Innovation and new products were the hallmark of both predecessor companies. INA sold the first fire and theft policy on an automobile, insured the first expedition to scale Mount Everest, and developed the first package insurance policy, the well-known homeowner's policy. Connecticut General was a pioneer in group life insurance and offered the first group major medical coverage.

CIGNA's International Operations

In the late 1800s INA marketed insurance on three continents through general agents and later through foreign offices. Connecticut General entered the international market through its acquisition of Aetna Insurance Company in 1962. Aetna was a member of the American Foreign Insurance Association (AFIA), a consortium of insurance carriers based in the United States and doing business overseas. When an AFIA company entered a foreign country, it typically shared the insurance business with other AFIA association members through reinsurance agreements. CIGNA acquired AFIA in 1984 for $215 million and merged it into its own international business to form CWW, one of the largest international insurance operations headquartered in the United States.

Before the acquisition, AFIA and CIGNA both maintained area offices in Belgium and had established operations throughout most of the EC. After acquiring AFIA, CIGNA consolidated the two insurance portfolios and personnel into one office in Brussels. The acquisition increased the percentage of CIGNA revenues derived from multinational corporations from 6% in 1984 to 12% in 1987. *Exhibit 4.2* summarizes information from the CIGNA/AFIA merger.

EXHIBIT 4.2 Selected information on CIGNA/AFIA merger

Country	1983 Headcount			1983 Net written premiums ($ millions)			1988 CIGNA Europe	
	CIGNA	AFIA	AFIA + CIGNA	CIGNA	AFIA	Combined	Headcount	Net written ($ millions)
United Kingdom	355	363	718	$129.7	$ 96.4	$226.1	575	$267.0
Ireland	9	34	43	5.9	11.0	16.9	42	16.5
France	105	339	444	35.0	54.8	89.8	360	123.7
Spain	34	104	138	1.7	5.8	7.5	89	22.3
Netherlands	68	59	127	17.8	27.8	45.6	81	49.7
Belgium[a]	93	86	179	4.6	9.7	14.3	80	25.7
West Germany	57	81	138	8.9	19.1	28.0	113	48.1
Italy	81	248	329	9.1	26.4	35.5	254	53.2
Greece	1	42	43	0.2	4.0	4.2	23	3.3
Denmark	17	16	33	1.4	3.6	5.0	13	6.8
Portugal	0	0	0	0.0	0.0	0.0	5	0.1
Total	820	1,372	2,192	$214.3	$258.6	$472.9	1,635	$616.4

[a]Luxembourg income was reported with Belgium's revenue figures.

EXHIBIT 4.3 Selected financial information for CIGNA Europe

	United Kingdom		France		Italy	
	1987	1985	1987	1985	1987	1985
Premiums written ($ millions):						
Gross written premiums (GWP)	$454.6	$582.1	$166.5	$160.6	$72.5	$ 89.2
Net written premiums (NWP)	267.0	227.6	123.7	106.5	52.2	60.2
Earned premiums (EP)	270.2	234.4	125.4	109.7	53.4	60.3
Losses incurred	217.3	177.2	74.5	84.0	26.2	50.2
Commissions (Comm)[b]	48.3	30.7	22.5	13.9	9.7	11.6
Taxes	0.9	2.5	2.4	5.5	2.7	3.4
Local overhead	24.3	32.8	17.9	18.7	7.1	10.9
Underwriting results	(20.6)	(8.9)	8.0	(12.3)	7.7	(15.8)
Investment income (IIN)	29.8	24.6	14.7	11.2	13.9	6.3
Operating profit	$ 9.2	$ 15.7	$ 22.8	$ (1.1)	$21.6	$ (9.5)
Share of EC profit (%)	16.9%	495.7%	45.1%	−60.9%	43.4%	−336.2%
Loss ratio (Losses/EP)	80.4	75.6	59.4	76.6	49.1	83.3
Commission ratio (Comm/NWP)	18.1	13.5	18.2	13.1	18.6	19.2
Expenses + taxes ratio (Expenses + taxes/ NWP)	9.4	15.5	16.4	22.7	18.8	23.8
Combined ratio	107.9	104.6	94.0	112.3	86.4	126.3
Retention rate (NWP/GWP)	58.7	39.1	74.3	66.3	72.1	67.5
Expense ratio (Expenses + taxes + Comm/NWP)	27.5	29.0	34.6	35.8	37.4	43.0
Investment ratio (IIN/NWP)	11.1	10.8	11.9	10.5	26.7	10.5

[a]Luxembourg premiums were reported under Belgium financial information.
[b]Commissions included fees paid to brokers and agents, as well as commissions received from other insurance companies as part of reinsurance agreements.

Most CWW business was written through individual agents and brokers in competition with local insurers. Over 75% of each nation's CWW premiums was derived from business closely associated with the country in which it was written. Most CWW employees were nationals of the country in which they worked. These individuals were well versed in the nuances of the local language and customs, familiar with local laws governing contracts, and attuned to the needs of the local

Netherlands		West Germany		Belgium[a]		Spain	
1987	1985	1987	1985	1987	1985	1987	1985
$ 65.1	$ 102.9	$81.1	$ 88.8	$37.0	$53.8	$ 33.5	$ 35.5
48.7	58.4	47.1	32.9	25.7	28.0	21.3	19.7
56.0	55.6	48.7	32.5	25.8	26.2	18.9	19.9
57.5	49.8	31.1	12.1	17.2	19.5	14.2	25.3
10.5	7.3	8.5	2.4	4.5	3.7	3.4	3.1
0.4	0.5	0.8	1.7	0.8	0.9	0.8	0.7
4.4	6.9	5.9	6.5	3.1	4.1	2.9	3.1
(16.8)	(8.8)	2.5	9.7	0.1	(2.0)	(2.4)	(12.4)
1.4	6.1	5.8	3.5	2.9	2.9	2.3	2.1
$ (15.4)	$ (2.7)	$ 8.3	$ 13.2	$ 3.0	$ .9	$ (.1)	$ (10.3)
− 33.6%	− 112.4%	17.1%	408.6%	5.0%	18.0%	− 1.4%	− 346.4%
102.6	89.6	63.9	37.2	66.7	74.4	75.1	127.1
21.6	12.5	18.0	7.3	17.5	13.2	16.0	15.7
9.7	12.7	14.2	24.9	15.2	17.9	17.4	19.3
134.0	114.5	96.0	69.6	99.6	105.5	108.3	162.4
74.8	56.8	58.0	37.0	69.5	52.0	63.6	55.4
31.3	25.2	32.2	32.2	32.7	31.1	33.4	35.0
2.8	10.5	12.3	10.5	11.4	10.5	11.0	10.5

(*continues on next page*)

insurance community. CWW supported its salespeople with direct marketing (13 million pieces mailed in 1987 versus 9 million in 1985) to generate leads.

CIGNA Worldwide in 1988

CWW's international marketing programs were tailored to meet local insurance needs. With strong support from the home office in Philadelphia, CWW tried to delegate as much authority as possible at the point

EXHIBIT 4.3 *(continued)*

	Ireland		Denmark	
	1987	1985	1987	1985
Premiums written ($ millions):				
Gross written premiums (GWP)	$20.3	$20.8	$ 8.8	$ 10.2
Net written premiums (NWP)	15.5	8.6	6.2	3.5
Earned premiums (EP)	13.6	7.8	6.3	3.0
Losses incurred	9.9	5.1	2.7	2.1
Commissions (Comm)[b]	2.2	−0.3	1.3	0.1
Taxes	0.1	0.1	0.0	0.0
Local overhead	1.6	1.7	1.4	1.0
Underwriting results	(0.1)	1.3	0.9	(0.2)
Investment income (IIN)	2.7	0.9	0.4	0.4
Operating profit	$ 2.6	$ 2.2	$ 1.3	$ 0.2
Share of EC profit (%)	5.0%	64.1%	2.3%	1.4%
Loss ratio (Losses/EP)	72.8	65.3	42.9	70.0
Commission ratio (Comm/NWP)	14.2	−3.5	21.0	2.9
Expenses + taxes ratio (Expenses + taxes/ NWP)	11.0	21.0	22.6	28.6
Combined ratio	97.4	82.0	86.3	101.7
Retention rate (NWP/GWP)	76.0	41.4	70.5	34.1
Expense ratio (Expenses + taxes + Comm/NWP)	25.2	17.5	43.6	31.5
Investment ratio (IIN/NWP)	17.5	10.5	6.3	10.5

of sale by giving country managers the final say in writing a policy. Most country offices were self-sufficient with their own underwriters, clerical staff, and data-processing operations. Hoping to keep more of its business in-house, CWW was reinsuring fewer policies with other carriers than previously. This reinsurance strategy increased CIGNA's risk exposure but also enlarged its upside profit potential. As a result of the new strategy CWW's net premiums were growing faster than gross premiums.

Greece		Portugal		Total	
1987	1985	1987	1985	1987	1985
$ 7.7	$ 3.0	$ 0.2	$ 0.0	$947.3	$1,146.9
3.3	1.5	0.1	0.0	610.8	546.9
3.0	0.7	0.1	0.0	621.4	550.1
1.4	0.9	0.0	0.0	452.0	426.2
0.9	0.5	0.0	0.0	112.0	73.0
0.1	0.1	0.0	0.0	9.0	15.4
0.4	0.2	0.4	0.1	69.2	86.0
0.2	(0.9)	(0.4)	(0.1)	(20.8)	(50.3)
0.4	0.2	0.0	0.0	74.3	58.1
$ 0.6	$ (0.7)	$ (0.4)	$(0.1)	$ 53.5	$ 7.4
1.1%	− 28.0%	− 0.8%	− 3.8%	100.0%	100.0%
46.6	128.6	0.0	0.0	72.7	77.5
30.0	33.3	0.0	0.0	18.3	13.3
15.2	9.0	400.0	0.0	12.8	18.5
87.8	172.2	348.9	0.0	103.8	109.3
43.2	48.3	78.9	0.0	64.5	47.5
45.2	42.3	400.0	0.0	31.1	31.8
11.2	10.5	1.5	0.0	12.2	10.5

CIGNA Insurance Company of Europe (CIGNA Europe) was a CIGNA, Inc. subsidiary and part of the CWW organization. CIGNA Europe operated in Austria, Belgium, Cyprus, Denmark, France, Germany, Greece, Ireland, Italy, the Netherlands, Norway, Portugal, Spain, Sweden, and the United Kingdom. Recent financial results and information for CIGNA Europe are summarized in *Exhibit 4.3*. Product mix information for CIGNA Europe is summarized in *Exhibit 4.4*. Some CIGNA executives thought that CIGNA Europe's recent financial

EXHIBIT 4.4 Selected information for product mix, product growth, and staffing in 1985 and 1988 for CIGNA Europe

	United Kingdom	France	Italy	Nether-lands	West Germany	Belgium	Spain	Ireland	Denmark	Greece	Portugal	Total
1985 Product mix[a]												
Property	24.2%	53.4%	38.3%	61.3%	48.3%	58.7%	44.8%	47.1%	53.3%	43.7%	0.0%	37.3%
Casualty	12.6	21.2	15.9	11.5	15.7	15.9	26.7	31.2	11.1	32.5	0.0	15.1
Marine	45.9	7.1	14.8	23.6	24.6	17.2	13.7	1.0	15.4	22.0	0.0	30.5
Accident and health	17.2	18.4	31.0	4.0	11.4	8.2	15.0	20.8	20.2	1.8	0.0	17.1
1988 Product mix[a]												
Property	50.7	59.0	46.8	49.3	64.6	65.0	56.6	54.9	42.1	62.4	96.0	54.1
Casualty	4.1	15.1	15.8	8.1	7.7	14.5	8.5	23.2	3.5	22.1	0.8	10.3
Marine	31.4	5.4	13.1	36.5	12.5	10.6	13.1	0.4	3.5	15.0	1.1	18.6
Accident and health	13.8%	20.5%	24.3%	6.2%	18.0%	9.9%	21.8%	21.5%	50.9%	0.5%	2.1%	16.8%
Total staff 1988	575	360	254	78	113	80	89	42	13	23	5	1,635
Professional, management	277	174	76	40	49	38	42	22	7	7	3	804
Clerical	298	186	178	38	64	42	47	20	6	16	2	831

[a]Product mix represents each line of business as a percentage of net written premiums.

growth was overstated on CIGNA, Inc.'s financial statements because of the devaluation of the U.S. dollar and CWW's retention of a higher percentage of its own policies.

The broker and agent system accounted for 95% of the premiums for CIGNA Europe. Broker-generated income averaged 80% of total premiums for other European carriers. CWW worked almost exclusively with tier one brokers writing policies for multinationals and large risk companies. The top 10 brokerage firms in Europe wrote 80% of CIGNA Europe's policies. In 1987 CWW's sales comprised 10% of CIGNA, Inc.'s total revenues (13% of CIGNA, Inc.'s total revenue and 7% of its operating income were foreign-based). CIGNA Europe's revenues, in turn, represented 54% of CWW's total revenues in 1987. Within the European Community, the United Kingdom and France accounted for 64% of CIGNA Europe's net premiums. *Exhibit 4.5* summarizes selected financial data for CWW.

EXHIBIT 4.5 Selected financial information for CIGNA Worldwide

Consolidated results for years ended December 31, 1985–1987

	1987	1986	1985
Property and casualty (U.S. $000)			
Gross written premiums	1,603,734	1,623,586	1,730,871
Net written premiums	1,081,604	1,052,194	948,896
Net earned premiums	1,110,307	1,022,543	955,657
Losses and expenses	1,164,799	1,088,183	1,061,820
Underwriting results	(54,492)	(65,640)	(106,163)
Investment and other income	106,900	101,298	99,395
Life (U.S. $000)			
Premiums	311,937	213,772	143,067
Earned premiums	300,268	209,435	139,289
Investment and other income	183,035	129,799	69,414
Benefits and expenses	473,869	328,646	202,636
Operating income	9,434	10,588	6,067
Combined operating income (loss) before noninsurance expenses and income taxes	61,800	46,246	(701)
Property and casualty statutory ratios (%)			
Loss	65.5	66.6	72.4
Expense	39.4	39.8	39.4
Combined	104.9	106.4	111.8

MARKETING IMPACT OF 1992

The EC, which represented 20% of all world trade flows, had agreed to remove its internal trade barriers by 1992. The integration of the European market would create the largest single market in the world (325 million consumers), surpassing the United States's 226 million and Japan's 121 million consumers. The European Economic Community, often called the "Common Market," was created in 1957 by the Treaty of Rome as a devastated Europe sought to rebuild its economy after World War II.

The EC believed that unification would create economies of scale, leading to lower prices, greater investment, and economic growth. Less efficient companies would be driven to become more productive, merge, or go out of business. However, despite earlier efforts, many internal barriers still remained by the mid-1980s. Recognizing the need to facilitate flows of people, goods, services, and capital, the EC embarked on a program to pull down many of these remaining physical, technical, and fiscal barriers among countries by December 31, 1992.

Background to 1992

In 1957 the Treaty of Rome established the European Economic Community (EEC). In 1968 the European Coal and Steel Community, the European Atomic Energy Commission, and the EEC merged to form the EC. Initially, the EC made progress in eliminating customs duties, but progress slowed because of the economic recession in the mid-1970s.

Following the slow growth of the late 1970s, the prime ministers of the EC countries pledged to complete the common market at an EC meeting in 1982. A White Paper, published by the Commission in June 1985, delineated a plan for achieving a single market. The EC plans were approved by the member nations and ratified in the Single European Act of 1986, amending the original Treaty of Rome.

The Single European Act became effective on July 1, 1987. After that date member states voted on legislation to remove the physical, technical, and fiscal barriers to a unified market. Legislation voting was expected to proceed more quickly because of the newly-instituted majority rule versus the previously required unanimity agreement. Many EC experts saw the technical standards and regulations, administrative barriers, and value-added tax (VAT) rate harmonization as the major obstacles to realization of the 1992 plan.

Physical barriers included customs posts, frontier control, immigration checkpoints, as well as terrorist and agricultural checks. Frontier formalities imposed monetary costs for salaries and administration and wasted time. Most experts agreed that removing these barriers would provide a visible sign of progress on unification and increase the efficiency of industry by lowering transportation costs.

Technical obstacles prevented goods and services legally manufactured and sold in one member state from competing in another state. Such obstacles were the result of disparate national policies on consumer product, health, environmental, and safety regulations. The result was that many products could not be sold without costly modifications, which reduced the length of production runs, increased manufacturing costs, and raised prices. Reaching complete agreement on standards would have been a very lengthy process for the EC member nations. Instead, as a compromise the EC developed the concept of mutual recognition, by which a product legalized for sale in one member country could be sold throughout the EC.

Fiscal barriers included restrictions on capital movements, as well as disparities in VAT levels and excise duties. Varying tax rates led to price distortions among EC countries and necessitated customs posts. Because most countries had three rates (reduced, standard, and higher), a two-rate VAT system was proposed by the Commission because it was politically impossible to agree on one rate.

EC Progress Update

Many people believed these numerous barriers made European firms less competitive than their United States and Japanese counterparts, which benefited from serving much larger domestic markets than any single European nation's market.

By November 1988, one third on the 285 legislative reforms detailed in the 1985 White Paper had been adopted by the EC, and over 100 others had been sent to the Council of Ministers for approval. The Commission expected to have 90% of the measures ready for adoption by the end of 1988. Directives already adopted included toy safety regulations, a single document for border crossings, abolished customs formalities, mutual recognition of higher education diplomas, and a directive allowing the sale of P&C insurance across borders.

Leaders of some nations outside the EC were disturbed by the prospect of an increasingly protectionist "fortress Europe." The United States and Japan, the largest trading partners of the EC, exported over $110 billion in goods and services to the EC in 1987. These two countries were particularly concerned about market exclusion.

EFFECT OF 1992 PLAN ON THE EUROPEAN INSURANCE MARKET

Insurance had been the focus of several major EC decisions since the signing of the Treaty of Rome in 1957. Most analysts considered the insurance industry cyclical, with low entry and exit barriers. Although reinsurance was traditionally international by virtue of the flows of trade among countries, the gradual breakdown of barriers to selling insurance products across national boundaries was expected to create opportunities in the P&C and life insurance segments.

Increasing regulation of the industry during the 1960s and 1970s had made it more difficult for insurance companies to operate throughout Europe and the number of foreign insurance firms had declined significantly in the past 25 years. In 1957 the Treaty of Rome introduced two acts that were crucial to establishing a Pan-European insurance market. These acts were freedom of establishment and freedom of services.

Freedom of Establishment

Freedom of establishment was defined as the right of a company in one member state to establish branches or agencies in other member states. This EC directive outlined a common procedure for granting operating licenses and prescribed a common standard for calculating the minimum solvency margin to be maintained.[3] Therefore, an insurer with its head office in one member state was entitled to set up branches elsewhere in the EC. By 1988 freedom of establishment had been realized, and most large insurance companies had offices in many EC countries.

Freedom of Services

Freedom of services permitted insurance companies to market a full range of products throughout the EC without having a branch in every member state. Some countries, however, were not honoring freedom of services. (The exception was reinsurance companies, which had been free to write cross-border insurance since the early 1900s.) In December 1986 the European Commission, concerned with the lack of progress in freedom of services, opened proceedings against Denmark, France, Germany, and Ireland. This action raised important issues about freedom

---

[3]Solvency margins and technical reserve requirements were intended to ensure that an insurance company could meet its future obligations toward the insured.

of services, and the court established additional guidelines. In January 1989 the status of freedom of services was as follows:

1. **Nonlife insurance.** The EC's 1988 nonlife directive allowed insurance firms to provide across-the-border services in nonlife insurance beginning January 1, 1990. The directive distinguished cross-border insurance for large risks and mass risks.[4]

    a. Large risks: Purchasers of insurance for large risks were believed to be able to protect their own interests and decide from whom they should buy insurance. A large risk was defined as meeting at least two of the following three criteria:

        Up through December 31, 1992:

            500 or more employees

            minimum of ECU 24 million revenue (U.S. $29 million)[5]

            minimum of ECU 12.4 million assets (U.S. $14 million)

        January 1, 1992 and after:

            250 or more employees

            minimum of ECU 12 million revenue (U.S. $14.5 million)

            minimum of ECU 6.2 million assets (U.S. $7 million)

    b. Mass risks: Mass risks involved consumers for whom, under the present state of EC law, national protection by the host state was still considered justified. Most analysts predicted that freedom of services for mass risks would not pass until the mid-1990s. Nevertheless, the prospect of such a change in 1992 was already altering company executives' perceptions of the European market.

Because of the availability of brokers and agents, insurance buyers were accustomed to a high level of personal contact. Such service expectations could restrict the ability of some companies to write commercial lines of insurance across borders. International companies which had their own operations within a country, or which were closely associated with local brokers, could provide the necessary service on policies providing international coverage. As barriers were removed in other industries, experts believed that cross-frontier trading would increase dramatically and expand demand for insurance services.

The 1988 nonlife directive would become effective in 1990. At that

---

[4]Industry experts estimated that this directive would apply to approximately 90% of the commercial and industrial insurance in the United Kingdom and 70% in Germany, France, and Italy. Also, marine, aviation, and transport business was automatically classified as large commercial risk business.

[5]The ECU was a European monetary unit which was a weighted unit of currency representing 10 member-state currencies (Portugal and Spain were not included).

time companies would no longer be forced to invest premiums in local government bonds but could seek higher returns on investment income in other countries.

2. **Life insurance.** The Commission introduced a proposal on freedom of services in the life insurance industry at the end of 1988. However, analysts believed it was unlikely to be in effect before 1994. Life insurance was much more politically sensitive than nonlife coverage because it involved individuals' savings and national government policies. Life insurance premiums varied enormously among the EC's 12 member states.

OPPORTUNITIES IN THE EUROPEAN INSURANCE MARKET

Many analysts predicted that the second nonlife directive would encourage insurance buyers to shop around and could lead to lower overheads for insurers and lower premiums for policyholders. One analyst explained, "Extensive cross-border corporate risk business should be written in the area of large corporate risks, but 1990, not 1992, will be the big year for this business in most EC nations." Large risk insurance markets in Spain, Portugal, Greece, and Ireland were scheduled to be liberalized from 1996 through 1998.

Many analysts believed that EC subsidiaries of foreign insurers were currently at a competitive disadvantage because they were obliged to meet solvency margins with local assets as opposed to corporate assets. In 1988 regulations prevented most insurance carriers from writing Pan-European insurance policies for companies with businesses in more than one EC country. Because of their open markets and competitive pricing structures, the United Kingdom and the Netherlands were expected to be the major beneficiaries of the 1992 plan. Yet, in 1988, these two nations received only 10% of their insurance business from the rest of the EC. The tightly regulated markets in West Germany and Italy, together with France, which was burdened with extremely high premium taxes, were thought especially likely to lose insurance business.

Because of the EC's low per capita spending for insurance ($468 in 1986), many insurance companies were expected to position themselves to take advantage of the eventual single market for mass risks by establishing operations throughout Europe. Premium growth potential was considered greatest in Italy, Spain, and Portugal. In these countries premium levels per capita were very low, particularly in the area of life

TABLE B   Relative sizes of EC insurance market, 1986 ($ billions)

	Number of operating companies	Nonlife premiums	Nonlife World share	Nonlife EC share	Life premiums	Life World share	Life EC share
West Germany	516	$34.4	7.7%	32.5%	$25.3	6.2%	31.5%
United Kingdom	712	18.6	4.2	17.6	27.2	6.6	33.9
France	482	22.3	4.9	21.1	14.8	3.5	17.6
Italy	207	11.8	2.6	11.2	2.6	0.6	3.2
Netherlands	439	6.2	1.4	6.0	5.3	1.3	6.5
Spain	520	4.3	0.9	4.1	1.1	0.3	1.4
Belgium[a]	302	3.7	0.8	3.5	1.4	0.3	1.4
Denmark	235	2.2	0.5	2.1	1.6	0.4	1.9
Ireland	63	0.9	0.2	0.9	1.3	0.3	1.6
Portugal	231	0.7	0.1	0.7	0.07	0.02	0.09
Greece	154	$ 0.3	0.07%	0.3%	$ 0.14	0.03%	0.1%

[a]Luxembourg information reported with Belgium figures.

insurance. *Table B* summarizes the relative sizes of EC insurance markets.

Some industry experts believed that firms with limited financial resources would concentrate on the life insurance market, where entry barriers were lower than was the case with nonlife because of lower initial capital requirements. *Exhibit 4.6* summarizes growth rates of life and nonlife insurance within the EC. *Exhibit 4.7* highlights the relative costs of various insurance products as indicated in an EC Commission study.

When the nonlife insurance market opened in 1990, experts predicted that competition would intensify. "Companies must become more efficient and cost-effective," said one industry executive; "premium margins will become razor-thin in some nations, with only the strong surviving."

To compete more effectively within the EC, many carriers were examining their options. A Swiss insurance executive offered the following options for U.S. insurers: "U.S. carriers can either make an outright acquisition, or they can set up a strategic alliance with an EC-based insurance company. Acquisitions are more difficult and expensive to carry out than they were in past years because Europeans are snapping up

EXHIBIT 4.6 EC insurance growth rates

Growth in premium income (%)[a]

Member state[b]	Total business		Life insurance		Nonlife insurance	
	1985–1986	1984–1985	1985–1986	1984–1985	1985–1986	1984–1985
United Kingdom	19.4%	6.3%	18.6%	5.5%	20.6%	7.4%
France	11.0	6.1	25.7	21.5	3.3	−0.6
Italy	11.2	7.8	30.4	23.0	7.6	5.4
Netherlands	8.7	3.3	5.9	7.1	11.2	0.2
West Germany	6.4	4.2	10.0	4.3	4.0	4.2
Belgium	10.1	1.3	9.6	1.7	10.3	1.2
Spain	22.0	4.7	67.9	14.6	14.0	3.3
Ireland	4.9	−6.9	−2.3	−14.7	17.3	10.3
Denmark	−2.7	21.8	−14.4	45.8	7.6	6.2
Portugal	12.1	1.8	9.0	20.4	12.5	0.1
Luxembourg	10.6%	7.4%	10.4%	9.2%	10.6%	6.8%

Forecasted nonlife premium income growth 1988–1992, index: 1987 = 100

	1987	1988	1989	1990	1991	1992
United Kingdom	100	110	118	126	134	142
France	100	105	112	118	125	133
Italy	100	110	118	127	137	148
West Germany	100	104	109	113	118	124

Forecasted life premium income growth for 1988–1992, index: 1987 = 100

	1987	1988	1989	1990	1991	1992
United Kingdom	100	117	128	136	146	157
France	100	111	120	130	140	147
Italy	100	125	150	173	190	209
West Germany	100	109	113	119	124	129

Source: Swiss Reinsurance Company.

[a]Growth has been adjusted for inflation.

[b]No premium income was reported for Greece.

111

EXHIBIT 4.7 Insurance price comparisons

	Life insurance[a]	Home[b]	Motor[c]	Commercial fire, theft[d]	Public liability[e]
Belgium	+78%	−16%	+30%	−9%	+13%
France	+33	+39	+9	+153	+117
Italy	+83	+81	+148	+245	+77
Luxembourg	+66	+57	+77	−15	+9
Netherlands	−9	+17	−7	−1	−16
Spain	+37	−4	+100	+24	+60
United Kingdom	−30	+90	−17	+27	−7
West Germany	+5%	+3%	+15%	+43%	+47%

Percentage differences in prices of standard insurance products compared with the average of the four lowest national prices in 1986

Source: EC Commission.

[a]*Life insurance* — Average annual cost of term (life) insurance.

[b]*Home insurance* — Annual cost of fire and theft coverage for a house valued at 70,000 ECU. Contents were valued at 28,000 ECU.

[c]*Motor insurance* — Annual cost of comprehensive insurance for a 1.6 liter car. Driver had 10 years experience.

[d]*Commercial fire and theft* — Annual coverage for premises valued at 387,000 ECU and stock valued at 232,000 ECU.

[e]*Public liability* — Annual premium for engineering company with 20 employees and an annual turnover of 1.29 million ECU.

most available takeover targets. A strategic alliance will enable a U.S. company to obtain help from its EC partner in adjusting its products to ensure that they meet local needs."

Many analysts believed several large insurance companies would dominate the new EC market. The CEO of a British insurer noted: "In 10 years, we will see a concentration of 10–15 large European insurers. The rest will be niche players." According to one European insurance association, EC insurers were involved in 121 mergers and acquisitions between June 1984 and September 1988. Of these mergers, 73 involved companies in the same country, 25 were mergers of companies in different EC nations, and 23 were mergers between an EC-based company and a firm outside the EC. Companies were attempting to acquire the necessary economies of scale in order to meet anticipated consumer demands more effectively. In 1987 the largest European insurers were Allianz (Germany), with $10.1 billion in net written premiums; Generali (Italy), $6.3 billion; Zurich (Switzerland), $6.2 billion; Royal (U.K.), $5.8 billion; and Prudential Corp. (U.K.), $5.6 billion. Several of these companies were expanding their presence in the U.S. market.

Internal mergers and acquisitions were believed most likely to occur in Spain and France. Each country had over 450 operating insurance companies. The CEO of Allianz stated: "After 1992 all European insurance companies will feel additional pressure with respect to premiums and commissions. As a result, economies of scale will become decisive." Analysts noted that Allianz had the largest dedicated agent sales force within the European insurance industry. This factor would probably give Allianz a distinctly competitive edge within a barrier-free EC market.

Among CWW's principal competitors in Europe was New York-based American International Group (AIG). In 1989, AIG announced that it would merge most of its European operations into a single company based in Paris, replacing 13 different national companies, using 6 separate computer centers with one central cash control and no corporate identity.[6] AIG's planned investment in its European operations was $200 million by 1992. An AIG marketing director noted: "Client companies will want consolidated insurance packages for their subsidiaries throughout Europe." AIG had a stronger reputation than CIGNA as a product innovator, particularly in the area of property and casualty insurance.

"The opportunities in the large risk market must first be exploited by brokers," commented an executive of the EC's Insurance Directorate. "If national habits are going to be broken down, brokers will do the job." A Belgian broker stated: "To take advantage of 1992 opportunities, brokers will need to be more informed about conditions, prices, and regulations in other member states, so they can better advise their clients. To properly serve multinational accounts, brokers will need to import favorable foreign rates and conditions and export home advantages to foreign clients." Another broker noted: "Our clients will look for Japanese-style, zero-defect service. Price will not be the driving issue; it will be taken for granted. The business will go to the broker who gets the right price; issues documentation instantly; and above all, obtains timely payment of claims."

---

[6]"Who's That Knocking on Foreign Doors? U.S. Insurance Salesmen," *Business Week,* March 6, 1989, pp. 84–85.

CWW's 1992 CHALLENGE

CWW executives believed their company was already well placed for the 1992 challenge. As Steve DeBrovner, senior vice president of marketing, pointed out, "We're much better positioned than are companies that are not yet even in the EC. Because of our experience with the 1984 CIGNA/AFIA merger, we know how long it takes for a company to become fully operational after an acquisition. The merging of two insurance sales networks can create many more problems than solutions. How to reconcile computer systems, design new policies, and deal with overlapping sales agents are among the problems that arise. Many competent people will be 'on the street' after some of these mergers, and we hope to add some of these quality producers to our staff."

According to analysts, other major U.S. insurers were poorly positioned to take advantage of the 1992 plan. In the past many of them had participated in international insurance through the AFIA insurance pool, which was acquired by CIGNA. Bruce Howson, president of CWW, noted: "Most U.S. insurers without international penetration will have difficulty if they begin now to take advantage of developments in the EC. It would mean the investment of millions of dollars and a 10-year process to deal with licensing requirements." Another executive added: "In 1984 most insurers were doubtful that the 1992 plan would ever be implemented. However, CIGNA management felt the plan would come to pass and purchased AFIA as a means to prepare for the change."

Many CWW executives believed the company's main strength was the large volume of business CWW transacted throughout Europe and the fact that it had fully staffed offices in every EC nation. Other strengths included CWW's capacity to write large risks, good name recognition, and a strong reputation for claims service among company risk managers. One country manager stated: "We know that our local service and our tailored products are of utmost importance to our present customers. We must not alienate our customers because they pay our bills." CWW spread the word about its large capacity through an advertising campaign built around the message, "Size has its advantages." *Exhibit 4.8* shows a recent advertisement that CIGNA Europe ran in the print media. *Exhibit 4.9* summarizes expenditures on advertising and marketing.

CIGNA Worldwide had excellent relationships with major U.S. insurance brokers. As a result, CIGNA Europe could rely upon its U.S.-based brokers to provide high-quality insurance packages for its customers within the EC. CWW was also extremely expert in writing large

EXHIBIT 4.8 CIGNA Europe — recent print advertisement

SIZE DOES HAVE ITS ADVANTAGES.

When you're navigating the unsure waters of today's insurance market, you need stability.

You need a provider backed by the resources of a worldwide company. One with experience to match. As Insurance Company of North America and former AFIA-member companies, we accumulated nearly a century of experience in the property and casualty market in Europe. Now that we've become *CIGNA Insurance Company of Europe S.A.-N.V.*, we also have all the resources you're likely to need. Of course, we've always had an extensive range of services.

Our Marine and Aviation Divisions lead the industry with innovative products and a unique underwriting capability.

At CIGNA, we can meet the needs of all kinds of businesses by offering specialized property and marine coverages as well as comprehensive commercial casualty products. We specialize in developing worldwide insurance programs.

Clearly, we're not just bigger. We're better. And you can learn how much better we are by writing to CIGNA Insurance Company of Europe, S.A.-N.V., CIGNA House, 8 Lime St., London EC3M 7NA, England or to the CIGNA office in your country (listed below).

An insurer with the ability *and* stability you're looking for. It's one more example of CIGNA's commitment to personalized service to business.

Vienna. Austria • Brussels. Belgium • Copenhagen. Denmark • Paris. France • Frankfurt. Federal Republic of Germany • Athens. Greece • Dublin. Ireland • Rome. Italy
Rotterdam. The Netherlands • Oslo. Norway • Lisbon. Portugal • Madrid. Spain • Stockholm. Sweden • Zurich. Switzerland • Istanbul. Turkey • London. United Kingdom

EXHIBIT 4.9 Advertising and mass marketing expenditures, CIGNA Europe ($000)

	Mass marketing[a]	
	1987	1985
Belgium-Luxembourg	$ 56	$ 114
Denmark	266	0
France	652	379
West Germany	599	443
Italy	648	383
Netherlands	104	81
Portugal	0	0
Spain	358	169
Ireland	173	96
United Kingdom	1,650	424
Total EC[b]	$4,506	$2,089

Note: CIGNA Europe's 1985 advertising expenditures were $249,000. 1987 advertising expenditures were estimated to be about four times larger than 1985 figures.

[a]Mass marketing includes costs of mailing and promotional materials.

[b]No expenditures were reported for Greece.

policies (especially for P&C coverage) designed for the international market. A CWW country manager pointed out: "We are the only U.S. carrier with an established European flagship, backed by the resources of a large parent company." According to many analysts, European markets were nationalistic, and U.S. insurance firms had a reputation for entering and exiting markets at "the drop of a hat" because of the cyclical nature of the business. CWW did not have this reputation. Most brokers and risk managers considered CWW to be a "national" company in each country in which it operated.

CWW executives believed the company's strengths outweighed its weaknesses. However, they knew improvements were needed in order for CWW to remain competitive. CIGNA Europe country managers operated their divisions as 12 independent entities. With little structured exchange of ideas among managers, communication occurred mostly informally. Computer systems in some EC countries were not compatible with those in other countries and, of course, outputs were in different national languages. Therefore, CWW personnel shared little information about product revenues, expenses, successes, and failures. One country manager commented, "The ability to exchange product, research and development, and financial information will become critical as 1992 approaches. We need a marketing information system that will allow us to do that. Also, we don't have enough competitive intelligence on the market players and this situation makes competing even more difficult than it normally would be." Computer systems would be addressed at the next task force meeting.

The P&C property segment comprised 60% of CIGNA Europe's total business compared to 40% of CIGNA, Inc.'s total revenues. CWW executives estimated that 70% of its property business would be opened to new competitors by the 1988 nonlife directive. This segment was relatively easy for competition to enter because of the large volume written and rewritten each year. Some CIGNA Europe managers felt that CWW was perhaps too focused on large accounts, while many of its competitors had systems in place to service medium-sized P&C accounts and personal lines. CWW's EC managers also maintained that the CWW management team was conservative and slow to implement change. One of the managers noted: "CWW's organizational reporting structure is not flexible enough to allow for quick decisions so we can take advantage of opportunities arising on the country level."

Although CWW was already highly regarded by other European insurers, CWW wanted to develop a corporate identity as strong as it enjoyed in the United States among brokers, agents, and clients in Europe. In a recent survey focusing on CIGNA's U.S. image, 63% of risk managers and 79% of brokers indicated that CIGNA provided "high-quality service." CWW also wanted to emulate the cost structure of its parent, CIGNA, Inc. because the expense side of the financial statement was the key to increasing CWW's competitiveness in Europe. As Howson stated: "Currently we have too many cooks and clerks supporting our salespeople."

Commenting on the fact that only 200 out of 1,700 CWW employees were underwriters, Howson noted: "CIGNA Europe's expense ratio is running at 40%, but our European competitors have 35% expense ratios. Some German and French insurance firms are even showing expense ratios of 27%–30%. If we can't remedy this five-point (or more) cost differential, we'll be at a disadvantage as insurance product prices fall in 1990. However, we need to decide what our goals are before we start cutting heads to lower expenses. Our 66% loss ratio for CWW is a great loss ratio and we can't expect to improve on it by much, but we need to focus on other key performance ratios." *Table C* summarizes key performance ratios.

TABLE C   CIGNA Europe performance ratios

	1988	Objective for January 1, 1993
Underwriting ratio[a]	14.0%	9.0%
Commission ratio[b]	18.0	19.0
Area office expense ratio[c]	3.2	2.0
Home office expense ratio[d]	5.0	2.5
Total expense ratio	40.2%	32.5%

[a]Underwriting expenses as a percent of sales.
[b]Commissions paid as a percent of sales.
[c]Allocated EC area office expenses as a percent of sales.
[d]Allocated U.S. home office expenses as a percent of sales.

Howson continued: "It is up to the country managers to grow the business and bring these ratios into line. Our responsibility as European managers is to get on with our 1992 changes now and not wait until 1992, or even until 1990. We can't wait for directives from the home office on these issues."

CWW executives understood the need for a coordinated effort in Europe. However, they also realized there were vast differences across the insurance markets of the EC countries. As one CWW European country manager stated: "Some companies will make the mistake of looking at the EC as a whole, offering 'Euro-insurance' products when there are still tremendous differences among nations. If these disparities are not recognized through niche product offerings, these companies might fail to satisfy any of the 325 million consumers in the EC. The key is to continue to think globally but to act in a manner that addresses local needs."

THE TASK FORCE MEETING

Nieuwenhuizen opened the task force meeting by outlining some key questions for his country managers: "How should CWW react to the changes occurring in its environment? What changes in market structure and competition were likely? What might happen to distribution channels? What countries would be most affected by the transformation? What are CWW's marketing options and how can CWW exploit its strengths to better position itself for 1992?"

After six hours of discussion and deliberation, the task force emerged with an initial outline of the critical issues, opportunities, and threats that 1992 posed to the organization. The country managers felt the critical issues for CWW in Europe were its sales effectiveness (marketing, distribution, and product mix) and cost effectiveness (cost containment, economies of scale, and technology).

Many managers thought product research and development could play a vital role in driving CIGNA Europe's future market share and revenue. One manager stated: "We need to develop new products to meet this fast-changing market. We need to look at what is changing technologically within various industries and then target products and services to meet the needs of a specific segment. In this way we can build our business." Another executive noted: "We should consider approaching the banks because we can offer our expertise in direct marketing and the banks will give us an additional distribution channel."

The challenges posed by 1992 stemmed from the probability of more intense price competition and the possibility of delay in reducing the expense ratio handicap. Another threat was voiced by one country manager as follows: "If the EC changes the definition of 'capital' in a future insurance directive, CWW could be relegated to foreigner status. We would need to maintain dramatically increased monetary reserves in each country. Such a situation would put a real kink into our 1992 plans."

As they left the task force meeting, CWW executives could not be sure how broad the EC's future insurance directives would be or how these directives would influence the way CWW did business. One executive commented: "The firms that will do well in the Common Market will be those with enough patience and capital to stay in for the long haul." The managers were certain, however, that 1990 would be an important year for insurance services and an opportunity for CWW to gain a stronger foothold in the European insurance marketplace.

EDITORS' COMMENTARY

CIGNA must first take inventory of its strengths. CIGNA is well known among risk managers and the larger brokers for its ability to write complex property and casualty insurance policies for multinationals and large national companies. In addition, CIGNA's country organizations enjoy a strong reputation for customer service, particularly in the area of claims administration.

CIGNA could continue to concentrate on large, complex risks that currently account for most of the company's European business and which are particularly subject to more intense competition as a result of the EC directives. A continuing focus on large risks will require that CIGNA develop further its product innovation skills where it apparently lags behind its principal American rival in Europe, AIG. In addition, greater coordination among CIGNA's largely autonomous country subsidiaries will be necessary, led perhaps by a new EC regional head-quarters. Another requirement will be investment in leading-edge information systems that will enable the risk managers of multinationals to access the status of their risks worldwide at any time.

An alternative strategy would be to target medium-risk business or to use such business to supplement the revenues obtained from serving the large multinationals. CIGNA's existing country organizations, staffed largely with local nationals, seem better equipped to address this segment than the large risk market. The option of pursuing small risk business seems ill-advised since the number of CIGNA salespeople in Europe precludes intensive coverage, CIGNA's name is not well known, and CIGNA's multinational experience is least relevant to this segment. On the other hand, CIGNA's direct marketing expertise, developed in the United States, might be a transferable capability to address the larger, small risk market.

Whichever strategy is chosen, it will be necessary for CIGNA to strengthen further its broker relationships and to reduce its expenses to become more profitable. This might involve a reduction in nonsales support staff and the consolidation of certain back-room tasks, currently carried out by each country organization, at a European regional office. However, CIGNA must be careful not to jeopardize the morale of its country organizations or the quality of service it currently provides to customers, since this is apparently a source of competitive advantage.

CHAPTER 5

Defending Global Market Leadership

Nokia-Mobira Oy and the Mobile Telephone Market

EDITORS' INTRODUCTION

In 1988, the Finnish company Nokia-Mobira Oy was the largest producer of mobile telephones in the world, with a 14% share of the world market. The company's strong market position was due in part to the fact that mobile telephone networks had evolved more rapidly in Scandinavia than in other countries. In addition, Nokia-Mobira had moved early to establish distribution in the growing U.S. market via a joint venture with Tandy's Radio Shack chain of retail outlets. In spite of these advantages, the company had relatively high costs and was little known outside Scandinavia.

In the EC countries, there were six different, largely incompatible, types of mobile telephone systems in operation. Market penetration of mobile phones was below 1% in all of the EC countries.

In mid-1987, the European Commission issued a "Green Paper" outlining proposals for the development of telecommunications services and equipment in the integrated EC market. The system that was envisaged would allow users to place and receive calls anywhere in the EC. The "Groupe Special Mobile," representing the EC countries' PTT organizations, was also recommending that the new system be capable of accommodating data and picture transmissions in addition to voice. Nokia-Mobira, like other key suppliers, was involved in a joint venture (with AEG and Alcatel) to develop equipment that would satisfy the new EC standards once they were established.

There was considerable uncertainty about the growth of the EC market for mobile telephones in the 1990s. It seemed likely, however, that price competition among producers would intensify, that new distribution channels might emerge, and that heavy advertising would be needed to establish brand awareness.

What strategies should Nokia-Mobira adopt to maintain its competitive position in the EC and in the world market?

Nokia-Mobira Oy

Ilkka Lipasti and John A. Quelch

Executives of Nokia-Mobira Oy met at company headquarters in Helsinki, Finland, in December 1988 to review their European marketing strategies. Nokia-Mobira was currently the world leader in the production of mobile phones but was facing increasingly stiff competition from Japanese and American manufacturers.

The European marketing strategy had to be considered in light of the European Community (EC) program to remove internal trade barriers by 1992. Between 1978 and 1986, the worldwide telecommunications industry grew rapidly but the EC share of world exports declined from 40% to 20%. Analysts attributed the decline to the fragmentation of European production which resulted from the continued application of different national equipment standards and type-approval policies. The market dominance of publicly owned telecommunications monopolies (PTTs) resulted in duplication of R&D efforts and increased costs. Between 1979 and 1989, telecommunications equipment was 80%–100% more expensive in Europe than in the United States.

Through EC-funded research programs and the harmonization of national technical standards, the EC hoped to rejuvenate its telecommunications industry. As a company headquartered within Europe but outside the EC, Nokia-Mobira was concerned about the marketing opportunities and challenges these developments presented.

THE EVOLUTION OF MOBILE TELECOMMUNICATIONS

Between 1920 and 1970, mobile telecommunications technology changed little except that the size of the equipment decreased significantly. Products consisted primarily of closed radiophone systems ("walkie talkies") and car radiotelephones. The limited number of free radio frequencies restricted the growth of the industry until the introduction of citizen band radios (CBs), which allowed a large number of users to communicate in a limited frequency and within a limited geographical area. To some extent, the CB replaced the public mobile phone in countries like the United States that did not have a wide network of radio stations for car phones. However, CBs, like mobile phones, were not connected to any telephone network, nor did they allow much privacy.

In the late 1970s, the industry changed dramatically. Paging and public mobile radio technologies were introduced, and cellular technology and closed cordless telephone systems soon followed. In addition, as indicated in *Exhibits 5.1* and *5.2*, through the adaptation of digital technology, several of the many new services facilitated by these tech-

EXHIBIT 5.1 Timing of innovations in telecommunications services

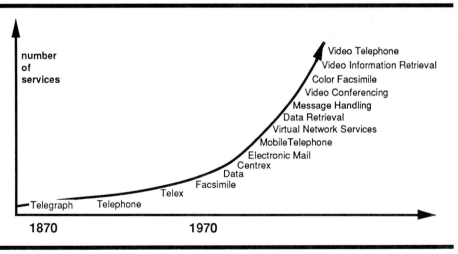

Source: L.M. Ericsson AB.

EXHIBIT 5.2 The evolution of telecommunications services

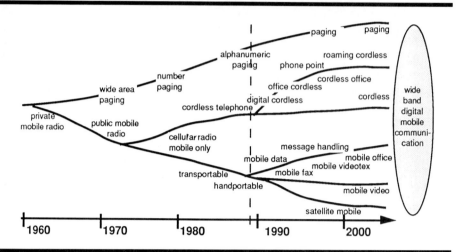

Source: Nokia-Mobira Oy and Consortium British Telconsult/Consultel/
Delecon, et al.

nologies could be integrated. Along with technological innovation came a restructuring of the industry. These new products and services were not introduced by the large, traditional telecommunications firms but by entrepreneurial firms in the semiconductor and the office automation industries. Learning curve effects had been rapid, and consequently, prices had dropped significantly, especially in countries with deregulated distribution of equipment and air time.[1]

Cellular Radio

A cellular system consisted of a central computerized telephone exchange that controlled several base stations, which in turn connected to the user's mobile telephone. The system had evolved from computer technology that allowed a more economical use of frequencies. Instead of each available frequency being restricted to one caller at a time, the new technology, which originated in Japan and in the Nordic countries in the late 1970s, allowed many callers to use the same frequency simultaneously. *Appendix A* describes cellular technology in more detail.

---

[1]*European Mobile Communications*, Quarterly Report, 1988: Issue 5.

In 1984, the United States introduced the AMPS cellular system, the Nordic countries introduced the NMT system, and the Japanese, the NTT system. The United Kingdom launched the TACS system in 1985. Between 1985 and 1988, the number of nations with operational cellular networks grew to 53, with the AMPS, NMT, and TACS systems claiming the largest bulk of subscribers.

Although the market was fragmented, the Nordic countries offered a geographical area with a common cellular system that allowed transfer of calls across national boundaries. Due to deregulation in the United States and the United Kingdom, the subscriber growth rate in these countries was the most rapid; the United States accounted for 55% of the 3.2 million subscribers worldwide, as opposed to Europe's 36%. However, the Nordic countries still recorded the highest cellular penetration.[2] Because of overcrowding of the systems, analysts expected digitalization to be the next technological advance to be tested in early 1990. Cellular telephone (and paging) were currently the fastest growing sectors in the telecommunications industry.[3]

In 1989, there were three main product applications for cellular radios: mobile, transportable, and handportable phones. The segment sizes varied widely by country, depending on the system capacities available and also on the timing of each product's introduction. For example, the handportable phone segment in the United States was small compared to that of the United Kingdom, due to differences in system capacity, and consequently, in price. In Scandinavia, the handportable segment was also very small, but this was due to the late introduction of the NMT-900 system[4] (see *Exhibit 5.3*).

Most of the companies involved in the cellular industry also had expertise in either telecommunications, radio communication, office automation, or consumer electronics. Like all telecommunications industries, the cellular business was regulated to some extent by international and national standards. Three regions of the world — North America, Europe, and Southeast Asia — each had their own central standards organizations, which usually included representatives from the relevant PTTs. Internationally, the standards-setting process was regulated to a modest degree by the CCITT organization in the International Telecommunications Union.

---

[2]"The Benefits of Completing the Internal Market for Telecommunication," Commission of the European Communities Report, 1988.
[3]*European Mobile Communications,* op. cit.
[4]Ibid.

EXHIBIT 5.3 Cellular product segments in major market areas, 1988

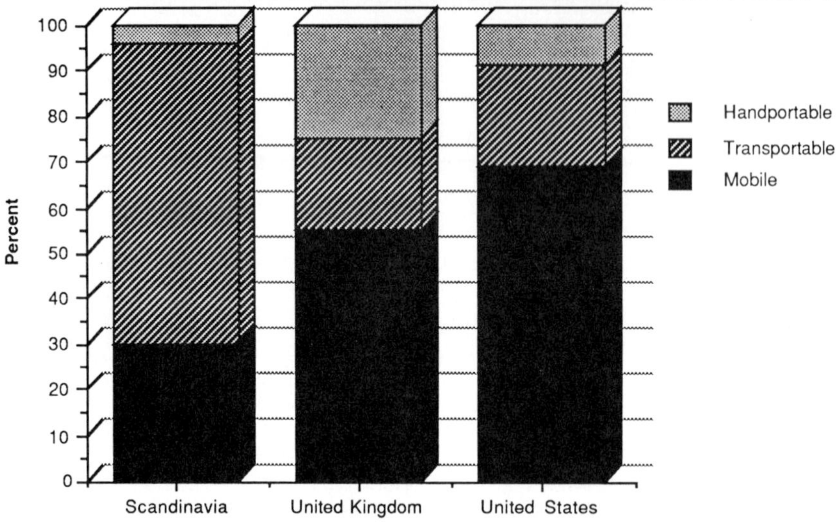

Source: Nokia-Mobira and *European Mobile Communications,* EMC.

In most countries, the cellular radio end user was typically a senior executive or a small business owner. Because of this upmarket bias, prices were generally high, and the market sizes small. However, in the United Kingdom and Scandinavia, the markets were considerably different — much larger and characterized by lower prices and a greater variety of business customers. In 1987, the market share accounted for by corporate purchases in Britain was estimated at 37%, while small business owners and self-employed people accounted for a 57% portion.[5] Consumers, at 2–3%, still represented a small portion of the market, but this market segment was expected to grow as prices dropped and networks improved. In terms of distribution, large corporations in the United Kingdom and other more developed markets tended to purchase directly from the manufacturer or the importer, while the other two segments purchased the product either from a telecommunications specialty store or from a consumer electronics outlet.

---

[5]Business Decisions Limited report, 1987.

COMPANY BACKGROUND
AND ORGANIZATION

Nokia Oy was established in Finland in 1865 as a manufacturer of paper and rubber products. In the mid-1970s, the firm began to expand internationally and to develop a business in high-technology products. By 1987, Nokia was Finland's largest company in terms of market capitalization and had sales of $3.4 billion. Its electronic division was both the fastest growing and the most profitable of its four divisions — electronics, cables and machinery, paper and chemicals, and rubber and floorings. Electronics sales totaled $1.6 billion, and profit, $170 million in 1987. Half of Nokia's electronics sales were made by companies it had acquired in West Germany and Sweden, which continued to market their products under their own trademarks.

Mobile Telephones Subsidiary

Nokia-Mobira Oy, a wholly owned subsidiary of Nokia Oy, designed, manufactured, and marketed mobile telephones and wide-area paging equipment, as well as cordless telephones and terminals for mobile data transmission. Nokia-Mobira limited itself strictly to end-user equipment, leaving the system infrastructure to Nokia Cellular Systems, another subsidiary of Nokia Oy.

When Nokia Oy acquired the first Finnish radiophone company, Televa, in 1925, the business that would later become Nokia-Mobira began operations. It produced its first radiophones in 1963, distributing them to the Finnish Army. In 1971, it introduced the public mobile phone. In 1979, the Mobira company was established as a joint venture between Nokia and Salora. By 1980, sales in Finland and Sweden totaled $12 million. In 1981, Mobira established a Swedish subsidiary and began distribution in seven other European countries. In 1982, Salora sold its share in Mobira to Nokia and the company then became Nokia-Mobira.

In 1987, Nokia-Mobira's sales were $270 million. Sales for 1988 were expected to be over $320 million, of which one-quarter would be domestic sales. Nokia-Mobira employed about 2,400 people and claimed a 14% world market share. Moreover, in important product markets such as the AMPS system and the NMT system, Nokia was the market leader.

When the U.S. market began to develop, Mobira needed an American business partner with an existing distributor network. In 1984, Mobira made an agreement with Tandy Corporation to set up a joint venture manufacturing plant in South Korea and to distribute phones through Tandy's Radio Shack outlets under the Radio Shack brand name. By 1988, Mobira had subsidiaries in the United Kingdom, the Federal Republic of Germany, Sweden, Norway, Denmark, the United States, and Canada; it also had joint ventures in South Korea and France.

Company Organization 1980–1988

In 1980, Nokia-Mobira had two factories. One produced mobile phones and pagers, while the second concentrated on support stations for dedicated networks and on standard radiophones. However, by late 1982, the growth expectations for NMT cellular radios and the introduction of new cellular systems in Germany, the United Kingdom, and France,

EXHIBIT 5.4 Nokia-Mobira organization chart, 1987

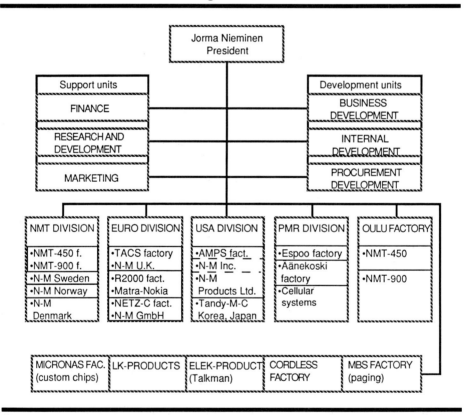

prompted Nokia to add independent production plants for each system. The organization is depicted in *Exhibit 5.4*. The fragmentation of production into a large number of fairly small units provided the company with flexibility as well as the motivation that came from decentralization. However, it also meant duplication of product costs. It became clear by early 1988 that the company could not compete with the cost structures of its main competitors.

Under a new president, Timo Louhenkilpi, the firm continued to refine its organizational structure to achieve greater cost effectiveness. Louhenkilpi counseled: "We must learn more from others' experiences and increase interrelationships in the company." *Exhibit 5.5* shows the

EXHIBIT 5.5 Nokia-Mobira organization chart, 1988

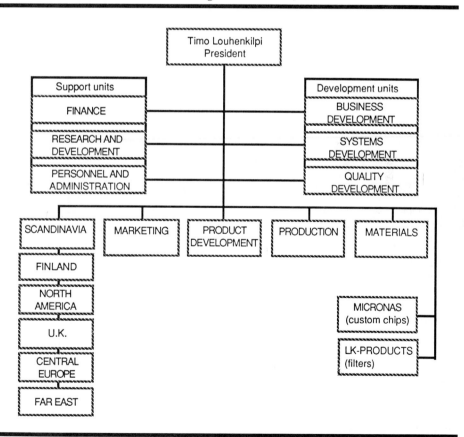

organization established in 1988. The newly formed management team looked for synergies between the various Nokia divisions. Nokia Cellular Systems was established as an independent company with exclusive control of the cellular systems product line.

CELLULAR MARKET DEVELOPMENT IN EUROPE

European Cellular Networks

In 1988, there were 18 cellular networks in Europe, which served over a million subscribers.[6] There were six different types of systems in operation — NMT, TACS, Radiocom 2000, C-450, RTMS, and Comvik — described in more detail in *Appendix B.* Not only were these systems largely incompatible but networks that operated under the same system were also not always compatible. For example, the NMT-450, the predominant system in terms of subscriber volume, was not produced to uniform specifications, and therefore its own network components were not always compatible with one another.

There were three main groups of countries within which networks could be connected across national boundaries: Scandinavia, The Benelux countries, and the United Kingdom and Ireland. As indicated in *Exhibit 5.6,* the two major systems used throughout Europe were NMT and TACS; NMT was losing share to TACS. The other four system types had not thus far succeeded in establishing a significant share of subscriber volume.

Cellular Penetration by Country

During 1988, the number of European subscribers grew at about 6% each month. However, the main sources of this growth were the United Kingdom and the Nordic countries, with the United Kingdom responsible for about 45% of the most recent annual increase, and the Nordic countries for 27%. *Exhibits 5.7* and *5.8* illustrate the wide range of penetration rates in European countries. For example, the United Kingdom market was characterized by medium penetration and high growth; the Nordic countries' market, by high penetration and medium growth; Germany and France, by both low penetration and low growth. In terms of penetration, Norway led all countries with 3.3%, while the Scandi-

---

[6]Most of this section is based on *Europe Mobile Communications,* Quarterly Report, 1988: Issue 5.

EXHIBIT 5.6 European cellular systems subscriber bases, 1981–1988

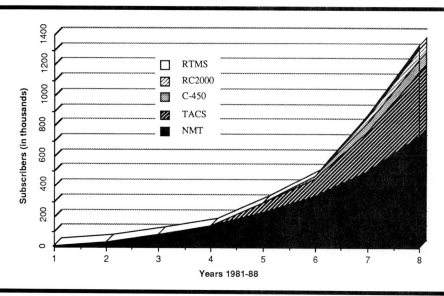

Source: *European Mobile Communications*, Quarterly Report, 1988: Issue 5.

navian countries generally enjoyed high penetration levels. The United Kingdom followed some distance behind with 0.65%, and with the exception of Austria (0.41%) and Switzerland (0.23%), none of the remaining European countries exceeded 0.2% penetration.

Observers attributed this wide variance in market penetration from country to country to the age of the systems, the different degrees of deregulation, competition, and marketing efforts, as well as to the type of network being implemented. For example, the slow growth in Germany was attributed to the technical complexity of Germany's national network and to the resulting poor connection quality and high tariffs. On the other hand, analysts credited Iceland's high growth to a delayed adoption of an already proven system, NMT, which served well the needs of its fishing fleet. Scandinavia's high-growth rates may have been encouraged by the sparseness of population and by the PTT's early market orientation.[7] In the United Kingdom, growth was mainly

---

[7]Survey on Mobile Communications, *Financial Times*, September 12, 1988.

EXHIBIT 5.7 **Speed of market penetration by country**

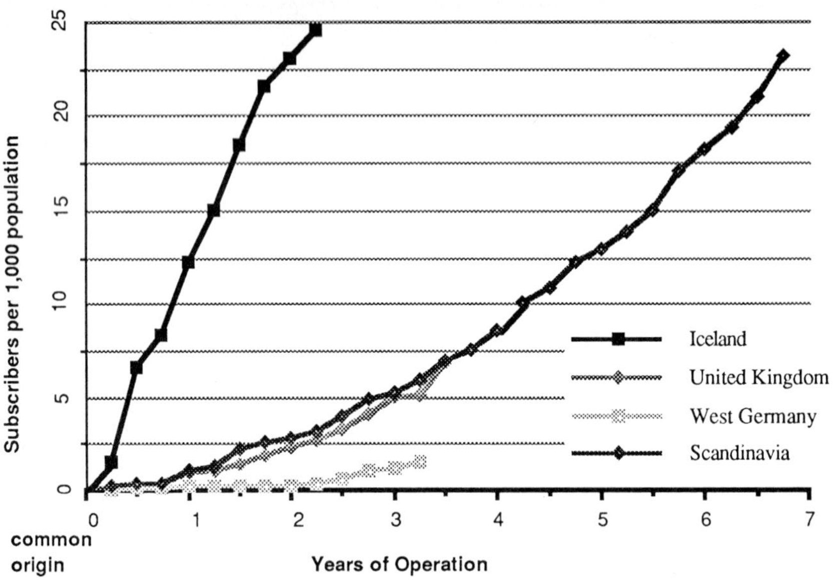

Source: *European Mobile Communications*, Quarterly Report, 1988: Issue 5.

spurred by the competition; two competing networks ensured aggressive marketing and more rapid market penetration.

Competition

Network Operations. As of 1988, among 16 European countries, only the United Kingdom and Sweden had competing networks within their boundaries. In Sweden, Televerket, the public telephone company, competed with a small network run by Comvik. Comvik's subscribers numbered only 14,000 versus the PTT's 193,000. In the United Kingdom, strong competition existed between two privately owned cellular networks, Cellnet and Vodafone. The privatized British Telecom owned 60% of Cellnet while Securicor owned 40%; Racal owned Vodafone 100%. The British distribution system was also unique. British network operators did not sell air time directly to end users. Instead, independent service providers sold air time, either directly or through a dealer network. The British approach to distribution was expected to become

EXHIBIT 5.8 Cellular penetration by country, 1988

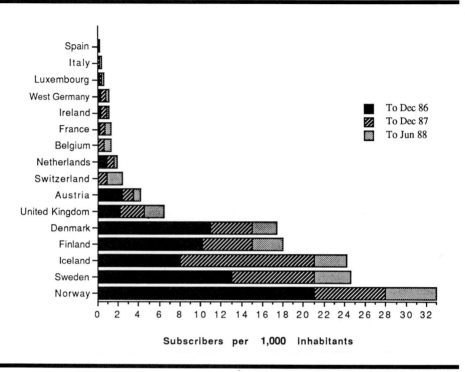

Source: *European Mobile Communications,* Quarterly Report, 1988: Issue 5.

more widespread in Europe.[8] *Appendix C* describes the British marketing system for cellular in more detail.

In 1987, France joined Britain and Scandinavia in allowing domestic competition in cellular networks. Its second system was expected to begin operations in 1989, at which point the PTT, France Telcom, with its Matra-designed Radiocom 2000 system, would begin to lose its monopoly position. However, all other cellular networks in Europe were still monopolies as of 1989.

Competition was believed to have had a stronger impact on cellular equipment prices than on air-time rates. In the United Kingdom this may have been because networks competed more on coverage than in

---

[8]A study of distribution strategies for cellular equipment in the United Kingdom, Juha Pinomaa, Helsinki University of Technology, 1988.

tariffs. As shown in *Exhibit 5.9*, the equipment prices in the United Kingdom were by far the lowest in Europe in 1988 — almost as low as those in the United States. British air-time rates, on the other hand, were only slightly below the European average.

Equipment Distribution. By 1988, the distribution of cellular equipment in Europe had for the most part been liberalized. Only Italy and the Netherlands limited the distribution of equipment to their PTTs. However, the degree of liberalization in the equipment markets varied considerably among European countries. With the exception of the United Kingdom, European distribution channels consisted of national network operators, telecommunications specialty stores, and importers.

EXHIBIT 5.9 World price levels, 1988
Equipment prices and air time rates in Europe (in GBP)

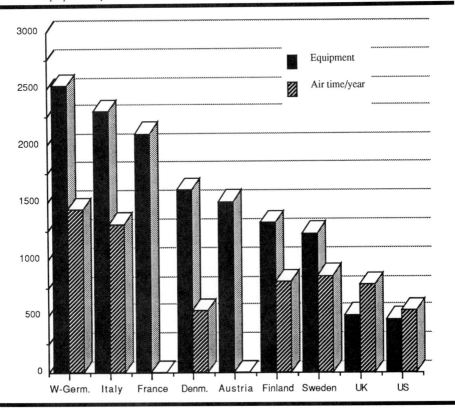

Source: *European Mobile Communications*, EMC.

Yet, despite the similarity in distribution systems, almost all countries had unique type-approval standards and other technical entry barriers that effectively blocked the use of standard products. In addition, domestic producers were emerging in most countries. Particularly in Germany, continuously changing specifications represented a serious barrier to entry.

Substitutes for Cellular

The major substitutes for cellular radio were amateur and citizen's band radios, radio paging, cordless phones, and private mobile radios. *Exhibits 5.10* and *5.11* provide data on these substitutes. New forms of electronic data communications, such as facsimile and electronic mail, tended to complement rather than substitute for cellular. Mobile radios were not a major threat to cellular radio because they were primarily used when a closed system was appropriate. Only cordless phones were in direct competition with cellular. Because they were cheaper and provided access to the public telephone network, the first generation of cordless phones also replaced some in-company mobile radio systems.

EXHIBIT 5.10 Cellular substitutes in the United Kingdom

The U.K. mobile communication market in 1988	Mobile communication growth rates in the United Kingdom in 1988

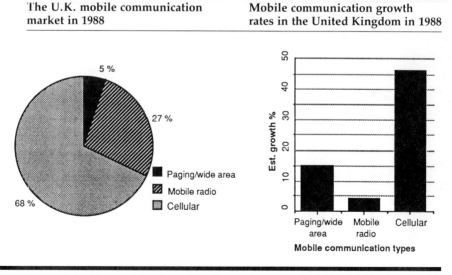

Source: Juha Pinomaa's Study on Distribution Strategies for Nokia-Mobira in the United Kingdom.

EXHIBIT 5.11 Rating the options for mobile communication in the
United Kingdom

	Payphone	Telepoint (CT2)	Car cellular	Portable cellular
Unit costs ($)	None	180–360	900–1080	1440–2700
Call cost (above PSTN[a])	25%	18¢/minute	45¢/minute	45¢/minute
Call type	Outgoing only	Outgoing only	Two-way	Two-way
Convenience				
Handset needs	None	One person	In car	One person
Call location	Fixed	Fixed	Mobile	Mobile

Source: Logica pls and Nokia Cellular Systems.
[a]Rates for public switched telephone network

Using a special radio network similar to that of the cellular network, the second generation of cordless phones could operate outside of an office, making them a serious threat to the handportable cellular radio. The other advantages of the second-generation cordless, also known as CT2, were its relatively low equipment and usage costs, its small size and its light weight. However, it also had disadvantages: it required a separate radio pager to receive messages; and there was only a limited number of "phonepoints" where this type of phone was operable. Nevertheless, the CT2 was being marketed in the United Kingdom where it was developed. Because its standards had been approved by the member states of the EC in 1989, it was expected to be adopted in other EC countries as well. Three major equipment manufacturers — Philips, Motorola, and Nokia-Mobira — had become involved in system development in the United Kingdom. Nokia had participated in the design of the new system through a joint venture with Shaye Communications, Ltd.

EQUIPMENT MANUFACTURERS IN EUROPE

Competitor Strategies

There were 31 cellular equipment manufacturers in Europe in 1988. With representation in 14 out of 16 European countries, Nokia-Mobira had the widest coverage. *Exhibit 5.12* lists the manufacturers with type approvals in Europe as of 1988. *Exhibit 5.13* shows worldwide and European market shares for cellular equipment as of 1988. Only 6 of the 31 cellular manufacturers operating in Europe were also major global players: Nokia-Mobira, Motorola, NEC, Panasonic, Novatel, and Mitsubishi. The European manufacturers whose markets were limited in Europe — Philips, Siemens, Ericsson, and Technophone — were almost invisible in markets beyond Europe, for example, in the United States. On the other hand, the European markets were not dominated by the Japanese manufacturers as were most of the other world markets. NEC, Panasonic, and Mitsubishi together held almost half of the world market, while in Europe, they had a combined market share of only 28%. Companies with significant shares of the United States market that had not yet entered the European market, such as OKI and Toshiba, were expected to do so as the market developed further.

In Europe, the clear market leader was Motorola, the American semiconductor company that had entered the EC market through the purchase of Storno, a Danish cellular firm. Relative to Motorola, Nokia was weak in the United Kingdom market but still the market leader in Scandinavia.

Nokia-Mobira's principal competitors in Europe were Motorola, NEC, Panasonic, Technophone, Mitsubishi, Novatel, Philips, and Ericsson.[9] In 1987, NEC, Panasonic, Philips, and Mitsubishi had on average triple the resources invested in communications technology that Nokia had. They were on average five times bigger than Nokia in sales, and they all had extensive experience in other information-related technologies such as telefax machines, copiers, and computers. Motorola and Ericsson were similar to Nokia in terms of sales and communications technology resources, although Motorola's know-how in integrated circuits was superior to Nokia's. All of these firms, particularly Philips and Motorola, increasingly pursued joint ventures and strategic alliances with other telecommunications companies in order to share development risks and costs and to develop more varied products. Nokia's two smaller, nonconglomerate competitors, Novatel and Technophone, had less than half Nokia's sales but they focused on only cellular radios. Moreover, Technophone had specifically targeted the handportable segment.

Various of Nokia-Mobira's major competitors employed the generic strategies of cost-leadership, differentiation, and focus as indicated in *Exhibit 5.14.* Companies like Motorola and NEC, with products in the

[9]Technophone and Mitsubishi marketed handportables only.

EXHIBIT 5.12 Cellular manufacturers in Europe

| Area | | | | | Scandinavia | | | | | | | Benelux | | | | | | | | |
| Country | | | | | | | | | | | | | | | | | | | |
Manufacturer	#	Note	S	DK	IS	N	SF	UK	IR	B	NL	LX	F	D	E	A	I	CH
AEG	1													X				
AT&T/Hitachi	1							X										
Autophon	1												X					
Bosch	1	1											X					
Cetelco	5	2	X	X		X	X											X
Dancall	9	3	X	X	X	X	X	X		X						X		X
Ericsson	9		X	X	X	X	X								X	X		X
Hitachi	1	4						X									X	
Italtel	1	5															X	
JRC/Cleartone	2							X	X									
Kokusai	7		X	X		X	X	X								X		X
Matra	1	6										X						
Mitsubishi	9		X	X	X	X	X	X	X	X					X			X
Mobira	14		X	X	X	X	X	X	X	X	X	X	X			X		X
Motorola	10		X	X	X	X	X	X	X	X						X		X
NEC	8		X	X	X	X	X	X	X									
Novatel/Astec	2							X	X									
OTE	1	5															X	

Company	S	SF	N	DK	IS	UK	IR	B	NL	LX	F	D	A	I	Ch
Panasonic	8	X	X		X	X	X	X		X					X	X
Philips AP	12	X	X	X	X	X	X	X		X	X	X	X		X	X
Philips PKI	1												X			
Racal-Orbitel [7]	1						X									
Radiotel	1													X		
Siemens	10	X	X		X	X	X	X		X	X		X		X	X
Simonsen	6	X	X		X	X				X						X
Storno	10	X	X		X	X	X	X		X	X		X		X	X
Talco	1													X		
Technophone [8]	7	X					X	X	X	X		X		X		X
Telettra [5]	1												X			
Toyocom [9]	2	X					X								X	
Number/country		15	12	10	13	13	15	8	6	3	7	4	3	9	3	14

Notes: Table does not include products supplied on a "badge engineered basis." (S = Sweden; DK = Denmark; IS = Iceland; N = Norway; SF = Finland; UK = United Kingdom; IR = Ireland; B = Belgium; NL = Netherlands; LX = Luxembourg; F = France; D = West Germany; A = Austria; I = Italy; Ch = Switzerland.)

1. Bosch is present as a distributor of cellular phones in several countries, but has its own products only in France. It is developing its own product for C-450 in Germany.

2. Only NMT-450, NMT-900 in planning stage.

3. Dancall markets through Autophon in Austria and plans to do the same in France.

4. Hitachi has made two entries into United Kingdom. First, indirectly as a supplier of the radio side of the Racal-marketed AT&T VIP product and second with a handportable through British Telecom.

5. There are three national manufacturers for Italy's RTMS-450 network: Italtel, OTE, and Telettra.

6. Matra's entry to equipment markets was heavily supported by Nokia-Mobira technology.

7. Racal's Citifone handportable was designed in collaboration with E.F. Johnsen.

8. The U.K.-manufactured technophone is marketed by Comvik in Sweden, BBC in Switzerland, ATR in France, SEL in Germany (SEL financed the development costs), and by Alcatel and Elin in Austria.

9. Toyocom products are marketed by STC in the United Kingdom and Comvik in Sweden.

139

EXHIBIT 5.13 Worldwide and European equipment market shares, 1988 (percent)

	Worldwide market share	European market share
Nokia-Mobira	13.8%	12.2%
Motorola	13.4	19.4
NEC	11.9	14.4
Panasonic	9.4	10.1
Toshiba	8.2	
Mitsubishi	8.1	3.1
OKI	5.9	
Novatel	5.9	4.7
Uniden	3.4	
Ericsson	2.8	7.2
Philips	2.5	6.4
Siemens	2.4	6.2
Others	12.4%	16.3%

low-price segment of the market pursued a cost-leadership strategy; Nokia, Panasonic, Philips, and Mitsubishi, which produced high- and middle-priced products, followed a strategy of differentiation; and Novatel and Technophone, operating in only one product-market segment, implemented a focus strategy.

Companies pursuing cost leadership tended to command higher market shares. Those pursuing differentiation seemed to have enjoyed higher profits, although consumers were not always willing to pay more for extra features. This was especially true in the United Kingdom and in other more developed markets.

Each manufacturer coordinated the range of products and systems it made according to its generic strategy. For example, those that pursued cost leadership manufactured for a broad range of systems. The majority of Nokia-Mobira's key competitors marketed equipment for multiple systems and product-market segments, although only Nokia-Mobira, Motorola, Technophone, and Philips had equipment for every cellular system in operation. Novatel and Ericsson were the only major players to focus on only one or two systems.

EXHIBIT 5.14 European strategies of major cellular manufacturers

STRATEGIC ADVANTAGE

	Uniqueness Perceived by the Customer	Low Cost Position
Industrywide	DIFFERENTIATION • Mobira • Panasonic • Philips • Mitsubishi	OVERALL COST LEADERSHIP • Motorola • NEC
Particular Segment Only	FOCUS	
	• Ericsson (NMT)	• Novatel (AMPS, TACS) • Tecnophone (handportable)

STRATEGIC MARKET (vertical axis label)

Product-Market Strategies of Major Manufacturers in 1988

PRODUCT SCOPE

SYSTEMS SCOPE	Wide	Focus
Wide (all)	• Mobira • Motorola • Philips	• Tecnophone
Wide (major)	• NEC • Panasonic • Mitsubishi	
Focus (1-2)	• Ericsson • Novatel	

Sources: *European Mobile Communications*, EMC, and Nokia-Mobira, among others.

...

Brand Choice Criteria

Through dealer surveys, Nokia mapped the most important end-user purchase criteria, both for the mobile and for the handportable cellular radio. Research results indicated that, for the mobile radio, price reliability, reception, design, and brand were considered especially important. In the case of handportables, battery life, size, and reception were the most important product features to end users. According to two consumer surveys summarized in *Exhibit 5.15,* Finnish end users considered reliability and brand image to be the most important product features, and British users were more concerned with price and design. These variations reflected not only differences in user preferences but also differences in industry structure and market maturity.

Another survey, summarized in *Exhibit 5.16,* measured the ability of

EXHIBIT 5.15 Brand choice criteria in the United Kingdom and Finland

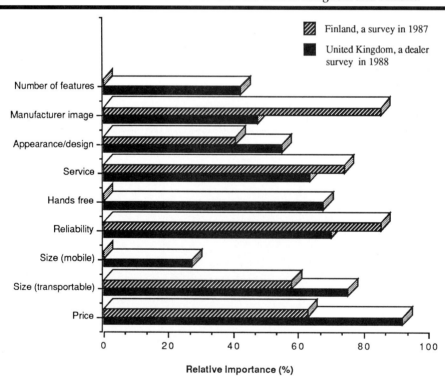

EXHIBIT 5.16 Relative customer perceptions of major U.K. manufacturers

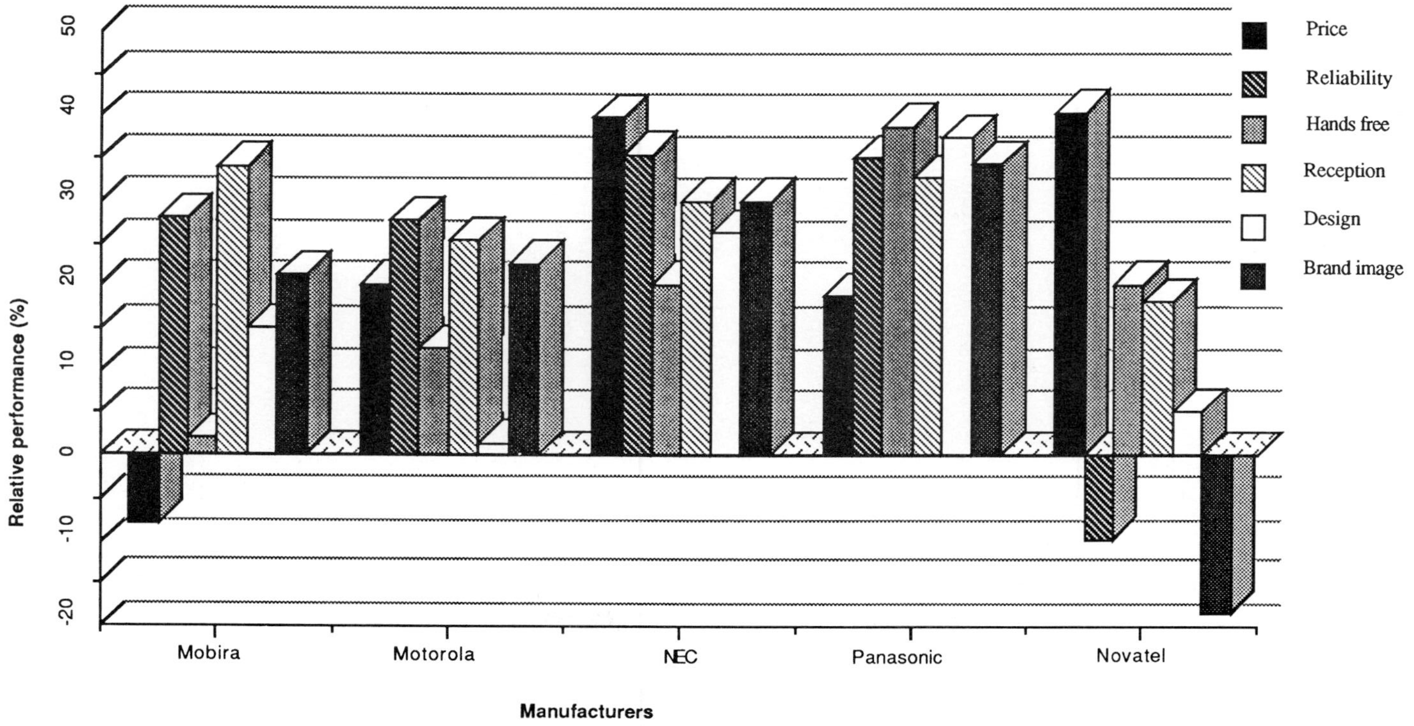

143

European manufacturers to meet user criteria. While Nokia outperformed some of its major competitors in reliability, reception, and brand image, the firm was less competitive on price and on design. The lack of a "hands-free" feature was another serious drawback to Nokia's product offering, although Nokia outperformed all major competitors in battery life and reception. Nokia was also constrained by its cost structure and the fact that its brand name was relatively unknown outside of Scandinavia.

Distribution

The major cellular radio manufacturers followed varied market entry, distribution, and brand strategies both within and across geographical markets, as indicated in *Exhibit 5.17*. Philips, the European consumer electronics giant, almost always used direct distribution as a market entry mode; whereas Technophone, a relatively small company, invariably distributed through importers, OEM agreements, and joint ventures. The big Japanese companies — NEC, Panasonic, and Mitsubishi — usually entered a new international market via an OEM agreement or an importer, and later introduced their own brands and direct distribution. In contrast, Novatel supplied both the British and the American market under various brand names through a single distributor, the Carphone Group, whose network included Volvo and Ford dealers.

The distribution penetration and brand awareness level of both Ericsson and Nokia-Mobira were very good in the Nordic countries and satisfactory in other markets. However, their cost positions were poor, particularly that of Nokia-Mobira in the United Kingdom. Both Nokia-Mobira and Ericsson had been relatively successful in penetrating regulated markets, either through joint ventures with cellular system developers, or through the local public telephone companies. Philips and Siemens had also enjoyed some success through joint ventures — Siemens in Austria, and Philips and Siemens in Switzerland. In contrast, Motorola had a very good cost position and intensive distribution but relatively poor channel control. NEC in pursuing a cost leadership strategy had introduced several brands distributed through multiple channels. Panasonic based its differentiation strategy on high product quality but distributed its products broadly through importers and wholesalers. Hence, its channel control was poor, though its market coverage was good. Novatel gained good market share through the use of exclusive, well-selected importers.

Most competitors marketed under their own brand names in the

EXHIBIT 5.17 Market entry strategies by manufacturers in six European countries

Manufacturers	AUSTRIA Market share %	FRANCE Market share %	W. GERMANY Market share %	SCANDINAVIA Market share %	SWITZERLAND Market share %	UNITED KINGDOM Market share %
Subscribers (June 1988)	34,408	68,870	70,290	522,964	13,970	366,000
Mobira	27	25?	new	20	?	6
Motorola	2-4	?	>20	17	?	33
NEC	-	-	-	5	?	25
Panasonic	-	?	-	7	?	10
Technophone	new	-	new	-	?	(23)
Mitsubishi	-	-	-	7	?	3
Novatel	-	-	-	-	-	10
Philips	20	-	>20	9	?	0,1
Ericsson	14	-	-	15	?	-
Large, local competitor	Siemens (assembly j-v)	Radiotel and Talco	AEG and Siemens	23	?	JRC, licensed to Cleartone

Note: Arrows indicate direction of development, market leaders are indicated with a grey tone.

more highly developed markets, such as the United Kingdom and Scandinavia, but used joint ventures or OEM manufacturers in closed or regulated markets such as France. As might be expected, companies pursuing a differentiation strategy used their own brand names and direct distribution to ensure tight control. On the other hand, companies pursuing a cost leadership strategy were more interested in wide coverage and efficient distribution, typically using several brands and distributors. Philips, Nokia-Mobira, Motorola, and Technophone had begun to supply air time in order to assist their dealers in promoting their products.

Market Communications

Almost all manufacturers using direct distribution invested heavily in promotion to support their dealer networks. Manufacturers such as NEC employing a cost leadership strategy pursued intensive distribution and were among the heavier advertisers. Motorola and Philips emphasized sales promotion instead of advertising because their brand awareness was already high, whereas Nokia-Mobira and Ericsson (and Technophone in the United Kingdom) did use advertising to create brand awareness. On the other hand, NEC, Panasonic, and Mitsubishi tended to rely instead on wholesalers and importers to handle their product advertising. Novatel and all manufacturers using OEM agreements — Hitachi, Technophone outside the United Kingdom, and others — delegated promotion to their importers and wholesalers. With the exception of Novatel, the result was often poor promotion.

Summary

Analysts believed that the European markets were at varying stages of the product life cycle. The lesser-developed markets — Italy, Germany, and France — were still in the introduction stage. In these countries, cellular radio had an upmarket image. Marketing channels, primarily specialty stores and manufacturer's representatives, emphasized customer service and high prices. The United Kingdom and Scandinavian markets were in the growth stage, perhaps in the late growth stage in the case of some subcategories such as transportable phones. Prices in these markets were low or falling as in Scandinavia.

THE IMPACT OF 1992

Toward a Competitive EC Telecommunications Market

On June 30, 1987, the Commission of the EC submitted a Green Paper that focused on the development of telecommunications services and equipment. The Commission listed the following objectives:

- Phased opening of the terminal market.
- Competition in all value-added services.
- Community-wide interoperability.
- Opening of public network procurement.
- Separation of regulatory and operational activities of PTTs.
- Continuous review of the activities of PTTs and private providers.
- Cooperation at all levels.
- Consensus in technical standards, frequencies, and tariffs.
- Establishment of the European Telecommunications Standards Institute by April 1988.

Two overarching ideas in the Green Paper were interoperability and a consensus on tariffs. From the cellular equipment manufacturers' point of view, the Green Paper offered several promising opportunities. First, the opening of public procurement would eventually end the PTTs' favoritism of local manufacturers. Second, mutual recognition of each country's type-approval criteria for terminal equipment, scheduled for December 1990, would remove entry barriers to new equipment from nonnational suppliers. Third, analysts expected cost-based tariffs and full competition in value-added services to lead to a price-competitive market structure similar to that in the United Kingdom, and hence to increased demand for cellular phones.

Groupe Special Mobile (GSM)

CEPT, a cooperative organization of European PTTs, formed GSM to ensure Europe's competitiveness in cellular technology, particularly against Asian competition. GSM's major objective was to create and implement standards and specifications for a Pan-European digital cellular system. A time line was set for the coordinated implementation of a digital cellular network. By the end of 1988, several operators in Europe had begun to award letters of intent to successful bidders for digital systems. The first systems were slated to start operation in June 1991. The new digital system had several important characteristics:

- *Pan-European roaming.* The system enabled an individual in any European country that had adopted the GSM system to receive and transmit calls throughout the system. To reach this goal, several billing-related problems had to be solved. However, the Green Paper emphasized that the GSM operation should not be given to a monopoly. Difficulties to be resolved included determining what the caller's choice should be in a border area where networks of more than one country could operate, and how the caller would be billed.
- *Call-handling capacity.* Analysts estimated that the analog networks in Europe could handle about 4.35 million subscribers, while the digital network could handle over 6 million subscribers in one country alone. This added capacity was important because, by 1989, the existing analog cellular networks in some EC countries had already become quite congested.
- *Special services.* The aim of the GSM working group was to design a state of the art system that would offer transfer of data, picture, and voice all through the same channel. Some manufacturers had complained that the system was too elaborate, that services such as the transmission of text data were not really necessary, and that the system would be costly to implement. Several surveys indicated that speech would remain the most important form of data transmission in cellular systems for the next several years.

Nokia-Mobira was developing both systems and equipment for GSM in a joint venture with AEG and Alcatel. Most of the other key European suppliers — Bosch, Ericsson, Matra, and Philips — were similarly involved in system development through different joint ventures. Motorola was also heavily involved in research and development work and had submitted competitive bids in Scandinavia, the United Kingdom, and Spain. Nokia-Mobira had also formed an alliance with AT&T to develop the semiconductors that were critical to successful GSM equipment. Motorola, and the major Japanese competitors (NEC, Toshiba, and Mitsubishi), had highly developed semiconductor technology. One-third of the manufacturing costs for cellular radio was in the special integrated circuits needed for digitalization. Moreover, the need to incorporate the new technology and special features of the system into small and lightweight handportables made the task even more challenging.

Cellular Equipment Demand in 1992

Analysts believed that the key factors that would determine the demand for digital cellular systems were the following: the increasing congestion in existing analog cellular services, competitive network operations, attractiveness of the equipment, and special features of the system. Although demand estimates varied widely, some analysts forecast 5 million systems would be required by 1996. Other more skeptical analysts wondered whether European bureaucrats had "shot themselves in the foot" while trying to ensure European competitiveness by specifying an overly complex system. Based on a comparison of European digital cellular system development with that of the United States, they predicted that 1996 demand would only amount to 2 million systems.

In Europe, the PTTs or manufacturers provided the specifications for each new system, but in the United States open competition determined the most widely used system. The result in the United States was a more effective and simpler system than in Europe. Though the U.S. market was more open to foreign competition, this ensured lower costs and competitive prices. Some skeptical analysts believed that digital cellular radio in Europe would not be able to compete effectively against the analog networks, particularly the NMT-900 system in Scandinavia and possibly the new French and German systems. A key question was whether or not the new French and German systems would ever be compatible with the current Scandinavian, and possibly the future Swiss, Dutch, and Belgian NMT-900 systems, thereby facilitating Pan-European roaming.

Another factor that could limit the growth of the digital cellular market in Europe was the development of both Europe-wide radio paging, ERMES, and the second-generation cordless, CT2. Market demand would be further limited if the prices for digital cellular equipment did not drop and if the size of the equipment could not be adequately miniaturized. On the other hand, demand for Pan-European cellular radio would probably be enhanced by the increased travel within the EC following the removal of border controls and by cost reductions due to learning curve effects in analog cellular equipment manufacturing, as had occurred in the United States and United Kingdom. Moreover, competition at the service provider level could accelerate the building of network coverage. New user groups could include ships and boats in the Mediterranean, trucks and vans on the continent, and business people calling from planes, airports, and private cars. A 1988 survey established that 2 million out of the 4 million car owners who crossed EC borders regularly were interested in cellular services. In addition, a third of the EC's 9 million farmers used private mobile radio systems, and many could be attracted to cellular radio. As suggested in *Exhibit 5.18*, there could be over 8 million subscribers in the EC in 1992 versus the 1.4 million in 1988 assuming that the penetration reached in Scandinavia in 1988 would be the 1992 European penetration level. Most of the growth would probably take place outside Scandinavia, particularly in Germany, France, Belgium, and the United Kingdom.

Price. Analysts expected price competition to intensify in Europe as 1992 approached, thanks to the emergence of competing network op-

EXHIBIT 5.18 Cellular demand forecast for Europe

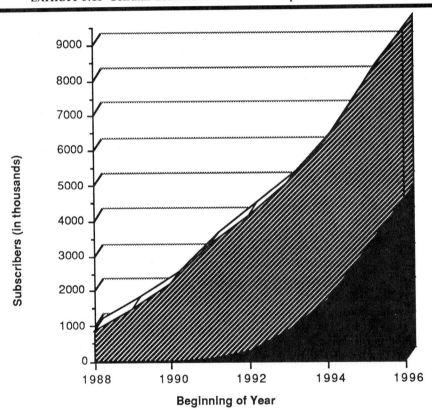

Source: *European Mobile Communications*, BisMacintosh, and Nokia-Mobira Oy.

erators and the opening of the terminal markets. Moreover, market expansion was likely to occur in response to progressively lower prices, and premium-priced products were expected to hold a decreasing market share.

Distribution. Competition among distributors might increase the demand for cellular radio. However, analysts saw distribution primarily as a result rather than as a determinant of demand. The introduction of cellular radio would not in itself cause any dramatic changes in distribution methods or channels. More likely, the distribution of digital equipment would follow the pattern for analog cellular equipment.

Many thought that the handportable phone would open a broader range of distribution channels for cellular phones. Because they did not require any installation or special services, these phones could be mass marketed. For example, in the United States, they were already being sold by mail order. In Hong Kong, specialty stores distributed them as "hot phones," registered and ready for immediate use. Prices and margins were expected to decrease as distribution expanded.

Specialty outlets were expected to lose their position as the principal channel by 1992, while direct business-to-business operations were expected to continue their strong growth. Consumer electronics outlets were thought likely to concentrate on selling lower-priced equipment. Products were expected to become more differentiated as technologies converged. Standard equipment would be mass marketed while specialty phones would be sold through more focused outlets. Overall, however, standard phones were expected to dominate the market for the next several years and to be offered increasingly as optional or even standard equipment in new automobiles.

Another factor transforming the distribution system was the emergence of increasingly powerful chains of consumer electronics outlets in Europe. Lower inventory costs, increased bargaining power, and the promise of free movement of labor and capital in 1992 had already prompted several hypermarkets in France, Spain, Belgium, and the Netherlands to form cross-border chains. These chains were likely to introduce their own brands and press for lower prices, as they had done in the United States and the United Kingdom. Such a trend would force European suppliers to select clearly either a differentiation or a cost leadership strategy. Suppliers that decided to sell only through OEM agreements would have to be prepared for intensive price competition.

Marketing Communications. Growing demand, changing distribution patterns, and the proliferation of new broadcast and print media presented new opportunities for marketing communications in Europe as 1992 approached. The increasing emphasis on business-to-business selling required larger direct sales forces and better brand awareness. Selling through consumer electronics outlets required strong brand awareness among trade customers and good product quality control (since the servicing capabilities of selling outlets would be limited) and the use of proven sales promotion methods. Since the likely end user was a frequent traveler within Europe, there would be an opportunity for Pan-European advertising and sales campaigns. To create a new Pan-European brand would require substantial advertising. Existing, well-known brands could more readily support such communications programs.

CONCLUSION

Industry experts agreed that the major marketing impacts of the 1992 program on the cellular industry would be in the areas of market demand, price, distribution, and marketing communications. Demand was expected to grow substantially. Price competition would intensify, and a standard product would probably dominate the market for a few years. Subsequently, as technologies converged, other features would be bolted onto cellular phones, and product differentiation would resurface. New distribution channels would emerge, primarily as a result of the handportable phone. Mass marketing through consumer electronics outlets and direct business-to-business selling would be the dominant forms of distribution by 1992. Finally, the promotion costs to develop Pan-European brands were expected to be high. An eventual industry shakeout of less well known manufacturers was predicted. Given all of these trends and expectations, Nokia-Mobira management had to determine the likely impact of the European market integration program and to decide how to compete most effectively in the years preceding and following 1992.

APPENDIX A: Structure of the Cellular System

THE CELLULAR SYSTEM

Cellular technology, developed initially in the 1950s, enables duplex communication (simultaneous receiving and sending) from a mobile radio terminal to the public telephone service (*Exhibit A.1* shows the structure of the cellular system). The system requires the use of modern computer technology, and it is made up of the following component parts:

Mobile Telephone Exchange (MTX)

MTX is the brain of the system and is technically the most complicated part. The cellular system is divided into a number of traffic areas. Each traffic area belongs to a single MTX. The exchange forms the interface between the cellular network and the fixed telephone network. It also switches the calls within the cellular network and controls the operation of the base stations.

Base Station

The base stations are intermediary links without a switching function between the wire and radio transmission. They consist of a low-powered transmitter with computer controller so that more calls can be handled in the same frequency band. In a traffic area, there are a number of base stations spaced about between 8–80 km apart. All base stations in the area are connected to the MTX of the traffic area, and all traffic in the area is channeled through it.

Mobile Station

The mobile stations, i.e., the subscriber equipment, come in various forms; they can be handportable, vehicle-borne or a coin-box type. Each mobile station is registered in a so-called home MTX, usually the MTX controlling the traffic area in which the subscriber normally resides.

A call from an ordinary telephone subscriber is connected on the basis of the first digits of the mobile subscriber's number to his home MTX. The latter stores data on the caller's present location and transmits a call signal over all base stations in that traffic area. The mobile station answers automatically with a call acknowledgement, and the MTX then assigns the mobile station a traffic channel. The call is set up. If the mobile subscriber is in a traffic area of some other MTX, the home MTX hands over the call to the MTX in the visited area. The system enables the mobile station to move between several base stations and even traffic areas without any interruptions in the conversation.

EXHIBIT A.1 Structure of the cellular system

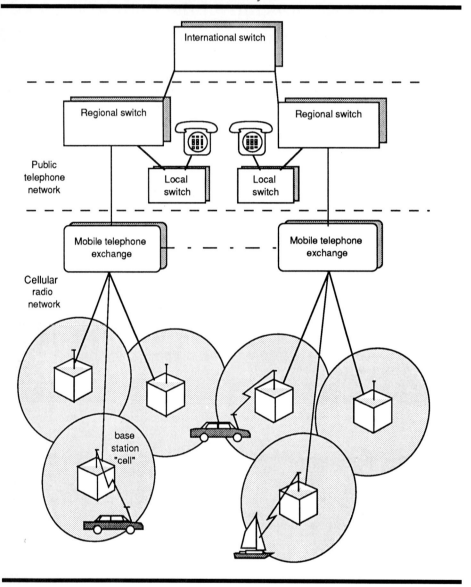

APPENDIX B: European Cellular Systems

NMT-450 and NMT 900. Nordic Mobile Telephone (NMT) was currently the only analog European cellular system offering multinational compatibility and international roaming. The system had been introduced and developed by the Scandinavian PTTs and by radiophone companies in the late 1970s. There was also an international roaming capability between the Scandinavian countries and Switzerland's NMT-900 network, which had opened in 1988.

Another region offering compatibility was the Belgian, Luxembourg and Netherlands NMT-450 network. However, other NMT-450 networks, such as the Austrian and Spanish ones, were not operationally compatible with other NMT systems. The operating NMT networks in 1988 were the following:

NMT-450	NMT-900
Denmark, Finland, Norway, and Sweden	Denmark, Finland, Norway, and Sweden
Iceland	Switzerland
Belgium, Luxembourg, and Netherlands	
Faeroes	

TACS. Total Access Communication System (TACS) was a refinement of the American 800 Mhz AMPS system. It operated in the 900 Mhz region and had been used in the United Kingdom and in Ireland since 1985. International roaming was expected to be possible between Ireland and the United Kingdom in 1989.

Soon after the airwaves began to become congested in 1988, an E-TACS system, operating in two new frequencies, was introduced in Central London. E-TACS users could operate in a TACS network, but not vice versa. The higher filtering requirements of E-TACS made the design of handportables more difficult than for TACS.

Radiocom 2000. Developed by Matra Company in 1985, this 'noncellular' system was used only in France. It operated at both 200 MHz and 20 MHz.

C-450. Siemens developed the system in 1985 in Germany. It was also being implemented in Portugal.

RTMS. The RTMS-450 network was developed independently in Italy in 1985. Only Italian suppliers were involved in it. A 900 MHz network was under development in 1988.

COMVIK. Comvik was a simpler cellular system to that of NMT, and it was used under the Comvik network in Sweden. It was about one-twelfth the size of the competing NMT network.

APPENDIX C: Cellular Market Structure in the United Kingdom

In the U.K. competition existed at each level in the cellular industry. The two networks, Cellnet and Vodafone, were prohibited by their licenses from selling either services or telephones directly to the end user. Hence both operators had invested over £200,000 in their networks of service providers. These air-time retailers billed end users for their calls. In 1988 there were over 50 service providers and many were subsidiaries of companies involved in the telecommunications industry. Some were equipment manufacturers and some were more service based, like the Automobile Association. Competition among the service providers centered on intensity of distribution and brand recognition. Their profits came mostly from air time rather than equipment sales.

To gain market share rapidly, the service providers signed up dealers to sell both air time and the equipment. The service providers competed mainly through commissions, dealer bonus schemes, low equipment prices, attractive billing methods, and efficient connection service. In 1988 there were over 2,000 dealers in the United Kingdom. The dealers fell into two main categories: traditional telecommunications and service oriented dealers, and discount operations. The first group of dealers relied on good after-sale service and tried to make profits from equipment sales. The second group sold equipment at a discount and made their profits from air-time commissions, thus pushing the equipment prices down. The market structure in the United Kingdom is illustrated in *Exhibit C.1*. Over 75% of the equipment was wholesaled through service providers and dealers, the rest being sold directly through service provider/ manufacturer sales forces.

EDITORS' COMMENTARY

Nokia-Mobira *appears* to have a strong competitive position in the world market for mobile telephones, but this appearance is deceptive. The company's success up to 1988 has been based on early entry and aggressive development of the Scandinavian market, high-quality products, and a joint-venture approach to the U.S. market. However, the company has high manufacturing costs, depends on others for key product components and technology, and is virtually unknown to users and distributors in the major EC countries. Consequently, the antici-

EXHIBIT C.1 Cellular market structure in the United Kingdom

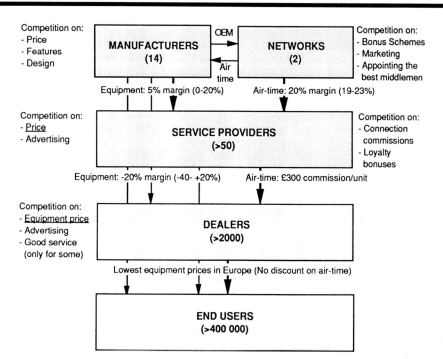

pated growth of the EC market following 1992 could well benefit other producers much more than it benefits Nokia-Mobira.

Nokia-Mobira has to make a basic strategic choice: Will it continue to be a large-scale manufacturer and a product developer in Europe or will it be more a differentiator and buyer of technology? The first alternative would mean huge investments in production, product development, distribution, and marketing communication. The other alternative would make Nokia-Mobira more a niche manufacturer, with a much smaller market share than it now has, but still with an opportunity to increase sales significantly. There would not be a need for as heavy an investment, but more of a need for significant changes in product positioning and organization.

If the first alternative is chosen, Nokia-Mobira should strive to achieve critical mass through acquisitions, strategic alliances, and joint ventures. It should aim to develop a widely recognized Pan-European brand like Philips. The company should try to exploit every possible synergy from the Nokia consumer electronics division, starting from distribution and brand policy and ending in production, product development, and sourcing. The costs should be lowered in order to ensure price competitiveness. Pricing of new products should aim at high market share rather than high profits for a short period of time. The company should establish its own direct sales offices and subsidiaries in Europe and increase its market presence. In addition, Nokia-Mobira should upgrade its European management capabilities.

CHAPTER *6*

Strategic Alliances

Biokit S.A. and the Biotechnology Market

EDITORS' INTRODUCTION

In mid-1987, the directors of Biokit, a Spanish biotechnology company with revenues of $7.6 million, were considering alternative marketing strategies for the future. The company, founded in the 1970s, had achieved rapid growth in the laboratory reagents market. After developing its own technical capabilities, Biokit had relied primarily on exports of bulk and private brand sales to distributors in other countries, thus allowing the company to concentrate its resources on R&D. It had received some R&D funding from the EC's EUREKA program. In 1985, the company had introduced self-contained diagnostic kits under its own brand, sold direct to laboratories, in several countries. This approach had worked well in West Germany but had "mixed results" in France. Biokit also marketed its products in the United States and Japan via wholly owned subsidiaries that sold primarily to large customers.

Although Biokit had achieved impressive results in terms of growth and profitability, management was concerned about the company's lack of control over distribution in key markets. It was considering a move to direct distribution under Biokit's own brand name in three EC countries and elsewhere. The advent of EC market integration, which was expected to make procurement of laboratory reagents more open to "foreign" suppliers, increased the urgency of resolving Biokit's distribution strategy for the future.

159

Biokit S.A.

Jose Luis Nueno and John A. Quelch

On June 1, 1987, the board of directors of Biokit S.A., a Spanish biotechnology firm, met to consider its marketing and research and development strategies for the coming decade.

Established in 1973 by IZASA, a diversified supplier of medical equipment, scientific and analytical instrumentation, single-use materials, and reagents, Biokit had grown rapidly. Biokit had developed its R&D, key to its success, with a broad range of alliances including research associates, business partners, consultants, subcontractors, licensers, and academics holding fellowships. For each of its research projects, which comprised a complex web of subprojects executed in various renowned institutions or in its own premises, Biokit had always managed to secure proprietary control of the key aspects. Francesc Duran, the firm's scientific director, had always maintained that the only way a small European company could excel in biotechnology was by subdividing projects and recruiting the right collaborators for each.

By 1987, Biokit had an extensive product line, but lacked the resources necessary to market it successfully; brand image and corporate identity had yet to be promoted to achieve an image of quality. Management understood that a market orientation was essential if Biokit was to be a significant worldwide competitor. On the other hand, this market orientation had to be achieved without drawing funds away from R&D, on which Biokit spent more than 30% of sales. *Exhibit 6.1* supplies the balance sheet for 1987 and *Exhibit 6.2* the income statement.

COMPANY BACKGROUND

IZASA S.L., Biokit's parent, was a subsidiary of a large, diversified family-owned holding, with interests in several industries and a total turnover of $1 billion in 1987. To encourage its executives to be entrepreneurial, IZASA pursued an "intrapreneurship" strategy in its new ventures. Most executives' salaries had a fixed and a variable structure,

EXHIBIT 6.1 Balance sheet for 1987 (millions of pesetas)

Fixed assets and long-term investments		Equity	
Net property, plant, and equipment	200	Capital	265
Goodwill	500	Retained earnings	
Total R&D	900		325
Depreciation	(400)		
Financial assets	70		
Liquid assets		Liabilities	
Inventories	80	Short-term	200
Receivables	350	Long-term	
Cash	90	Banks	100
		R&D support institutions	400
Total assets	1,290	Total equity and liabilities	1,290

Note: One U.S. dollar = 117 pesetas.

EXHIBIT 6.2 Income statement for 1987

	Millions of pesetas	**Percent**
Sales	807.0	100.0%
Other income[a]	84.7	10.5
Total income	891.7	110.5
Cost of materials	177.5	22.0
Selling expense	56.4	7.0
Production expense	24.2	3.0
Quality assurance	24.1	3.0
Administrative expense	32.3	4.0
Personnel (without R&D)	217.9	27.0
R&D	242.1	30.0
Depreciation	56.5	7.0
Gross income	60.5	7.5
Net income	40.3	5.0
Cash flow	96.9	12.0

[a]From research grants.

the latter averaging 40% of total compensation and related to achieving previously agreed-on objectives. Through this scheme, the executive identifying an opportunity not directly related to his or her current activity (budget) would have an incentive to bring it to the group and even participate in a profit-sharing scheme of the new activity. Some executives had found interesting projects that led to joint ventures, acquisitions, start-ups, and projects in which the group served as a venture capitalist.

Biokit, which started as a company in the chemical-pharmaceutical industry, was a rare example of a fully Spanish-owned company in the field of human laboratory diagnostic reagents.[1] Fully integrated, it covered all the phases of the productive process: research, manufacture, and sale of reagents for the diagnosis of medical conditions such as rheumatism, sexually transmitted diseases, birth abnormalities and pathologies, and viral diseases. *Exhibit 6.3* provides sales forecasts for these reagents by end users.

Biokit's strategy was based on increasing the product line in the above-mentioned areas of medical diagnosis through proprietary skill and technology. For this reason, the company was investing 30% of sales in R&D, compared with an industry average of 10%. According to Jos Manent, Biokit's general manager, competition in the human laboratory diagnostic reagents industry was global because R&D expenses in the product and manufacturing process could not be justified on the basis of a national or even regional market. If research was important, quick worldwide market coverage was critical as soon as a product was

EXHIBIT 6.3 Percentage of actual and forecasted U.S. sales in dollars by end-user segment for selected immunodiagnostics techniques

	1986	1987
Viral diseases		
Corporate laboratories	30%	29%
Hospitals	50	41
Doctors' offices	20	30
Sexually transmitted diseases		
Corporate laboratories	10	15
Hospitals	11	15
Doctors' offices and blood banks	79%	70%

Source: Robert First.

---

[1]A reagent was any substance, possibly used in combination with other substances, that performed an analytical diagnostic laboratory procedure. The simplest possible example was the glucose test: to determine the level of glucose in urine, a reagent that changed color when in contact with the glucose was used. This change in color depended on the radicals that attached to the reactive. A simple visual comparison with a predetermined color scale indicated the concentration of glucose in the urine.

available. Because Biokit's products were limited to laboratory analysis and did not require contact with the human body, once developed to the point of delivering a satisfactory performance, they could be marketed. However, introduction of a product required either penetrating an existing market, supplanting another product on the basis of better performance (e.g., quality, price, speed, prediction of results), or creating a market with a reagent that implemented a test with a level of accuracy that was not previously possible.

When considering a potential market, the company set the following criteria:

- Minimum world market of $9 million;
- Minimum yearly growth of 15% in units per year;
- Gross margin of 80% to 85%;
- Maximum product development period of three years;
- Product appeal to major foreign distributors;
- Acquisition of both the antigen[2] and the antibody[3] by Biokit. To make the antibody, an antigen was traditionally supplied to an animal. Recent developments in genetic engineering had resulted in the monoclonal antibody technique, by which a specific antibody was produced "by design," generally by an abnormal plasmatic cell;
- Product focus on sexually transmitted diseases, abnormalities and the aging process.

In addition to these priorities was the need to keep pace with the latest technological developments, while the average three-year life cycle of the diagnostic products was a constant pressure toward product diversification.

Biokit had 95 employees in 1987. Most managers held MBAs, all R&D personnel held PhDs in biology or chemistry, and the production personnel was also highly qualified. The average age of the management team was 38 years.

---

[2]An antigen was a molecule or a part of a protein molecule that had the capability of producing an immunological response.

[3]An antibody was a protein produced by the plasmatic cells (the cells of the immunological system) as a reaction to specific antigens. The antigen and the antibody were obtained by Biokit if the monoclonal antibody technique was used. They were obtained separately if the antibody was obtained by supplying an antigen to an animal. The monoclonal antibody technique was preferred because it secured the production of the specific antibody to a single antigen, a property that could not be assured if the antibody was supplied by an animal (which may have contracted other diseases aside from the one for which it was inoculated).

Biokit exports to several European countries. The United States and Japan accounted for more than 70% of its sales during the previous five years. The investment requirements for forthcoming R&D projects required not only increasing the overall sales figure but also maintaining the percentage of sales dedicated to R&D.

Biokit was founded as one of the manufacturing branches of IZASA, which had been importing from the United States the antigen and antibody for the diagnosis of the rheumatoid factor. With an original investment of two million pesetas,[4] three technicians were brought in from IZASA to begin to develop the reagent in-house. The reasons for this vertical integration strategy were first that the reagent had a substantial market in Spain, and second that the U.S. manufacturer expressed its intention to establish a wholly owned distribution company in Spain. Such a move could leave IZASA without a source of supply. As a by-product of the R&D effort on the reagent for the rheumatoid factor, Biokit derived the Antigen Estreptolisin O (AEO). To capitalize on this research success was a challenge because many firms worldwide were manufacturing AEO. AEO was practically the only product Biokit could sell in 1973, and distribution was sought through the Spanish subsidiary-distributor of a Swiss pharmaceutical firm that competed with IZASA. In marketing the AEO that it produced itself through the Swiss subsidiary, Biokit was competing with IZASA, which continued importing the product from its foreign supplier.

The subsidiary-distributor was extremely successful distributing AEO and when, in 1977, Biokit finally derived the reagent for the rheumatoid factor (RRF), was appointed sole and exclusive distributor for the product. Through aggressive pricing, Biokit captured a 15% share of the Spanish market for RRF in its first year.

THE LABORATORY REAGENTS INDUSTRY[5]

To understand the role of immunological chemistry procedures, one should contemplate its predecessor: the chemistry reagents procedures industry. The growth of both industries was parallel, and most of the pressures that affected one also affected the other.

The science of clinical laboratory medicine was fairly recent. The goal of clinical chemistry reagents, kits, standards, and controls was to

---

[4]$1 = 117 pesetas.

[5]This section is based on the 1986 Frost and Sullivan report on the Clinical Reagents Industry.

aid the physician in providing a specific diagnosis and, in some cases to predict a possible pathology before the patient demonstrated any symptoms. It was not until 1948, with the introduction of the indirect and direct Coombs tests (also called erythroblastosis fetalis or, more commonly, the Rh factor test), that clinical laboratory medicine became firmly established. Until then, physicians had had to rely on classical medical history and physical examination for diagnosis. A new industry also developed to supply instruments, apparatus, reagents, supplies, disposables, and animals to clinical laboratories. Clinical chemistry machinery and reagents represented the largest dollar shares of clinical laboratory product expenditures.

In the United States, widespread malpractice litigation contributed to dramatic sales growth; risk-averse practitioners were prone to order numerous tests for their patients. Growth was fueled also by the emergence in the early 1970s of automated testing, which led to the establishment of large sophisticated laboratories such as National Health Laboratories. Small operations became "collecting stations," subcontracting the testing to major laboratories that could provide a greater range of services at lower prices.

This trend also occurred in Europe. Only large laboratories were able to supply the most sophisticated tests, and the smaller operations became collecting stations. However, increased efficiencies in testing did not mean lower health care costs for the patients because the small operations physicians and collecting stations persisted in absorbing the savings as margin. In the United States, as much as 40% of physicians' income was derived from charging exceptionally high (preautomation) margins for the tests that commercial labs billed at reasonable (postautomation) prices.

Another trend that characterized the 1970s was the emergence of disposable laboratory supplies.

In the 1980s many pharmaceutical companies saw the diagnostic products market as a natural extension of their businesses. There were low-entry barriers, with the typical entrant being a spin-off of a university research team, sometimes started in humble quarters with very limited financial resources but often with a breakthrough product. The biotechnology market in medical and analytical applications was very fragmented. Companies tended to specialize in groups of products that could be obtained from certain technologies they had mastered. Companies pushed their technological skills to the limit, thereby improving their products and developing new ones. As in the computer industry, it was possible to talk about first-, second-, and third-generation products, with the difference being the degree of advancement of the technologies on which the products were based and their resulting improved performance.

Since the late 1950s, the clinical laboratory diagnostics market had been growing at an estimated 15% per year. By 1986, due to government efforts to control the rise in health costs experienced in the preceding decade and the regulatory and market pressures of government and third-party reimbursement agencies, respectively, this growth had slowed to 8%. In the same year, approximately $670 million was spent in the United States for immunodiagnostics reagents, kits, controls, and standards. Total expenditures in Western Europe, the United States and Japan approached $1.8 billion. *Exhibit 6.4* presents information on the growth of the various immunodiagnostic techniques for selected diseases; *Exhibit 6.5* and *Exhibit 6.6* break down sales forecasts for the worldwide immunodiagnostic market.

EXHIBIT 6.4 Market growth for selected immunodiagnostic techniques for selected diseases in the United States

	Forecast		
	Volume, 1990 (U.S.$ millions)	Yearly growth (%)	**Biokit entry**
Viral diseases	$118	10.8%	
Hepatitis B	44	12	1987
Rubella	20	3	1987
Streptococcus A	16	19	1987
Hepatitis A	11	9	1987
Mononucleosis	8	2	1986
Asto O	3	−2	1980
Citomegalovirus	4	20	R&D
Epstein-Barr virus	4	30	R&D
Sexually transmitted diseases	175	10	
AIDS	134	10	R&D
Syphilis	7	5	1980
Chlamydia	9	25	1987
Herpes	4	10	R&D
Neisseria gonorrhea	8	80%	R&D
Others	$ 8		

Source: Robert First.

EXHIBIT 6.5 Market forecast for all immunodiagnostic techniques in Europe (U.S.$ millions)

	1988	1989	1990	1991
France	$130	$154	$185	$225
Italy	296	327	361	389
United Kingdom	64	88	111	135
West Germany	224	265	320	400
All others	$183	$220	$252	$284

Source: Frost and Sullivan, *Immunodiagnostic Reagents Market in Europe,* 1986.
Note: Immunodiagnostic techniques include RIO, EP, antisera, serology, pregnancy tests, particle counting, LIA, FIA, EIA, and RIA.

EXHIBIT 6.6 Sales of immunodiagnostics by geographic market, 1986

	Percent	U.S.$ millions
United States and Canada	40%	$720
Europe	35	630
West Germany	6	110
France	4	80
Italy	5	100
Japan	15	270
Others	10%	$180

Source: Robert First.

THE BIOTECHNOLOGY INDUSTRY IN THE 1990s

Competitive developments in biotechnology in general and in immunodiagnostics in particular were hard to predict. First, the timing and nature of new technology was always uncertain. Second, changing regulations and different national health care systems around the world complicated marketing strategies and precluded standardization.

The trends that experts expected during the late 1980s and early 1990s were the following:

■ New diagnostic procedures, such as the increasing use of nonsurgical diagnosis in heart conditions and in-vivo (within the patient's body) testing.

- Increased use of computer technology by large laboratories that processed a high volume of tests. Computerization also facilitated the increasing sophistication of some of the test-screening methods.
- Emergence of new therapeutic processes that would require new diagnostic tests, especially in the areas of birth defects and abnormalities and in the control of sexually transmitted diseases.
- Emergence of a "volume" market for blood sample testing in blood banks, due to the risk of intravenous contamination posed by AIDS and hepatitis viruses.
- Growth in the consumer market for self-testing products purchased in local drug stores, a trend that emerged in Europe in the early 1970s with pregnancy and blood/glucose-level tests. Tests for urinary tract infections and sexually transmitted diseases were expected soon in local pharmacies. By the early 1990s, 15 to 20 categories of diagnostic tests were expected to be available as over-the-counter kits.
- The importance of high-technology products based on immunological procedures stemming from recombinant DNA research was expected to increase the possibilities of the field. Recombinant DNA allows the production "by design" of an infinite variety of reagents, enabling scientists to govern a cell's genes. The variety, quantity, and cost of the reagent obtained promised to be much more favorable with this technique.
- Increased participation of the pharmaceutical industry in the clinical diagnostics market. By 1978, pharmaceutical firms started to establish in-house biotechnology R&D programs. By 1992, Du Pont was spending $120 million in biotechnological R&D, Monsanto $62 million, Eli Lilly $60 million, and Hoffman-La Roche $59 million, compared with $9 million and $8 million for large biotechnological firms such as Biogen and Genex, respectively. Regulatory pressures by the national health care systems were both a restriction for the pharmaceutical industry and a cause of growth for the reagents industry. By entering the reagents industry, pharmaceutical firms balanced these regulatory pressures. A portion of their budget devoted to biotechnological R&D would be allocated to externally sponsored R&D. Pharmaceutical firms had a relative advantage over their biotechnological counterparts from their experience in handling large-scale manufacturing and marketing activities.
- Some immunodiagnostics (e.g., radioimmunoassay) were approaching market maturity and encountering severe regulatory restrictions, given the risks involved in manipulating radioactive

materials. Other markets, such as chemibioluminescence, were expected to grow rapidly.[6]

- Because medical practices in France, Germany, and Italy had reached the technical sophistication necessary to warrant the increased use of reagents, these were the markets expected to grow fastest. Some other countries, such as the United Kingdom, had reached the same level of sophistication, but their national health care systems self-supplied reagents which were developed and manufactured by government-owned research laboratories. For this reason, the United Kingdom was a less attractive market in terms of expected growth.

- Acquisitions and mergers were expected to increase in the immunodiagnostics market. Participants were of two types. The first group of firms were those founded by or in conjunction with university scientists. Their capabilities lay principally in R&D. The second group were pharmaceutical firms with capabilities in and the capital to finance the downstream stages of innovation, process development, manufacturing, product testing, promotion, marketing, and distribution. These stages required not only expertise in conducting them, but also enormous sums of capital. While many pharmaceutical firms sought to develop their own R&D in biotechnology, this complementarity of competitive advantages and the increasing difficulty of raising capital for new start-ups were expected to encourage more joint ventures, mergers, and acquisitions.[7]

INDUSTRY REGULATION FOR 1992

Although a common health care policy was one of the European Community's (EC) goals for 1992, the European Commission had worked through seven draft proposals by 1987 without securing agreement by the member states.[8] Industry experts expected the EC to supply general

---

[6]Traditionally, the antigen/antibody complex and its properties were detected by means of a radioactive "marker" or label. Radioimmunoassay required the use of radioactive isotopes. For this reason, other less risky procedures were being developed based on colorimetric or fluorescent methods.

[7]Gary P. Pisano, Weijan Shan, and David J. Teece, "Joint Ventures and Collaboration in the Biotechnology Industry," in *International Collaborative Ventures in U.S. Manufacturing*, David C. Mowery, ed., Chapter 6, pp. 183–222 (Cambridge, Mass.: Ballinger, 1988).

[8]*The Economist* Intelligence Unit, 1988.

guidelines without identifying the specific classes of products that could or would not be manufactured. Such a move would provide the appearance of a Pan-European policy but be of little help to firms looking to develop Pan-European products.

Each country had its own regulations concerning issues such as the release into the environment of new life forms and other genetically engineered materials based on animal embryo research and plant research. Each country also had its own regulations for the research, production, and marketing of such developments. In some cases, these regulations were the same or similar across several countries. For instance, legislative restrictions on radioimmunoassay were similar in all EC countries, based on the restrictions placed on the use and importation of radioactive materials. As far as Pan-European standards or mutual recognition were concerned, the prospects were bleak. Each country required that its own agencies authorize each new product introduction. This was an extremely time-consuming and costly process in the case of in-vivo reagents (those used inside the patient's body) but merely an administrative procedure for in-vitro reagents (those used outside the patient's body).

On the other hand, the pharmaceutical industry had developed the European Pharmacopoeia that was accepted throughout the EC. This permitted the same pharmaceutical products to be available in all 12 EC countries. The entry of pharmaceutical firms in the biotechnology industry and the efforts of the European Commission were expected to lead eventually to a similar Pan-European standard for biotechnological products.

Some observers believed that the biotechnology industry might follow trends that were apparent in the pharmaceutical industry. Though there was some agreement among EC countries on pharmaceutical product standards, each country continued to apply its own regulations for advertising, samples, in-store promotions, and the like. This practice advantaged low-cost producing countries like Spain, whose pharmaceutical industry was experiencing booming exports through "gray" marketing. Multinational firms manufacturing in low-cost countries were subject to regulatory price controls which reduced their margins. As a result, there were large differences between the prices charged to consumers in the low-cost and the high-cost countries. These differences allowed local distributors to divert pharmaceuticals produced in low-cost countries to high-cost countries. The EC was not averse to gray marketing, because it was competitive and helped to reduce health care costs. Any similar trend in the reagents industry was likely to be welcomed by local governments and also by the European Commission.

1992 AND THE BIOTECHNOLOGICAL INDUSTRY

In 1987, the distribution of medical and scientific products in Europe was not consistent from country to country. The leading buyer in most countries was the government because health care was state-provided. In France, Italy, and Spain, the health care market was at least 80% financed by government, and in the Netherlands it was almost 90%. Therefore, France tended to buy from companies established in France; Italy, from companies established in Italy; and so on. Some American, Japanese, and European companies had their headquarters in a European country and subsidiaries elsewhere. Many American, Japanese, and European producers sold to distributors located in different countries. There were no Pan-European companies acting exclusively as distributors, although some manufacturing companies distributed goods from other companies together with their own products. Distribution was very fragmented in countries like West Germany, with hundreds of small distributors, or concentrated in countries like Spain, where a few foreign subsidiaries, IZASA (the leading Spanish distributor), and two or three other Spanish distributors accounted for 80% of sales. The removal of trade barriers in 1992 was expected to promote further industry concentration and increased competition, particularly if important differences among the 12 EC health care systems were also reduced.

Even if the single market program was implemented in 1992, Biokit managers wondered about the extent to which a Spanish manufacturer would be able to sell directly to the French or the Italian government-controlled hospital laboratory systems. In addition, given the specificity of biotechnological products, a close contact between user and seller was necessary. For years Biokit had been selling through distributors, some of whom were worldwide leaders in production and sales of pharmaceuticals and reagents for clinical analysis. Management thought that, by 1988, Biokit would have obtained sufficient market share in several European countries to justify a direct selling organization.

END USERS AND DECISION-MAKING PROCESSES

The end users of clinical laboratory market reagents were clinical laboratories, both hospital-based and independent. An emerging segment was group practice laboratories that performed tests exclusively for physician outpatient offices and primary care centers. In the United States, 15,500 such laboratories performed 9 billion tests in 1983, generating revenues of $22.6 billion. Most hospitals maintained their own clinical laboratories, although cost-reduction pressures were forcing some to share their facilities. In addition, an increasing number of hospitals were contracting out their clinical laboratory operations to commercial laboratories. These contracts usually included an initial up-front payment to the hospital, followed by a percentage override of annual revenues generated through the hospital. The correlation between the number of tests performed and hospital bed size was not precise. Specialty hospitals such as psychiatric institutions did less testing. However, the number of tests performed per patient each year was increasing. *Exhibit 6.7* estimates the number of United States hospitals with different test volumes.

In addition there were about 8,500 commercial clinical laboratories in the United States, ranging from small independents to large facilities that were part of national chains. There were also 44,000 laboratories based in physicians' offices and about 4,000 group practice clinical laboratories that performed routine diagnostic procedures for the group's member physicians. *Exhibit 6.8* shows the nonhospital segment breakdown by type of location.

In Europe, the size of the clinical market for immunodiagnostics varied by country, depending partly on the health care reimbursement system. For instance, in France, reimbursement levels had been increasing during the early 1980s, because of the government's socialized health care policy. The number of specialists, general hospitals, and laboratories and the certifications necessary to perform immunological tests were the other factors determining market size. *Exhibit 6.9* provides details on the health care systems in three EC countries.

End users cited "product quality," meaning consistency and reliability, as a key dimension driving their buying decisions. Errors resulting from unstable biochemicals could distort interpretation of the test results. Price was not a key concern among end users, but, given equivalent perceived reliability, price could be a tie-breaker. Other factors that played a role in the decision-making process were delivery, technical service, size of the product line, the nature of the interaction with the salesperson, literature citations, recommendations of other professionals, advertising, and appearance of the producer in technical publications. One consistent trend was the increasing sophistication of the buying practices followed by end users. Bidding techniques and centralized group purchasing tended to reduce the importance of distributors who responded by specializing in carrying deep assortments of a particular range of products, or by merging to form larger corporations themselves.

EXHIBIT 6.7 U.S. hospital-based clinical laboratories ranked by test volume, 1983

Annual test volume	Estimated number of hospitals	Percent of total
Up to 49,999[a]	900	12.6%
50,000–99,999	1,940	27.8
100,000–249,999	1,780	25.5
250,000–499,999	1,030	14.8
500,000 or more	1,350	19.3%

Source: Frost and Sullivan, *Clinical Laboratory Reagents Market in the United States,* 1984.

[a]To be read: "Nine hundred hospitals (12.6% of the total number of hospitals performing tests in 1983) each performed 49,999 or fewer tests per year."

EXHIBIT 6.8 Nonhospital commercial clinical laboratories by type of location and rank by volume in the United States, 1983

	Estimated number of labs	Percent of total
Type of location		
Single, one location	6,570	77.3%
Multiple locations	1,930	22.7
	8,500	100.0%
Rank by annual test volume		
Up to 99,999[a]	6,330	74.5%
100,000–249,999	963	11.3
250,000–499,999	430	5.1
500,000 or more	777	9.1%

Source: Frost and Sullivan, *Clinical Laboratory Reagents Market in the United States,* 1984.

[a]To be read: "6,330 laboratories (74.5% of the total number of laboratories performing tests in 1983) each performed 99,999 or fewer tests per year."

EXHIBIT 6.9 **Characteristics of three European reagent markets**

Country	Reimbursement system	Number of specialists	Hospitals		Number of pharmacists	Laboratories	
			Total	With comprehensive facilities		Total	Large labs
France	Allowance levels	30,000	2,500	127	30,000	4,400	880
Italy	Predetermined grants and allowances	9,000	1,900	250	1,200	10,000	2,500
West Germany	Negotiated fee level between insurance company and government intermediary agency	62,000	1,600	na	28,000	na	300

Source: Frost and Sullivan, *Clinical Chemistry Diagnostic Reagents Market in Europe*, 1985.

MARKETING OPPORTUNITIES

Manufacturers of immunodiagnostics in the EC were focusing on product and distribution strategies to increase their market penetration. The screening tests with the greatest market growth potential — such as gonorrhea and monoclonal antibodies tests — were widely known and became the focus for many companies' product R&D efforts.

Product bundling was seen as another opportunity for growth. Some competitors were offering to supply instruments free or at low cost in exchange for long-term purchasing arrangements. Others offered multisystem instruments that could be used with a variety of tests.

In recent years, manufacturers of clinical laboratory supplies were increasingly selling direct. Traditionally, the role of the distributor had been to identify sales leads and then introduce the manufacturer's representative to the key decision maker in the clinical laboratory. Larger distributors were increasingly emphasizing the specialized knowledge of their salespeople and were therefore able to take a more important role in the closing of the sale. The distributor's role was critical for new manufacturers that lacked the personnel or financial resources needed to go direct. These manufacturers used distributors until they achieved the sales volume necessary to justify going direct.

The alternative to distributors was direct selling through a manufacturer's own sales force. Given the increasing technical sophistication of reagents, several companies had switched to direct selling to ensure that highly technical information was communicated accurately to end users. Others were entering joint ventures with reagent and/or instrument manufacturers for the marketing and/or distribution of their products. Such joint ventures were seen as inevitable, given increasing concentration in the immunodiagnostics industry and the interest of pharmaceutical producers in participating in the industry.

EXPORT STRATEGIES BEFORE 1988

The market for human laboratory diagnostic reagents was largely controlled by multinational companies, which, in the early 1980s, were going through a process of concentration. *Exhibit 6.10* presents the market shares of the principal competitors. Western Europe, the United States and Japan accounted for 90% of world sales. Biokit managers believed that to compete in this "market of giants," they had to emphasize growth and develop both a brand image and international distribution.

Although both assets were intertwined, Biokit focused first on exports of bulk and private-brand product. Bulk product involved the ex-

EXHIBIT 6.10 Manufacturers of tests for sexually transmitted diseases: worldwide sales and market shares of principal industry participants

	Sales, 1986	Market share
	(U.S.$ millions)	(%)
Abbott Diagnostics	$53.5	49.3%
Electro Nucleonics	20.0	18.4
BBL-Microbiology	5.6	5.2
Syva	4.2	3.9
Whittaker M.A. Bioproducts	2.1	1.9
Difco Laboratories	1.5	1.4
Behring Diagnostics	0.9	0.8
Others	$16.5	15.2%

Source: Robert First, 1987.

port of only the technological basis of the product and the largest share of its value added, leaving to the importer, generally a distributor, the final steps of the manufacturing process including separating the bulk product into individual doses, packaging, and labeling. Private-brand operations involved full production of the reagent for another manufacturer or distributor that distributed to end users under its own brand name.

This strategy brought Biokit several advantages. First, specializing in bulk production resulted in substantial volume economies in procurement and manufacturing. Second, Biokit was able to increase its market share with a very lean marketing organization and low marketing expenses. Biokit's strategy was product-oriented; the key success factor was being able to supply large quantities of product of a consistently high quality. Third, the strategy permitted Biokit to concentrate its limited resources on R&D and manufacturing rather than dilute its initial effort through marketing expenses. Fourth, the need to achieve the quality standards required by multinational manufacturers and distributors that bought Biokit's in-bulk products required that Biokit's manufacturing operations be of the highest standard.

Further, to achieve international recognition, Biokit needed to develop relationships with well-known multinational customers, particularly because Spain was not a recognized source of high-quality medical products. Some Biokit marketing managers maintained that the firm could focus on exporting its products to developing countries instead of the highly industrialized markets that it pursued for in-bulk sales. However, the combined market of these developing countries was quite small, end users were less sophisticated, and payments were often delayed. On the other hand, proponents of the developing countries alternative maintained that the in-bulk strategy made Biokit dependent on the multinationals. They also claimed that in-bulk and private-label sales commoditized a specialized high-technology product, making delivery and cost the only two bases for competition. Gross margins were lower, yet sales uncertainty was high because customers could drop Biokit as a supplier with minimal notice. Further, given the nature of competition and the percentages of sales that Biokit was dedicating to R&D, reliance on high-volume, low-margin customers could result in slower growth.

By 1983, the firm's top management was becoming more sensitive to overreliance on multinational customers. A barrier to any change in strategy that might result in Biokit's competing with its own multinational customers was that the in-bulk and private-brand operations were at full capacity. To minimize retaliation by current customers, the marketing department suggested distributing a self-contained diagnostic test kit under the Biokit brand. The kit was introduced in West Germany, Italy, and France, where the existing customers did not perceive this new product as directly competitive.

The kit strategy allowed Biokit to sell a product under its own brand in an industry where end user brand loyalty was a key dimension of competition. It also resulted in improved margins, because the bundling of all the elements necessary for the performance of the test permitted Biokit to charge a higher price than those obtained for private-brand and in-bulk sales. The introduction of the kit was a success. As a result, Biokit extended the kit approach to other products. By 1987, it sold such kits in the five most important markets of the world.

In West Germany, Biokit decided to adopt a dual marketing approach, selling both through a distributor, Labor Diagnostica GmbH, and directly to large end users. It was also able to maintain its bulk and private-brand sales. Since the kit sales were fueled by the trend toward self-testing and increased use of disposable materials, virtually no cannibalization of private-brand sales occurred. Biokit was quite satisfied with the relationship with its German distributor.

In France, the dual approach was also followed, but with mixed results. The distributors that Biokit approached were less willing than those in West Germany to make strong commitments to the company, and, partly for that reason, no exclusive agreements were signed. Bulk and private-label sales were equally important. Biokit sold directly to some large end users and signed agreements with three regional distributors. However, sales through the distributors were discouraging; coverage seemed limited to the area surrounding Paris, which accounted for two-thirds of the sales.

The sales breakdown in Italy was similar to that in West Germany. A single distributor, Biomedical Services S.p.a., had been appointed, with mixed results. Sales orders were uneven and unpredictable, causing production scheduling problems. On the other hand, coverage was satisfactory. Additionally, in-bulk and private-brand sales were cannibalized by kit sales because the Italian market had not experienced the disposable and self-testing growth evident in West Germany. However, Biokit had not experienced any direct manufacturer retaliation.

In Japan, Biokit adopted a different strategy, establishing Nippon Biokit Ltd. to sell directly bulk and private-label product. The sales of this subsidiary equaled those of West Germany, Italy, and France combined, encouraging some Biokit executives to favor direct distribution in Europe as a next step. On the other hand, sales of Nippon Biokit were concentrated in the commodity segment, and although the idea of selling under private brand were being explored, the risks of retaliation by manufacturer-customers could be high.

In the United States, Biokit established Biokit USA Inc. Sales to the United States started in 1981, when private-brand sales were initiated with the American Dade division of American Hospital Supply Corporation. Through this client, a 22% market share in syphilis reagents was achieved. Sales in 1987 were principally private-brand and in-bulk, as in Japan. The success of the American Dade relationship made management reluctant to explore the introduction of branded products. On the other hand, the United States was a "showcase" market for biotechnological reagents, and a success in marketing branded products there could facilitate their introduction in other markets.

RECONSIDERING THE DISTRIBUTION STRATEGY

Despite these international sales successes, management believed that Biokit lacked sufficient control over its international channels. Reliance on distributors precluded the establishment of a coherent brand policy. Reagent distributors carried too many products to give substantial attention to any one. They paid little attention to Biokit's requests for more sales push and were not specially receptive to Biokit's offers of sales support. Concerned that Biokit might consider selling directly once sales

EXHIBIT 6.11 Biokit sales in 1987 by channel of distribution

	Sales[a]	Sales
	(millions of pesetas)	(%)
Bulk	108	23%
OEM	234	49
Branded	133	28%

Source: Company records.
[a]IZASA not included.

reached the necessary volume, the distributors supplied little information about their markets. *Exhibit 6.11* reviews Biokit's 1987 sales by distribution channel, and *Exhibit 6.12* summarizes Biokit sales forecasts for
the period 1988–1992.

   Jos Manent, Biokit's general manager, was concerned also about the
breadth of the product line. By June 1987, it exceeded 30 product items
in 4 high-growth segments of biotechnology: rheumatism reagents; ve-
nereal disease diagnostics such as syphilis and gonorrhea; viral disease
reagents for toxoplasmosis, mononucleosis, and hepatitis; and fertility.
By the end of 1989, two new products were expected to be ready for
market: chlamydia and cytomegalovirus diagnosis reagents.

   Under these circumstances, Manent was contemplating vertical integration in distribution in at least five of Biokit's most important markets: France, West Germany, Italy, Japan, and the United States. He
estimated that the extra cost of such a strategy would be $2 million, $3.2
million and $3.9 million for the first, second, and third years, respec-
tively. Among the issues to consider in executing this strategy were the
type of organization to establish in each country, the degree of partici-

**EXHIBIT 6.12 Biokit sales and earnings forecasts, 1988–1992
(millions of pesetas)**

Year	1988	1989	1990	1991	1992
Sales	870	980	1,421	2,060	2,987
Earnings	260	294	440	659	985
Earnings/sales	30	30	31	32	33

Source: Company records.

pation by Biokit in each venture, the criteria for and eventual choice of partner, and the arrangements that would have to be made with existing distributors and multinational customers.

NEW ATTITUDE TOWARD STRATEGIC ALLIANCES

Many European companies facing the challenge of a more integrated market after 1992 were considering whether they were large enough to survive. High-technology industries, including biotechnology, were seen by industry experts as ripe for mergers, acquisitions, and other cooperative strategies involving both European and non-European firms. The pace of technology change and short product life cycles, perhaps more so than the prospect of EC integration in 1992, accounted for this trend. *Exhibits 6.13, 6.14,* and *6.15* summarize the number and pattern of recent strategic alliances[9] involving European high-tech companies. *Exhibit 6.16* reviews the motives for strategic alliances in biotechnology.

The business climate for mergers and joint ventures varied among the EC countries. The United Kingdom, Ireland, and Spain actively encouraged alliances involving both European and non-European firms. In France and Italy, a more protective environment, bureaucratic formalities, and tangled ownership structures were major obstacles. In West Germany, the public policy posture was neutral but the capital structure of companies and their dependence on the banking system impeded takeovers, especially if they were unfriendly. Greece was extremely protectionist and differed from the other southern European countries in not viewing the joint venture as an important means to acquiring more advanced technology and more rapid business expansion. Nevertheless, the 1992 program was thought likely to reduce the existing legal restraints on mergers that could be imposed by each country.

There were multiple motives for biotechnology alliances. Joint ventures between large and small firms were caused by the small firms' need to gain access to markets and capital to launch their new products. Unilever, for example, had acquired several small European firms to

---

[9]Strategic alliances were formal industrial, commercial, financial, or technological alliances established between two or more firms with such purposes as achieving the size necessary to compete, rationalizing or restructuring their processes, and achieving economies of scale, resources for innovation, or marketing efficiencies.

EXHIBIT 6.13 Alliances between European and non-European high-technology companies, June 1987 to Sept. 1988

	Europe–Europe[a]	EC–U.S.[b]	U.S.–EC[c]	Japan–EC	Total
Takeovers and mergers	69	74	71	17	231
Joint ventures and alliances other than mergers	134	← 94 →		42	270
Total	203	← 239 →		59	501

Source: *The Economist* Intelligence Unit, 1988.

[a]Including alliances involving non-EC companies from Finland, Sweden, and Switzerland, in 8 takeovers and 21 joint ventures.

[b]Alliances initiated by EC companies.

[c]Alliances initiated by U.S. companies.

EXHIBIT 6.14 Sector breakdown of competitive alliances involving European high-technology companies, June 1987 to Sept. 1988

	Mergers	Other cooperative ventures
Biotechnology	14	23
Pharmaceuticals	4	15
Chemicals	11	21
Computer hardware	2	9
Computer software	9	11
Electricals	13	25
Machinery	7	14
Others	9	16
Total	69	134

Source: *The Economist* Intelligence Unit, 1988.

EXHIBIT 6.15 Joint venture activity in Europe by country of participating company, June 1987 to Sept. 1988

Belgium	15	Japan	42
Denmark	12	Netherlands	45
France	53	Portugal	5
Greece	11	Spain	36
Italy	34	United Kingdom	97
West Germany	82	United States	94

Source: *The Economist* Intelligence Unit, 1988.

EXHIBIT 6.16 Cross-sectional comparison of the motives for collaboration in biotechnology

Function	Pharmaceuticals	Diagnostics	Animal health	Specialty chemicals
R&D	34%	17%	36%	40%
R&D and marketing	13	10	21	10
Manufacturing	7	10	0	10
Marketing	21	31	36	20
Supply	2	21	0	0
Technology transfer	22	10	7	20
Other	1	0	0	0
Total	100%	100%	100%	100%

Source: Based on Pisano, Shan, and Teece, op. cit.

gain access to biological reagents. Other biotechnology companies used alliances to pursue research links with companies in Japan and the United States. Fisons (United Kingdom) and Novo (Denmark) had been particularly active in Japan and the United States, respectively. L'Oreal (France) had established joint ventures with U.S. and Japanese firms.

The EC and its member countries had launched a number of programs to support technology development and innovation. The EC budget for technology development programs in 1986 was about one billion ECU. Most EC or Pan-European support programs could be tapped along with other sources of support at the country or regional level.

Technology alliances had become more prevalent since 1984, when several EC organizations were established to review and fund project proposals. The most important of these frameworks were: ESPRIT (European Strategic Program for Research and Development in Information Technology), BRITE (Basic Research in Industrial Technologies for Europe), and RACE (Research and Development in Advanced Communications Technology for Europe). All these programs funded alliances only to develop technology, generally between partners from different EC states. More than 1,000 companies participated in these programs by 1987.

EUREKA in particular was initiated under the leadership of France's President Francois Mitterrand. European countries (including non-EC members such as Switzerland, Sweden, Austria, and Norway) agreed to launch an initiative to stimulate innovation in Europe and to strengthen European high-technology industries in competition with Japan and the United States. The focus on EUREKA was development rather than basic research. Each country set up a national EUREKA secretariat to administer the program. To qualify for EUREKA, projects had to be submitted by corporations or institutions from more than one of the EUREKA member countries. This forced cooperation was intended to avoid duplication and boost efficiency.

The Spanish secretariat of EUREKA resided at CDTI, an autonomous institution attached to the Ministry of Industry and Energy. CDTI served as a government venture capital corporation, granting loans for R&D. These loans were paid back through royalties on sales of the resulting products. If an R&D effort failed, CDTI could not claim the return of the money.

Because Biokit had a strong reputation at CDTI after years of successful use of R&D loans, CDTI encouraged Biokit to participate in one EUREKA program. Biokit was at the time negotiating the joint development of a product with A.P. Technologies, a British laboratory. A.P. Technologies performed contract research and, according to Biokit's scientific director, was one of the world leaders in several key technologies involved in developing their proposed new product. Biokit and A.P. Technologies obtained joint funding for this project under the EUREKA program. In Spain, as well as in other EC countries, EUREKA projects received up to 50% of the funds required in the form of either a grant or a loan. In addition to the subsidy, the EUREKA funding brought valuable publicity. Stories on Biokit appeared in the *Wall Street Journal*, the *Financial Times*, and other leading business publications.

Biokit had been involved in one other strategic alliance in R&D. In 1987, it started a project with a U.S. and an Italian university for the development of testing equipment based on a patent purchased from the Massachusetts Institute of Technology. No strategic alliances had been initiated in distribution, although this was an option that Biokit management contemplated for the future.

MARKETING STRATEGY FOR THE 1990s

Manent reasoned in front of the board of directors that the market for branded reagents was becoming more global and, therefore, more similar to the markets for in-bulk and private-brand reagents. Regulatory changes pointed toward a progressive normalization of standards and practices in the biotechnological industry. To be successful as a small biotechnological firm researching and manufacturing in Spain and facing the removal of intra-EC trade barriers in 1992, Biokit's perspective had to be global. Particularly important was the decision on Biokit's distribution strategy for the 1990s.

Manent's proposal to the board was to develop further Biokit's own distribution network so that, unless a distributor willing to make the necessary commitments could be found, Biokit would sell directly under its own brand name. Manent thought that, before 1992, he should have distribution points in all the major EC countries. The United States and Japan could be handled by strengthening the current subsidiaries. In spite of 1992, he thought that each major European country would still require an individual approach. Given the limited resources of Biokit, he thought that the best solution would be to establish distribution alliances as had been done in the R&D area. He was confident that the company could implement a coherent sales program while sharing ownership of the channels.

Manent determined to approach the best distributors of reagents in various countries and convince each of them to establish an independent joint venture to sell Biokit's products. He knew that the success of this strategy depended on Biokit's products maintaining their excellent quality, on the manufacturing system continuing to benefit from the learning curve and lower costs, and the R&D laboratory maintaining its creativity and high productivity.

EDITORS' COMMENTARY

Biokit's strategy up to 1987 has been based on developing and maintaining proprietary technology. The company is investing 30% of sales in R&D, and with a relatively small total volume it has been forced to pursue low-cost methods of distribution. For this reason, Biokit has emphasized OEM and private-label sales (72% of total sales in 1987). The United States and Japan — the world's two largest health care markets — accounted for 70% of company sales.

The 1992 market integration process will lead to greater competition in the EC biotechnology market. Government agencies, the principal buyers of laboratory reagents, are supposed to give equal consideration to all qualified suppliers — but there is no guarantee that this will actually happen. At the same time, maintaining an adequate R&D program requires a "global" scale of operations. Biokit wants to achieve control over its distribution in key markets, but its resources are very limited. Thus it seems impractical for the company to invest in establishing its own wholly owned subsidiaries *and* to maintain an adequate R&D program at the same time. The most promising approach seems to be one of forming "strategic alliances" with one or more other firms, probably a major multinational pharmaceutical producer or several primarily national companies that can provide the required distribution facilities in each EC country.

CHAPTER 7

Redefining Product-Market Strategy

Chloride Lighting and the Emergency Lighting Market

EDITORS' INTRODUCTION

Chloride Lighting was a recently constituted strategic business unit of Chloride Group, a United Kingdom-based manufacturer of batteries and other electrical products. The Lighting unit, with headquarters in Connecticut, included two plants and sales networks in the United States and a British operation that sold both branded and OEM products. Collectively, these operations comprised the second-largest producer of emergency lighting fixtures in the $660 million world market. Chloride's sales in EC countries other than the United Kingdom, however, were negligible; in most countries the leading suppliers were strictly national in scope.

Cross-border trade in emergency lighting, like many other products related to construction, had traditionally been severely limited by differences in national product standards and preferences for national suppliers in government and government-influenced purchasing. The process of EC market integration was expected to result in common product standards and (in principle, at least) equal treatment for all EC-based suppliers by purchasers (building contractors, architects, and wholesale distributors).

In the fall of 1988, the Managing Director of Chloride Lighting, Robert McCue, and the SBU's Planning and Development Director, Mark Geering, identified five strategic options for Chloride during the 1990s. These included direct entry into the major EC markets, acquisitions, and various types of possible joint ventures. McCue believed that the company could not simply "stand pat" in the face of the changes that were coming. Which strategic approach offered the greatest chances of success?

Chloride Lighting Strategies for Emergency Lighting in Europe

Robert D. Buzzell and Tammy Bunn Hiller

In early November 1988, Bob McCue, managing director of Chloride Lighting, Chloride's emergency lighting strategic business unit (SBU), was deep in discussion with Mark Geering, the SBU's planning and development director. The two men were finalizing the 1992 impact statement and action plan which they were developing to present to Roger Holmes, Chloride's corporate operations director and the coordinator of a corporatewide 1992 task force. Holmes had requested that each SBU of Chloride submit to him, by November 7, a document assessing the potential impact on the SBU of European Community (EC) directives aimed at creating a single internal EC market by the end of 1992.

"Our current European emergency lighting operation is really a U.K. business," admitted McCue to Geering. "However, the introduction of a single EC-wide emergency lighting standard, a part of the EC's 1992 reforms, promises to open opportunities for us in the rest of Europe and create threats for our U.K. position. We must develop a strategy now which will ensure us a competitive position in post-1992 Europe."

COMPANY BACKGROUND

Chloride was established in 1891 as an English battery manufacturer. A century later, it described itself as a global electrical energy company.

Principally, it manufactured and sold lead acid batteries and associated products, power supplies, power electronics, and emergency lighting. Chloride was one of the world's leading manufacturers of rechargeable batteries and the world leader in manufacturing motive power batteries, which powered electric vehicles. Its Powersafe battery line was the preeminent battery used for telecommunications and standby power in the United Kingdom. Chloride also produced a range of electronic products and systems, including uninterruptible power supply systems (UPS) which were designed to support critical loads on computers and telecommunications systems. The company also designed and manufactured a wide range of emergency lighting equipment and ranked second in world emergency lighting sales.

Headquartered in the United Kingdom, Chloride was dependent on its home market for over one-third of its sales. In the fiscal year ending March 31, 1988, Chloride's sales were distributed as follows: 35% from the United Kingdom, 24% from the rest of Europe, 16% from Asia, 14% from Africa, and 11% from the Americas.

Historically, Chloride operated in a cartel with each major competitor maintaining a monopoly in its assigned markets, protected from competition by a combination of government protectionist policies, tradition, and inertia. Chloride organizations in different countries developed independently of each other with very little coordination among country managers. Through the mid-1980s, the company focused its managerial efforts on manufacturing supply versus creating and responding to market demand. The markets in which Chloride sold, however, were becoming increasingly competitive as customers for many of Chloride's products began to source and operate globally.

Chloride suffered poor financial performance in the first half of the 1980s. *Table A* gives its revenues and profits (losses) for fiscal 1981 through 1986.[1]

TABLE A   Chloride sales and profits (millions of pounds)

	1986[a]	1985	1984	1983	1982	1981
Net sales	309.7	412.0	373.5	359.9	380.7	351.9
Profit (loss) before extraordinary items	(10.0)	1.5	2.3	(8.9)	(11.6)	(20.2)

[a]For years ending March 31.

---

[1]The exchange rate used in this case is £1 = $1.80.

In December 1986, Kent Price was appointed chief executive officer of Chloride. He determined to regenerate the company. He spearheaded strategic divestments and acquisitions designed to strengthen Chloride's global position in its core product markets. Chloride was restructured worldwide into strategic business units. Each SBU was assigned responsibility for developing and implementing an integrated strategy for its product lines. In addition to Chloride Lighting, SBUs had been established for Automotive Products, Standby Power and Defense, Motive Power, Power Supplies, and Power Systems. Each of these SBUs was responsible for product design and development, product sourcing, marketing, financial management, and personnel on a worldwide basis. The managing director of each SBU was charged with "determining the most effective method of managing his/her business in each country in which the unit operates." In contrast, under the company's traditional organization structure, country general managers had been responsible for all Chloride activities in their respective territories.

In his first two years as CEO, Price also sought to develop a stronger market orientation throughout Chloride. A consulting firm developed a standard "Marketing Process" which was adopted in mid-1988 as the companywide framework for strategic business planning. The Marketing Process was featured in a series of seminars conducted by business school professors and attended by key managers from the SBUs and operating divisions.

Revenues declined to £273.4 million in fiscal 1987 but rebounded to £307.9 million in fiscal 1988. Profit before extraordinary items expanded to £5.7 million in fiscal 1987 and £7.9 million in fiscal 1988.

The restructuring of Chloride into SBUs was gradual. In October 1987, the final and smallest SBU, the emergency lighting SBU, was formed. Initially, it consisted of two facilities — one in North Haven, Connecticut, and the other in Southampton, England.

The North Haven plant, originally an emergency lighting company named Mallard Teal, was purchased by Chloride in 1972. Renamed Chloride Systems, the company manufactured and sold emergency lighting under the Chloride brand name. Prior to the 1987 reorganization, Chloride Systems was an operating unit of Chloride Power Electronics (CPE). CPE was a division of Chloride America until the 1986 disposal of Chloride's U.S. automotive businesses made CPE Chloride's only business unit in the United States. CPE included two power supplies plants in addition to the North Haven emergency lighting plant. Although nominally one company, the three plants had operated as stand-alone entities, each with its own information systems, finance, engineering, and marketing functions. In 1987, a power supplies SBU was formed, and Chloride Systems became a nuclear unit.

The English half of Chloride Lighting began in 1963 as Chloride Bardic. Prior to October 1987, Chloride Bardic was one of three divisions of Chloride Systems Limited, the U.K. electronics subsidiary of Chloride. Chloride Bardic manufactured and sold emergency lighting systems under the brand names of Bardic and Security Lighting. It also sold fire detection systems under the Bardic brand name. The other two divisions of Chloride Systems Limited specialized in manufacturing UPS systems and motive power chargers. Prior to October 1987, when the three divisions joined separate SBUs, they shared sales, engineering, and product development functions and management information systems.

Chloride Lighting was headquartered in North Haven. It was one of only three Chloride SBUs headquartered outside the United Kingdom and was located in the United States because of the individuals involved. Bob McCue, the general manager of the North Haven facility, was appointed to head the SBU. However, he also retained his responsibility as North Haven general manager, making North Haven the logical site for the SBU. In addition, McCue served as general manager of the Southampton facility until a full-time candidate was appointed in September 1988.

In August 1988, Chloride Lighting acquired Exide Lightguard, the emergency lighting division of Exide Electronics Corporation. Located in Cary, North Carolina, Exide Lightguard had been producing emergency lighting for over fifty years. It sold primarily to the industrial sector, whereas Chloride focused on commercial applications of emergency lighting. In addition to the manufacturing facilities and the Exide Lightguard product line, Chloride Lighting purchased the rights to use the Exide Lightguard brand name for three years.

During Chloride Lighting's first year, McCue concentrated on bringing substance to the SBU. The Southampton facility, divorced from its old sister divisions, created its own sales, engineering, and personnel functions and began to align its information systems with those of North Haven. By November 1988, the Cary facility was dependent on North Haven for engineering and purchasing support. Additionally, Exide Lightguard had begun to market some of North Haven's products. Finally, although U.S. designs had been offered to the United Kingdom, the cost of Anglicization appeared to be too high to use them. However, the United Kingdom did initiate a product rationalization program using U.S. practice as a model.

In November 1988, Chloride Lighting was organized as shown in *Exhibit 7.1*. SBU management consisted of four people, only one of whom, Mark Geering, worked solely for the SBU. Bob McCue was both

EXHIBIT 7.1 Organization chart

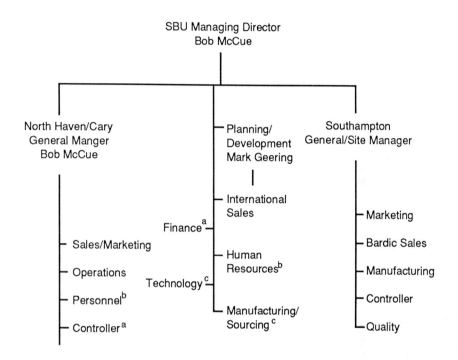

[a]These two roles are performed by one person.
[b]These two roles are performed by one person.
[c]These two positions are currently unfilled.

managing director of the SBU and general manager of the North Haven and Cary facilities. The SBU finance and human resource managers were also the controller and personnel manager, respectively, of the two U.S. plants. Chloride Lighting's stated mission was "through innovation, commitment and achievement, to serve our global markets and customers profitably and, in every other way, better than our competition."

EMERGENCY LIGHTING

Product Description

Emergency lighting was designed to supply illumination when the power supply to normal lighting failed. It included both escape lighting (which functioned to identify the means of escape from a building) and standby lighting (which enabled normal activities to continue or to be terminated safely).

Maintained emergency lighting was always on: a single fixture was powered either by normal (mains) current or by an emergency source. Nonmaintained emergency lighting only operated when normal lighting failed. Single point units (SPUs) were self-contained emergency lights. They contrasted with central systems in which several emergency lights were energized from a central emergency power system located outside the fixtures.

Emergency lighting was a low-technology product. All units consisted of three basic parts: a light source (lamp), a power source (battery), and control circuitry (printed circuit board). Some units also had an invertor which converted direct current into alternating current. This basic design had not changed for forty years and was not expected to change over the next ten years. *Exhibit 7.2* contains pictures of several Chloride and Bardic brand emergency lighting models.

Market demand for emergency lighting was driven by the need to satisfy safety regulations for industrial and commercial buildings. Most customers were not sensitive to technological differentiation. Their objective was to source readily available products which met the relevant standards at the least cost. For most buyers, emergency lighting was a "grudge buy." They would not pay extra for features that regulations did not require. Consequently, the emergency lighting industry had little incentive to develop innovative technology. Existing emergency lighting designs incorporated technologies developed by the regular lighting and automobile headlight industries.

Manufacturing of emergency lighting was a light assembly operation that created little value added. Direct labor accounted for only 6% of Chloride Lighting's sales, whereas direct materials cost over 45% of sales. The single most costly component, the battery, represented up to 50% of the cost of a unit, depending on the model. Production economies of scale were insignificant. Chloride executives believed that the only significant opportunity for achieving economies of scale was in the sourcing of parts. They reasoned that the larger the percentage of a supplier's business they represented, the better price they could negotiate for parts.

EXHIBIT 7.2 Illustration of emergency lighting units

STANDARD FEATURES

- Maintenance-free battery
- 120/277 volt selectable input
- Thermoplastic housing
- Primary disconnect
- Tools not required to position heads
- ACCU-CHIP reliability

Listed
Standard
924

871C

Model QT6
6 VOLT / 12 WATT
Emergency Light

ACORN CIRCULAR AND SQUARE

ACORN 8 WATT INTERIOR/ EXTERIOR LUMINAIRES

XL2 AND XL4
EMERGENCY
EXIT EXIT

The predominant power source employed in emergency lighting differed between the United States and Europe. The standard in the United States was the sealed lead acid battery. In Europe, nickel cadmium (NiCad) batteries were the preferred source. Sealed lead acid batteries were cheaper than NiCad ones, but had a shorter life. The cost of NiCad batteries was steadily rising due to raw material price increases coupled with explosion in demand for NiCad batteries from the battery-powered hand-tool industry. One producer, Saft, had a virtual monopoly on supply of NiCad batteries in Europe and was hard pressed to meet demand. No alternative power source for European emergency lighting was immediately feasible, however. Europeans had rejected sealed lead acid batteries in the past. Lithium batteries might eventually fill the gap, but industry observers believed their successful application to emergency lighting was several years off.

"Hidden is best" summarized most users' preference of inconspicuous or otherwise aesthetically pleasing emergency lighting. Sales of conversion kits, which converted mains lighting fixtures to emergency lights, were growing rapidly in both the United States and the United Kingdom. In November 1988 conversion kits represented approximately 20% of the U.S. market and 10% of the U.K. market. Furthermore, this segment was growing faster than total emergency lighting in the two markets. Although emergency lighting product standards in all EC countries except France permitted the use of conversion kits, continental Europe had been slow in embracing their use.

Customers

Three different groups of customers — architects and designing engineers, distributors, and contractors — influenced the emergency lighting buying decision for a given construction project. Architects and engineers were the first link in the buying chain. They designed buildings and in the process drew up wiring diagrams. From these diagrams they wrote up bills of materials that included emergency lighting requirements. Their needs for emergency lighting were that it comply with all applicable building and fire code standards and that it meet the client's design demands. Occasionally, architects and engineers insisted on a specific brand and model of emergency lighting. More often they simply specified which standards the lighting must meet. The most common practice was to specify a particular brand and model of emergency lighting but qualify the directive by adding the phrase "or equivalent."

The second link in the buying chain was distributors. According to a Frost and Sullivan report, 97.1% of U.S. emergency lighting sales occurred through distributors rather than direct from manufacturers. A similar situation existed in Europe. In both the United States and Europe, emergency lighting was sold through general electrical wholesalers who carried a broad range of electrical goods and averaged over 1500 product lines carried. They typically represented several brands of emergency lighting, some of which they held in stock and others that they only ordered at a contractor's request. Distributors promoted the brands of the manufacturers who met their needs, which included earning good margins, receiving consistent delivery with a fast turn-around time on orders, and receiving sales support in the form of training about manufacturers' products.

The final link in the chain, the contractors, performed the actual purchase of emergency lighting. Their needs included low price, ready availability, and easy installation. Most construction projects that required emergency lighting were built by contractors who won the jobs through bidding. Their revenues were thus predetermined, and they maximized their profits by minimizing the cost of construction. Consequently, they generally opted to buy the least expensive emergency lighting product that met the standards specified by their architects. However, availability was also key. Most contractors did not buy their emergency lighting until they were ready to install it. Construction delays due to unavailable product translated directly to cost overruns. Therefore, contractors were often willing to pay more for an emergency lighting brand that was in stock than for one that had to be ordered.

For commercial buildings such as office complexes, hotels, schools, and hospitals, first cost was usually the only cost considered when choosing emergency lighting. For industrial buildings such as factories and warehouses, however, owners often insisted that the cost of maintaining emergency lighting be balanced against first cost in choosing a brand. Aesthetics were less important in the purchase decision for industrial buildings than for commercial ones.

World Market

No "global market" existed for emergency lighting. Products differed by country due to varying product standards and codes of practice. The prime determinant of the size of the market for emergency lighting in a given country was the level of enforcement of the country's emergency lighting legislation. In fact, only countries with relatively mature economies had any legislation requiring emergency lighting. In countries whose infrastructure was less developed, emergency lighting was esoteric. Gross domestic product per capita was a good barometer of the existence and enforcement level of emergency lighting legislation within

TABLE B **World emergency lighting market (millions of pounds)**

Region	Market size
12 EC countries	175
Non-EC Europe	10
United States	111
Far East	56
Oceania	10
Middle East	5
Total	367

a country. In general, the higher a country's GDP per capita, the more strongly its emergency lighting standards were enforced; therefore, the more emergency lighting was consumed. Within each country, demand in any given year tracked closely the level of construction starts of new nonresidential buildings.

In 1988, the United States and Europe accounted for 80% of the world emergency lighting market. Annual world sales of £367 million were distributed as given in *Table B.*

Acquisition activity in the United States during 1988 altered emergency lighting manufacturer world rankings significantly. Emergi-Lite moved from fourth to first place with the purchase of Light Alarms, and Chloride Lighting rose from third to second place with its acquisition of Exide Lightguard. Dual-Lite was shifted down from first to third place and Saft from second to fourth. Lithonia and Menvier maintained their fifth and sixth place positions, respectively. Most emergency lighting manufacturers were heavily dependent on their home markets. Emergi-Lite, for example, sold only in the United States and Canada. Therefore, world rankings had questionable significance.

THE U.S. EMERGENCY LIGHTING MARKET

U.S. emergency lighting product standards and layout specifications were set by the national Fire Protection Association Life Safety Code. Underwriter's Laboratory tested emergency lighting products and conferred approval to those models that conformed with the national code. Nonapproved emergency lighting could legally be sold, but most fire marshals would not approve buildings in which unapproved emergency lighting was installed. Therefore, approximately 90% of the market for emergency lighting was in approved lighting.

In the United States, emergency lighting was sold as a small part of a total lighting package. Following World War II, approximately 4,000 U.S. companies manufactured lighting. Most were small companies that concentrated on producing a few types of lighting. A system of manufacturers' agents arose in the lighting industry. These independent businesspeople represented the lines of many manufacturers and became technical experts on lighting. They worked with architects and engineers to assemble packages that met all of the lighting needs for new buildings, including emergency lighting. The agents then sold these total lighting packages to contractors through distributors to whom they sold the products of all the manufacturers they represented. These lighting agents became so powerful that a key to success in the lighting industry was to be represented by agents with strong lines.

Then, in the mid-1970s, lighting manufacturers began consolidating. The total number of U.S. lighting companies dwindled to less than 400. Through mergers, acquisitions, and internal expansion many lighting manufacturers grew from specialty companies to broad line manufacturers. These large lighting companies (LLCs), as they were known in the industry, began to create their own lighting packages. Some LLCs manufactured all the lights needed for full packages, including emergency lighting. Other LLCs manufactured a complete array of regular lighting but did not produce specialty lighting such as emergency lighting and outdoor lighting. Agents who represented those LLCs combined their products with specialty lighting produced by other companies to form complete lighting packages.

In 1988, emergency lighting was a $200 million market in the United States, merely 3% of the total $6 billion U.S. lighting market. Although not a customer, the lighting agent was the most important link in the distribution chain for emergency lighting. LLCs were pushing to consolidate their selling leverage by offering all their lines through a single agent in a given territory and pressuring that agent to become a de facto factory man, representing only that LLC's products. Such pressures from LLCs on agents were reducing market access for smaller lighting companies. To be successful, independent emergency lighting manufacturers needed to align themselves with agents who had line cards from which they could create strong packages, but who did not represent an LLC that manufactured its own emergency lighting.

Market Trends

Between 1983 and 1987 the emergency lighting market grew at a compound annual rate of 4.5%. Estimated sales and compound annual growth rate by type of construction project are shown in *Exhibit 7.3.* Due

EXHIBIT 7.3 U.S. emergency lighting market by building type
(estimated 1987 sales in $ millions)

Building type	Estimated sales	CAGR[a]
Industrial	$ 13.6	(1.3)%
Office	52.4	2.3
Hotel	10.2	4.7
Other commercial	46.0	11.5
Educational	12.2	14.0
Hospital	2.9	(4.3)
Other public	18.4	–
Federal[b]	7.9	–
Residential multiunit	23.2	–
Other	10.3	–
Total	$197.0	4.5%

[a]Compound annual growth rate is for 1983–1987.
[b]Federal does not include buildings funded by the federal government that are included under other headings such as educational or hospital.

to a relatively flat construction market, industry observers predicted a 2%–2.5% annual growth rate for the emergency lighting market between 1988 and 1992.

Industry trends were toward lower price, lower-performance emergency lighting products sold out of distributor stock. According to *U.S. Industrial Outlook 1988*, contractors decided which brands to buy on 70% of the dollar value of total lighting purchased in 1987. Architects and engineers made the call on 20% of lighting purchased. Building owners determined the brand on the remaining 10%. No change in decision-making patterns was anticipated.

Major Competitors

Between 1978 and 1988, new emergency lighting competitors, Emergi-Lite and Lithonia, gained share at the expense of older brands such as Chloride. During 1988, emphasis shifted from organic expansion to growth by acquisition, and the market became increasingly concentrated. By November 1988, the four largest firms controlled over 70% of the market.

Emergi-Lite, a 1978 start-up, grew to become number two in the market in just ten years. In 1988 it purchased Light Alarms and leapt into the number-one position in both the United States and the world. Its projected 1988 sales were $54 million, $32 million under the Emergi-Lite brand, and $22 million under the Light Alarms brand.[2] When Emergi-Lite was first established, it hired away several key executives from Chloride, who then wooed away many of Chloride's best lighting agents. Chloride executives attributed Emergi-Lite's rapid growth to an excellent agent network, street savvy, flexibility, and aggressive pricing. Emergi-Lite products were often packaged with Emerson mains lighting.

Emergi-Lite planned to maintain Light Alarms as a separate manufacturing and marketing operation, but to centralize the engineering functions and component purchasing of the two companies. Previously a family-owned company, Light Alarms had long dominated the metropolitan areas of New York, Chicago, and Philadelphia. Its prices were among the most competitive in the industry. Product quality was indifferent but, although not innovative, the company was quick to adopt popular features introduced by competitors. Light Alarm's products were not aligned with any particular LLC's package.

Dual Lite had projected 1988 sales of $36 million and was in second place in the United States emergency lighting market. Its sales had been flat over the past few years. The company's parentage had changed during the past year and further changes were expected. Dual Lite enjoyed a reputation for excellent marketing and extensive field coverage emphasizing long-standing relationships. Its products were usually packaged with GE/U.S. Industries' mains lighting.

Lithonia had projected emergency lighting sales of $26 million and total lighting sales of $531 million in 1988. Started in 1979, Lithonia's emergency lighting business grew rapidly to fourth place in the U.S. market through packaging with Lithonia's mains lighting. The company was increasingly pressuring both its agents and distributors to carry its complete product line, including emergency lighting. Although Lithonia's emergency lighting line was limited to only a few models, as the leading LLC in the United States, Lithonia was a formidable competitor.

With Cooper Lighting as its parent company, Surelite could potentially enjoy the same strengths as Lithonia, but had been less successful at exploiting the benefits of association with an LLC. Surelite's projected

---

[2]All competitors' sales figures included in this case are estimates made by Chloride Lighting executives.

1988 sales were $4.5 million and its parent company's were $510 million. Acquired by Cooper Lighting in 1983, Surelite had suffered a series of management changes. Its brand was not widely recognized, its range was incomplete, and it was always packaged with Cooper lighting products.

In the early 1980s, Chloride Systems had lived off a "Rolls Royce" reputation for quality. Its product line of high-end models ignored the market shift to simpler products. Consequently, the company's sales stagnated and new competitors flourished. Between 1983 and 1986, Chloride Systems rejuvenated its product line to meet market demand. As a result, Chloride's sales and market share had improved significantly by 1987. With the 1988 acquisition of Exide Lightguard, Chloride moved out of fifth into third place in the U.S. market. The profitability of Chloride Lighting's U.S. operations had declined from the early 1980s up to 1985, but by 1988 it had improved to what McCue characterized as a "satisfactory" level.

In 1988, Chloride Lighting sold its two brands of emergency lighting through separate networks of lighting agents who packaged them with a variety of mains lighting brands and sold them through over 3,000 of the United States' 6,500 electrical wholesalers. Only a few hundred distributors, however, purchased as much or more than $10,000 of Chloride Lighting products annually.

A group of Chloride Lighting sales and marketing managers developed a list of factors that they believed contributed to success in the emergency lighting industry. They weighted each factor based on their perception of its importance in customers' purchase decisions. They also graded each brand's performance on each success factor. *Exhibit 7.4* shows the matrix which they developed. The executives created it in order to expose their brands' relative strengths and weaknesses and to help them plan future strategies.

Chloride Lighting's U.S. Strategy

Chloride Lighting concentrated on selling through large distributor buying groups and medium-sized wholesalers that were resisting LLC pressures to develop exclusive arrangements. Its objective was to increase volume through existing distributors rather than to sell to new ones. In addition, it pursued OEM and private label manufacturing arrangements.

Electrical codes described emergency lighting standards so tightly that little scope existed for meaningfully differentiating products. Chloride Lighting believed that the greatest opportunity for creating a com-

EXHIBIT 7.4 U.S. emergency lighting success factors and competitive rankings

Success factor[a]	Weight[b]	Sure Lite[c]		Emergi-Lite[c]		Light Alarms[c]		Dual Lite[c]		Lithonia[c]		Chloride[c]		Exide[c]	
Innovation	2	1	2	2	4	1	2	4	8	2	4	3	6	2	4
Product breadth	2	1	2	4	8	2	4	3	6	1	2	3	6	2	4
Quality of agents	3	3	9	3.5	10.5	2	6	3.5	10.5	4	12	3	9	2	6
Communication	2	1	2	3	6	1	2	4	8	2	4	3	6	2.5	5
Price response	2	1	2	3.5	7	4	8	3	6	3	6	3.5	7	2.5	5
Packaging	3	3.5	10.5	3	9	1	3	3.5	10.5	4	12	3	9	3	9
Customer service	3	1	3	3	9	3	9	3	9	3	9	2.5	7.5	3	9
Brand awareness	1	1	1	3	3	2	2	4	4	4	4	2	2	4	4
Product quality	3	2	6	3	9	1	3	3	9	3	9	3	9	3	9
Total	21		37.5		65.5		39		71		62		61.5		55
Percentage of possible			45%		78%		46%		85%		74%		73%		65%

[a]"Innovation" refers to innovation in product design. "Product breadth" measures the breadth of the product line. "Quality of agents" includes the professionalism of agents, their reputation, and the breadth and strength of their line card. "Communication" measures quality of literature on new item introductions, etc. "Price response" measures how willing a company is to continue lowering price to get business. "Packaging" measures strength of mains lighting packages with which a brand is usually/always coupled. "Customer Service" is detailed in *Exhibit 7.5.* "Brand awareness" measures the brand's awareness level across all three types of customers. "Product quality" measures reliability and quality of build.

[b]Weight represents importance of factor in purchase decision.

[c]First column under each competitor corresponds to raw score: 1 = Poor, 4 = Good; second column is equal to product of raw score and weight.

petitive edge lay in differentiation through the quality of service provided to the customer. *Exhibit 7.5* shows Chloride Lighting's definition of the elements included in customer service. Toward its goal of delivering exceptional and valued services, the company had recently strengthened its field sales presence, had reduced its product failure rate from 6% to 0.04%, and had initiated an industry-unique quick-ship program that guaranteed 48-hour delivery of Chloride's top-selling emergency lighting models. These models represented only 20% of Chloride's product line but accounted for 80% of its sales.

Longer term, Chloride Lighting's U.S. strategy was to create a sub-package grouping of specialty lighting companies. This strategy assumed that LLC's would not devote the time, effort, and resources

---

EXHIBIT 7.5 Elements of customer service

Delivery
Knowledgeable contacts within plant
Quality, timely literature
Quote turn-time
Delivery of core products
Hearing customer . . . language
Making it easier for customer to do business with us
Policies . . . black, white, and grey
Personal rapport with customer
Accessibility
Telephone image/background noise
Internal communications
Contemporary product line
Postsale service
Credit processing time
Product quality
Transactional accuracy/quality
Problem resolution time
Pricing
Convenience
Attitudes of customer contact personnel
Quality of field personnel . . . agents/RSMs
Packaging
Customer training . . . quality/frequency

---

required to dominate the small specialty lighting segments. A group of specialty lighting companies, offering contemporary products and under coordinated control, could complement LLC packages and attract the better manufacturers' agents. The acquisition of Exide Lightguard, whose industrial product line complemented Chloride's commercial one, was the first step in the execution of this strategy.

THE EUROPEAN EMERGENCY LIGHTING MARKET

Collectively, the EC countries represented the world's largest emergency lighting market. *Exhibit 7.6* shows the EC market breakout by country. Annual demand of £175 million made the combined market over 50% larger than the U.S. one. Propelled by a buoyant construction sector and increasing enforcement of legislation, the market had grown rapidly in

EXHIBIT 7.6 Emergency lighting market in EC Europe

Country	1987 gross domestic product	Emergency lighting sales		
		SPUs	Central systems	Total
West Germany	621.7	20.0	25.0	45.0
United Kingdom	368.3	30.9	8.1	39.0
France	488.9	27.0	5.0	32.0
Italy	417.8	20.0	2.0	22.0
Spain	160.0	14.0	3.0	17.0
Netherlands	119.4	4.0	5.0	9.0
Belgium	77.2	4.0	1.0	5.0
Denmark	56.1	4.0	1.0	5.0
Greece	26.1	1.0	0.1	1.1
Portugal	20.0	1.0	0.1	1.1
Ireland	16.1	0.7	0.2	0.9
Luxembourg	3.3	–	–	–
Total	2,374.9	129.7	45.8	175.5

Note: Gross domestic product figures are in billions of pounds; all other figures are in millions of pounds.

recent years. In the United Kingdom and France, for example, market value grew by 15% and 25%, respectively, in 1987. Growth in the first half of 1988 was faster still.

Emergency lighting product standards and codes of practice varied widely from country to country in Europe. Standards were set by national fire safety and electrical commissions. In order to sell an emergency lighting product in a given country, its design had to meet the nation's standards, and it had to receive approval by the country's national testing laboratory. Such testing cost several thousand pounds and took a year or more to complete.

The EC market was highly fragmented. The EC market leader, Saft, had only 10% of the market. The top four companies, Saft, Menvier, Beghelli, and CEAG, accounted for less than 30% of the market, which compared to combined shares of over 70% and 60% for the United States' and the United Kingdom's top four companies, respectively. In fact, the top ten companies in the EC accounted for less than 53% of EC emergency lighting sales. Chloride held seventh place in the EC market.

In general, manufacturers enjoyed close relationships with authorities in their home countries. EC governments were large customers of emergency lighting, accounting for at least 15% of the annual dollar volume of each country's sales. In the United Kingdom, over 30% of annual emergency lighting sales were made to the government. Governments' preferential treatment of local manufacturers hampered market penetration by outsiders.

Contrary to U.S. practice, in Europe, emergency lighting was not usually sold as part of a total lighting package. It was considered to be fire safety equipment, and contractors tended to purchase it with fire alarms and other fire safety devices rather than with lighting packages. Emergency lighting companies did not usually link their products with those of mains lighting companies, even when selling conversion kits. Rather than selling through agents, it was standard practice for European emergency lighting companies to employ direct sales forces that sold their products to electrical goods distributors through which contractors purchased all of their fire safety needs.

Chloride Lighting, for example, employed a direct sales force in the United Kingdom. These salespeople spent approximately 50% of their time selling to distributors, teaching the distributors' salespeople about the merits of their products, and encouraging them to promote them to contractors. The other half of their time was spent calling on architects and contractors, trying to sell them on insisting on Bardic or Security Lighting brands for their construction projects.

The U.K. Market

In Europe, Chloride Lighting's strength lay in its U.K. home market, where it vied with JSB Electrical for second place. Its projected sales to other European nations in fiscal 1989, of which over two-thirds would be to EC countries, represented less than 6% of the Southampton plant's anticipated fiscal 1989 turnover. A similar quantity of sales was planned for the Middle East, Africa, and the Pacific Basin.

In 1980, Chloride Bardic was the leader in the U.K. emergency lighting market with over 40% share. In the early 1980s, contractors began demanding simpler, more energy-efficient, cheaper models of emergency lighting. Chloride Bardic's competitors went after this commodity business, while Chloride Bardic concentrated on the high end of the business through which it had earned its market leadership. Chloride Bardic products had set the standard for emergency lighting in the United Kingdom, and the management at that time regarded its leadership position as secure. Throughout the early 1980s, Chloride Bardic steadily lost market share. In 1987 its market share bottomed out. After the creation of the Chloride Lighting SBU, a new U.K. general manager was appointed, new operating standards were instituted, and a new product line was developed that was targeted toward the commodity market. By November 1988, Chloride Lighting had recovered several U.K. share points.

Chloride Lighting sold emergency lighting under two brand names in the United Kingdom, Bardic and Security Lighting. Bardic was the primary brand. Half of Security Lighting's annual sales were to OEMs who relabeled the products with their own brand names. In September 1987, Chloride Bardic relaunched its fire detection systems with a new line of smoke alarms, heat detectors, control panels, and a variety of ancillary equipment. These devices were manufactured for Chloride Bardic by another company that labeled them with the Bardic brand name. In fiscal 1988, fire detection systems accounted for a small percentage of Chloride Lighting's U.K. sales.

Between 1986 and late 1988, the U.K. market grew by 40%. Over this same period, the market became increasingly concentrated with the share controlled by Chloride Lighting, Menvier, and JSB rising from 38% to over 50%. In 1988, the top six manufacturers accounted for 74% of sales.

The market leader, Menvier-Swain Group, had projected 1988 emergency lighting sales of £8.4 million in the United Kingdom and £13.9 million worldwide. Total projected 1988 company sales were £18.3 million. Originally an electrical contractor, Menvier's sales grew at a compound annual rate of 23% between 1984 and 1988, with growth propelled by emergency lighting sales. In addition to the United Kingdom, Menvier had operations in the Netherlands, the United States, and Australia. Its Dutch operation was a recent acquisition.

Menvier offered a complete line of emergency lighting and fire alarm products, all of which it manufactured in-house. The company pioneered the technology for converting standard fluorescent lights into emergency lighting. An additional 30,000 square feet of capacity was under construction at Menvier's U.K. plant and was due to be completed in early 1989. Menvier products competed head-on with Bardic ones, sharing the same wholesale distribution network. The company also competed against Chloride Lighting in the OEM business, although Security Lighting was the leader in this field.

Chloride Lighting's other major competitor in the U.K. market, JSB Electrical, had projected 1988 emergency lighting sales of £7.1 million in the U.K. and £8.7 million worldwide. Projected total company sales were £11.9 million in 1988. Like Menvier, JSB had grown rapidly since 1983. JSB marketed a full line of emergency lighting products and fire detection equipment. It also sold some general lighting products. Unlike Chloride Lighting and Menvier, JSB sometimes cut distributors out by dealing directly with contractors. The company had also been known to slash prices to secure business. JSB was vertically integrated in its manufacturing processes. It had sheet metalwork capability that gave it greater flexibility of manufacture than its competitors. It had also recently purchased an Isle of Man-based manufacturer of printed circuit boards.

In late 1988, Saft, a French producer of emergency lighting and the EC market leader in emergency lighting sales, obtained approval from the British Standards Institute to sell its emergency lighting in the United Kingdom. Saft's traditional markets were France and Spain. As of November 1988, the company had sold an insignificant amount of emergency lighting in the United Kingdom. Nevertheless, Saft potentially posed a serious threat to the established players in the U.K. market. In Ireland, Saft had recently quoted prices that were 15% below the going market rates there.

Saft was a subsidiary of CGE, a £6 billion conglomerate whose core business was telecommunications. Saft's primary business was the manufacture of NiCad batteries over which it held a virtual European monopoly. Chloride Lighting purchased all of the NiCad batteries required for the production of its emergency lighting from Saft. Saft's projected

1988 sales totaled £158 million, only 11% of which, £17 million, was in emergency lighting.

The Rest of EC Europe

Germany. In Europe, the largest market for emergency lighting was in Germany. In both Germany and the Netherlands, central systems made up the majority of the emergency lighting market, accounting for 56% of sales. In contrast, SPUs dominated the remainder of the EC market, outselling central systems almost seven to one. As in the United Kingdom, emergency lighting regulations in Germany covered both electrical safety and product performance requirements. To be sold in Germany, products had to be approved by the V.D.E., the German equivalent of Underwriter's Laboratory.

A large number of indigenous manufacturers sold emergency lighting in Germany. It was rare to find an imported product in the market. Chloride Lighting had no distribution in Germany. It had attempted in the past to create a joint venture with an independent German manufacturer of mains lighting that had expressed interest in emergency lighting. After protracted discussions, however, the companies decided not to proceed because of perceived difficulties in selling an imported product in Germany. The difficulties foreseen were those of gaining market acceptance of a non-German product rather than actual technical obstacles of meeting V.D.E. requirements.

France. The third largest European emergency lighting market, France, had the most complex and exclusive set of emergency lighting specifications in Europe. Defined in French NORMES, the regulations covered both electrical safety and product performance requirements and were rigorously enforced by the fire service. Approval testing was carried out by government-approved test laboratories. Unlike most of Europe, where at least a small market for nonapproved emergency lighting existed, there was no market for nonapproved products in France. Seventy percent of the French market for emergency lighting was in incandescent SPUs, the prices for which were extremely low.

The French market was served exclusively by French manufacturers. Over 70% of the market was split evenly between Saft and Legrand. Although Legrand confined its emergency lighting business to France, the company's mainline business in electrical fittings was sold internationally through channels ideally suited to emergency lighting distribution. Both Saft and Legrand had acquired several small French emergency lighting companies in recent years. The third- and fourth-place companies in the French market, Impex and Luminox, together accounted for 15% of the market.

Chloride Bardic had ventured unsuccessfully into the French market in a partnership with Coredel, a French distributor, which was terminated in 1985. Coredel was a subsidiary of Chloride with the primary business of manufacturing UPS. Although it proved possible to obtain approvals in France for U.K.-made products, it proved impossible to produce them profitably while meeting the market price. Saft, which dominated the committee that established French emergency lighting standards, reacted aggressively to Chloride Bardic's entry into the French market by pushing through continual changes in standards and testing requirements that kept Saft a step ahead of Chloride and prohibitively increased Chloride's cost of doing business in France.

Belgium. Belgian emergency lighting regulations covered both electrical safety and product performance requirements. The regulations were rigorously enforced by the fire service. Two separate approvals were relevant to emergency lighting. MTP approval applied to all emergency lighting installed in public sector buildings in Belgium. Buildings not covered by the MTP standards needed emergency lighting products with NBN approval. NBN regulations were recently adopted and were more severe than those of MTP.

No manufacturers had yet obtained NBN approval. Four indigenous manufacturers had MTP approval — ETAP, Mitralux, CET, and Saft. Chloride Lighting also had MTP approval. Belgium was the most important of Chloride Lighting's export markets. Its fiscal 1988 sales accounted for approximately half of Chloride Lighting's non-U.K. EC sales. Chloride Lighting projected 20% growth in its Belgian sales in fiscal 1989. All of Chloride Lighting's Belgian sales were through one distributor, Helpelec, a small company of seven people that specialized in emergency, explosion-proof, and portable lighting. Chloride Lighting products represented the bulk of Helpelec's sales. Prices in the Belgian market were very competitive and had trended downward in recent years.

Ireland. Installation regulations similar to and based upon the British standard existed in Ireland and had been rigorously enforced since the "Star Dust" disco fire in Dublin in 1983. The British ICEL product standards were widely recognized and specified by architects and engineers but were not mandatory. There were no local product approvals required.

All of the major U.K. competitors had distribution in Ireland. In addition, there were several small local manufacturers of emergency lighting. Chloride Lighting's Irish distributor, Project Lighting Ltd., assembled most of the Bardic emergency lighting it sold from components. This practice was begun at a time when a "guaranteed Irish content" was a prerequisite for participation in any government project. Although this requirement had softened, the arrangement had continued in order to keep Chloride Lighting competitive with local manufacturers. Chloride Lighting's fiscal 1988 Irish sales were second in importance to its Belgian sales. Emergency lighting prices in Ireland were significantly below U.K. levels.

Netherlands. The Netherlands had no national regulations for emergency lighting. Requirements were left up to each local fire service to decide. In practice, however, most of them followed the emergency lighting regulations drafted by The Hague fire service. Until 1987, no national product approval process existed. In 1987, a requirement to obtain KEMA approval was enacted. Concerned mainly with electrical safety, the standards were equivalent to those of the British Standards Institute.

The Dutch market was divided among products produced by several local manufacturers and U.K. and German imports. Chloride Lighting sold a small amount of emergency lighting in the Netherlands in fiscal 1988. The company was seeking to change distributors there because its current distributor, Chloride Holland, was reluctant to increase its emergency lighting activity.

Portugal. Portugal had emergency lighting regulations that were ill-defined and applied to only a limited category of buildings. No national approval was required to sell emergency lighting in Portugal. Consequently, a large number of suppliers were active in this small market. Competitors included importers from France, Spain, and the United Kingdom and two small local manufacturers. Chloride Lighting products had been represented in Portugal for nearly twenty years by Casa Palissy, an old established electrical distributor in Lisbon. Chloride Lighting's fiscal 1988 Portuguese sales were small and were projected to remain constant in fiscal 1989. Emergency lighting prices were low in Portugal.

Denmark. In Denmark, emergency lighting regulations were concerned mainly with electrical safety and not with product performance. Products had to be approved by DEMKO in order to be sold in Denmark.

The market was served largely by local manufacturers. In late 1988, Chloride Lighting appointed a distributor in Denmark and submitted products to DEMKO for approval. It expected to receive approval by late 1989.

Spain. A Spanish national standard existed for emergency lighting, but it was not technically demanding and could be met with a simple product. To be sold in Spain, emergency lighting required approval by an independent laboratory. A number of local manufacturers produced emergency lighting to minimum requirements and at low cost. The predominant competitor was the Spanish subsidiary of Saft, which sold an obsolete model from Saft France. Imported products were not evident on the Spanish market. Chloride Lighting had appointed a distributor in Spain but did no business there.

Italy and Greece. Both Italy and Greece had ill-defined legislation and were served by very low-cost local manufacturers. Beghelli, number three in the EC emergency lighting market, was the leading Italian manufacturer. Chloride Lighting had pursued neither market.

Non-EC Europe

Chloride Lighting sold emergency lighting in three non-EC European countries — Norway, Sweden, and Finland. With the exception of Sweden, emergency lighting regulations in these countries were concerned exclusively with electrical safety, not with product performance. Each country required approval by its national testing agency in order to sell emergency lighting there. Each market was dominated by three or four local manufacturers. The relatively high cost of production in these countries allowed Chloride Lighting to compete effectively and achieve acceptable margins.

THE IMPACT OF 1992 ON THE EUROPEAN EMERGENCY LIGHTING BUSINESS

The expression "1992" was shorthand for a campaign to turn the 12 EC member countries into one barrier-free internal market by the end of 1992. The community's goal was to create a market of 322 million people in which the free movement of goods, services, people, and capital was ensured. In 1985, the European Commission, the EC's executive arm, which was composed of commissioners appointed by national governments and sworn to act in the interests of the community as a whole, authored a White Paper that proposed 286 specific legislative reforms designed to create a wholly unified internal market in the EC. Many of the proposed directives were industry specific and designed to tear down technical barriers to cross-border trade such as varying national product standards. Others were directed toward eliminating all physical frontier barriers and controls. Still others were designed to tear down fiscal barriers by harmonizing VAT rates and excise taxes within narrow ranges across the EC. The European Commission set December 31, 1992 as the deadline for passing all of the White Paper reforms. As of November 1988, one-third of the proposals had been adopted by the EC and made into Eurolaws. Over 100 others had been drafted by the European Commission and sent for approval to the Council of Ministers, the final decision-making body of the EC that was drawn from top national politicians.

Included in the construction product directive drafted by the European Commission were the essential requirements needed for CENELEC, the European Committee responsible for electrotechnical standardization, to draw up the technical specifications for a harmonized emergency lighting product standard. Created by CENELEC subcommittee TC 34Z, whose primary area of interest was the mains lighting industry, a draft document was issued to national standards-making bodies for opinion and possible amendment in mid-1988. The document was based on a standard first proposed by the International Electrotechnical Commission. It did not differ significantly from the existing British product standard. Apart from one or two local deviations, industry observers did not expect member nations to make many changes to the draft document. Voting on a definitive standard was expected to be complete by mid-1989, after which the harmonized standard would be sent to the CENELEC Technical Board for rubber stamping. Member governments would have up to 30 months to replace their existing standards with the new one. After the 30-month deadline, the new standard would become the Eurostandard. A country not complying with the Eurostandard could be prosecuted by the powerful European court.

The proposed emergency lighting product standard defined the various types of emergency lighting. It also set standards for product labeling, construction, external and internal wiring, provisions for grounding, protection against electric shock, creepage distances and clearances, terminals, endurance tests and thermal tests, resistance to dust and moisture, insulation resistance and electric strength, photometric performance, high temperature operation, battery chargers for self-contained luminaires, changeover operation, and resistance to heat, fire and tracking.

The evolution of the European emergency lighting market post-1992 hinged not only on the implementation of a harmonized product standard, but also on a harmonized code of practice. The code of practice specified the amount of illumination emergency lighting was required to provide in a given building type. It also dictated details such as where emergency lighting had to be placed in a building and how close together individual units had to be. The code of practice, therefore, impacted the design of emergency lighting products by influencing such design elements as the size of lamp and strength of battery needed in an emergency lighting unit.

CEN, the European Committee for standardization, was working to develop a harmonized code of practice for emergency lighting. However, progress on this front was far less advanced than on that of a harmonized product standard. Final definition and adoption of a harmonized code of practice into Eurolaw was not expected much before the 1992 deadline. Chloride Lighting executives anticipated that the harmonized code of practice would be based on present German custom because the Germans were providing the secretariat to the technical committee responsible for drafting the harmonized code.

Implications of Emergency Lighting Standards Harmonization

The introduction of a single European emergency lighting standard and code of practice opened up a spectrum of opportunities and threats for Chloride Lighting and its competitors. Once the Eurostandard was adopted, all EC countries would be forced to require emergency lighting to be installed in all new commercial and industrial buildings covered by the harmonized code of practice. Manufacturers would no longer be required to design products to differing technical standards for each European market. Moreover, a product that was approved to the Eurostandard by a testing laboratory in one EC country would automatically be eligible for sale in all EC countries, thereby greatly reducing the time, cost, and aggravation required to enter new markets. In addition, existing competitors in a given nation would no longer be able to stave off outsiders by lobbying for continual changes in national standards, as Saft had previously successfully ousted Chloride from France.

Several of the 1992 directives were designed to liberalize government procurement practices throughout the EC and ensure that local companies were no longer treated preferentially. A large proportion of emergency lighting sales were for government projects. The combination of a harmonized emergency lighting standard with a more open bidding process for public works' construction implied greater opportunity for companies to supply public projects outside their traditional markets.

In addition to competitors already active in the emergency lighting industry, companies from outside the industry could be attracted to enter the market by the combination of the new Eurostandard and the rapid growth projected for the European emergency lighting market. Possible new entrants included large lighting companies wishing to complete their lines, specialty lighting groups wishing to expand their lines, and manufacturers of allied security/safety products such as fire alarms.

Although introduction of a Eurostandard for emergency lighting meant decreased product differentiation, it did not mean that one model of emergency lighting would satisfy customer needs throughout Europe. Even after standard harmonization, different markets would have different product demands. Some markets would insist on low-cost products, while others would demand higher-cost products with more features. Companies would still need to produce a range of products in order to meet EC-wide demand.

The new Eurostandard would guarantee EC-wide market access to emergency lighting manufacturers; however, it could do nothing to guarantee customer acceptance of unfamiliar products and brand names. In order to convince architects and engineers to specify new brands, distributors to stock them, and contractors to buy them, all three groups had to be conversant with the new Eurostandard and code of practice and be convinced that the new brands offered benefits that were missing from the brands upon which they had relied in the past. Most emergency lighting buyers were national in scope at best. In 1988, no European electrical wholesaler operated across national boundaries. In 1987, less than 2% of architects and designing engineers' turnover came from inter-Europe work. That same year, construction expenditures in the 12 EC countries totaled an estimated $380 billion. Only $17.2 billion were awarded to nondomestic contractors.

Sudden realignment of prevailing commercial practices and national preferences in the European construction industry was unlikely. However, a myriad of construction standards would become harmonized by various 1992 directives. Therefore, over time, Europeanization of architectural and engineering consulting firms and contractors was feasible, as was the expansion of electrical distributors across national boundaries.

CHLORIDE LIGHTING'S STRATEGIC OPTIONS

The action plan that Mark Geering took to his meeting with Bob McCue is contained in *Exhibit 7.7*. Geering estimated that Chloride Lighting would need only four weeks of design time to modify its existing range of emergency lighting to conform to the new Eurostandard and code of practice, once they were enacted. Furthermore, approval testing based on modification of existing equipment took only three to four months, compared to 12 months for totally new products, and, once granted, product approval would be recognized throughout Europe. Consequently, the hurdles that Chloride Lighting would have to leap in order to emerge a winner in the post-1992 European emergency lighting market were not technical ones.

The challenge, Geering believed, was to develop a strategy that would give Chloride Lighting enough "local color" in each market to succeed throughout Europe, while at the same time remaining flexible enough to meet a variety of different post-1992 European construction market scenarios. In item six of his action plan, Geering listed the several strategic options he perceived Chloride Lighting to have in Europe.

The options were five. First, Chloride Lighting could create a joint venture with a European emergency lighting manufacturer headquartered outside of the United Kingdom, preferably in Germany or France,

---

EXHIBIT 7.7 Geering's proposed action plan

1. Maintain close contact with the regulatory authorities. Ensure maximum representation and strive to mitigate German influence in standard setting.
2. Improve knowledge of the major European markets, especially distribution and end-user practices.
3. Be ready to invest resources in developing products meeting harmonized standards.
4. Prepare education programs to take out to sales force, consultants, contractors, and distributors.
5. Maintain close watch of competitor activity. In particular, prepare defensive strategy to protect existing business.
6. Investigate ways of expanding activity in mainland Europe via any of the following routes:
   Acquisition
   OEM-type customer base development
   Joint marketing with specialty lighting company or manufacturer of allied product
   Establishment of regional sales office or warehouse or assembly activity staffed by local national(s)
   Joint design of "Euro"-range

to jointly design and market a "Euro"-range of emergency lighting products. Geering believed that this option would be the least costly, but also would provide the least potential benefit. It was unclear what added value the two companies could bring to one another.

Second, Chloride Lighting could pursue OEM arrangements. It could seek to supply mains lighting manufacturers, allied safety products manufacturers, and/or electrical distributors throughout Europe with unbranded emergency lighting products that each OEM would then sell under its own brand name. A benefit of this approach was that the number of potential OEM customers was small. Therefore, Chloride Lighting would need to devote little sales resource to this strategy. A danger was that Chloride Lighting would lose control of how its products went to market, with its OEM customers becoming, in essence, its sales agents. Moreover, sales to OEM customers would not command as high a price as would sales of branded products to distributors.

The third option was to establish a joint venture with a continental European specialty lighting company or manufacturer of allied products such as fire alarms. For example, Chloride Lighting could link up with a German company that produced fire alarms under a popular German brand name but which sold no emergency lighting. The two companies could supply product to each other, Chloride Lighting sending emergency lighting to the German company in exchange for fire alarms. Each company could then market the full line of products under its brand name in its home country and other countries in which its brand name was well established. Such a venture could give Chloride Lighting quick access to markets and distributor networks at a relatively low cost, allowing Chloride Lighting to piggyback on an established brand name from an allied market. One disadvantage of such a joint venture would be that Chloride Lighting would not have full control of the marketing of its products.

The fourth option, acquisition, would allow Chloride Lighting to maintain greater control over the marketing of its products than any of the preceding strategies. Acquisition could take the form of buying a company with an established brand of emergency lighting or of buying one with an established brand of allied products outside of Chloride Lighting's home market. An acquisition would buy both access to local distribution channels and local marketing expertise. It would be more expensive than a joint venture, but would give Chloride Lighting greater control over the marketing of its products. One drawback was that most of the possible acquisition targets were small family-owned companies. Cultural differences between Chloride Lighting and its acquired companies could lead to managerial difficulties.

The final option was to establish regional Chloride Lighting sales offices, and/or assembly/warehousing operations staffed by local nationals in countries in which Chloride Lighting currently had no presence. Such offices would be charged with developing demand for Bardic brand emergency lighting in countries in which it was currently unknown. This strategy would depend on recruiting local managers with previous emergency lighting experience who could convince distributors, architects, and contractors to buy the Bardic brand. Its success was highly dependent on hiring the right people, which might include disaffected employees of competitors. Establishing a regional office would probably cost slightly less than an acquisition. It would take longer to establish local color, but, if done well, had the potential for the biggest payoff in the long run.

DECIDING A STRATEGY

After discussing the five strategic options that Geering had included in his action plan, McCue leaned toward Geering and exclaimed:

> I question whether "four and five percenters" [competitors with 4% and 5% EC market share] will still be around in Europe in the year 2000. My goal is for our SBU to grow into the leading world player in emergency lighting by the turn of the century. Achieving that goal demands that we earn 10–20% market share in the EC emergency lighting market. Today our SBU is defined by emergency lighting. Will that take us where we want to go? Should we broaden that definition to include specialty lighting or safety equipment in order to achieve our emergency lighting goals?
>
> Furthermore, can our experience in the U.S. market provide learning which will help us succeed in the changing EC environment? Equally important, is our SBU organized in such a way as to allow us to take advantage of opportunities and ward off threats in Europe?
>
> If only as a result of the publicity 1992 has generated, the European emergency lighting market will change. I am committed to shaping that change into success for Chloride Lighting.

EDITORS' COMMENTARY

Chloride Lighting's situation, in the context of EC market integration, is typical of that facing many small enterprises. Chloride, in common with other EC producers of emergency lighting, serves a national market in the United Kingdom, with only a nominal volume of export sales. Its previous efforts to establish distribution in France, Germany, the Netherlands, and Portugal have yielded little in the way of results. The company's operations in the United States seemingly have little or no connection to those in the United Kingdom. Potential scale economies in manufacturing are negligible, according to Chloride executives; only in component procurement are there significant prospects for reducing costs via larger-scale operations.

Under these conditions, how is the integration of the EC market likely to affect Chloride and the emergency lighting business in general? It could be argued that not much will change — why should German contractors change their established (and presumably satisfactory) sources of supply? What inducements can Chloride offer to customers, given that opportunities for scale economies and product differentiation are so limited?

While a good case can be made that 1992 will be a "nonevent" for emergency lighting producers, there are indications that one competitor, Saft, is taking steps to establish its products in additional markets. (Saft already marketed its products in Spain and Belgium.) This may be a prelude to entering the U.K. market and threatening Chloride's "home base" directly. Saft's approach is apparently based primarily on the sale of obsolete models and/or price cutting.

Chloride's strategic options are outlined in the case. Which of these offers the best chances of success will, of course, depend on the specific acquisition candidates or joint-venture partners that can be identified and on the terms of any deal that might be made. Based on the information in the case, it appears unlikely that simply combining Chloride with another emergency lighting producer would accomplish much. A more productive approach may be one based on product innovation — possibly emphasizing "conversion kits" for regular lighting fixtures. Another possibility might be combining emergency lighting with fire alarms, smoke detectors, and other specialty products (e.g., outdoor lighting). With either of these approaches, Chloride may find it necessary to reduce costs by manufacturing in a country with lower labor costs than the United Kingdom — perhaps Spain or Portugal. Although manufacturing scale economies may be unimportant, differences in relative labor and other costs among EC locations may be substantial.

A final possibility — not mentioned in the case — is for Chloride to sell the business to Saft or another producer. This solution was adopted by the company in late 1988 for its automotive battery business. The attractiveness of this strategy depends on the company's alternate uses of the resources.

CHAPTER 8

Identifying a Sustainable Niche

Canadian Imperial Bank of Commerce and the Banking Services Market

EDITORS' INTRODUCTION

By 1992, a banking license obtained in one EC country would permit establishment of offices and freedom to sell services throughout the EC. In June 1989, following agreement among the EC ministers of the member states, this directive was sent to the European parliament for its second reading. Other directives covering the solvency ratios required of financial institutions and insider trading were also in process. American and, to a lesser extent, Canadian and other foreign banks were concerned that the EC might use the principle of reciprocity to justify restrictions on the scope of their business activities. Under current U.S. legislation, EC banks would not enjoy the same freedom of access to the American market due to state licensing regulations and restrictions on banks entering the securities business. On the reciprocity issue, the second banking directive of June 1989 stated that the European Commission should draw up proposals for the European Council of Ministers to negotiate comparable access.

The banking directives were expected to permit more open competition and to erode differences in the cost of financial services from one EC country to another. In the face of likely increased competition, considerable industry consolidation was taking place, particularly in the more fragmented banking markets such as Italy and Spain. As the remaining EC banks became stronger and both broadened and upgraded their range of services, it would be even harder for foreign banks to compete without the benefit of low-cost funds supplied by a retail branch network — and there was no reason to expect that 1992 would prompt European consumers to place their savings with foreign banks.

In the material that follows, Dr. John Pattison first presents an over-view of the impact of 1992 market integration on the EC banking ser-vices sector. He highlights the different marketing strategies that will be appropriate depending on each bank's competitive position. He then focuses on the market position and strategic marketing options con-fronting the Canadian Imperial Bank of Commerce (CIBC).

What role should CIBC play in Europe after 1992 beyond satisfying the European banking needs of its principal North American multina-tional clients? Could CIBC build on its existing capabilities to establish a stronger yet profitable presence in selected niche markets, perhaps in cooperation with existing EC-based banks? Given the continuing uncer-tainty about the Commission's position on reciprocity, were investments to enhance CIBC's European operations too risky?

Bank Marketing Strategies in the EC

John C. Pattison

Banking, although not the oldest profession, is arguably the oldest or-ganized business, with its roots planted firmly in European soil. The development of banking took little notice of national frontiers and was instrumental both in financing international trade and in financing na-tions. London developed a key role in finance, with Barings and Roth-schilds providing loans to European nations and Hambros financing the unification of Italy in the mid-1800s. Today, London continues to play an important role in European banking.

It is with these historical trends in mind that it is necessary to ask whether the advent of 1992 offers any new challenges. The answer is a resounding yes, for the following reasons. First, banking has become an intensely regulated industry, and each nation has developed very dif-ferent rules governing competition, prudential controls, and techniques of monetary policy. In 1992 all but the monetary policy techniques will change. Second, banking products and services have proliferated but at

different paces in different countries. The single market will cause banks
to offer products in markets in which they have never been offered before. Third, banking serves many different market segments in each
country, with positioning strategies differing significantly even among
so-called full-service banks. In 1992 banks will be required to reconsider
their positioning in Europe. Fourth, the individual customer today is
being viewed more and more as a retail client along the same lines as
those of department stores and other retail chains. Fifth, the economics
of banking, together with the spread of new products, including securities, has focused attention on methods of distribution. These last two
factors in the context of 1992 have led to a reconsideration of the ability
and the methods by which international banks might offer retail services
in foreign markets heavily dominated by national institutions. The importance of the advent of 1992 rests, as much as anything, in forcing
those banks with significant European activity to rethink their fundamental business and marketing strategies to a degree that would not
otherwise have been thought necessary.[1]

The purpose of this overview is, first, to assess the impact of the
advent of 1992 on the marketing strategies of different types of banks
and, second, to focus on the challenges facing the Canadian Imperial
Bank of Commerce (CIBC) in particular.[2] In this context banking is defined as encompassing the full range of services offered by banks in
Europe, including securities, mutual funds, and investment banking.
The dramatic changes that occurred in international financial markets in
the 1980s, particularly the emergence of London as the principal European financial center, must be considered as a backdrop to assessing the
impact of 1992's changes. In addition, Europe must also be seen in its
global context. For many non-European banks, European activities support the local operations of multinational companies. This is true for
Japanese and U.S. banks, but it is also true to some extent for Canadian,
Australian, and other banks. European offices also provide international
investment banking products and investment management services to
wealthy individuals from many countries. European banks' strength-

---

[1] In the United States most banks are concerned today with such matters as their entry
into the securities business and interstate banking. However, in many European
countries banks have been allowed to provide a much wider array of products,
including securities, and branching is not restricted.

[2] The advent of 1992 will have important impacts on capital flows and the cross-rates
of exchange between European currencies, and hence on the European Monetary
System. These factors will have an impact on bank marketing decisions. Although it
is possible to analyze them, doing so would go beyond the scope of this case.

ened European operations will enable them to provide a better and wider array of services to customers outside Europe. As a consequence, the advent of 1992 promises to be an event whose impact does not stop at Europe's frontiers.

THE REGULATORY IMPLICATIONS OF 1992 ON MARKETING STRATEGIES

In 1989, banking was an open industry in much of Europe, with the right of establishment already in place for foreign banks. However, banks could not sell their services across national frontiers, in most cases, without a local establishment regulated by the host country. An additional difficulty was that varying business powers were granted to banks in each country, with serious restrictions on securities in a few European countries. Spain and Italy restricted foreign acquisitions of local banks. The goal of the European Commission, the policy-making body of the European Community (EC), was "for such freedoms as are already enjoyed, sometimes on a rather tenuous basis, to be secured, and for the full scope of freedom to provide services to be made generally available, so that the competitive marketing of these services can take place."[3] The creation of a single market was intended to include three areas of reform: the free movement of capital, the right to sell across frontiers *without* a local establishment, and the right of establishment in other member countries of the EC without authorization by host country regulators.

A large number of enabling laws were required to implement the single market of 1992. The centerpiece of the plan was the Council of Ministers' second directive on credit institutions, which, together with four technical directives, would establish the single banking license valid for both establishment and freedom of services throughout the EC by 1992. (A directive is a binding policy that each member state is free to implement in its own way.) A directive on mutual funds (unit trusts) was adopted earlier, to be implemented progressively from 1989;[4] a directive on investment services was sent to the Council of Ministers at the end of December 1988. The principle of authorization by the home

---

[3]Commission of the European Communities, *European Economy: The Economics of 1992* (Luxembourg: Office for Official Publications of the European Communities, 1988), p. 86.

[4]Although unit trusts and mutual funds differ in some important legal respects, they are used synonymously here for purposes of exposition.

country, as opposed to the host country, was controversial because of the need for host countries to protect depositors and consumers of financial services. Partly for this reason, host countries were given responsibility for the regulation of marketing and advertising, as well as for monetary policy.

The advent of 1992 would not result in a federal European banking license. Rather, a license issued in one country would be valid in all EC member countries. Such mutual recognition would be valid for specified activities, including leasing, securities, trading, and portfolio management, as well as for the full range of traditional banking activities.

Mutual recognition was a powerful principle. It allowed banks to conduct activities that might not even have been permitted to domestic institutions in the host country. On the other hand, if a bank's home state did not allow an activity that the host state did allow, the bank could not carry out the activity in either place. Competition would likely force each member state to broaden its banking powers until they covered, at a minimum, those specified in the second directive.

Subsidiaries of non-EC banks could also benefit from the mutual recognition principle in establishing branches or marketing products throughout the community with a single license. However, a subsidiary was essential: mere branches of foreign (non-EC) banks did not have such rights.

The second directive required reciprocity before a subsidiary could be established or before an acquisition or a participation could be made in a credit institution of the EC. Reciprocity covered the entire EC, not merely the state in which a foreign institution wished to be active. Therefore, all member states had to enjoy reciprocity with the foreign nation.

In early 1989 it was not yet known how reciprocity would be interpreted by the European Commission. At one extreme, reciprocity would necessitate that third countries grant the same treatment to all EC members that was allowed in the most liberal European member state of the community. There was also uncertainty as to how reciprocity would be applied, for example, to new products or to acquisitions or to the establishment of new companies to facilitate specialized activities or transactions. However, the European Commission had clarified that reciprocity implied a lack of discrimination and would not be applied to institutions that were already established in the market.

Market forces and each step toward 1992 put pressure on national governments to make their laws and regulations converge. In addition, the European Commission progressively assumed the role of policy maker for European financial regulation. Fortunately, enabling directives and legislation increasingly reflected the technical realities of the financial services industry. The common prospectus rules for new issues of securities had to be modified; otherwise, they would have ground the Eurobond market to a halt or driven it out of the community since the speed with which new issues were launched in this market would not allow time to comply with these rules. The industry's concerns were heard and appropriate modifications made.

One further area of regulatory reform that was part of the preparation for 1992 was the harmonization of tax policies that discriminated among institutions or protected local markets. Without such harmonization, French residents would benefit by transferring their savings from France to other member countries. Experts agreed that tax harmonization would be an especially difficult step for national governments to achieve fully because of conflicting domestic political pressures.

MARKETING SCENARIOS FOR DIFFERENT TYPES OF BANKS

The advent of 1992 presented different marketing opportunities and competitive threats for European banks, non-European banks, and banks with varying mixes of business — retail, corporate, and investment banking. In retail banking there was considerable scope for product differentiation both in home markets and in other European countries. Because corporate treasurers were cost sensitive, there was less room for differentiation except in customer service. The major opportunity for product differentiation was expected in domestic markets that were uncompetitive because of current regulations, competitive conditions, or historical traditions.

Corporate Banking — Member Countries

To unravel the likely impact of 1992's changes, one must consider first corporate banking for member-country banks. The 1992 agenda offered this group of banks the greatest opportunities. These included taking existing specialized expertise and services from the home market and selling them in other suitably targeted markets; extending services that were already being provided to multinational companies from the home country in other European locations; providing competitive services to multinationals from other countries in the home country (the multinationals' host country) and in other European countries; and expanding trade finance activity as EC exports involve value-added, and hence export guarantees, from a number of countries. In addition, the single market could lead to more financing opportunities both domestically and across European borders because of the stimulus given to trade and investment flows.

The threats were also compelling. First, large, well-capitalized banks from other member countries were expected to enter previously protected domestic markets that traditionally had been served by domestic banks through branches, subsidiaries, acquisitions, joint ventures, and other approaches such as networking marketing agreements. Second, those banks that were better positioned to serve multinational companies were expected to try to take clients from domestic banks, particularly smaller or regional banks. The wide range of services that a foreign bank might be unable to provide — including payroll services, cash management, or domestic mergers and acquisitions advice — could be a deterrent to shifting principal banking relationships in a home country but could be an inducement in a host country.

Corporate banks habitually wrestled with the issue of whether close to a full range of services was necessary to attract, hold, and develop corporate customers. In the 1980s this question became linked with the strategic necessity of offering investment banking services. Two factors needed to be considered. First, banks without investment banking capabilities often had to refer growing companies with which they had established relationships to other banks to handle the profitable underwriting and distribution of debt and equity for these maturing businesses. Second, corporate treasurers economized on the number of banks with which they maintained relationships for the sake of convenience and the facilitation of their own financial management responsibilities. Hence, banks that could not supply a full line of services often had limited access to corporate treasurers and therefore would miss opportunities to bid on transactions.[5]

In early 1989 a report on European capital markets questioned the need for a full-service strategy.[6] The report argued that corporate treasurers in fact preferred to shop around for each product and required

---

[5]See, for example, "National Westminster Bank a Difficult Child," *The Economist*, October 22, 1988, p. 82: "As NatWest's large corporate clients were switching their borrowing from bank loans to the capital market, the bank decided — with a little help from McKinsey . . . — that it could best keep them loyal by offering a full range of investment-banking services." The same article, page 84, went on to say that "Lloyds Bank and Midland long ago stopped trying to offer the whole caboodle."

[6]"Corporates Shun Europe's Financial Supermarkets," *International Financial Review*, January 28, 1989, p. 8.

access to the top transactional professionals in each specialized market. This preference was undoubtedly true for price-sensitive transactions for which the time involved in soliciting price quotes was minimal (for example, interest rate and currency swaps and the issuance of securities in well-defined markets with standardized documentation and covenants). Even so, a history of service and experience was necessary to secure a place on the short list of bidders when the number of competing institutions could be 50, 60, or more. However, for most mainstream corporate banking products, a sufficiently wide range of products, or acknowledged superiority in one, was necessary to attract the time and interest of those European corporate treasurers confronting more intra-European financial needs. Consequently, investment banking services in 1992 would require a different approach from that of the credit-related products.

Another report argued that the typical investment banker of the 1990s would shed his or her ambition to be all things to all people and would "concentrate on acting as an international niche player."[7] The report suggested that investment banks would concentrate on establishing a global superiority in a selected range of products and that this range of products would be reduced according to each firm's strengths and weaknesses.

National differences in methods of raising corporate finance appeared on the surface to represent a barrier to banks wishing to market existing services in other European countries. However, such differences allowed foreign banks perhaps their greatest opportunity for product differentiation. For example, in Germany the large, universal banks were the principal source of corporate finance, whereas the United Kingdom had a wide range of merchant banks and stockbrokers that provided, in contrast, a more equity-based system. In the United Kingdom 2,061 domestic companies were listed on the stock exchange in 1988. Germany had only 507.[8] This difference was expected to provide opportunities for merchant banks based in the United Kingdom to raise equity capital for German companies, particularly those with international name recognition.

Two services require special note — mergers and acquisitions, and

---

[7]"Investment Banking on the Knife Edge," *International Financial Review,* February 11, 1989, p. 5.

[8]R. Swannell, "The Strategy for M&A in Countries with Limited Stock Markets," Paper presented at the F T European Mergers and Acquisitions Conference, London, February 1989.

stockbroking. Mergers and acquisitions were particularly important services for corporate banks as the prospect of the single market fueled an increased amount of cross-border activity involving both EC- and non-EC-based companies. Analysts expected this process to be stimulated further by the release of pent-up demand. For many years there was a reluctance, except in the United Kingdom, to undertake or even allow takeovers of major companies. This reluctance started to break down in the late 1980s, and the restructuring stimulated by 1992 promised to unleash highly profitable merger and acquisition activity for banks positioned as experts in this business. Merger and acquisition activity was expected to grow not only because the European Commission's single market strategy would eliminate market barriers but also because the directives on information disclosure on takeovers, common prospectus rules, and changes in national legislation and regulations would make transactions easier.

As multinational firms restructured their European operations, there would be considerable advisory work to be won. Foreign banks with merger and acquisition skills, such as Morgan, Citicorp, and others, were expected to receive this business because of relationships with non-European head offices of multinationals, although European banks could plausibly argue their case based on local market knowledge.

The case for stockbroking as an important ancillary service for corporate bankers in Europe was based partly on the fact that banks in some European countries already provided full services. It was also based on the demand for and supply of corporate information to assist with restructurings, mergers, and acquisitions. The argument was also made that the single market would result in wider cross-border portfolio investments. However, most important were the restrictive practices in some European countries that invited greater competition.

Market Structure

The market structure of corporate banking was an important consideration for marketing strategy. Concentration ratios showed the importance of a small number of large banks in each European country. There were four major banks in the United Kingdom, three in France, and three in Germany. This degree of concentration was expected to increase even further. In 1989 one analyst noted that "today there are about 25 banks in the 12 nations of the European Community and Switzerland that matter globally. Come the mid-1990s there will probably be 10 or

15."[9] (See Exhibit 8.1.) However, this high degree of concentration existed alongside freedom of entry and competitive market conditions, which often resulted in narrow margins against referenced lending rates such as Libor (London inter-bank offered rate — a basic interest rate in international finance). The key explanatory variable was the differential cost of funds.

The large domestic banks had access to a permanent base of funds provided by their branch systems. Even considering the overhead and variable costs of the branch systems, their basic interest cost of funds was especially favorable relative to that of foreign banks, which had to access local currency funds via the wholesale or interbank markets. However, pricing, volume, and prudential asset-liability management limited this advantage. As a consequence, foreign banks usually competed without the benefit of a local branch network and would often do so by a combination of means, including higher margin loans reflecting a move to smaller size customers. Another approach that foreign banks used, often concurrently with the first, was to offer large, wholesale loans, with low margins, but also low administrative costs, to major domestic corporations. Their purpose was to secure a foot in the door in order to make future sales of other products such as foreign exchange, trade finance, and treasury products.

More price competition was expected in protected national markets, with a trend toward cross-border price convergence. A study conducted for the European Commission[10] showed considerable pricing disparities for products in different European member countries even when the theoretical range of price margins was reduced by 50% to allow for measurement problems. Banks attempting to build a broader customer base used price to access major customers in new markets in which they had, at least initially, a restricted range of products, little customer awareness, and difficulty opening doors.

Corporate Banking — Nonmember Countries

Much of the analysis above is also relevant to banks from non-member countries. The differences, however, are worth noting. First, the defensive nature of marketing strategies designed to protect existing business would suggest that European banks had relatively more to lose by fail-

---

[9]P. Koenig, "The No Idea Man at Crédit Lyonnais," *Euromoney*, January 1989, p. 27.

[10]Commission of the European Communities, *European Economy: The Economics of 1992.*

EXHIBIT 8.1 Europe's 25 top banks in 1987: four ways to measure

Ranked by assets	U.S.$ billions	Ranked by return on assets	%	Ranked by equity	U.S.$ millions	Ranked by proportion of equity to assets	%
1 Agricole	$216.8	1 Crédit Suisse	0.53%	1 NatWest	$9,165.26	1 Crédit Suisse	6.23%
2 BNP	182.7	2 Paribas	0.53	2 Agricole	8,741.16	2 UBS	6.14
3 Crédit Lyonnais	168.3	3 NatWest	0.52	3 Barclays	7,707.28	3 SBC	6.06
4 Deutsche	165.8	4 Rabobank	0.49	4 UBS	7,626.19	4 Rabobank	5.79
5 NatWest	161.9	5 UBS	0.49	5 Deutsche	7,111.66	5 NatWest	5.70
6 Barclays	158.0	6 SBC	0.49	6 SBC	6,855.09	6 Midland	5.54
7 Société Générale	153.0	7 Algemene	0.35	7 BNP	5,379.40	7 Lloyds	5.33
8 Dresdner	129.0	8 Amro Bank	0.34	8 Crédit Suisse	5,174.34	8 Paribas	5.25
9 UBS	124.6	9 Société Générale	0.34	9 Midland	4,839.98	9 Barclays	4.98
10 Paribas	122.3	10 BNP	0.32	10 Rabobank	4,716.17	10 Deutsche	4.22
11 SBC	113.4	11 Commerzbank	0.28	11 Lloyds	4,475.01	11 Algemene	3.96
12 Commerzbank	100.6	12 Crédit Lyonnais	0.27	12 Dresdner	4,231.87	12 Agricole	3.74
13 West LB	94.4	13 Générale Bank	0.27	13 TBS Group	3,887.08	13 Amro Bank	3.55
14 Bayerische	93.5	14 Deutsche	0.26	14 Monte dei Paschi	3,872.40	14 Dresdner	3.31

Rank	Bank	Value	Rank	Bank	Value	Rank	Bank	Value	Rank	Bank	Value
15	Midland	90.1	15	Barclays	0.24	15	BCI	3,529.46	15	BNL	3.11
16	Algemene	84.9	16	Dresdner	0.23	16	Crédit Lyonnais	3,500.99	16	Hypo-Bank	3.07
17	Lloyds	83.6	17	Agricole	0.23	17	Cariplo	3,407.57	17	Commerzbank	2.95
18	Crédit Suisse	83.3	18	Crédit Industriel	0.21	18	Paribas	3,326.97	18	West LB	2.72
19	Rabobank	81.9	19	Hypo-Bank	0.21	19	Algemene	3,288.33	19	Crédit Industriel	2.63
20	Amro Bank	81.0	20	Bayerische	0.16	20	Société Générale	3,182.02	20	BNP	2.54
21	Hypo-Bank	78.9	21	DG Bank	0.15	21	San Paolo	3,157.43	21	Bayerische	2.43
22	DG Bank	78.4	22	West LB	0.07	22	BNL	3,009.49	22	Société Générale	2.38
23	BNL	76.1	23	BNL	0.01	23	IMI	2,939.54	23	Générale Bank	2.16
24	Crédit Industriel	62.9	24	Lloyds	−0.48	24	Amro Bank	3,873.14	24	Crédit Lyonnais	2.12
25	Générale Bank	60.8	25	Midland	−0.82	25	Credito Italiano	2,692.04	25	DG Bank	1.81
	CIBC	$ 66.0		CIBC	0.50%		CIBC Shareholders' equity	3,176.08		CIBC Shareholders' equity	4.81
							Total capital	$4,289.77		Total capital	6.73

Sources: *Euromoney*, January 1989, p. 32; the IBCA and CIBC company records.
Note: All figures end 1987.

ing to prepare for 1992 than did non-European banks. Among non-European banks, Citicorp had by far the most extensive European network. Walter Seipp, the chairman of Commerzbank, remarked that Citicorp was the only truly European bank.[11] Second, because of the large amount of intra-European business, non-European banks' lack of branches and offices would not only allow banks from member countries to offer better service but also place the non-Europeans at an even greater disadvantage in terms of market intelligence and knowledge of developing transactions. Third, the growth of intra-European trade, the development of member-country banks, and the requirements for full-service suppliers would lead corporate treasurers to drop non-EC-based banks, particularly those providing specialist services but lacking true superiority, in favor of EC banks if trade and other forms of cross-border finance were important in their companies' business. Therefore, while European banks needed to protect local markets from other European institutions, banks from nonmember countries faced considerable disadvantages in challenging European banks in their home markets.

As discussed earlier, foreign banks often established a foothold via large loans with low administrative costs. The Japanese banks were particularly noted for such loans partly because of their much higher leverage ratios. These leverage ratios allowed the banks to achieve a higher return on equity at narrower margins than less leveraged banks achieved on higher margins. These lower margins for Japanese banks offset the local market disadvantages, including a lack of access to local retail funds in building a customer base. The promise of 1992 prompted the most important Japanese banks to move into all major European markets. This move seemed likely to enhance their ability to establish a foothold with clients on a price basis. Banks from the United States were at more of a disadvantage because of their relatively poorer capital positions.

Investment Banking — Member and Nonmember Countries

Foreign firms faced serious disadvantages in the securities field in EC markets. First, although trading skills could be transferred, an intimate knowledge of distribution practices and well-developed relationships

---

[11]G. Melloan, "German Banks Flex Their 'European' Muscles," *Wall Street Journal*, January 17, 1989, p. A19.

with local firms were essential to assessing inventories, funds available for investment, trading strategies, and portfolios of major investors. Second, many countries had regulatory barriers preventing foreign firms from becoming members of stock exchanges. In the late 1980s some of these barriers were relaxed, and much of the resulting action came from intra-European moves. Banks and merchant banks purchased brokerage firms and investment banks in other European countries. Also, for various reasons many institutions, not only those from the EC, acquired brokerage firms in London in the mid-1980s. One reason was the growth of international equity trading and distribution based in London. Another reason was access to the many international companies whose securities were traded on the London Stock Exchange. A London broker allowed some banks, such as the French, to conduct business that was not permitted in the home market. In mergers and acquisitions as well as other types of advisory work, the skills are easily transferable; but the knowledge and trust of local entrepreneurs often rest domestically rather than internationally.

There has been a substantial amount of international investment banking activity since the 1970s. Much of this activity, particularly in the Eurobond, Eurocommercial paper, and international equities areas, occurred in London. Accordingly, the mid-1980s brought a modest reshuffle, with sales desks for domestic debt sold internationally, together with some of the nondollar Eurobond business moving to European centers. European banks were likely to build up their investment banking skills in advance of 1992 at both the national head offices and in London, Europe's financial capital, where firms could work together most easily on international transactions.

Retail Banking — Member Countries

Considerable retail marketing opportunities were expected to exist within the EC after 1992. These opportunities stemmed from the differential penetration of banks and financial institutions in each country; different sets of competitors, resulting in variations in pricing for almost every product; cross-subsidization of different products in each country; different approaches to the packaging of financial services; and differences in the use of financial services according to the demographic characteristics of the populations. An example of this last opportunity was the underservicing of the mortgage market in Spain relative to the age, income, and family formation profile of consumers. The extent of cross-border branching was minimal. A Henley Centre study indicated that in 1984 there were 135 cross-border branches within member countries, of which 19 belonged to British banks.[12] One specialized cross-border segment was that of expatriates, of whom there were over 7 million in the EC. That number was expected to double in the 1990s.[13]

The complexity of and differences among these individual country markets and the increasing professionalization of retail bank marketing increased the need for Pan-European market research by European banks contemplating moves in retail banking. A retail bank would need to analyze carefully social stratification, age profiles, savings and investment behavior, knowledge of competing investments, and locational factors before making any move into nondomestic markets and ensuring a clear positioning in its home market. Banks' experience with and customer attitudes toward alternative approaches to pricing were also relevant to attempts to make incursions into markets where price differentials existed.

The most important issue in retail banking concerned methods of distribution. The need for retail outlets was a major barrier because customers would not readily do business with foreign banks to which they did not have ready access. No matter how sophisticated a customer, the safety and security of local retail outlets as well as the ability to make convenient and low-cost enquiries represented significant switching costs. The use of direct mail was sure to be limited to very specialized products, such as mutual funds, and to credit and related card services. A company such as American Express, with proven customer acceptance, could use its unique card system as a base to sell other financial services more readily than could foreign banks, which often competed with domestic banks offering the same card. However, since most banks already provided customers with transaction cards that allowed access to automated banking machines (ABMs), there were some possibilities for making creative use of the existing technology and accounting systems to market new products on a Pan-European basis through networking with ABMs in other countries.

Other retail products, such as mortgage lending, lent themselves to joint ventures between a local firm with an ability to originate new mortgage applications and a foreign bank with the mortgage credit skills and the finance capability. Joint-venture agreements between banks and nonbank companies were seen as a way of substituting for a branch

---

[12]Henley Centre, *The United Markets of Europe — The Market Report* (London: Henley Centre, 1988), p. 20.

[13]See P. Knox, "Funds Gear Up for Europe's Big Bang," *Equity International*, September 1988, no. 9, pp. 11–14.

distribution network. Banks could have such agreements with financial institutions such as insurance companies, store chains, and even petroleum distribution companies because of their branches and credit card use.

The retail equity business was expected to grow on a cross-border basis for banks offering such services because of legal changes and because this business was often conducted by telephone with confirmation and payment by mail. The potential existed for other banking services, such as lending and custodian services, to be integrated with this business via transaction cards.

A special market segment of retail banking was private banking, catering to individuals with high net worth. Most major banks expanded into this niche in the late 1980s, and it was identified by European banks, such as Deutsche Bank, as a specific opportunity offered by 1992's single market because of the access to wealthy clients across Europe.

Retail Banking — Nonmember Countries

Private banking in its various forms was the only segment of retail banking that had been identified across a broad spectrum of foreign banks as an area for concentration and growth. Even here it was not necessarily the European customer base that was the prime attraction, but rather wealthy non-Europeans interested in the European trusts and banks in tax havens such as Luxembourg, Guernsey, Jersey, and the Isle of Man. Chase Manhattan, for example, decided to concentrate on two areas after 1992: wholesale corporate banking and private banking services for wealthy individuals.[14] Its European strategy was expected to be centered on the United Kingdom, although it owned a bank in Spain that would be tailored toward the individual client. Hong Kong and Shanghai Bank followed a similar strategy of pursuing individuals with high net worth, using the fund managers of their affiliate, Wardley. One main advantage that 1992 would bring to private banking for non-EC banks was the ability to market services to targeted wealthy clients in each country without the need for a local establishment.

The mortgage market was another specialized market segment thought likely to grow with the advent of 1992. Following the United

---

[14]D. Lascelles, "Chase Adjusts European Strategy," *Financial Times*, November 15, 1988, p. 28.

Kingdom experience, mortgage lending capacity in Europe was expected to increase, with networks of affiliated institutions, as described earlier, used to identify customers and originate products.

MARKETING STRATEGIES

A bank's marketing strategy in preparation for 1992 depended first on its domestic strength. A bank needed market research to determine the competitive advantages that it could exploit and export as well as the dangers to which it was exposed by virtue of domestic weaknesses. Looking next at foreign markets, the bank had to analyze its strengths and weaknesses in the context of an environment in which the foreign bank would still be at a disadvantage.

Cost and revenue estimates had to be carefully prepared for each strategy. For a bank with an extensive European base, the interrelationships between the national markets required examination in terms of the products and services used by its international customer base to see if the expense involved in a Pan-European strategy would be rewarded by customer acceptance on a sufficient scale to make the investment profitable.

The challenge was to create competitive advantage by exploiting existing core businesses while either holding down the overhead costs of entry or having the entry costs produce an acceptable return on equity over a reasonably short time horizon. With Japanese banks focused on expanding their European base, the consequent, likely downward trend of pricing promised to make successful entry strategies very difficult. Japanese banks, given their high price-earnings ratios and low cost of capital, could afford to take a longer term view than non-Japanese banks.

Many non-European banks agreed with Chase Manhattan about the difficulty of competing directly with the major local banks. Thomas Labrecque, president of Chase, said, "It would be insanity for me to think of spending a dollar on that."[15] However, Japanese banks not only increased their representation through the establishment of European subsidiaries but also upgraded local offices, improved the quality of local staff, and restructured their account management organizations. Representative offices of Japanese banks were converted to branches by the Industrial Bank of Japan, Bank of Tokyo and Fuji Bank in Paris, and Fuji Bank in Milan. Japanese banks and brokerage houses both sought

---

[15]Ibid.

listings on European stock markets to broaden awareness of their banks among European financial market participants.

The principal marketing challenges for any European bank were how to position the bank in its markets; how to construct a delivery system; and, consistent with these, how to orchestrate account management for corporate business. The chief executive of Deutsche Bank, Alfred Herrhausen, said that "it will take a wider network of offices for us to be able to offer our extensive range of services locally and it is precisely for the medium-sized firm that, in many cases, an integrated European market will open up scope for additional business."[16] Herrhausen outlined three possible strategies: "acquiring banks in other countries or expanding holdings that already exist; establishing a more tightly knit European branch network by setting up branches in other countries; or cooperating with leading banks in other European countries, possibly including reciprocal equity holdings."[17]

National Westminster Bank was considering a somewhat different strategy. Chief Executive Designate for International Business John Tugwell stated that "the bank had already had a good experience of joint ventures in Europe and had decided that this was the best way to penetrate foreign markets and gain acceptance for the NatWest name."[18] What differentiated NatWest's strategy from the options listed by Herrhausen was that the partners need not be banks but could include other financial institutions, such as insurance companies, or could even be telephone companies with long client lists. Tugwell focused on the key issue of distribution: "I don't see how a bank is going to sell broad-scale products unless it gets into distribution arrangements with a partner — we need to have skillful local management."[19] NatWest's large U.K. competitor, Barclay's Bank, announced that it would follow a single-handed strategy in those countries in which it had established a presence. It intended to concentrate on its credit card system, Barclaycard. In contrast, NatWest shared its credit card operations with other banks in the United Kingdom.

The potential existed for banks to increase their scope by using investment banking or stockbroking activities as a basis for an expanded

---

[16]A. Herrhausen, "Three Options for the Banks," *Euromoney,* Special Supplement, September 1985, p. 45.

[17]Ibid.

[18]Reported in D. Lascelles, "Developing a European Branch Network," *Financial Times,* October 17, 1988, p. 31.

[19]Ibid.

European push. Through cross-selling a bank could use its European office to develop a client base for other products. For example, Barclay's stockbroking subsidiary, Barclay's DeZoete Wedd, opened offices in Paris, Amsterdam, and Madrid in the late 1980s.

Examples of a wide range of possible business development strategies also existed. Deutsche Bank pursued growth through acquisitions — for example, with the purchase of the Italian bank, Banca d'America e d'Italia, from Bank of America. It acquired MDM Sociedade de Investimentos in Portugal and a stake in Banco Commercial Transatlantico in Spain. Where legally possible, Deutsche Bank aimed for control, not simply cooperative arrangements, so that its own products could be sold with maximum push and control to a wider market without the possible impediments stemming from conflicts with local partners. Its German competitor, Commerzbank, the smallest of the three big German banks, followed a strategy of joint ventures and strategic investments. For example, it acquired a 10% holding in Banco Hispano Americano in Spain and discussed a similar stake in Crédit Lyonnais of France. In the investment banking arena, Midland Bank of the United Kingdom acquired control of Euromobiliare, the second most powerful Italian investment bank. One advantage of this merger was access to the customer list of clients with a high net worth served by a fund manager acquired earlier by Euromobiliare.

To build a distribution network, banks pursued strategies ranging from plans for large mergers — for example, between the large Netherlands and Belgian institutions, Amro and Générale de Banque — to a mutual strategic stake of 6% between the relatively small Hambros Bank and Banco San Paolo di Torino in Italy. Mortgage companies such as the U.K. building society, Abbey National, acquired stakes in mortgage lenders in other community countries.

Conspicuously absent in many of these plans, at least as publicly reported, were details about how products would be chosen for sales through affiliates; how these products would be marketed; and how account management would deal with the information requirements of the product bases of both companies, their own marketing teams, and product management and pricing. This issue was particularly important when the balance sheet of one institution was used to finance transactions originated by another. Potentially, account managers would confront a conflict in the use of their time and be unwilling to spend time introducing to the sales force new products with less immediate profitability.

It was always difficult for financial institutions to motivate cross-selling of products that required commission payments or other compensation to affiliates or other parts of the institution. These problems were likely to be exacerbated in some of the new European financial institution alliances, even when an acquiror achieved full control.

LONDON'S ROLE IN EUROPEAN MARKETING

London had emerged as the product center for European investment banking, for trading in Euro-securities, and for mergers and acquisitions activity. London was also the marketing hub for many investment banking products as well as the marketing and administrative center for most non-European banks' European operations. The domestic U.K. market was also an enticement to a London base, however, and language and history had much to do with this evolution. Much of the world's bank pricing was done from a London base — Libor — and London was the major commodities center for Europe.

There was concern about whether the advent of 1992 would reduce London's dominance and cause bank marketers to shift their product or currency mixes or to allocate fewer resources to London. First, some experts argued that customers involved in cross-border transactions would demand deutsche marks (DMs) or products denominated in European Currency Units (ECU — a book-entry currency composed of a weighted amount of individual European currencies). Because the pound was not part of the European Monetary System, clients using sterling would experience greater exchange rate risk in their transactions. It could not yet be determined whether 1992's changes would lead to more financial activity in Frankfurt or whether ECU activity would be centralized for purposes of trading and pricing in one European financial center. Second, deregulation of financial services by EC governments meant that activities that were carried on in London because they could not be done at home, such as stockbroking in London for French banks, could move closer to the home country client base. Third, the future of London as the premier European financial center was being questioned because London had one of the highest costs of any financial center in the world aside from Tokyo. The single market of 1992 offered an opportunity to develop less costly European distribution methods for securities sold to local clients and thereby permit a reduction in marketing costs for European business previously conducted in London. Overall, however, most experts believed that London would not lose its preeminence as the European financial center, but that DM and ECU transactions and the relative importance of Frankfurt would definitely grow.

CONCLUSION

For European banks looking ahead to 1992, the advent of the single, European market had serious potential consequences. It was also important to Citibank and many Japanese city banks. But to the majority of foreign banks whose presence in Europe was limited to London and to major international transactions and treasury activity, it was of little significance.

For European banks in particular, and for a few foreign banks, the threats to existing markets and client relationships were significant. Opportunities to develop new distribution or product origination (e.g., loan) business appeared substantial. There was, however, a risk that too much attention paid to imaginative solutions to the distribution/origination challenge could result in too little attention being paid to other important issues — in particular, to consolidating and protecting existing home markets or recognizing the challenges to domestic pricing and profitability, to competitive product innovation by new entrants, or to the successful management of cross-border accounts of home country multinational corporations.

The Canadian Imperial Bank of Commerce

John C. Pattison

Regardless of its trading characteristics, one characteristic of Europe 1992 is that it is going to be a very big market and if you have any visions of being a global corporation, you had better be there. My own recommendation would be to get there now and muddle through the integration process from the inside rather than waiting for all the facts to be known and then sitting on the outside looking into a done deal.

Edmund B. Fitzgerald
Chairman and Chief Executive Officer
Northern Telecom Limited
February 7, 1989

In January 1989, Holger Kluge, executive vice president, Eastern Canada, Europe, and the Middle East, pondered the implications of 1992 for the Canadian Imperial Bank of Commerce's (CIBC) European strategy. Kluge wondered whether he and his colleagues at Toronto headquarters and in Europe had considered all of the implications and whether they had examined sufficiently both the marketing opportunities and the problems that 1992 and its changes presented. For European banks, at least, the ground rules were clear. They were proceeding to reorganize the management of their European branches and subsidiaries; make acquisitions and divestitures; and make strategic investments in other financial intermediaries, with the goal of networking the sale of broader lines of products and services. Overseas banks, however — particularly those in the United States, Canada, Japan, and Australia — faced the potential danger that a lack of reciprocity would be used as a barrier; that is, that the inability to offer European banks operating in these countries the same powers that foreign banks enjoyed in Europe would be used as a reason to limit the activities of foreign banks in the European market.

HISTORY OF CIBC

CIBC was founded in 1867. By 1988 it was the second-largest bank in Canada, with assets of $94,687 million (Canadian). Net income for the fiscal year ended October 31, 1988, was $591 million, up from only $241 million in 1984. Like most major North American banks, CIBC's balance sheet had needed improvement in the early to mid-1980s. This improvement occurred when CIBC sold some of its third world loans, made substantial provisions against the remaining loans, achieved better management of its corporate loans portfolio, and added retained earnings and new issues of common equity. Unlike many banks with third world loans that were greater than the banks' capital, CIBC's true net exposure had declined to less than 25% of capital by 1988. Therefore, Kluge could make business decisions for Europe without being preoccupied with CIBC's capital position.

In 1986 Chairman and Chief Executive Officer Donald Fullerton dispensed with CIBC's International Division and reorganized the bank into four strategic business units (SBUs): the Corporate Bank, the Investment Bank, the Individual Bank, and the Administrative Bank. Each SBU had a worldwide mandate. Kluge's territory extended from Montreal to the Middle East, and Europe was a vitally important component of this business. Kluge's responsibilities were limited to the Corporate Bank, but this part of CIBC had the largest amount of European activity. Kluge was responsible for coordinating the bank's European strategy in preparation for 1992.

But what was the bank's mission in Europe? In 1988, the Canadian Imperial Bank of Commerce undertook a worldwide marketing plan to become known as CIBC. Previously, telephone operators in London, England, had answered the phone with "Canadian Imperial"; others knew the bank as CIBC or Bank of Commerce; while in Milan, years in the local market had caused the bank to be known simply as "Banca Canadese," a complimentary name but one likely to generate confusion. CIBC under Fullerton pursued the strategy of being a selective specialist outside Canada. The bank made no commitment to being all things to all people nor even to being present in all "major" markets. CIBC's mission statement was "to be recognized by our clients, our employees, and our shareholders as a world leader in providing quality financial products to the global markets we serve." Its European activities were organized as follows:

The *Corporate Bank* in Europe was headed by Derek Newman in London, who reported to Kluge. Newman, a British banker who had joined CIBC from Chemical Bank in London, had increased profits substantially since 1984 by entering specialized local markets such as residential mortgage lending, real estate financing, acquisition financing, leasing, and trade financing. He hired market specialists in targeted lending areas rather than relying on generalist lenders with a regional base, as had been done previously. He introduced new investment banking products to his customers and provided extensive product training programs for his account officers. He also reduced the number of high-cost teller services that the Corporate Bank's London office ran mainly for visiting Canadian customers.

In addition to his responsibilities in the United Kingdom, Newman oversaw corporate banking offices in Paris and Frankfurt and a finance company in Milan. A holding company for European subsidiaries had been established in Amsterdam because of a favorable tax treaty between the Netherlands and Canada; however, because of changes to this treaty, the representative office in Amsterdam was to be closed.

Nonetheless, the largest share of assets and earnings was in the United Kingdom, as shown in *Exhibits 8.2* and *8.3*. The credit quality of CIBC's Corporate Bank's assets proved to be very good; nonaccrual loans to European customers had declined from $12 million in 1984 to very close to zero in 1988.

The *Investment Bank* was undergoing considerable reorganization because of its 1988 acquisition of Wood Gundy, a leading Canadian investment dealer. Wood Gundy had European offices in London and Paris. It dealt mainly in Canadian debt and equity issues and in the Eurobond market, in which it often had a leading market share for distributing new issues of Euro-Canadian bonds. CIBC also had a good Eurobond team whose success rested primarily on relationships with non-Canadian clients in the so-called currency sector — non-U.S. currencies — of the market. Unfortunately, the profitability of this business had been declining with little sign of improvement, leading many firms to exit the market.

The Investment Bank had foreign exchange and money market operations in London and Frankfurt and a bank in Geneva. This Swiss bank engaged in investment management, the underwriting of Swiss franc bonds, private client business, and the trading of foreign exchange

EXHIBIT 8.2 Geographical distribution of assets for the major Canadian banks (millions of Canadian dollars)

	1987		1988	
	Amount	Percent of total assets	Amount	Percent of total assets
Europe (including United Kingdom)				
CIBC	$ 7,218	8.3%	$6,344	6.7%
Royal	10,143	11.6	8,756	9.4
Montreal	7,523	9.1	4,883	6.3
Nova Scotia	7,748	11.7	5,841	8.3
Toronto Dominion	1,636	3.0	1,824	3.1
United Kingdom				
CIBC	4,060	4.7	3,881	4.1
Royal	4,318	5.0	3,807	4.1
Montreal	2,988	3.6	1,674	2.2
Nova Scotia	2,592	3.9	2,251	3.2
Toronto Dominion	$ 775	1.4%	$1,422	2.4%

Source: Annual reports for 1988.

EXHIBIT 8.3 Total interest income by place of booking, taxable equivalent basis (millions of Canadian dollars)

	1986		1987		1988	
	Amount	Percent	Amount	Percent	Amount	Percent
Canada	$5,496	74.9%	$5,312	73.4%	$6,036	73.7%
United States	790	10.8	831	11.5	957	11.7
United Kingdom	424	5.8	449	6.2	505	6.2
Europe, excluding United Kingdom	187	2.5	159	2.2	140	1.7
Asia-Pacific and Australasia	220	3.0	260	3.6	294	3.6
Latin America, Caribbean, and Other	225	3.0	226	3.1	259	3.1
Total	$7,342	100.0%	$7,237	100.0%	$8,191	100.0%

Source: Canadian Imperial Bank of Commerce, *1988 Annual Report*, p. 22.

and money market instruments. The Swiss activities were modestly profitable, and the three-year-old operation was performing slightly ahead of early plans. CIBC also owned a brokerage firm and an investment management company in London.

The *Individual Bank* had no European retail operations, but it did have a successful and growing worldwide network of private banking offices catering to wealthy clients from North America, Europe, Asia, and the Middle East. In Europe it had a team of private banking marketing officers based in London, Guernsey, and Geneva that offered a full range of services through branches of the bank; offshore trust companies in Guernsey, Nassau, and the Cayman Islands; investment management companies in London and Hong Kong; and stockbrokers in London, Australia, and Hong Kong. In addition, it offered the services of Wood Gundy, which was a member of all the major U.S. stock markets and futures exchanges as well as those in Canada. CIBC also has a successful bullion operation serving both corporate and individual clients in gold, silver, and platinum.

The quality of CIBC's European staff continued to improve. Managers were drawn from the local markets and chosen for their skills and drive. Over the years CIBC had reduced the number of expatriate Canadians in Europe to a minimal number in order to control costs and to increase knowledge of local markets.

CIBC did not focus solely on the equivalent of Europe's *Fortune* 1000 firms. Newman also targeted specific segments among medium-sized businesses for which CIBC had particular products or services that were attractive and for which being a foreign bank without a full range of domestic products was not a major disadvantage. He also brought product specialists to bear on this market. The major banks of the world all targeted the top firms, hoping to develop relationships that would result in sales of everything from acceptances to zero coupons. The net result of this competition was thin margins on lending business that often would not compensate for the higher capital requirements being imposed by national regulators.

CIBC was not bound by any preconceptions about its positioning in Europe. Newman's profitable move into the mortgage market would not have been consistent with the traditional mandate of a corporate banker. The initial success of the mortgage business was based on forming links with United Kingdom insurers, which originated and referred mortgage applications to CIBC for its own credit review. CIBC subsequently approached the customers directly. The bank's views on the mortgage market were often sought; the BBC, for example, interviewed CIBC officers for the prime-time evening news.

Newman's team was ahead of the rapidly changing European markets in other ways as well. For example, when the sterling commercial paper market was first opened, CIBC had already completed a survey of corporate treasurers, which was sent to customers and which received timely press coverage.

BARRIERS TO ENTRY

CIBC's head of compliance and regulatory affairs, John Pattison (formerly the managing director of CIBC's London investment banking subsidiary), advised Kluge that the Europeans did not have much of a case to make against Canada on grounds of reciprocity. Canada was much less exposed to allegations of a lack of reciprocity than the United States and Japan. There were, however, three minor problems.

First, there was a ceiling on loans by foreign banks in Canada of 16% of total bank lending (reduced to 12% for non-U.S. banks with the passage in 1988 of the free-trade agreement between Canada and the United States). Current levels were well below this threshold. Second, no individual investor was allowed to own more than 10% of a large Canadian bank (beyond a point defined by capital and leverage), and foreign investors were limited to 25% ownership in any Canadian bank. However, European banks could engage in any banking activities they chose coast-to-coast in Canada and could engage in investment banking through a subsidiary. Under the anticipated revisions to the Canadian Bank Act, they also could enter the insurance or trust businesses, most probably via subsidiaries. Even the ownership ceilings allowed a foreign bank to grow to a substantial size before any restraints were imposed. Kluge felt that no member state of the European Community would willingly allow one of its top banks to become foreign controlled so the ownership issue was unlikely to cause a problem. The third problem, however, was potentially the greatest: Canada required foreign banks to establish subsidiaries rather than branches. This requirement mandated separate capitalization, and therefore higher costs, and was a sore point with foreign banks.

Although there was a danger of protectionism in Europe, Kluge felt that Canada had created a substantially open market and that the real targets of the European Commission would be the United States and Japan. Pattison had confirmed with senior officials of the Canadian government after they had made a tour of European capitals that they did not feel at risk on the reciprocity issue, although differences between Canada and the European Commission might need to be negotiated.

A NICHE STRATEGY AND GLOBAL LINKS

Kluge had a difficult challenge in Europe. On the one hand, CIBC was a foreign, selective specialist, relatively small in continental Europe — a niche player in some markets. On the other hand, CIBC was a lender to major European and other large corporations. It also provided European services for the bank's clients in Canada, the United States, and other countries such as Australia or Hong Kong, where the bank had a solid and profitable customer base. For example, in trade finance, the bank used the Italian, state-sponsored export finance agency (SACE) to finance Italian exports to Australia. It used outside insurers to finance the export of products from subsidiaries of U.S. multinationals in the United Kingdom to countries in Africa. These transactions were not only of above-average profitability, but also of below-average risk. Kluge knew that he could continue to develop new business. However, he wondered whether the strengthening of European banks' European networks after 1992, if only as a defensive strategy, combined with a possible resurgence of nationalist sentiment, would reduce both his current access to select clients and his ability to provide unique services without the full range of the European banks' services.

In every market in which foreign banks were prominent, they capitalized on lower overhead costs to provide a pricing advantage. However, each market was different. In many cases, domestic banks achieved a substantial cost advantage over foreign banks by having a lower cost of funds as a result of their long-term investment in a branch network and the loyalty of their national customers. The costs to a foreign bank of acquiring such networks were prohibitive, and they therefore constituted an effective barrier to entry. These differential costs of funds also dictated the kinds of business for which foreign banks were able to compete.

Kluge wondered whether 1992 would mean more intense competition even if it did not mean more regulation. He felt that the management and staff in Europe were capable of meeting this competition. With the increasing professionalism of its management, the bank had achieved enormous strides since the 1970s, when foreign banks in Europe were interested mainly in the lucrative syndicated loan markets. The latter required relatively little knowledge of local markets.

The interest of the other Canadian banks was mixed. Some had little interest in Europe and had closed branches there. Others were more positive. Some banks were very clear about their strategies, as exemplified by the Bank of Montreal's *1988 Annual Report*:

> *The focus outside of North America is upon services and products which support the Bank's core North American customer base, upon international investor clients and upon overseas-based multinational customers with North American interests, to whom the Bank's unique North American capability represents a useful competitive advantage.*
>
> *Emphasis was shifted away from low-margin lending to indigenous corporations and focused on multinational corporations with major interests in North America. [p. 23]*

The Royal Bank of Canada ranked its markets in its 1988 annual report. While stating that "the U.S. is our priority market outside of Canada," the report went on to say:

> *The European Common Market, the second largest trading area in the world, also represents an important target market, especially as the realignment of 1992 approaches. Our European headquarters group in London underwent major restructuring during the year, enabling closer coordination of our corporate banking and treasury operations with the investment banking capabilities of our subsidiary, RBC Dominion Securities Limited. [p. 24]*

The Bank of Nova Scotia had a European network encompassing 13 offices, of which 3 were in the United Kingdom, 3 were in Greece, and 2 were in Ireland. Its 1988 annual report stated:

> *Fiscal 1988 was the first full year following a major restructuring to sharpen the focus of our Corporate Banking operations in the U.K. and Europe. Despite fewer offices, Corporate Banking assets generated in the U.K. and Europe have*

increased sharply over the past year. Return on these assets has also improved. Scotiabank is looking for continued strong growth in this market, based on an ability to respond quickly to market opportunities with creative corporate financing packages. [p. 16]

United States banks appeared to be approaching 1992 cautiously, targeting the large corporate and government borrowers; high net worth individuals for their private banking services; and selected segments in the securities business, particularly international securities. Some U.S. banks, including Citicorp and Morgan, provided European products and services to a select Canadian client list, particularly in the capital markets and for syndicated loans. Other banks had sold European subsidiaries. Citicorp was likely to be the only U.S. bank with a Pan-European presence. Overall, U.S. banks had considerable respect for the power of the small number of national banks firmly entrenched in each domestic market.

Japanese banks were establishing branches and subsidiaries ahead of 1992, when reciprocity might become a problem. The target markets were large borrowers and the European subsidiaries of Japanese multinationals. These banks were emphasizing securities activities as well because they needed financial assets to sell in Japan and because domestic restrictions had caused many corporate finance activities to be moved to Europe, such as the underwriting and distribution of equity warrants for Japanese companies.

Accepting the challenge of 1992 in Europe rather than withdrawing was not at issue for CIBC. The question was how Kluge, Newman, and their teams should position CIBC as a selective specialist against full-service European banks, European specialists, the low-margin Japanese, and the U.S. money center banks. Since financial markets changed so frequently, did it even make sense for CIBC to plan a detailed product strategy when its existing flexible strategy of moving into niches to exploit new market opportunities had yielded improved profits for the past few years? These profits, however, had declined as a share of total bank profits. In addition, some of the previously profitable niche markets had not proved defensible as competitors eventually noted their above-average profitability and moved in, driving down margins. The Canadian dollar Eurobond market was an example.

Another relevant issue would be the structuring of account management, although Kluge felt that the challenge would be the same after 1992 as before. In such markets as France, Germany, and Italy, CIBC had always had to balance national representation and geographic expertise with product specialists in treasury and securities, corporate finance, or trade finance, and with other managers with industry specializations such as real estate, chemicals, and petroleum.

Senior management also wanted to marry CIBC accounts with the investment banking skills of Wood Gundy. In 1988, Wood Gundy and Union Bank of Switzerland (UBS) vied for the number one position worldwide in the Canadian dollar sector of the Eurobond market; UBS won by a deciding transaction just before the market closed for Christmas. There was a lot of European business for Wood Gundy even in the Canadian dollar sector of the Eurobond market since interest rate swaps meant that issuers were less concerned than in the past with the currency involved. The existing strategy of industry specialization, relying on local advice for sensitive account information and calling on product specialists as necessary, seemed to be working well.

Finally, management had to consider what types of market research would be most helpful in sorting out the unknown or questionable elements in their strategy. One of the market research tools most widely used by CIBC was syndicated market studies. These studies were available through Greenwich Associates and covered a number of geographically defined markets, from the large corporate market to specific markets such as foreign exchange and securities markets. They provided valuable insight into the bank's competitive situation by using customer attitudes toward CIBC and its competitors to help identify strengths and weaknesses. Custom-designed research was also used when a specific need was identified, and secondary research provided valuable ongoing input on market dynamics.

CONCLUSION

Newman and the private banking staff received an electronic mail message one afternoon in January 1989, asking them for a summary of their situation analysis and marketing strategy recommendations in preparation for 1992. The summary was to include product recommendations given the likelihood of more intense European competition both in national markets and from Pan-European banks — such as Citicorp, Deutsche Bank, or Barclays — whose networks reached all corners of the world.

EDITORS' COMMENTARY

What role should CIBC play in Europe? At a minimum, it should service the needs of its principal multinational customers to the extent that such service is necessary to defend and reinforce its core business in North America. This defensive approach was being pursued by other foreign banks. In May 1989, for example, the Royal Bank of Canada announced the sale of several European subsidiaries to focus on corporate banking services for large companies having or seeking solid connections with North America. The profitability of such strategies was likely to be limited by the increasing preference among corporate treasurers of multinationals to source their financial services from multiple banks at lowest prices rather than to emphasize convenience by securing all their needs from one or two banks.

In the face of increased competition from the full service EC banks, EC specialist financial institutions, U.S. money center banks, and the low-margin Japanese banks, CIBC's only viable role in Europe is as a niche player. The strategic question is how CIBC should define its niche — by focusing on specific products and services, on specific countries, or on specific types of customers? Variations in profitability make defining the niche especially important. For example, Eurobonds have declined in profitability, and the price sensitivity of the large multinationals is increasing. At the same time, most analysts believed that customized, selective markets would experience less incremental price competition as a result on the 1992 reforms than would be evident in credit and payment services.

While a niche approach is essential, CIBC should not define its strategy too rigidly. Doing so might preclude the kind of profitable opportunism displayed by CIBC's U.K. management, which identified new market opportunities and developed creative financial packages to exploit them before imitative competitors drove margins down. Permitting such local initiatives boosts profits and enables CIBC to attract quality management with an entrepreneurial flair despite being a niche player.

CHAPTER *9*

Managing the Product Line

Nissan Motor Company, Ltd. and the Automobile Market

EDITORS' INTRODUCTION

European automobile manufacturers have long been concerned about the negative impact of open Japanese competition on their share of sales. Though the Japanese have voluntarily limited their exports to 10% of the EC car market, France, Italy, and Spain have continued to maintain their own severe bilateral quotas on imported Japanese cars. The 1992 market integration program promises to end these quotas.

Nissan has been a long-standing player in the European automobile market, having exported its first cars to Finland in 1959. Nissan was also one of the first Japanese car manufacturers to respond to protectionist sentiment against Japanese imports by investing in a £735 million assembly plant in Europe. Nissan has a lesser share than Toyota in the domestic Japanese market but a larger share in Europe; thus the success of Nissan's European strategy is vital to its overall performance.

The issue facing Nissan management is how to take advantage of the opening up of the southern European countries once bilateral quotas are removed. In particular, Nissan must decide whether to emphasize an upper-medium-size car, the Bluebird, or a small-size car, the Micra, in its initial efforts to penetrate these countries. This decision requires consideration of such factors as sales and profit streams, likely competitive retaliation, and the best way to establish the Nissan brand and strong dealer networks in the three countries.

Nissan Motor Co., Ltd.: Marketing Strategy for the European Market

Kyoichi Ikeo and John A. Quelch

In February 1989, in anticipation of the European Community (EC) market integration in 1992, Kiyoshi Sekiguchi, general manager, and Shu Gomi, deputy general manager, European sales group of Nissan Motor Co., Ltd., were discussing how to expand Nissan's market penetration in three principal southern European countries: France, Italy, and Spain.

Japanese carmakers had voluntarily limited their total exports to Europe to a ceiling of about 10% of the EC market, which accounted for 90% of the total Western European market. In addition, France, Italy, and Spain had imposed severe restrictions on Japanese imports, resulting in quite small sales of Nissan in these countries. However, because Nissan started to export the Bluebird (equivalent to its Stanza model in the United States), which was manufactured in its U.K. factory, to the European continent in late 1988 and because the restrictions by individual EC countries on Japanese car imports were likely to be relieved at the advent of EC integration, Nissan believed that full-scale penetration into these three European countries would become possible.

Although Sekiguchi and Gomi needed to develop a marketing strategy for the entire European market in light of the tougher competition expected after 1992, the more immediate decision was how much marketing effort to allocate to two models, the 1800-cc upper-medium-sized Bluebird and a supermini car like the Micra (hereafter New Micra). Nissan manufactured the Bluebird in its U.K. factory, but it planned to manufacture the New Micra there as well until 1992. Of course, to serve the markets adequately, it needed to market a complete product line of five or six models, including exports from Japan. Among them, the models that were especially important strategically were the Bluebird and the New Micra. Because resources — especially for advertising — that could be allocated to France, Italy, and Spain were limited, Sekiguchi and Gomi had to decide which model to emphasize and how to promote

EXHIBIT 9.1 Nissan Bluebird and Nissan New Micra

The Nissan Bluebird

The Nissan New Micra

both of them in those countries and then recommend their decision to Yoshikazu Kawana, director of the European sales group. *Exhibit 9.1* shows the current Bluebird and Micra models.

COMPANY BACKGROUND

In 1935, Nissan Motor Co., Ltd., which had been established in 1933 by Gisuke Ayukawa, started the mass production of automobiles in Japan with a small 750-cc car. It eventually grew to include a full-sized 3670-cc car in its product line, expanding its production volume and becoming, along with Toyota and Isuzu, one of the leading companies in the Japanese automobile industry. However, due to shortage of material during

EXHIBIT 9.2 Nonconsolidated statements of income, 1984-1988 (in millions of yen)

	1984[a]	1985	1986	1987	1988
Net sales	3,460,123	3,618,076	3,754,172	3,429,317	3,418,671
Cost of sales	2,811,052	2,943,384	3,099,243	2,948,127	2,882,252
Gross profit	649,071	674,692	654,929	481,190	536,419
Selling, general, and administrative expenses	572,947	585,155	584,870	475,691	470,779
Operating income	76,124	89,537	70,059	5,499	65,640
Other income (expense)					
Interest income	67,559	72,325	70,494	58,989	50,548
Interest expense	(46,012)	(46,190)	(42,237)	(38,428)	(36,594)
Other net[b]	30,377	43,385	10,084	83,652	59,971
Total other income	51,925	69,520	38,341	104,213	73,925
Income before income taxes	128,049	159,057	108,398	109,712	139,565
Income taxes	57,517	84,780	43,648	63,105	100,978
Net income	70,532	74,277	64,750	46,607	38,587

[a]Years ended March 31, 1984-1988.
[b]*Other, net* consists of dividend income, net realized gain on sales of securities, and other sources.

World War II, Nissan was obliged to focus on truck production and to decrease its car output. The end of the war brought its production to a standstill.

Nissan's growth in truck and car production after World War II was due to the special procurement needs of the Korean War and the increased household penetration of cars in Japan beginning in the late 1950s. In particular, the enormous success of the new small-sized cars in the 1960s, when a major portion of vehicle demand moved from trucks and medium-sized cars for business use to small-sized cars for personal use, gave Nissan a firm footing in the Japanese automobile industry.

Exports of Nissan cars started in 1958 and increased from 10,000 units in 1960 to 400,000 in 1970. During the 1970s, partly because of the rise in gasoline prices, high-quality, fuel-efficient Japanese cars dramatically increased their share of the North American market. Nissan exported 1.46 million units in 1980.

By the 1988 fiscal year, Nissan sales totaled 3,400 billion yen. It manufactured 2.16 million units in domestic factories and 0.52 million units in foreign factories, and it exported 1.14 million units from Japan. *Exhibit 9.2* presents Nissan income statements for 1984 to 1988, and *Exhibit 9.3* summarizes total sales, in yen, of Japanese automobile manufacturers for 1983 to 1988.

EXHIBIT 9.3 Total sales of Japanese car manufacturers, 1983–1988 (in millions of yen)

	1983	1984	1985	1986	1987	1988
Nissan	3,187,722	3,460,124	3,618,076	3,754,172	3,429,317	3,418,671
Toyota	4,892,663	5,472,681	6,064,420	6,304,858	6,024,909	6,691,299
Honda	1,746,919	1,846,028	1,929,519	2,245,743	2,334,597	2,650,077[a]
Mazda	1,364,229	1,431,815	1,569,553	1,626,187	1,602,293	1,844,300
Mitsubishi	1,061,375	1,173,631	1,408,307	1,578,823	1,558,670	1,752,697
Isuzu	684,624	769,071	1,016,250	1,013,434	909,915	1,023,300
Suzuki	542,319	524,259	580,841	722,336	744,854	759,550
Subaru	580,052	602,735	672,071	768,424	715,717	686,238
Daihatsu	425,909	469,950	515,911	535,645	557,627	445,665[b]

Source: Company records.
[a]Thirteen months, due to alteration of settlement term.
[b]Nine months, due to alteration of settlement term.

PENETRATING THE EUROPEAN MARKET

Nissan's European market penetration began with exports to Finland in 1959. The company concentrated first on the northern European countries, not entering the EC countries until the late 1960s. Its exports to Europe increased from 3,600 vehicles in 1964 to 163,000 in 1973 and reached 240,000 in 1978.

However, protectionist sentiment against increased car exports from Japan began appearing in several countries in the late 1970s, resulting in the 1981 voluntary ceiling on exports to the United States and various restrictions and surveillances in European countries. Management expected this protectionist atmosphere to continue and decided in 1980 to begin to move local production overseas. In Europe, it acquired Motor Iberica, S.A. to make commercial vehicles in Spain and founded Nissan Motor Manufacturing U.K., Ltd. to make passenger cars in the United Kingdom. These decisive steps were in stark contrast to Toyota's strategy, which placed much less emphasis on local production.

Nissan Motor Iberica, S.A. (NMISA)

In 1980 Nissan acquired a 35.85% equity stake in Motor Iberica, the largest commercial vehicle manufacturer in Spain, participated in its administration, and helped make it a more efficient manufacturer. In 1983, it started to manufacture vehicles under its own brand, gradually increasing its share holdings to 68% by 1989.

In 1988, NMISA manufactured 76,000 commercial vehicles, of which 66% were Nissan's and the rest Motor Iberica's. Of all the commercial vehicles NMISA manufactured, 32% were exported, mainly to other European countries. NMISA's performance was favorable, and its cumulative losses were covered by profits in fiscal year 1988.

Nissan Motor Manufacturing U.K., Ltd. (NMUK)

To manufacture passenger cars, Nissan founded NMUK as a local subsidiary in 1984 and began constructing a factory in Sunderland, near Newcastle, in northeast England. Completed in 1986, the factory produced an upper-medium-sized car called the Bluebird. Because Nissan volunteered to manufacture with 60% value-based local content rising to 80% by 1991, the British government in January 1988 authorized the Bluebird as a U.K.-made car.[1] The EC Commission supported the U.K.

---

[1]Value-based local content was calculated by subtracting from the factory price of the

position. However, the French government insisted that local content had to reach 80% for EC approval and threatened to count U.K.-built Bluebirds against its 3% Japanese import ceiling until they reached 80% local content. The U.K.-made Bluebird began to be exported to other EC member countries in late 1988, by when it had reached 70% local content. In 1988, the Sunderland factory purchased components from 113 European companies. The French government finally conceded that the Bluebird could be exported to France without any restriction or duty, though the possibility of reducing quotas on car imports from Japan to France remained.

Although it would be some time before NMUK would be operating in the black because of the huge initial investment,[2] production volume grew smoothly: 5,079 in 1986, 28,797 in 1987, and 56,744 in 1988. Nissan planned to expand production even further, to 100,000 a year in 1990, when it would introduce a new version of the Bluebird, and to 200,000 by 1992, when it would add the New Micra. By 1988, NMUK had invested 50 billion yen and planned to invest an additional 80 billion yen before full production was reached in 1992. Although Nissan's U.K. cost structure was not publicly available, *Exhibit 9.4*, which shows Nissan's cost structure for selling in the Netherlands, can be treated as an approximation.

MARKET INTEGRATION OF THE EC

A major impact on Nissan's European operations was the planned market integration of the EC in 1992. An integrated EC would liberate the movement of products, services, people, and capital within the Community and consolidate technical standards that hitherto had been determined by individual member countries. Much progress had already been achieved toward harmonization of technical standards for cars. By 1988, 41 of 44 voluntary technical directives proposed in 1970 had been adopted by all EC member states. The remaining three — on tires, windshields and towing weights — were expected to be tabled soon by the

---

car the value of components and materials imported from outside the EC. Some protectionists advocated the use of cost-based local content, which took into account the full production cost, including all overheads as well as design and engineering costs. However, this approach was much harder to monitor and police. Others demanded local manufacturing of specific components such as engines, transmissions, axles, and electronic components. To achieve 80% local content, it was, however, necessary for either engines or transmissions to be locally sourced.

[2] The U.K. government, motivated by the additional employment opportunities the plant would bring to the northeast, contributed £125 million of the investment.

EXHIBIT 9.4 Cost structure of Nissan for selling in the Netherlands

	Nissan's U.K.-made cars		Nissan's Japan-made cars (average)
	Bluebird[a]	New Micra[b]	
Retail price	100%	100%	100%
Dealer margin	18	18	18
Distributor selling price	82	82	82
Distributor margin	12	12	12
Nissan selling price	70	70	70
Transportation cost	3.5	4	8
Duty	0	0	10
Labor cost	8	10	12
Parts & material cost	39	40	32
Overhead & selling cost	12%	10%	3%

Note: Figures are a percentage of retail price, excluding taxes other than duty.
[a]1988 figures.
[b]Estimated figures for the year production began.

European Commission, and all were expected to be made mandatory by 1990, permitting single-type approval for the entire EC market.

Thanks to a more efficient allocation of production facilities, and concentration and reduction of inventories, production and logistics costs were expected by industry analysts to decrease as a result of the 1992 program. According to the EC Commission, such cost reductions were valued at 853 billion yen. If all these cost savings were passed through as lower prices, average retail auto prices would be lowered by 5.7%, and consequently, the market would expand by more than 6%. Market expansion would be especially strong in countries such as Spain and the United Kingdom where harmonization of value-added taxes and excise taxes on cars would substantially reduce retail prices.

At the same time, market integration was expected by analysts to intensify competition in the automobile industry and, thereby, to magnify the differences among companies. Therefore, in preparing for 1992, European auto companies made great efforts to expand, modernize, or reallocate their production resources.

Market integration promised to affect import restrictions on Japanese automobiles. Although the voluntary EC-wide ceiling on all Japanese imports was expected to remain, the bilateral import quotas on

Japanese cars imposed by France, Italy, and Spain had to cease. French officials, in particular, pressed for maintenance of the EC-wide ceiling on Japanese imports, for an 80% EC-wide local content requirement, and for higher exports of EC-made cars to Japan. They were also sensitive to the possibility of Japanese companies shipping U.S.-made cars to Europe to circumvent the EC-wide quota. Realistic observers foresaw a transition period whereby restrictions on Japanese automobile imports would be phased out gradually to give national producers such as Fiat and Renault time to improve the efficiency of their operations before they had to face open Japanese competition.

In addition, the possibility of cost reductions made local production more attractive for the Japanese. In this respect, Nissan had an advantage over other Japanese companies: a proven record in Spain and the United Kingdom. However, the other Japanese automobile companies, such as Toyota and Mazda, were moving toward local production in Europe. *Exhibit 9.5* summarizes these endeavors. Some executives of European automobile companies worried that Japanese local production would bring overcapacity and price erosion to the European market. But countries with no automotive industry, such as Greece and Ireland, welcomed the Japanese as a means of increasing price competition in their markets. In addition, certain EC countries, particularly the United Kingdom, actively sought additional Japanese investment in car production following the decline of their domestic manufacturers.

MIDDLE-RANGE PLAN FOR THE EUROPEAN MARKET

Although Japanese automobile sales in Europe were small when compared with domestic or North American counterparts, there was large potential for growth if their plans for local production were put into practice and EC market integration were carried out. In particular, Nissan, which trailed Toyota and was closely followed by Honda in share of the domestic and North American markets, had capitalized on its competitive advantage in the European market where it had the largest market share among the Japanese companies, thanks in part to its early establishment of local production facilities. *Exhibit 9.6* shows the overall market shares of Japanese and major European companies in the Western European car market.

Given the importance and rapid growth of the European market (car registrations increased 5% in 1988), Nissan management formulated a

EXHIBIT 9.5 Movements of major Japanese automobile companies toward local production in Europe

Company's name	Country	Outline[a]
Nissan	Spain	Manufacturing 76,000 commercial vehicles a year (in 1988).
Nissan	U.K.	Manufacturing 57,000 upper-medium-sized cars a year (in 1988).
Toyota	West Germany	Planning to manufacture 15,000 small trucks a year (from 1989) in a Volkswagen factory in Hanover.
Toyota	U.K.	Planning to manufacture 200,000 upper-medium-sized cars a year (from 1992).
Honda	U.K.	Manufacturing 84,000 medium-sized cars a year (in 1987) jointly with the Rover Group.
Mazda	Spain	Considering the manufacture of 25,000 commercial vehicles a year.
Mazda	Undecided	Considering the manufacture of 200,000 upper-medium-sized cars a year (from 1992) in a Ford factory with which Mazda is affiliated.
Isuzu	U.K.	Manufacturing 5,400 commercial vehicles a year (in 1987) in a joint venture with General Motors.
Suzuki	Spain	Manufacturing 25,000 small four-wheel-drive off-road vehicles a year (in 1987) jointly with Land-Rover Santana.
Subaru	France	Considering the manufacture of 30,000 vehicles a year in northwestern France.

[a]Excludes knockdown productions.

EXHIBIT 9.6 Western Europe — Overall market share in car market, 1983–1988

	1983	1984	1985	1986	1987	1988[a]
VW group[b]	13.02%	13.56%	14.37%	14.70%	14.95%	14.44%
Ford Europe	12.47	12.80	11.90	11.67	11.93	11.45
Fiat group[c]	13.78	14.48	13.74	14.01	14.20	15.35
Peugeot group[d]	11.71	11.50	11.52	11.38	12.12	12.83
GM Europe[e]	11.07	11.04	11.36	10.95	10.55	10.29
Renault group	12.63	10.90	10.65	10.61	10.62	10.34
Total Japanese:	10.06	10.27	10.77	11.71	11.38	11.00
Nissan	2.79	2.83	2.89	3.00	2.93	2.84
Toyota	2.25	2.24	2.58	2.88	2.81	2.66
Honda	1.02	1.14	1.11	1.17	1.03	1.11
Mazda	2.01	1.97	1.91	2.05	1.90	1.88
Mitsubishi	0.98	1.09	1.10	1.21	1.22	1.10
Suzuki	0.42	0.43	0.47	0.58	0.65	0.66
Subaru	0.29	0.30	0.38	0.44	0.45	0.40
Daihatsu	0.27%	0.24%	0.28%	0.32%	0.30%	0.25%

Source: DRI World Automotive Forecast Report.
[a]Estimate.
[b]VW group consisted of Volkswagen and Audi until 1985. In 1986, SEAT joined the VW group.
[c]Fiat group consisted of Fiat, Autobianchi, Lancia, and Ferrari until 1986. In 1987, Alfa Romeo joined the Fiat group.
[d]Peugeot group includes Peugeot, Citroen, and Talbot.
[e]GM Europe includes Opel and Vauxhall.

plan in the fall of 1988 to strengthen its competitive position until 1992. The main goals to be achieved by 1992 were as follows:

1. Raise Nissan's market share in the European car market to 4.5% by 1992 and increase car production in the United Kingdom to 200,000 and truck production in Spain to 100,000.
2. Improve Nissan's brand image by reinforcing the quality of its sales and service organizations in Europe.
3. Further decentralize Nissan's responsibility for European operations, including product design, production, marketing, and sales.

According to the plan, Nissan's sales increase in Europe would be accomplished mainly through its U.K.-made cars, because exports from Japan had to contend with trade restrictions, political friction, and a decrease in per unit contribution and price competitiveness due to appreciation of the yen. Reinforcing the sales and service organization and localizing overall European operations were measures to achieve the market penetration needed to justify increased production, achieve further scale economies, and increase productivity.

To coordinate European operations, Nissan established a European Technical Center (NETC) in the United Kingdom in 1988 and planned to start the operation of Nissan Europe N.V. in the Netherlands in 1990. Whereas Nissan had previously developed all of its products in Japan, NETC would through the combined efforts of Japanese and European staff produce new cars to meet European consumer needs. Moreover, because models for local production, which were designed in Japan, often required special orders from European parts suppliers, materials costs increased. NETC's objective was to design cars that incorporated standard parts available in Europe at lower costs — for example, a new Bluebird model to be launched in 1990, the New Micra to be launched by 1992, and any new commercial vehicles that would be manufactured in Spain.

Nissan Europe N.V. would be responsible for coordinating all development, production, logistics, and marketing in Europe, most of which had been done in Tokyo. And it would formulate overall marketing strategy for Europe, in place of the Europe Sales Group in Tokyo. Distributors in each country would continue to draft national marketing plans that were integrated with the regional plan.

Furthermore, Nissan Europe would play a key role in consolidating logistics under EC integration, which would facilitate the free flow of goods within the EC community and unify the technical standards. Nissan's plan was to gather orders from local distributors in each country and to relay them to the United Kingdom, Spain, and Tokyo. Also, Nissan Europe would totally oversee the transportation from each factory to each dealer via the large-scale collection and delivery center and predelivery inspection facility, which were under construction in Amsterdam. Therefore, transportation and inventory functions for cars and commercial vehicles, which had been shared by Nissan and local distributors, would be performed by Nissan Europe and its subsidiary logistics company. The only logistics function left to distributors would be that for parts.

TRENDS IN THE EUROPEAN MARKET

The European car market in 1987 comprised 12.4 million units, one-third of the total world market, and 10 million of these sales were accounted for by five countries: West Germany, the United Kingdom, France, Italy, and Spain. *Exhibit 9.7* shows new car sales in European countries and other major markets. *Exhibits 9.8* and *9.9* provide new car sales data for European countries in 1987 and 1988. *Exhibits 9.10* and *9.11* provide market segmentation data for each major European country. *Exhibit 9.12* shows profiles of European countries. *Exhibit 9.13* profiles Nissan's distributors, and *Exhibit 9.14* lists the car models Nissan marketed in Europe and their retail list price ranges.

To catch up to the Japanese, European car makers needed to improve productivity by one-third; it took Japanese workers 20 hours to assemble a car, whereas the European average was 36 hours and the U.S., 26½ hours. While local content restrictions were designed to make Japanese assembly in Europe more costly, industry analysts believed that, even with a 90% requirement, Japanese plants in Europe would be more efficient than those run by the European manufacturers.

West Germany

West Germany had the largest car market in Europe, with sales of about 3 million units a year and no restrictions imposed on imports; therefore, Japanese companies were able to achieve considerable car sales. However, with highly competitive companies like Volkswagen, the West German market was regarded as having the stiffest competition in Europe. Generally, West German consumers, known as serious readers of car magazines, were knowledgeable about cars and apt to consider numerous data before purchasing. *Table A* shows the relative importance of product attributes in major European countries. Regarding vehicle size,

TABLE A Relative importance of product attributes by country

	West Germany	United Kingdom	France	Italy	Spain
Performance	*	*			
Fuel economy					*
Price		*	*	*	*
Styling			*		
Quality	*				
Accessories				*	
Maintenance	*				

Source: Estimate of Mr. Shu Gomi, deputy general manager
Note: An asterisk (*) indicates a particularly important attribute. Its absence does not mean a lack of importance.

EXHIBIT 9.7 New car sales — Overall world market, 1983–1989 (000s of units)

	1983	1984	1985	1986	1987	1988[a]	1989[a]
West Germany	2,427	2,394	2,379	2,829	2,916	2,730	2,660
France	2,018	1,758	1,766	1,912	2,105	2,217	2,146
United Kingdom	1,792	1,750	1,832	1,882	2,014	2,195	1,939
Italy	1,581	1,636	1,746	1,825	1,977	2,131	2,002
Spain	547	520	572	686	925	1,039	1,089
Netherlands	459	461	496	561	556	485	550
Belgium	339	352	360	395	406	435	426
Other EC countries	329	342	388	402	353	388	531
EC total	9,492	9,213	9,539	10,492	11,252	11,620	11,343
Sweden	217	231	263	270	316	331	352
Switzerland	274	267	265	300	303	322	327
Other western European countries	486	450	540	572	509	505	599
Western European total	10,469	10,161	10,607	11,634	12,380	12,778	12,621
United States	9,181	10,393	11,043	11,452	10,227	10,699	10,623
Canada	842	964	1,137	1,089	1,057	1,013	1,196
North American total	10,023	11,357	12,180	12,541	11,284	11,712	11,819
Japan	3,136	3,096	3,104	3,146	3,275	3,609	3,497
World total	29,151	30,289	31,821	33,049	32,657	34,277	35,528

Source: DRI World Automotive Forecast Report.

[a]Estimate.

EXHIBIT 9.8 New car sales in major European countries, 1987 (000s of units)

	West Germany	France	United Kingdom	Italy	Spain	Netherlands	Belgium	Sweden	Switzerland
Total	2,915.7	2,105.2	2,013.7	1,976.5	924.8	555.7	406.2	316.0	303.3
By manufacturer:									
VW group	872.2	159.3	116.2	225.8	161.2	63.0	65.6	37.7	50.0
Ford Europe	300.8	143.4	580.1	78.4	142.1	56.0	39.5	34.3	21.2
Fiat group	132.8	151.8	74.3	1,179.9	69.6	35.3	18.5	8.2	29.5
Peugeot group	123.3	703.5	147.3	148.8	154.2	65.0	57.3	11.0	25.1
GM Europe	453.3	96.8	270.8	57.3	130.1	88.6	46.8	31.1	37.6
Renault group	89.6	641.7	78.7	154.2	209.4	22.6	35.3	5.1	16.6
Total Japanese[a]	441.4	63.1	225.4	13.7	6.8	144.0	83.5	68.5	87.6
Nissan	84.5	17.8	114.2	0.0	2.1	31.3	19.4	18.1	13.7
Toyota	93.3	14.3	38.3	2.0	2.1	31.2	26.8	22.8	26.6
Honda	41.5	10.2	24.7	0.2	0.5	11.9	8.5	4.1	7.6
Mazda	91.0	16.6	18.8	0.0	0.5	24.5	10.6	13.9	8.1
Mitsubishi	68.6	3.3	11.8	0.7	1.0	15.3	9.6	3.6	11.1
Suzuki	27.1	0.9	5.6	9.9	0.4	18.0	3.3	2.4	4.1
Subaru	16.7	0.0	5.0	0.4	0.1	4.7	3.0	1.8	14.3
Daihatsu	13.0	0.0	4.6	0.5	0.0	7.1	2.3	1.7	1.4

Source: DRI World Automotive Forecast Report.

[a]Total Japanese in Italy and Spain exceed the quotas on car imports from Japan because some parts of commercial vehicles, manufactured by Nissan and Suzuki in Spain and knocked down by Toyota and Mitsubishi in Portugal, are counted as passenger cars. Furthermore, in the case of Italy, indirect imports via other European countries boost the sales of Japanese cars.

EXHIBIT 9.9 Estimated new car sales in major European countries, 1988 (000s of units)

	West Germany	France	United Kingdom	Italy	Spain	Netherlands	Belgium	Sweden	Switzerland
Total	2,730.2	2,216.8	2,195.4	2,030.9	1,039.2	484.8	435.0	331.3	322.1
By manufacturer:									
VW group	797.0	168.8	125.4	220.3	196.5	54.7	70.7	36.8	50.9
Ford Europe	269.9	139.2	582.2	79.6	152.9	50.6	44.5	34.0	21.5
Fiat group	138.9	217.1	86.6	1,211.7	85.4	29.4	16.3	7.6	31.0
Peugeot group	108.4	740.2	187.1	165.1	197.4	60.6	65.6	14.7	23.9
GM Europe	418.4	104.1	302.2	71.6	136.6	69.0	50.4	28.7	38.4
Renault group	84.8	639.4	84.4	148.0	217.7	21.3	38.9	4.7	16.6
Total Japanese	390.0	65.0	247.5	10.7	8.3	127.5	88.4	81.4	100.0
Nissan	71.9	18.7	132.6	0.2	2.8	23.9	20.5	19.8	13.5
Toyota	77.2	14.9	39.2	0.6	2.2	23.3	29.1	25.5	31.0
Honda	45.7	10.6	25.9	0.5	0.6	12.0	9.0	5.5	8.3
Mazda	82.6	17.2	20.4	0.1	0.6	24.5	9.8	18.3	12.3
Mitsubishi	55.0	3.0	12.4	0.8	1.0	13.1	9.4	6.0	13.1
Suzuki	26.7	0.6	5.9	7.8	1.0	18.2	3.8	3.3	4.7
Subaru	13.7	0.0	4.5	0.2	0.1	5.1	3.3	1.6	14.1
Daihatsu	10.7	0.0	3.4	0.5	0.0	7.3	3.2	1.2	1.7

Source: DRI World Automotive Forecast Report.

EXHIBIT 9.10 New car sales by segment, 1987 (000s of units)

	West Germany	France	United Kingdom	Italy	Spain
Total sales	2,915.7	2,105.2	2,013.7	1,976.6	924.8
By segment:					
Utility	2.22%	4.06%	2.30%	18.50% ⎫	43.0%[a]
Supermini	14.46	40.31	25.51	38.94 ⎭	
Lower-medium	35.62	23.03	34.41	25.37	37.1
Upper-medium	22.92	22.25	25.48	8.06	13.9
Executive	24.76%	10.35%	12.31%	9.14%	6.0%[b]

Source: DRI World Automotive Forecast Report and company records.

[a]Includes Utility and Supermini.

[b]Includes sports cars such as the Nissan 300ZX. In other countries, sports cars are included in each segment according to vehicle size.

Note: Typical models included in each segment are the following:

Utility — Fiat 126, Renault R4, Suzuki Cervo; *Supermini* — Fiat Uno, Ford Fiesta, Nissan New Micra, Peugeot 104, Toyota Starlet, VW Polo; *Lower-Medium* — Fiat Tipo, Ford Escort, Honda Civic, Nissan Sunny, Nissan Violet, Toyota Corolla, Toyota Tercel, VW Golf; *Upper-Medium* — Audi 80/90, Ford Capri, Honda Accord, Nissan Bluebird, Nissan Prairie, Renault Fuego, Toyota Camry, Toyota Carina; and *Executive* — Audi 100/200, BMW (all models), Honda Legend, Mazda RX7, Nissan Cedric/Laurel, Nissan 280/300ZX, Nissan Silvia, Toyota Celica, Toyota Crown, Toyota Supra.

EXHIBIT 9.11 New car sales of Japanese companies by segment, 1987 (000s of units)

	West Germany	France	United Kingdom	Italy
Nissan				
Supermini	21.8	5.1	38.9	0.0
Lower-medium	31.6	6.2	36.7	0.0
Upper-medium	25.0	4.8	35.3	0.0
Executive	6.2	1.7	3.3	0.0
Toyota				
Supermini	16.6	0.0	1.2	0.0
Lower-medium	39.0	7.9	17.1	0.0
Upper-medium	28.7	3.1	9.8	0.0
Executive	9.0	3.3	10.1	2.0
Honda				
Supermini	0.1	0.0	0.0	0.0
Lower-medium	19.3	5.2	5.8	0.0
Upper-medium	21.9	4.8	18.2	0.2
Executive	0.2	0.2	0.8	0.0
Mazda				
Supermini	0.0	0.0	0.0	0.0
Lower-medium	47.9	9.7	11.9	0.0
Upper-medium	40.0	5.6	6.2	0.0
Executive	3.0	1.2	0.7	0.0

Source: DRI World Automotive Forecast Report.

EXHIBIT 9.12 Profiles of major European countries, 1987

	West Germany	France	United Kingdom	Italy	Spain	Nether-lands	Belgium	Sweden	Switzerland
Car sales (000)	2,915.7	2,105.2	2,013.7	1,976.5	924.8	555.7	406.2	316.0	303.3
Commercial vehicle sales (000)	113.7	369.4	252.8	163.0	170.0	69.6	28.8	29.5	24.3
Nissan's commercial vehicle sales (000)	2.9	3.1	10.5	4.0	33.7	3.1	1.5	2.8	1.3
Total sales (000)	3,029.4	2,474.6	2,266.5	2,139.5	1,094.8	625.3	435.0	345.5	327.6
Car production (000)	4,374	3,052	1,143	1,713	1,403	125	277	432	0
Car export (000)	2,451	1,681	226	641	707	112	228	340	0
Car import (000)	1,012	760	1,041	780	188	535	NA	226	NA
Number of cars per 1,000 people	468	385	360	392	264	340	351	400	423
Car price index[a] (exclusive of tax)	128	128	144	129	151	122	121	NA	NA
Car price index[a] (inclusive of tax)	105	124	129	112	139	135	109	NA	NA

Source: DRI World Automotive Forecast Report; BEUC Car Report; company records.

[a]The EC market with the lowest price is indexed at 100 in both cases.

EXHIBIT 9.13 Profiles of Nissan's distributors in major European countries

Country	Name of distributor	% of shares held by Nissan	No. of dealers	No. of Nissan employees
West Germany	Nissan Motor Deutschland	100%	734	4
France	Richard-Nissan	9.6	203	1
United Kingdom	Nissan U.K.	0	450	0
Italy	Nissan Italia	64.2	160	2
Spain	Nissan Motor Iberica	68	148	19
Netherlands	Nissan Motor Nederland	100	170	3
Belgium	N.V. Nissan Belgium	0	345	0
Sweden	Philipson Bil	0	50	0
Switzerland	Nissan Motor Schweiz	100%	284	3

Source: Company records.

EXHIBIT 9.14 Marketed car models and their retail list price ranges in major European countries (¥ thousands)

| Name in Europe: | 300ZX | Laurel | Maxima | Bluebird | Silvia | Sunny | New Micra | Prairie | Sunny-Wagon |
| Name in U.S.: | 300ZX | | Maxima | Stanza | 200SX | Sentra | New Micra | Stanza-Wagon | Sentra-Wagon |
Name in Japan:	Fairlady	Laurel	Bluebird	Auster	Silvia	Sunny	March	Prairie	Sunny-California
West Germany	4,088	2,023–2,138	2,861–3,035	1,613–1,873	2,791–2,962	1,315–1,912	962–1,179	2,093 2,512	
France	4,386–5,256			1,675–2,360	2,670[a]	1,364–2,308	972–1,262	2,027	
United Kingdom	4,533–5,394	3,339	undecided	2,110–2,965	3,440[a]	1,721 2,645	1,246 1,588	2,369–2,743[a]	1,453
Italy				undecided	3,689		undecided		
Spain	7,095			2,543–2,917	undecided	2,668	undecided	undecided	
Netherlands	5,493	2,872		1,788–2,257		1,260–2,347	1,086		1,046
Belgium	3,974–5,072	2,110–2,474		1,527–1,764	2,722–3,171	1,266–1,752	825–1,106	1,589	1,172
Sweden				2,056–2,144	2,826	1,645–2,215	1,373–1,416	2,661	
Switzerland	4,323			1,643–2,108	2,705–2,870	1,346–1,931	984–1,206	1,890–2,545	

Source: Company records.
[a]Old model is being marketed.

models larger than the Supermini had a large market share, especially when compared with their share in the southern European countries.

Among Japanese competitors, Mazda focused on West Germany, where it had a relatively high market share, followed by Toyota and then Nissan. Although Nissan hoped to increase its market share in West Germany as production volume in its U.K. factory increased, it was thought that the market could absorb only a limited quantity.

West Germany took the most liberal view toward Japanese competition in the automobile industry because its car companies dominated other EC car manufacturers in the Japanese market, holding a 2% market share (80,000 units) by 1988. In addition, an open EC car market with the French, Spanish, and Italian bilateral quotas removed would mean that the bulk of imported Japanese cars would no longer be forced on the northern EC countries as was currently the case.

United Kingdom

A unique feature of the U.K. market was that fleet sales, purchases by companies for use by their employees, accounted for more than half of the total car sales. Because most of the fleet sales were of upper-medium-sized 1600-cc to 2000-cc cars, this class held about a 25% unit share of the total car market. The U.K.-made Bluebird was an upper-medium-sized car suitable for fleet sales.

In addition to the voluntary ceiling on all Japanese imports to EC countries, Japanese car imports in the United Kingdom were limited to 11% of the total market by a gentlemen's agreement between each country's associations of automobile manufacturers. But, because Nissan's sales were so high when this casual agreement was made, it obtained a very favorable import quota, gaining 6% of the market, the largest share of all the Japanese imports, and vying with Volkswagen for fourth position in the market, following Ford, GM, and Peugeot. Owing to the growth of the U.K. market, Nissan sales reached more than 100,000, representing 35% of its European unit sales. Also, the U.K.-made Bluebird was sold mostly in the U.K. market from 1986 to 1988, partly because until 1987 the EC had treated it as a Japanese import.

On January 27, 1989, Toyota announced that it would construct a factory in the United Kingdom to manufacture, beginning in 1992, 200,000 units a year of an upper-medium-sized 1800-cc car. The local content was set to start at 60% and reach 80% as soon as possible. Local production by Toyota would inevitably make competition more severe because a considerable portion of Toyota's U.K.-made cars had to be sold in the U.K. market. Therefore, the extent to which Nissan could depend on the U.K. market was more circumscribed; when it increased U.K. production, it needed to depend more heavily on exports to the European continent.

The local distributor was Nissan U.K., which was 100%-owned by a local businessman and had 450 dealers. Nissan U.K. was an excellent distributor, as shown by its market share in the United Kingdom; however, Nissan wished to increase its own influence over marketing in the United Kingdom and to coordinate it under a single strategy for Europe and therefore planned to acquire the distributor. But negotiations between the two had not been successful so far, and it was somewhat uncertain that Nissan could control the marketing and logistics in the United Kingdom as it did in other countries.

France

Although France had a large car market, with about 2.2 million units a year, total imports of Japanese cars were limited to five manufacturers: Toyota, Nissan, Mitsubishi, Honda, and Mazda, which shared 3% of the market. The supermini class was the largest segment, followed by the lower- and upper-medium-sized cars. French consumers were thought to be price conscious and less sensitive to quality than consumers in West Germany and the Netherlands.

The French automobile companies, Peugeot and Renault, held more than a 60% market share, and the total share of imported cars was only one-third. Despite having the largest market share, Peugeot had not achieved productivity as high as had the Japanese manufacturers and, therefore, attempted to enlarge and modernize its production facilities in preparation for 1992. However, Renault was heavily in debt and lacked the capital to make substantial investments to raise productivity.

Nissan's marketing organization in France was weak because sales had been restricted. The exclusive distributor, Richard-Nissan S.A., of which Nissan owned 9.6%, was limited in management and marketing capability. Thus, Nissan was making efforts to strengthen the capability of Richard-Nissan. Richard-Nissan served 203 dealers in France, most of which sold only Japanese-made cars and Nissan's Spanish-made commercial vehicles. However, these dealers were relatively small in size, varying from family-run shops with 3 to 4 employees to companies with about 20 employees.

Italy

The Italian car market, highly restricted since 1957, represented about 2 million units a year; however, in 1988, Japanese car imports were restricted to only 3,300 units, of which 750 were off-road vehicles. Fiat, which was the largest automobile company in Italy, held the highest market share not only in Italy (60%) but in all of Europe (15.5%), due in part to its dominance of the domestic market and the launch of a successful new lower-medium-sized car. However, 54% of its sales were in Italy. Expecting an end to the Italian market's restrictive quota on Japanese imports by 1992, Fiat aggressively increased its investment in production facilities and R&D, shortened the time to develop new products, and improved productivity.

A unique characteristic of the Italian car market was the large market share of the utility-class car. Italian consumers, like the French and Spanish, but unlike the other Europeans, tended to be price rather than quality sensitive.

Nissan sold through 160 dealerships organized under Nissan Italia S.p.A., a joint venture of Nissan (64.2%) and NMISA (35.8%). However, because the company's car imports had been so restricted, these dealers were experienced mainly in selling Spanish-manufactured commercial vehicles, which accounted for 6,200 units in 1988. Therefore, because the average dealership had fewer than ten employees and sold other companies' vehicles as well as Nissan's, sales performance was not strong. Nissan Italia planned to recruit or establish larger dealerships that were expected to stock Nissan vehicles only.

Spain

The car market in Spain expanded rapidly from a plateau of 500,000 units in 1985 to more than 1 million units in 1988. However, in 1988, the total Japanese quota was still only 3,200 units, including imports via other EC countries. This quota was slated to increase to about 7,000 in 1990 and, eventually, be integrated into the voluntary ceiling on total Japanese imports into EC countries.

Spanish market characteristics were similar to those in France and Italy; car demand concentrated on utility, supermini, and lower-medium classes, and price tended to be more important than quality.

Although Spain's car market was the fifth-largest in Europe in unit sales, it had outstripped the United Kingdom in production to become the fourth-largest since 1984, because of heavy investment by foreign companies attracted by lower labor costs and Spain's entry into the EC. However, all Spanish car manufacturers were controlled by foreign companies. Among them, SEAT, an affiliate of Volkswagen, was positioned as a base for manufacturing smaller cars for southern Europe and considered fairly competitive.

Japanese companies had little business presence in passenger cars. However, regarding commercial vehicles, Nissan carried out local production through NMISA and held about a 20% market share in 1987. Also, Suzuki bought 17% of a local commercial vehicle manufacturer, Land-Rover Santana S.A., which made a small four-wheel-drive off-road vehicle in Spain.

Although NMISA had 143 dealers for selling its commercial vehicles, it served also as a local distributor of Nissan's passenger cars. With 70 to 80 employees, the dealerships were on average relatively larger than those in other European countries. But, because they handled mostly commercial vehicles, they had very limited experience in selling passenger cars. Recognizing the need to alter the dealerships, Nissan asked them to meet appropriate standards as to space, appearance, capital, organization, and other qualities conducive to selling passenger cars.

Other Countries

In addition to the "Big Five," the Japanese held more than a 30% market share in countries such as Ireland, Denmark, Finland, Norway, and Austria, which had no automobile industry and no restrictions on car imports. Even in other European countries, such as the Netherlands, Belgium, Sweden, and Switzerland, the Japanese held more than a 20% market share, except in Portugal, where quotas were enforced. Consequently, room for raising market share was limited. Also, because individual market sizes were small, Nissan could not depend much on additional sales in these countries as it expanded production in the United Kingdom.

However, the three major southern European markets — France, Italy, and Spain — were large in size and underexploited due to import restrictions. And in Italy and Spain, the U.K.-made Bluebird was expected to be approved for import as an EC-made car. Even in France, importation was close to being conceded, though some uncertainties remained. Therefore, it was mostly agreed within Nissan that to increase sales in Europe on a large scale, exploiting these three markets would be critical.

PROMOTION STRATEGY

Sekiguchi and Gomi consulted with their colleagues on Nissan's marketing strategy for southern Europe. All agreed that the European market was important and that the three southern countries needed to be exploited in order to retain the competitive advantage in Europe. And they agreed to market five or six car models, including the Bluebird and the New Micra, in the three countries. The major issue was how to allocate marketing resources between the two U.K.-made models, because both cars were strategically important yet available marketing funds for the three countries were limited.

The most significant constraint was on the advertising budget. Nissan advertising in Europe was placed by Nissan itself, by national distributors, and by local dealers. Nissan's advertising copy was created first in English, translated into the appropriate language, and exposed to all European countries at the same time with the same message. Consequently, it was not that easy to stress a particular model for a particular country.

Advertising by each local distributor was prepared separately, though guided by Nissan's total marketing strategy for Europe. Distributor advertisements were paid for mostly out of their 12% margins and placed mainly in print media. The importance of television advertising was increasing, though its role was still relatively limited compared with that in North America or Japan. Recently, the West German distributor, planning to run a large-scale TV campaign, had asked Nissan to bear some part of the cost. In France, Italy, and Spain the distributors' small sales volumes restricted the level of their advertising budgets. Any mass medium advertising in these markets would therefore have to focus on either the Bluebird or the New Micra, even if Nissan or Nissan Europe provided supplemental funds.

Dealer advertisements, which were placed mostly in print media, were often funded by local distributors — so long as the advertising met certain content criteria — usually up to 50% of their cost. These allowances to dealers reduced correspondingly the size of distributor advertising budgets.

BLUEBIRD VS. NEW MICRA

Executives supporting the New Micra pointed to the relatively faster growth in sales of small cars and emphasized that a higher percentage of consumers in the southern European countries purchased smaller cars. They asserted that these markets where more potential demand existed should be targeted. And, to establish strong distribution channels, Nissan needed a rapid sales increase, which was more likely to be accomplished by the New Micra than the Bluebird.

That the New Micra would not face direct competition with other Japanese companies was another important factor in its favor. Nissan felt uneasy about competitors of similar background and image, though it would also have to compete with local European companies. But the only other Japanese car company currently engaged in local production was Honda, which jointly manufactured medium-sized cars with the Rover Group in the United Kingdom. Although Toyota decided to start local production in the United Kingdom in 1992 and needed to exploit the French, Italian, and Spanish markets for the same reasons as Nissan, the model to be manufactured in the Toyota U.K. factory was an upper-medium-sized car. Moreover, Nissan executives were confident that no other Japanese car company could manufacture in Europe a supermini-class car like the New Micra, at least not before 1992. Therefore, the New Micra would be insulated from direct Japanese competition for a while.

One of the major reasons for supporting the Bluebird was that its profit margin per unit was higher than that for the New Micra. Also, emphasizing the Bluebird would generate further increases in unit profit contribution because of experience curve and scale economy effects in the U.K. factory. If the New Micra were emphasized, reaching break-even on Bluebird production in the U.K. factory would be delayed.

Another reason for supporting the Bluebird was the probability that the New Micra would attract more attention among Nissan's European competitors. Major southern European car companies like Fiat, Peugeot, and Renault, which were very influential in automobile-related policy making in their respective countries, focused mainly on the small-sized-car market, especially in southern Europe. Accordingly, stressing the New Micra meant head-on competition with these companies and, in the long term, could cause further trade friction, which in turn might result in regulations detrimental to Japanese car companies.

Furthermore, Nissan's image in Europe had to be considered. Formerly, European countries had been in advance of Japan in developing the medium- or small-sized car; therefore, Japanese car designers had some yearning for the European car. Then, Japanese car companies became competitive in the North American and European markets by improving production technology and manufacturing efficiencies. However, differing from North America, where the Japanese had earlier faced no direct local competition for medium- or small-sized cars, Europe had had several competitive local manufacturers in those classes of car. Thus, in Europe, the Japanese car had long been regarded as low-priced, and higher-priced Japanese cars had tended to sell poorly. But the image of Japanese cars was improving and they were now regarded as superior in quality to French and Italian cars, though still inferior to the West German.

At the same time, each Japanese company tried to create its own unique image. For example, Toyota featured high performance, Honda emphasized upgraded value-added cars, and Mazda focused on building market share in sophisticated, performance-oriented West Germany, making special efforts to develop cars tailored to the European market. Among these competitors, Nissan was seen as an average Japanese car maker. Hence, it sometimes happened that Nissan perpetuated the low-priced car image of the Japanese car, and focusing on the New Micra would reinforce this view.

However, in the three southern European countries, Nissan was not a well-known name, except in Spain, thanks to its locally produced commercial vehicles. Because sales were currently low due to import restrictions, Nissan executives believed it would be important to raise awareness immediately upon the lifting of the restrictions in order to obtain a favorable competitive position in these countries. The New Micra, with its broader appeal and promise of higher unit sales volume, seemed to be the model to emphasize.

EDITORS' COMMENTARY

After the Micra and the Bluebird are in production in Europe, which model should Nissan emphasize in trying to penetrate the southern European markets once its bilateral quotas on Japanese car imports are rescinded? More marketing resources should be allocated to the Micra for three principal reasons.

First, Nissan already has proportionately more of its sales than its Japanese competition in the small-car segment in those northern European countries where Japanese cars are already widely available. To emphasize the Micra in southern Europe would play to Nissan's existing strengths.

Second, the small-car segment is proportionately larger in the southern European markets. In addition, the consumer's perceived purchase risk would be lower for the small Micra than for the higher-priced Bluebird. For these reasons, Nissan's unit sales would be higher if the Micra were given more emphasis (though the Bluebird's unit contribution would be higher). As a result, Nissan would be able to build its brand name recognition and distribution network more rapidly. Satisfied Micra customers might trade up to the Bluebird later.

Third, competition among the Japanese manufacturers in southern Europe is likely to be more intense in the upper-medium segment than in the small-car segment. Neither Toyota nor Mazda will be able to manufacture two models in Europe before 1992, and both are likely to produce upper-medium cars first. Aggressive marketing of the Bluebird by Nissan would expand the size of the upper-medium segment but would also unfortunately prepare the market for a subsequent entry by Toyota with its much larger resources. On the other hand, focusing on the Micra would enable Nissan to enjoy any halo effect for Japanese quality that might result as other Japanese manufacturers battle in the upper-medium segment.

True, the Micra might provoke a stronger reaction than the Bluebird from the French, Italian, and Spanish car manufacturers that currently dominate the small-car segment in southern Europe. However, any negative consumer sentiment would typically be directed against the Japanese as a whole rather than against a single manufacturer. An advertising campaign stressing the Japanese quality built into the Micra could counter any such reaction.

Even if the Micra is later emphasized over the Bluebird in southern Europe, we must remember that an updated version of the Bluebird will be available ahead of the Micra. Improving the Bluebird's market share in the United Kingdom and West Germany in the short run will enhance Nissan's brand recognition and enable it to attract top-quality distributors in the southern markets.

In June 1989, the French government concluded that its opposition to the U.K.-made Bluebird was deterring Japanese companies from investing in France. Accordingly, the French recognized the Bluebird as U.K.- rather than Japanese-made, and its sales in France were therefore excluded from the bilateral import quota on Japanese car imports. Mr. Martin Bangemann, newly appointed EC Commissioner for industry, announced his objectives for the automobile industry in June: to end bilateral quotas on Japanese cars, facilitate a single EC-type approval, reduce national disparities in car taxes, and oppose any EC-wide local content rules. For their part, the Japanese would be expected to limit exports voluntarily for an as yet unspecified period.

Investment by Japanese car manufacturers in Europe continued at a rapid pace, with Toyota electing to build a new engine plant as well as its previously announced £700 million assembly plant in the United Kingdom. In car manufacturing, at least, concerns about Japanese "screwdriver" plants, low research and design investment, and dumping seemed to have abated by the middle of 1989.

CHAPTER 10

Organizing the Marketing System

David Del Curto S.A. and the Fresh Fruit Market

EDITORS' INTRODUCTION

David Del Curto S.A. (DDC) was one of the largest fruit-growing and exporting organizations in Chile. The company was one of the first (in the early 1970s) to establish large-scale facilities for grading, packing, and cooling fruit for shipment to foreign markets. DDC had played a major role in the "industrialization" of Chilean fruit growing, including carrying on research, advising farmers on planting, and handling export arrangements. The company's export volume in 1987–1988 reached 138,000 metric tons, with a value of $85.3 million. Almost one-third of this volume was sold in Europe. Chilean and other Southern Hemisphere producers of fruit — especially grapes and apples — had enjoyed substantial growth in sales during the 1980s, supplying European and North American markets during the "contraseason" when domestic crops were not available.

DDC and other Chilean exporters sold their products to retailers in the EC countries via independent agents. Chilean fruits were not branded or advertised. Both South Africa and New Zealand, in contrast, had marketing boards in the major EC countries. South African fruits, for example, were promoted under the "Cape" and "Outspan" brands through radio advertising and point-of-purchase materials. All imports of fruit into the EC countries were subject to tariffs and import quotas, which were designed to protect domestic producers.

The 1992 market integration reforms were expected to include harmonization of sanitary regulations affecting fruit. Some observers also predicted increasing similarity of consumer tastes and, possibly, receptivity to "Pan-European" advertising.

In mid-1989 Lothar Meier, president of DDC, was trying to evaluate the impact of the 1992 reforms and other marketplace trends on his company's operations. Among the possible strategies under consideration was either (1) establishing a wholly owned DDC subsidiary to handle marketing in the EC or (2) joining with other Chilean exporters to form a marketing board similar to those of South Africa and New Zealand.

David Del Curto S.A.

Jon I. Martinez and John A. Quelch

In June 1989, Lothar Meier, president of David Del Curto S.A. (DDC), reflected on his company's future in the European Community's (EC) impending integrated market. Headquartered in Chile, DDC was the largest private company in the Southern Hemisphere dedicated to the export of fresh fruit. Though it exported to more than 35 countries, its products were sold mainly in the Northern Hemisphere to supply "contraseasonal" (off-season) needs for fresh fruit.

Lothar Meier wondered whether the 1992 EC market integration program represented a threat or an opportunity to DDC. In addition, he pondered the decisions he would have to make about the company's entry strategy in Europe, its marketing organization, distribution channels, and branding and communications policies.

COMPANY BACKGROUND

In 1949, David Del Curto Libera emigrated from Italy to Chile, where he joined his uncle Antonio in running a small firm in the Aconcagua Valley, about 60 miles north from Santiago. The company exported onions, garlic, melons, almonds, chestnuts, and walnuts to Argentina.

In 1953, David Del Curto founded his own firm in the same business. In 1956, the new company started exporting and added some leguminous crops such as lentils, beans, and peas as well as honey to its product line. During a trip to West Germany, David Del Curto met Lothar Meier, a young German trained in foreign trade who worked in the cereals department of a DDC agent. David Del Curto offered Meier a job at DDC to promote cereals, and he arrived in Chile in 1958.

In 1958, DDC entered the fresh fruit business and began to export nectarines, peaches, and plums to the U.S. market. However, the firm's main exports were still grains and brans to West Germany and the United Kingdom, animal feeds to Scandinavia, melons to the United States, onions to the United Kingdom, garlic to Brazil, walnuts to Argentina, prunes to Europe, and honey to West Germany. In 1963, DDC became interested in exporting apples and pears and, four years later, bought its first orchard. By then, DDC was the fifth-largest Chilean exporter of fresh fruit.

Increases in its apple business prompted DDC to build in 1971 the first private fruit plant in Chile for selecting, standardizing quality of, packing, and precooling fruit to ensure resistance to damage during transportation and distribution. Subsequently, the company built six additional fruit plants, three in the 1970s and three in the 1980s.

In 1971, DDC became the third-largest exporter of fresh fruit from Chile, and four years later the largest. This rapid growth was due to DDC's leadership in three areas. First, because of David del Curto's knowledge of consumption patterns in foreign markets, the company was able to advise growers on which varieties to plant. It worked with Chilean and foreign agronomists specializing in fruit research to advise growers about plantation planning, soil fumigation, and other modern farming methods.

Second, DDC pioneered in plant engineering. Chilean fruit had not always arrived in good condition in world markets due to improper postharvest storage. David Del Curto persuaded growers that to combat this problem they had to take more responsibility for the appearance and quality of the fruit they cultivated. Hence, DDC obliged growers to participate in the final outcome of the selling process by accepting their fruit only on consignment — the same system imposed on DDC by its distribution agents.

Third, the company pioneered in opening several new markets for Chilean products, including the Middle East in 1974 and Southeast Asia in 1976. Because DDC understood each country's different consumer preferences and needs, the company was very successful in the European market from the outset.

In 1983, David Del Curto died in an air accident. Ownership of the company passed to his family and to Lothar Meier, Manuel Sánchez, and Ramón Guerrero, who had been shareholders since 1978. These executives became president, vice president, and executive director, respectively.

In the 1987–1988 season (from September to August), DDC became the first Chilean firm to break the 10-million-box barrier, exporting a volume of 13.7 million boxes (about 140,000 metric tons) valued at $85.3 million. This volume represented about 15% of Chile's total fresh fruit exports (*Exhibit 10.1* shows company exports and share of Chilean exports from 1980 to 1988). Net profit in 1988 was about $2.5 million, which represented a 16% return on equity. (*Exhibit 10.2* shows selected financial indexes.) Besides exports, DDC's revenues included $3 million in domestic fruit sales and sales of products and services worth about $7 million to growers.

Though its main activity was the export of fresh fruit, DDC defined itself as an "agroindustrial producer and marketer of fresh fruit, dry fruit and vegetables, with worldwide distribution." Its basic operating cycle consisted of six phases: production, selection, packing, shipping, distribution, and marketing of the fruit. The staff consisted of about 550 permanent employees and over 2,500 temporary workers due to the high seasonality of operations. DDC maintained some 25 to 30 employees in major ports abroad to supervise product unloading and clearance and to coordinate distribution.

Only 15% of the fruit the company exported came from its land and land held by the company's owners; the rest was provided by a network

EXHIBIT 10.1 Evolution of company exports

| | Volume | | | Share of |
Year	Boxes (000)	Tons[a]	Value ($000)	Chilean exports
1980	5,157	1,906	$43,897.6	23.7%
1981	7,126	515	54,003.6	28.5
1982	6,628	817	54,043.7	24.01
1983	5,871	384	42,899.2	16.48
1984	7,596	927	55,376.9	17.42
1985	8,808	602	61,745.8	16.83
1986	9,346	454	69,113.9	15.74
1987	9,889	442	76,742.7	13.79
1988	13,651 +	621	$85,278.7	15.2%

Source: Company records.

[a]Some dry fruit, such as walnuts, was exported in bags and therefore measured in tons. This column is *in addition* to boxes of fruit.

EXHIBIT 10.2 Selected financial indexes

	1987	1988
Liquidity ratios		
Current ratio	1.02	1.03
Quick ratio	0.78	0.78
Debt ratios		
Total debt/equity	4.84	4.83
Long-term debt/equity	67.44%	86.62%
Profitability ratios		
Gross profit margin	11.77%	11.27%
Net profit margin	3.67	2.65
Return on equity	23.03	16.02
Return on assets	3.79	2.67

Source: Company records.

of more than 800 independent growers in Chile. DDC maintained one-
to five-year contracts with these growers and provided several support
services. These services included technical assistance (on fertilization,
irrigation, pest and disease control, weed control, growth regulations,
pruning, thinning, maturity development, and harvest readiness), delivery scheduling, financing, and a computerized service that kept each
grower constantly informed about its fruit's progress and the average
prices in overseas markets.

DDC's main products were grapes, which represented about 50% of
its exports in U.S. dollars and 53% in volume; stone fruits, 19% and
18%, respectively; apples, 18% and 18%; pears, 6% and 5%; and kiwi
fruit, 2% and 2%. *Exhibit 10.3* illustrates some of the company's main
products. The shares of DDC exports accounted for by various destination markets were as follows:

	1986	1987	1988
United States and Canada	61%	61%	59%
Europe and Scandinavia	22	23	31
Middle East	12	12	7
Far East	4	4	2
South America	1	1	1

EXHIBIT 10.3 Main products and varieties exported

More detailed information about DDC's products and markets is presented in *Exhibit 10.4* (pp. 286–287).

THE FRESH FRUIT INDUSTRY IN CHILE

The fresh fruit industry accounted for over 1% of Chile's total GDP. In addition, it was the second most important generator of foreign currency in Chile, after copper mining. In the 1987–1988 season, fruit exports valued at $680 million represented 10% of the total Chilean exports that year. More than $800 million in exports was expected in 1988–1989.

Although Chilean fruit represented only 2.3% of all world trade in fruit, its relative importance was higher for selected products: 16% of grapes, 6.1% of apples, and 4.5% of pears. Chile was a major Southern Hemisphere supplier to the contraseasonal markets of North America and Europe. During winter and spring in the Northern Hemisphere, Chile accounted for 80% of world trade in grapes, 92% in peaches and nectarines, 31% in apples, and 23% in pears.

The area planted with fruit in Chile had grown almost three times in size since 1973, while export volumes had increased more than 20 times. Data on the two main crops illustrating this growth are presented in *Table A*.

The fruit industry in Chile comprised about 11,000 growers, most of whom sold abroad through nearly 100 exporting firms. Data on the first six, accounting for 57% of exports in volume, are presented in *Table B*.

All six leading companies competed worldwide and especially in Europe. The following is a brief description of DDC's main competitors:

TABLE A Evolution of planted surface (in hectares) and exports (in tons)

	1973	1978	1983	1988
Grapes:				
Surface	4,150	10,300	24,100	42,200
Exports	13,600	51,100	149,930	359,900
Apples:				
Surface	11,290	13,800	18,100	22,500
Exports	24,500	116,100	179,296	347,336

Sources: ODEPA and Asociación de Exportadores de Chile A.G.

**TABLE B Leading Chilean fruit exporters, 1987–1988 season
(in 000 boxes; 1 ton = 95–100 boxes)**

	Total exports	%	Exports to Europe	%
1. David Del Curto S.A.	13,661	15.2	3,694	11.5
2. Standard Trading	11,609	13.5	5,325	16.6
3. United Trading Company	8,050	9.4	2,775	8.6
4. Unifrutti Traders	6,933	8.1	1,799	5.6
5. Frupac Ltda.	5,299	6.2	1,605	5.0
6. Coopefrut Ltda.	3,909	4.5	2,065	6.4

Sources: Servicio Agrícola Ganadero and Asociación de Exportadores de Chile A.G.

- **Standard Trading:** a wholly owned subsidiary of the American multinational Castle & Cooke and one of the leaders in the world fruit business. It established operations in Chile in the early 1980s. It marketed in Europe under the Dole brand through a branch network that organized distribution.
- **United Trading Company:** owned by an important Arab consortium with several businesses in Chile. New to the fruit business, it began operations in Chile in the early 1980s. It sold in Europe through distribution agents, and in the United States through a joint venture with Californian partners.
- **Unifrutti Traders:** owned by an Italian family. It marketed fruit throughout Europe but particularly in Italy. It began operations in Chile in 1983. Its subsidiary, Unifrutti of America, distributed to the U.S. market, while elsewhere it marketed through distribution agents.
- **Frupac:** a Chilean firm owned by several growers who joined together in 1979 to export their own fruit. It was the first Chilean company to establish subsidiaries in the United States and Europe to import and market its own fruit. Frupac's operations were international in scope; it owned plantations in Peru and businesses in Argentina, and also marketed Mexican fruit worldwide.
- **Coopefrut:** a cooperative founded in 1964 by Chilean owners that focused on apples. It used two distribution agents in the United States and several in Europe. It had recently established a branch in Europe to import its own fruit and support the marketing activities of its distribution agents.

EXHIBIT 10.4 Shipments from May 31, 1988 to May 31, 1989 (boxes)

		U.S. East Coast	U.S. West Coast	Middle East	Far East	Europe	South America	Total maritime	Air and truck	Total
Nectarines	1987	270,901	143,398	65,434		52,542	744	533,019	47,450	580,469
	1988	376,989	363,907	28,655		85,221		854,772	54,247	912,019
	1989	357,761	508,930	54,008		97,136		1,017,835	79,300	1,097,135
Plums	1987	343,645	125,181	55,381		31,212	1,896	557,315	37,911	595,226
	1988	376,115	217,712	2,688		75,105		671,620	28,847	700,467
	1989	441,948	507,483	32,755	10,136	104,527		1,096,849	90,833	1,187,682
Peaches	1987	159,971	60,136	4,321			416	224,844	35,632	260,476
	1988	237,624	200,507	4,000		1,242		443,373	32,817	476,190
	1989	278,734	343,614	1,404		19,770		643,522	93,265	738,787
Apples	1987	138,273	65,807	319,175	188,832	944,109	12,458	1,668,654	624	1,669,278
	1988	108,234	47,138	469,251	41,903	1,167,277	15,948	1,849,751		1,849,751
	1989	140,238	150,897	407,310	36,000	1,279,914	23,592	2,037,951		2,037,951
Pears	1987	114,047	44,286	40,480	32,231	257,679	960	489,653	144	489,797
	1988	240,136	44,906	33,368	8,016	363,922		688,348		688,348
	1989	274,454	121,148	26,331	22,848	511,551		956,332	20	956,352
Grapes	1987	2,581,922	1,459,671	361,039	65,287	737,873	7,032	5,212,824	74,729	5,287,553
	1988	3,073,236	2,263,876	194,029	81,757	1,572,658		7,185,556	51,538	7,237,094
	1989	2,255,177	2,827,390	76,628	142,734	1,495,225		6,797,154	102,163	6,899,317
Cherries	1987	336	336					672	32,271	32,943
	1988	10,368	16,848					27,216	53,280	80,496
	1989	11,872	13,050					24,922	64,935	89,857
Apricots	1987	10,544	1,152	3,408				15,104	10,567	25,671
	1988	16,152	11,476	2,848				30,476	12,023	42,499
	1989	21,993	23,074	2,611	1,762			49,440	21,396	70,836
Melons	1987	39,941	12,270	3,890		930		57,031	2,785	59,816
	1988	4,005	1,335			19,071		24,411		24,411
	1989									
Onions	1987	16,218	6,720			55,523		78,461		78,461
	1988	27,646	8,634			128,070		164,950		164,950
	1989	11,280	11,568			129,687		152,535		152,535

		1	2	3	4	5	6	7	8	9
Watermelons	1987									
	1988	332		332	332					
	1989	1,358		1,358	1,358					
Lemons	1987									
	1988									
	1989									
Kiwis	1987	8,517		8,517	8,517					
	1988	309,087		309,087	278,199			17,928	12,960	
	1989	358,311	9,718	348,593	334,337			5,184	9,072	
Garlic	1987	3,228		3,228	3,228					
	1988	10,120		10,120	3,168			6,052		
	1989	4,752		4,752	2,640			2,112		
Persimmons	1987									
	1988									
	1989	3,963		3,963	3,963					
Asparagus	1987									
	1988	28,087	29,087							
	1989	41,310	42,210	100					100	
Artichokes	1987									
	1988	504		504					504	
	1989	80		80					80	
Nuts	1987									
	1988								504	
	1989								80	
Raisins	1987				6,053	23,506				
	1988	7,853		7,853	20,500	15,948			1,800	
	1989	33,350		33,350		24,592			10,800	
Prunes	1987	100		100	100					
	1988									
	1989						2,050			
Totals	1987	9,091,767	242,113	8,849,654	2,091,945	23,506	286,350	853,128	1,918,927	3,675,798
	1988	12,531,976	263,839	12,268,137	3,700,686	15,948	131,676	734,839	1,199,219	4,485,769
	1989	13,672,676	502,840	13,169,836	4,000,708	24,592	215,530	601,047	4,514,450	3,813,509

TABLE C   World trade in fresh fruit (000 tons)

	1963		1973		1983	
	Tons	%	Tons	%	Tons	%
Bananas	4,088	38.1	6,603	39.4	6,762	33.6
Oranges	2,923	27.3	4,543	27.1	4,994	24.8
Apples	1,588	14.8	2,448	14.6	3,535	17.6
Grapes	720	6.7	896	5.3	1,139	5.7
Other	1,415	13.1	2,310	13.6	3,711	18.3
Total	10,734	100.0	16,800	100.0	20,141	100.0

Source: FAO.

THE WORLD MARKET FOR FRESH FRUIT

The world production of fresh fruit was about 210 million tons in 1983–1985. The main producers were Brazil, the United States, Italy, Israel, and Spain in citrus; the Soviet Union, Italy, and the United States in stone fruits; the Soviet Union, China, France, and Italy in apples and pears; and Brazil, Philippines, India, and Colombia in bananas.

World trade in fresh fruit represented about 10% of world production, and almost doubled in volume between 1963 and 1983 as shown in *Table C*.

Europe was both the main exporter and importer of fresh fruit in the world. It accounted for 30% of world exports and 54% of world imports. The main exporting countries were Spain, 9%, the United States, 8%, Italy, 6%, and Ecuador, 5%, while the United States, 15%, West Germany, 14%, France, 9%, and the United Kingdom, 6% were the main importers.

THE EUROPEAN FRESH FRUIT MARKET

Basic Patterns

The per capita consumption of fruit differed markedly across countries in the EC. *Table D* shows the evolution of consumption (in kilograms per capita) for all fresh fruit except citrus, and for apples, the most heavily consumed fruit.

Consumption patterns in each country were rather stable, except in Greece, where per capita fruit consumption had increased significantly.

TABLE D   Evolution of fresh fruit consumption in Europe (kilograms per capita)

	All fresh fruit[a]		Apples	
	1973–1974	1984–1985	1973–1974	1984–1985
Belgium/Luxembourg	55	50	24	20
Denmark	42	38	14	19
France	56	55	17	16
Greece	56	77	21	22
Holland	66	64	36	33
Ireland	28	30	10	18
Italy	68	69	15	20
Portugal	NA	37	NA	9
Spain	NA	67	NA	21
United Kingdom	31	38	12	12
West Germany	86	79	22	22
Europe	60	60	18	19

Source: Eurostat.
[a]Not including citrus

However, there were great differences among countries. For instance, per capita consumption in West Germany and Greece was more than double that in Ireland and the United Kingdom.

Total EC production of fresh fruit reached 28.3 million tons in 1985, representing 13.5% of world production. *Table E* shows the production (in thousand tons) by country of all fruits, production of apples alone, and the percentage of fruit consumed in each country that was home-grown.

The countries that consumed the least fruit were those with the lowest self-supply ratios: Ireland, United Kingdom, and Denmark. The opposite was also true: Italy, Spain, and Greece, with self-supply ratios over 100%, were among the heaviest consumers.

European markets not only differed significantly in consumption per capita, but also in tastes and preferences for varieties, sizes, quality, and color. For instance, U.K. consumers preferred red apples with intense red color, excellent quality, in all varieties, and in medium to small sizes. Spaniards preferred streaky varieties, with little color, medium quality, but large in size. For Italians, variety and color were not impor-

TABLE E   Fresh fruit production in Europe, 1985 (000 tons)

	All fresh fruits[a]	Apples	Self-supply[b]
Belgium/Luxembourg	353	222	61%
Denmark	73	45	38
France	3,433	1,793	89
Greece	2,265	267	125
Holland	439	300	57
Ireland	15	9	15
Italy	6,802	2,014	128
Portugal	419	95	95
Spain	4,188	1,004	116
United Kingdom	494	301	22
West Germany	2,694	1,383	54
Europe 12	21,175[b]	7,433	87%

Source: Eurostat.
[a]Not including citrus.
[b]Part of this production was exported or was used for animal feed or in the food-processing industry.

tant features, but they insisted on big apples. Finally, Germans preferred small size, medium color, and were not as exacting on quality. In general, consumers in Mediterranean countries had stronger preferences regarding size and quality because these countries produced excellent fruit; conversely, consumers in northern Europe were not as demanding since they produced less.

EC imports of all fresh fruit except citrus, and of apples, were as follows (in thousands of tons):

	1983	1984	1985	1986
All fresh fruits[a]	1,393	1,573	1,642	1,517
Apples	419	504	475	508

Source: Eurostat.
[a]Not including citrus.

TABLE F Sources of EC fruit imports, 1986 (in thousands of tons)

	Deciduous	Citrus	Subtropical	Other	Total
South Africa	250	299	20	5	504
Chile	205	2	—	—	210
New Zealand	98	—	1	40	139
Argentina	50	86	—	—	136
Brazil	1	73	5	4	83
Uruguay	—	39	—	1	40
Australia	18	3	—	1	22
Total Southern Hemisphere	622	432	26	54	1,134

Source: Eurofruit.

Almost all the fruit imported into the EC during winter and spring came from the Southern Hemisphere. The main suppliers to the EC in 1986 are listed in *Table F.*

Key Markets

In 1988, The Marketing Unit, Saatchi & Saatchi affiliate, performed a study for the Chilean Association of Fruit Exporters. The study focused on the three main markets for Chilean fruit: West Germany, France, and the United Kingdom.

West Germany. The largest European fruit market was West Germany, with an annual consumption of about 5 million tons. It was a stable and mature market, increasing in value but static in volume. Due to its high per capita consumption (the highest in Europe) and its relatively low self-supply ratio average (54%), West Germany was the largest market for imports, with a well-developed contraseasonal market (approximately 30% of all apples). Its principal contraseasonal sources were Chile, 11%, South Africa, 9%, New Zealand, 7%, and Argentina, 3%.

The trade structure was very decentralized. There were many independent stores (125,000), local and regional (rather than national) chains and department stores (about 30,000), purchasing co-ops, and "symbol groups" which bought on behalf of individually owned stores. *Exhibit 10.5* diagrams the distribution system for fresh fruit in West Germany.

EXHIBIT 10.5 Channels of distribution of fresh fruit in West Germany

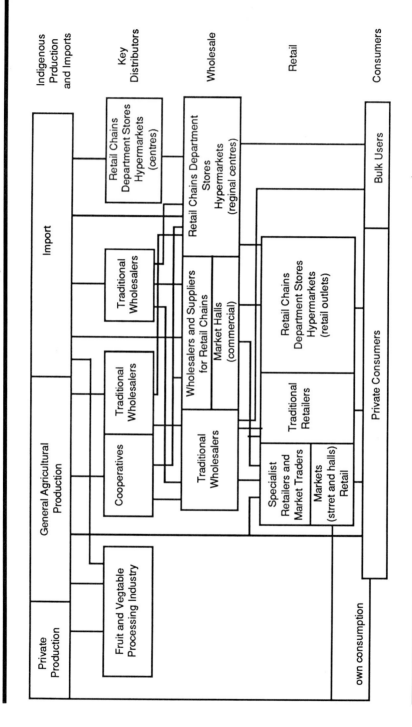

Source: The Marketing Unit

Both the independents and chains tended to be conservative. The worldwide trend toward retail concentration was developing fairly slowly in West Germany. There were also many regional differences with suppliers operating for the most part on a regional basis. Hence, a great number of primary wholesalers were needed to supply the West German market.

France. France was a mature market with an annual consumption of about 3 million tons. Due to its high self-supply ratio and per capita consumption a little under the EC average, its import volume was modest, but exports were high. The contraseasonal fruit market was still underdeveloped but growing, while the seasonal market was in slow decline. The apple market was dominated by the home-grown Golden Delicious variety; contraseasonal apple imports accounted for about 15% of consumption. The key contraseasonal suppliers were Chile, 35%, Italy, 20%, New Zealand, 12%, and South Africa, 11%.

The trade structure in France was rather fragmented, as indicated in *Table G.*

The distribution channels for fresh fruit in France are diagrammed in *Exhibit 10.6.* France had the most rigidly structured distribution system of any of the key EC markets. It was dominated at one end by a few large chains (hypermarkets/superstores), and at the other end, by a very large number of small independents selling fruits and vegetables. There were major regional differences between north and south in patterns of fruit consumption and channel structure. There was a gradual shift of share and trade power toward the major chains in the north. However, the rural south was more conservative, dominated by markets and small shopkeepers, and loath to accept imports.

TABLE G Retail channels for fresh fruit in France

	Number	Fruit share
Markets	9,000	29.4%
Supermarkets	11,000	22.7
General Stores	29,500	14.1
Greengrocers	5,000	11.4
Hypermarkets	550	9.9
Other	NA	12.5%

EXHIBIT 10.6 Channels of distribution of fresh fruit in France

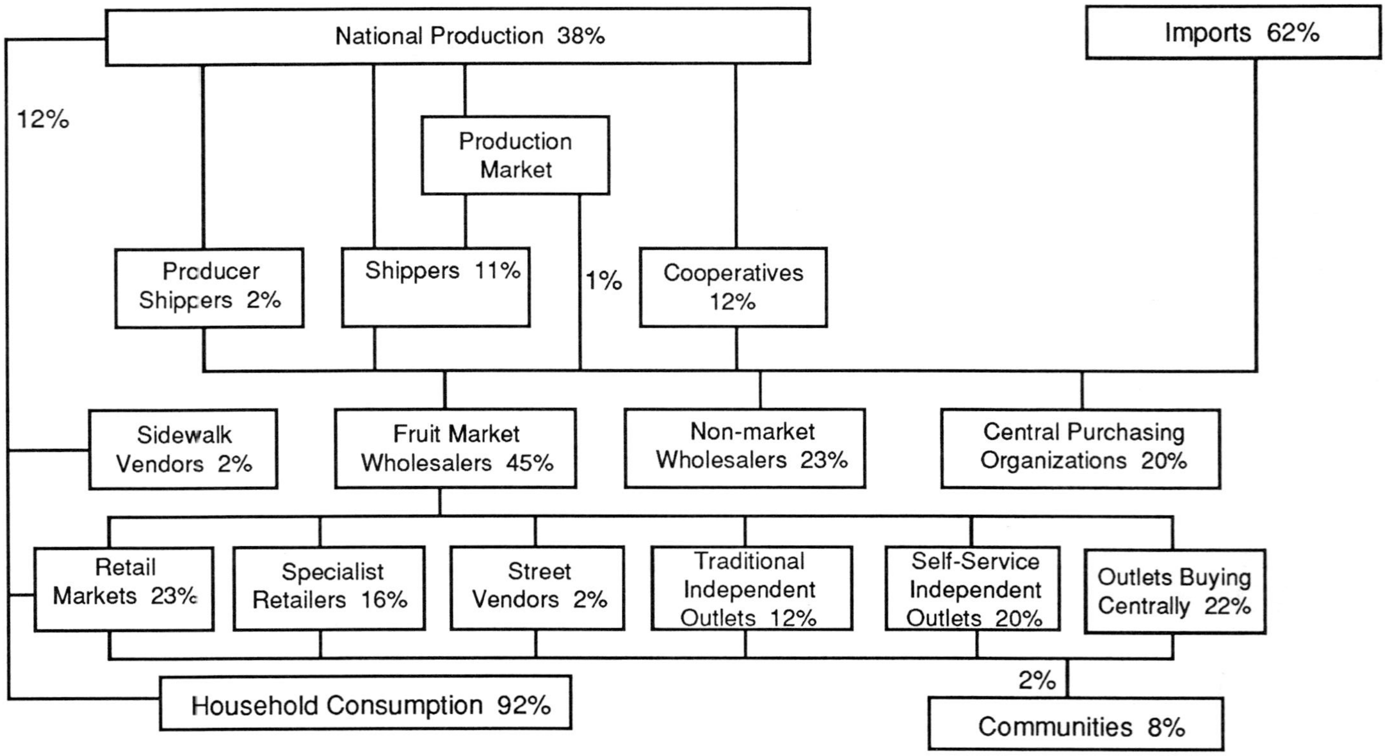

Source: The Marketing Unit.

Note: These descriptions are the standard ones used for the French retail/wholesale markets.

United Kingdom. The United Kingdom had one of the lowest per capita consumption levels in the EC. Like France and West Germany, it was a stable, mature market with declining consumption year to year, but increasing in value. With a low self-supply ratio, the contraseasonal fruit market in the United Kingdom was still developing, driven by the major chains. Its main contraseasonal suppliers were South Africa, 25%, New Zealand, 11%, and Chile, 7%.

Unlike in the other major markets, the U.K. trade structure for fresh fruit was highly centralized. Grocery retailing was dominated by only ten chains. The retail channels for fresh fruit were as follows:

	Number	Fruit share
Chains	> 30,000	> 45%
Greengrocers	> 15,000	> 30%
Independents	> 70,000	> 20%

All retailers bought through wholesalers/importers. Innovations were initiated and driven by the chains. The distribution system for fresh fruit in the United Kingdom is diagrammed in *Exhibit 10.7*.

Consumer Attitudes, Habits, and Trends

According to The Marketing Unit survey, consumer attitudes were basically similar in all three major markets. Consumers bought primarily on the basis of visual appearance. The fruit's country of origin, like Chile or South Africa, was not usually advertised at the point of sale, and consumers did not generally ask for this information.

The main factors that seemed to determine fruit purchasing were price, quality, varieties, visual appeal, trust in the retail outlet, seasonal habits, and fashion (as in the case of kiwi fruit). In some markets, like the United Kingdom, consumers tended to buy with their eyes and had a very low brand awareness of fruit. Branding of fruit was often precluded by the risk of bruising, especially in the case of soft fruit. Consumer recall of brands of fruit was low, though some brands like Cape (South Africa's brand) did have significant consumer awareness. Some analysts believed that branding had a greater benefit in marketing to the trade than to the end consumer.

EXHIBIT 10.7 Channels of distribution of fresh fruit in the United Kingdom

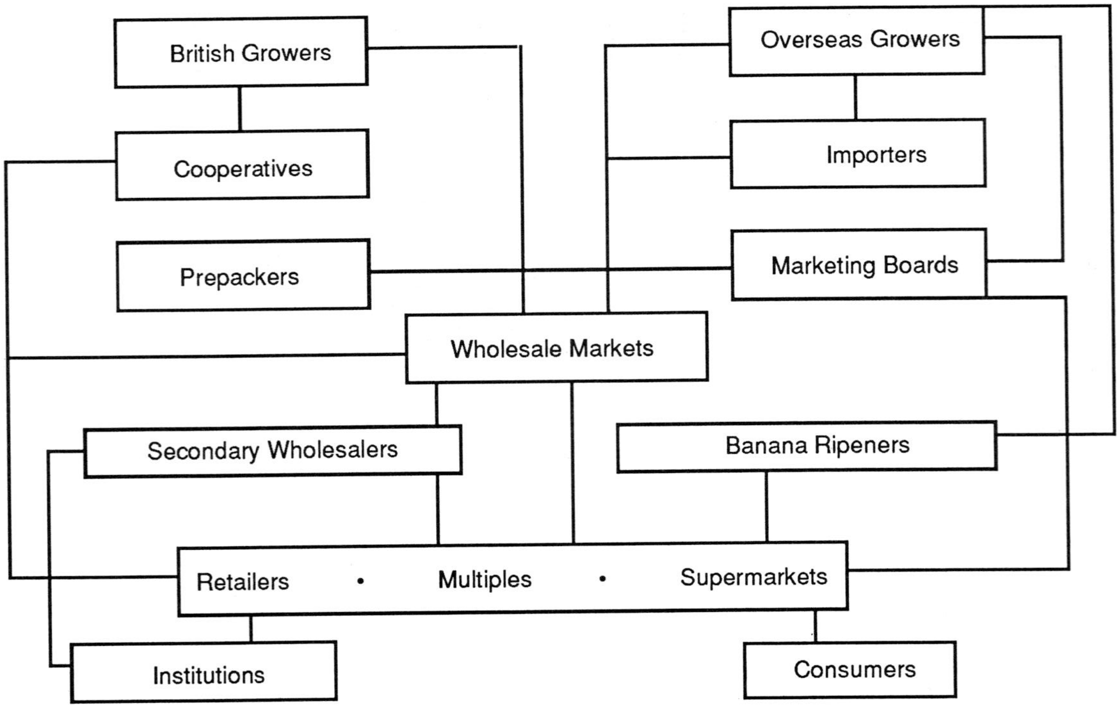

Source: The Marketing Unit.

Recently, consumers were showing more interest in exotic fruits, such as kiwi fruit, and better quality and new varieties of staple fruit. This upmarket trend was stronger in countries like the United Kingdom with a more concentrated trade where the major chains sought to boost their margins on a stable volume of demand.

Sourcing Patterns

Consumers did not determine sourcing patterns. These were decided by the trade. The key criteria used to select the country of origin and exporter were availability, consistency of supply throughout the season, quality of produce, price (adjusted for the exchange rate), and service.

CHILEAN FRUIT POSITIONING IN THE EC MARKET

Chile's share of the EC contraseasonal fruit market grew significantly in the 1980s. It was the leader in West Germany and France, with 11% and 35% market shares, respectively, and third after South Africa and New Zealand (its main competitors) in the United Kingdom. *Table H* shows the mix of Chilean products in these three key markets.

According to market observers, the key sources of competitive advantage for Chile were (1) a relatively neutral political profile compared to South Africa, (2) recent rapid increases in overall fruit quality, (3) a longer harvesting season, (4) a speed of delivery which rivaled that of South Africa, and (5) a broad and competitive range of deciduous fruits.

TABLE H Mix of Chilean fruits by volume and value in three EC markets

	Germany		France		United Kingdom	
	% Volume	% Value	% Volume	% Value	% Volume	% Value
Apples	81	72	69	56	58	41
Pears	7	8	15	13	4	3
Grapes	6	12	12	20	27	42
Plums	—	—	1	2	1	2
Peaches	—	1	2	5	1	2
Other	5	7	2	5	10	11

Image

Retail and wholesale perceptions of Chilean fruit quality varied across markets. West German and French distributors considered Chilean products to be of very good quality. Germans tended to believe that Chilean fruit had "little or no chemical treatment." Chilean exporters were viewed as responsive, particularly by French importers. In the United Kingdom, Chilean fruit was seen as fairly good in quality, but not as good as that from South Africa or New Zealand.

The main criticisms made by the trade about Chilean fruit concerned consistency of quality and consistency of supply. Other problems mentioned by the trade in Europe were the lack of consumer awareness of fruit originating from Chile, the lack of overall coordination among Chilean exporters which led to missed marketing opportunities, and the lack of standardization in packaging.

Trade Relations and Marketing

Both South Africa and New Zealand had marketing organizations in West Germany, France, and the United Kingdom. These government-controlled organizations were called "marketing boards" ("UNIFRUCO" and A.P.M.B., respectively). The mission of these organizations was to coordinate harvesting, shipping, importing, and marketing. The marketing boards distributed the fruit through a "panel" system. Panel appointments were franchises granted to wholesalers by producers to sell fruit on their behalf. Panelists were selected by the marketing boards and were reviewed on a yearly basis. They sold to retail customers on a fixed commission basis which ranged from 5 to 8%. The price at which the fruit was sold was set by the central marketing board. Panelists meant that the producers did not have to trade directly.

The marketing board was also in charge of all marketing activities. The main activities were advertising, promotion, and branding. For instance, South Africa's board UNIFRUCO created awareness for its brands "Cape" and "Outspan" through advertising (mainly on radio) and promotional material for the point of sale (posters, educational leaflets describing the fruit's nutritional value, mobiles, brand logos, brochures, carrier bags, and sometimes badges and T-shirts). In addition, UNIFRUCO advertised in trade magazines. It was estimated that UNIFRUCO spent in 1987 about $2.1 million in its communications program for the Cape brand in the United Kingdom, West Germany, and France.

Chile did not use a marketing board or panelists and operated in an "uncoordinated" way through distribution agents and importers in all three countries. Chile performed almost no marketing activities, and had very little direct contact with the major retailers. Except for Standard Trading's Dole brand, Chilean fruit was usually unbranded. Finally, Chilean exporters had never attempted to promote their fruit generically in Europe; only a few individual exporters advertised in trade magazines.

IMPLICATIONS OF 1992 FOR THE FRESH FRUIT MARKET

Although the impact of the 1992 market integration program on the fresh fruit market was not yet clear, some changes were expected. The EC Commission was expected to decrease agricultural subsidies because of the enormous cost of the Common Agricultural Policy (CAP). EC authorities were concerned about the continuing rapid growth of the CAP budget, caused by consistent excess production and large stockpiles of certain food products. In 1988, CAP net expenses reached 25.2 billion ECUs,[1] accounting for 65% of the EC's general budget. About 7% of these expenses subsidized fruit and vegetables.

However, analysts believed that, even if agricultural subsidies were reduced, some measures would have to be taken to protect agriculture, a sector that employed 8.8% of EC workers. There was growing pressure on the Commission from COPA (the European growers association) to restrict imports from Southern Hemisphere suppliers. The reasons were overproduction of apples (primarily in France and Italy) and the support of other growers of peaches, nectarines, and strawberries. Balanced against this pressure was the Commission's awareness that it had to ensure competitive prices for EC consumers.

These pressures had led to restrictions being imposed on Southern Hemisphere suppliers in the fresh fruit market — first on apples and then on grapes. The restriction on apples, applied in 1988, consisted of quotas on imports which, as shown in *Table I,* had grown significantly since 1984.

The producing country most damaged by the quotas was Chile, which, until 1987, had exhibited the greatest growth. Whereas South Africa was assigned a quota of 165,000 tons, Chile's quota was only 130,000; its capacity was 190,000. Finally, South Africa was actually allowed to supply 195,000 tons, but Chilean imports were halted at 142,130. Thousands of tons of product en route to Europe had to be thrown away. Chile had recourse to the General Agreement on Tariffs

---

[1] In 1988, one ECU was between U.S.$1.1 and U.S.$1.2.

TABLE I   EC Imports of apples, 1984–1989 (in thousands of tons)

	1984	1985	1986	1987	1988[a]	1989[a]
South Africa	157	147	164	170	195	188
Chile	98	87	151	161	142	168
New Zealand	77	96	97	105	128	135
Argentina	53	64	32	53	79	78
Australia	2	10	6	8	6	11
Total	387	404	450	497	550	580

Source: Eurostat.
[a]Quotas.

and Trade (GATT), and one year later the GATT Group of Experts passed judgment favorable to Chile in an unprecedented verdict. For 1989, the EC assigned 188,000 tons to South Africa, and Chile negotiated a voluntary agreement for 168,000.

Fruit imported from outside the EC was charged a standard tariff that ranged between 5% and 22% for all EC countries, depending on type of fruit and variety. Also, tariffs were higher at the beginning and end of the season to protect the sale of EC-grown fruit. For example, tariffs for apples were 8% from January 1 to March 31, 6% from April 1 to July 31, and 14% from August 1 to December 31. It was thought that these tariffs would not be higher, but would remain steady or even go lower. Besides tariffs, other restrictions included quotas, minimum prices, licenses to import some types of fruit, and sanitary regulations. The general trend, even before 1992, was to harmonize and standardize all sanitary regulations in the EC countries. Although these regulations varied from country to country, especially in Italy, the fruit that had passed the tests in whatever European port it had entered was allowed to move to other countries without further controls. Therefore, there already was a free movement of fruit across EC markets.

Consumer preferences after 1992 were difficult to predict. Despite the deep differences in tastes, habits, and patterns of consumption, experts forecast a slow but continuous homogenization of European markets. The free movement of workers, easier travel across countries without border controls, development of Pan-European television and other media, and an increasing concentration of distribution were among the factors that argued for further similarities among European consumers.

DDC OPERATIONS IN EUROPE

Markets and Products

DDC sold in all of Western Europe except Portugal. It could not sell in Eastern Europe because of a boycott on Chilean products since the overthrow of Allende's socialist government in 1973. DDC's European sales in 1988 were $17.83 million, which represented 20.9% of total company exports. The 3.7 million boxes exported to Europe in 1988, which accounted for 27.1% of company export sales by volume, had the following initial destination:

Holland and Belgium	22%
United Kingdom	20
West Germany	17
France	13
Italy	12
Sweden, Finland, Denmark, and Norway	11
Other	5%

DDC did not know where its fruit was finally consumed. Actual consumption in Holland and Belgium was only 5% of the shipments. The main markets for DDC's fruit were West Germany, the United Kingdom, France, Italy, and Scandinavian countries.

The types of fruit DDC exported to Europe in 1988 were grapes (43% of volume), apples (32%), pears (10%), kiwi fruit (8%), and stone fruits (4%).

Distribution

The company used different distribution arrangements in each EC market:

Holland, Belgium, Switzerland, and Austria	Distribution Agent 1
United Kingdom and Ireland	Distribution Agent 2
West Germany	Distribution Agent 3 and Central Purchasing Org. 1
France	Distribution Agent 4
Italy and Greece	Distribution Agent 5
Sweden, Finland, Norway, and Denmark	Central Purchasing Org. 2
Spain	Importers

For most of the EC markets, DDC used five distribution agents to sell and market its products. They were independent agents paid by commission who sold to various wholesalers and retailers, including most supermarket and hypermarket chains. Additionally, the company sold directly to two central purchasing organizations. One belonged to a West German supermarket chain and the other to the Union of Scandinavian Consumer Cooperatives. Finally, DDC's clients in Spain were three importers and producers of fruit.

The distribution agents worked exclusively for DDC during the contraseason, but represented othe. firms from Europe and other countries during the rest of the year.

DDC executives met each distribution agent personally twice a season to discuss the distribution strategy and prepare annual orders based on historical trends and expected changes during the next season. In these meetings they also analyzed the total supply situation in Europe: new varieties, countries of origin, qualities, types of packing, new transportation technologies, forecasted prices and volumes, and the mix of varieties to include in future shipments. Distribution agents also sent weekly market reports by telex or fax, which commented on volume sold that week, estimated prices, the general market situation, and future prospects.

Pricing

Due to fruit's perishable nature, its uncertain condition after transportation, and changing consumer tastes, fruit prices were highly volatile, both seasonally and from year to year. However, early contraseasonal prices were typically much higher because of the insufficient supply at the beginning of the winter, but then fell quickly. Thanks to the quality of its fruit, its prestige as the largest and oldest Chilean supplier, and dependable supply through the contraseason, DDC usually obtained prices a little higher than average in the market.

DDC used three methods to sell fruit: firm price, minimum guarantee, and free consignment. DDC employed the first method with Spanish importers, the second with German and Scandinavian central purchasing organizations, and the third with distribution agents. Under free consignment, the exporter delivered the fruit to the destination port distribution agent, who sold it to wholesalers and retailers at the highest possible price. After the sale, the distribution agent presented a "sales account" which detailed sales revenues for each product minus customs fees, duties, handling of fruit in the port, cold-storage, internal transportation, and other expenses.

Agents' commissions were normally 8% of the selling price. DDC's sales to wholesalers and retailers worldwide in 1988 totaled about $150 million. However, its net revenues were only $85.3 million. The difference, about $65 million, was used by distribution agents to pay their commissions (8% of $150 million), distribution expenses, port expenses, duties, and freight and insurance. From net revenues, DDC deducted a commission of 8%, which was standard among Chilean exporters. Other DDC income came from all services and products provided to growers. *Exhibit 10.8* shows a typical cost breakdown on fruit exported to Europe from Chile.

EXHIBIT 10.8 Cost breakdown of a typical export of apples and grapes to Europe

		Apples	Grapes
	Selling price to wholesalers or retailers in Europe	100%	100%
minus:	Distribution agent's commission (over selling price)	8%	8%
	Expenses in Europe (discounted by the distribution agent):		
	■ Port and distribution expenses (discharge, handling, trucking, storage, etc.)	7–8%	5–6%
	■ Duties	5–6%	11–13%
	■ Freight and insurance	34–37%	17–20%
equal:	FOB Chile	41–46%	53–59%
minus:	Exporter's commission (8% over FOB price)	3–4%	4–5%
	Expenses in Chile (discounted by the exporter):		
	■ Port expenses	0.9%	1.3%
	■ Domestic freight	2.0%	1.6%
	■ Cooling	2.1%	2.8%
	■ Packing service	3.5%	6.7%
	■ Packing materials	13.4%	12.5%
equal:	Grower's revenue	15–21%	23–30%

Source: Casewriter estimates based on information given by several fresh fruit exporters.
Note: Data from 1987–88 season for Granny Smith apples and Ribier and Thompson seedless grapes, the varieties most exported to Europe. Costs have been estimated over the following average prices per box: apples $13.5–14.5 (18.2 kilograms) and grapes $8.5–9.5 (5 kilograms).

Organization and Control

The company's commercial department consisted of a manager and four executives, as shown in *Exhibit 10.9*. Basically, it was structured according to geography. One executive was in charge of the U.S. West Coast market and dry fruit exports; another was responsible for the U.S. East Coast market; the third coordinated the European markets; and the fourth was in charge of South America and air shipments. Apart from managing the whole department, the commercial manager oversaw the Middle and Far East markets.

The executive in charge of the European markets was Rodrigo Falcone, who described his task in this way:

> *My objective is to maximize the revenues for the boxes sent to Europe. To accomplish this task, I have to be in close and permanent contact with each distribution agent so as to move the fruit toward the highest priced markets.*

Rodrigo Falcone's mission was to coordinate and control all shipments to Europe in order to secure the maximum possible price for the fruit delivered on consignment to distribution agents. First, the fruit was allocated to distribution agents from Chile, and then Rodrigo Falcone reallocated it to agents whose markets offered better prices at any time. This task required almost instantaneous decisions by phone, telex, or fax.

Rodrigo Falcone had no established travel plan; every year was different due to changing market conditions. However, he usually worked in Europe from March to August and in Chile the rest of the year. While in Europe, he worked in different markets, but resided in Hamburg, West Germany. His operations base was the Central Representation Office for Europe. The company did not own this organization, but used it exclusively during the contraseason. Like distribution agents, the organization worked with both European fruit and products from tropical countries. It had a permanent staff of six or seven people, all West Germans. Its functions were to (1) coordinate the logistics: regular shipments, charters, and the reallocation of fruit to different markets; (2) serve as the communications center: telex, fax, and mail; and (3) supervise the financial and administrative activities of DDC's European business: payments, collection, credit lines for ships, and handling of all kinds of formalities, documents and other papers. In sum, the organization focused not on the marketing of the fruit but on the coordination of operations.

Finally, DDC employed a full-time agronomist engineer in Rotterdam, the main port of entry for its fruit in Europe. Other agronomists

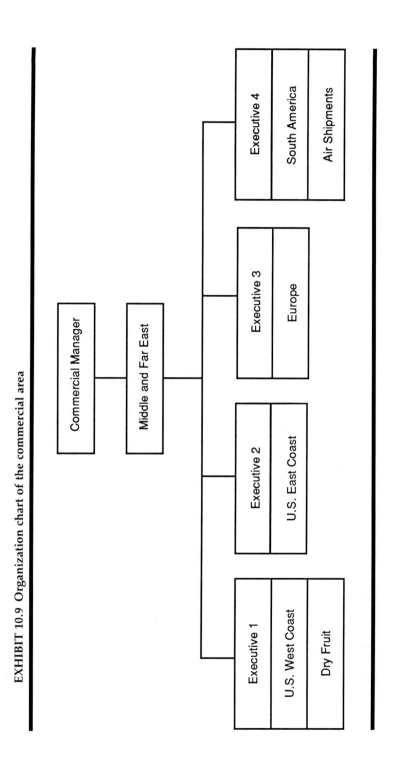

EXHIBIT 10.9 Organization chart of the commercial area

305

and technicians traveled from Chile to inspect the fruit's condition on its arrival in Europe. They ensured quality control and monitored the effectiveness of different experimental packing techniques.

Branding and Communications

DDC's fruit in Europe neither carried its own brand nor that of any distribution agent. Only a few supermarket chains used displays that included boxes with the logo "Del Curto-Chile"; normally these retailers did not brand their fruit. Merchandising activities were performed by neither DDC nor distribution agents. From time to time, chains offered special promotions of DDC products.

The company did not advertise its products to the final consumer; however, it did place some full color institutional or image advertisements targeted at the trade in specialized magazines such as "Fruchthandel" from West Germany and "Eurofruit" from the United Kingdom. These were bi-monthly publications sold by subscription to importers, distributors, wholesalers, supermarket chains, and exporters throughout the world. The distribution agents neither advertised nor promoted DDC's fruit, but only advertised their own firms' capabilities.

REVIEWING THE EUROPEAN STRATEGY

In mid-June 1989, Lothar Meier wondered whether the trends and expected changes in the EC fresh fruit market would necessitate modifying his company's strategy.

Organization

Meier's first concern was the suitability of DDC's organization and distribution in Europe. There were at least three alternatives: (1) to continue with the current way of doing business in Europe; (2) to create a subsidiary that could import, distribute, and market its own fruit; and (3) to foster the creation of a marketing board for all Chilean fruit, like the ones run by South Africa, New Zealand, and Israel. This last alternative was not considered by Lothar Meier but was a possibility suggested by some market observers.

Of the six main Chilean exporters, four had European sales subsidiaries or operated through their parent companies' European networks. DDC had previously rejected the idea of a sales office to import, distribute, or market its fruit in Europe. Lothar Meier concurred with the opinion of Rodrigo Falcone, the executive in charge in Europe:

> *If we had a sales branch in Europe, we would need at least 15 employees to manage our current volume, and this would reduce our flexibility. For instance, if the dollar goes up much, if there is a significant fall in demand, or the export of some product into the EC market is suddenly forbidden, we can divert our fruit to the USA and deliver less in Europe. If we did do this, we couldn't justify the fixed expenses of a subsidiary in Europe. Instead, by being the major private exporter from the Southern Hemisphere, DDC has the capacity to work with the best distribution agents in each country. After almost 30 years in this business, the company knows all the distribution agents in Europe and works with the best ones. That our main competitors constantly offer them opportunities to join their organizations demonstrates their quality.*

Lothar Meier added:

> *Besides being a matter of flexibility, it's a matter of cost. If we operate in the European market for just six months a year, we cannot absorb the overhead expenses for the whole year. With our current organization and distribution system we keep our costs low.*

Asked about running the sales office all year long and handling fruit of the Northern Hemisphere in the seasonal market, Lothar Meier stated that instead of continuing to grow in volume and embarking on new ventures, the company should consolidate its current activities.

The third alternative, to promote the creation of a marketing board with other Chilean exporters to coordinate the harvesting, shipping, importing, distribution, and marketing of Chilean fruit in the EC market, was suggested by The Marketing Unit to the Chilean Association of Fruit Exporters as a result of its study (see *Exhibit 10.10*).

Some of the large Chilean exporters were opposed to the marketing board idea. They believed that the central planning and coordination provided by such a board could not compensate for the flexibility and rapid response time that they enjoyed as independent entrepreneurs. To some the faster growth of Chilean exports compared with those from South Africa and New Zealand proved the superiority of the independent or uncoordinated approach. Lothar Meier agreed with this position. He believed that marketing boards had often failed because of inefficiency and the high costs of production and transportation.

Distribution

As previously mentioned, DDC operated directly with the central purchasing organizations of two major supermarket or cooperative chains in West Germany and Sweden. Asked about extending these arrange-

EXHIBIT 10.10 Excerpts from Marketing Unit report

Chile has no marketing organization on site in Europe.

- For Chile, the importers are the trade interface
- Therefore there is negligible coordination
- Activities in Europe are fragmented, opportunistic

This flexibility and opportunism has served Chile well:

- It has been an appropriate strategy during periods of open access to EC markets and buoyant EC economies
- Chilean exports to Europe have grown dramatically, due to:
    Increases in availability
    Incentives to importers including dating
    Exchange rates favorable to European currencies

But are flexibility and opportunism right for the new climate?

The New Climate in Europe

1. The EC is closing ranks (and frontiers) against Southern Hemisphere fruit suppliers. Chile has been singled out for close attention. Chile must expect rigidly applied limitations in the future.
2. Exchange rates expected to continue to move in favor of European currencies at least until the end of 1989.
3. The scope for further cost-effective direct incentives to importers is limited. Investment in marketplace impacts at the point-of-sale is likely to represent the most profitable use of support funds.

Strategy

The market now demands a strategic rather than a tactical approach. Such strategy requires:

- Systematic marketing planning for each major outlet
- Development of close trade relationships
- Ability to guarantee supply
- Point-of-sale merchandising support

A Marketing Board could perform these tasks.

Organization

Improved organization could improve dramatically the way in which Chile:

- Services the importers
- Services the retail trade
- Coordinates supply and demand
- Demonstrates size, stature, importance
- Maximizes visibility and presence in each market

A new organization should have the following capabilities/functions:

- Tightly knit, *dedicated* resource for *Chilean* fruit
- Ongoing Pan-European coverage
- EC liaison capability
- Handling importer and major trade relations directly
- Using outside consulting resources for Marketing Services and for Marketing Communications

Source: Adapted from "Chilean Winter Fruit: A Marketing Plan for 1988/1989 and Beyond, Covering: West Germany, France and the United Kingdom," by The Marketing Unit, February 1988.

ments to other large chains in Europe and forming joint ventures or strategic alliances, Lothar Meier answered:

> We can't do so much. Our company receives many proposals from important chains. As they are big retailers they want to buy in the country of origin, to have a link there. Currently, we reach all important chains across Europe through our distribution agents. To serve the chains directly, we would need a huge staff. We can't do all the business in the world. We are specialists in a part of the distribution channel.

Branding and Promotion

Finally, Lothar Meier wondered about making a greater marketing effort to increase consumer awareness and loyalty toward Chilean fruit and, in particular, toward DDC's fruit. Two crucial subjects were branding and communications. On these issues, Lothar Meier commented:

> Advertising to create awareness and loyalty in this business is expensive and ineffective, because it is directed toward the consumer who doesn't see the brand; he sees only apples and grapes. Building a brand in the international fruit market is very costly, and large volumes are needed to absorb those expenses. Chiquita, the famous brand of bananas, sells more than 120 million boxes all over the world. However, this is a brand for just one product shipped by one producer. No Chilean exporter has the volume to warrant such a huge investment.

EDITORS' COMMENTARY

David Del Curto (DDC) pioneered in the "industrialization" of fruit production, handling, and export distribution in Chile. But the company still relied on traditional marketing methods that have been employed by fruit producers and exporters for generations. DDC's apples, grapes, and other fruits were not branded, advertised, or promoted; they were sold in bulk to whichever customers would pay the best prices to the import agents. The agents represented DDC only on a seasonal basis.

Because DDC sells through agents and does not brand or promote its products, the company has no real contact with or knowledge about its customers. Indeed, it does not even know how much of its exports are consumed in each country, much less how much is bought by individual retail chains. DDC is in the classic "commodity marketing" situation, although it does (allegedly) enjoy a slight price premium by virtue of being a large, dependable supplier of high-quality fruit.

DDC's traditional method of sales and distribution in the EC has some real merits; fixed costs are low, and the system provides flexibility in directing supplies to the markets where the best prices can be realized. Thus, it is not surprising that company executives are skeptical about the benefits versus the costs of either a DDC subsidiary or supporting a joint marketing board along with other Chilean exporters. Mr. Meier, president of DDC, also expressed doubts about the effectiveness of consumer advertising for fresh fruit. Nevertheless, DDC should consider whether competition from other Southern Hemisphere fruit suppliers, some of which *do* have organized advertising and promotion programs, may force the Chilean producers to adopt similar approaches.

The fact that the EC has imposed import quotas, reducing Chilean producers' share of the business sharply in 1988, implies that there is an oversupply of "contraseasonal" fruit available. Despite alleged "political sensitivity" among consumers toward South Africa, the share of EC fruit imports coming from the latter country has held up better than Chile's; moreover, South Africa has been able to develop its own Cape brand in the market. Thus, it may be that DDC (or Chilean producers as a group) will be forced to compete in new ways in order to maintain volume.

A second factor that may affect DDC's business in the EC is the increasing consolidation of food retailing. The growing importance of large, professionally managed food chains may require a different selling approach on DDC's part. The 1992 reforms are likely to encourage even more concentration in EC food retailing in the future.

While DDC executives would clearly prefer to keep on "doing business as usual," increased competition and the continuing consolidation of major customers may require changes. The company should, in our opinion, at least explore whether a marketing board is feasible, and whether such a board should confine itself to advertising and promotion activities or should also organize distribution. A marketing board might have enabled the Chilean growers to respond more promptly to control the precipitous drop in demand that followed the discovery of two cyanide-contaminated Chilean grapes in a U.S. shipment in early 1989.

CHAPTER *11*

Expanding Distribution

FNAC and the Retailing of Cultural and Leisure Products

EDITORS' INTRODUCTION

In May 1989, the managers of FNAC,[1] a large French retail chain that sold leisure and cultural products, were reviewing the firm's long-term strategy in light of the changes that were anticipated in connection with the 1992 integration of the EC market. FNAC had been founded in 1954 as a consumer cooperative distributor of photographic products. By 1989 the company had 24 stores in France and 4 in Belgium. FNAC's 1988 sales of FF4.8 billion included consumer electronics, books, records, and sporting goods in addition to the original photographic product line. Also, 68 small "FNAC Service" shops offered film, photo processing, and blank tapes, and 7 outlets sold and installed auto audio systems.

While none of the proposed 1992 market integration directives dealt directly with retailing, FNAC executives did anticipate significant changes in the marketplace and competitive climate. Among these changes were increased cross-border shopping, growth in direct marketing, and the emergence of multinational retail groups similar to Benetton, the Italian apparel distributor. Already a U.K.-based retailer of recorded music, Virgin, had opened a store in Paris, and two photographic specialty chains were believed to be ready to enter the French market.

Among the alternatives under consideration by FNAC were establishing more specialized stores, carrying either only photographic prod-

---

[1]FNAC is an acronym for Federation Nationale d'Achat des Cadres.

ucts or only consumer electronics; developing smaller full-line stores for smaller communities; and opening full-line FNAC stores in other EC countries.

FNAC

Andre Tordjman and Jean-Francis Harris

In May 1989, Philippe Mondan, managing director of FNAC, the leading retailer of leisure and cultural products in France, was contemplating the company's long-term strategy in light of the 1992 EC market integration program:

> *Two years ago, we began to focus on improving FNAC's profitability, with good results. However, new foreign distributors are now entering our markets and competing for our customers.*
>
> *Will our 35-year-old concept be able to resist this new pressure? What is the growth potential for FNAC stores in France? Should we create new retail concepts to defend our home market or is it better to seek foreign growth, even if our entry into Belgium has yet to prove successful?*
>
> *Regardless, we must choose and implement a strategy that will maintain FNAC's leadership position.*

COMPANY BACKGROUND

Created in 1954 by two friends and former Trotskyists, Andre Essel and Max Theret, FNAC was originally a consumer purchase cooperative that enabled its members to receive 10% to 20% price reductions. Because no photography specialty stores then existed in France, FNAC's founders, both photography buffs, decided to sell photographic supplies at a discount and convert part of their Paris store into a Photo-Cinema Club. Two years later, they added tape recorders and, in 1961, electrical appliances and records. By then, FNAC had 100,000 members and 13.5 million FF in annual sales.

FNAC grew slowly as a specialty retailer that concentrated on selling four product lines: books, records, photographic supplies, and consumer electronics equipment. In 1969, it opened its first large store in Paris. A second opened in 1974. That same year, FNAC replaced its electrical appliances department with books. In 1979, one year before the company became listed on the Paris Stock Exchange, FNAC celebrated its 25th anniversary with the opening of its third and largest Paris store (5,090 square meters in size).

FNAC first ventured outside Paris in 1972 with the opening of a store in Lyon, France's third largest city. Stores were launched in other French cities at a rate of about one per year until 1985 when four new stores were opened. In 1981, FNAC opened its first store outside France in Brussels, Belgium. The store had a 2,000-square-meter sales area.

As FNAC expanded, it diversified into the sports equipment market (FNAC Sport), tourism (FNAC Tourisme), film development (Junacor), direct imports (AVI), and proximity services (FNAC Service and FNAC Autoradio). Except in the latter case, these diversification efforts generated only modest financial results and, coupled with insufficient financial resources to fuel expansion, led the firm to concentrate increasingly on its core business, photography.

During the 1970s and 1980s, several banks and insurance companies invested in FNAC. From 1985 to early 1989, FNAC had two main shareholders: Garantie Mutuelle des Fonctionnaires (GMF), an insurance company that controlled 70%, and Storehouse, a British retail group (owner of the Habitat and Mothercare chains) that controlled 20%. Due to difficulties in its home market, Storehouse sold its share to GMF; the remaining 10% of shares was offered to the public.

These changes of ownership were accompanied by turnover among the company's senior managers. From 1982 to 1989, FNAC had four CEOs and five managing directors. Partly as a result, sales growth from 1983 to 1989 was not matched by a similar growth in earnings (*Exhibit 11.1*). Declining profitability required FNAC to raise 150 million FF in additional capital from its two shareholders in 1987.

In the 1987–1988 fiscal year, FNAC's sales were 4.8 billion FF. The company had 4,300 employees. Thanks to the efforts of its new senior management, led by M. Mondan, the company's financial performance improved considerably.

THE FNAC CONCEPT

FNAC differentiated itself from its competitors through its retail strategy, its support of cultural events, and its pro-consumer stance.

EXHIBIT 11.1 FNAC sales and profits, 1978–1987

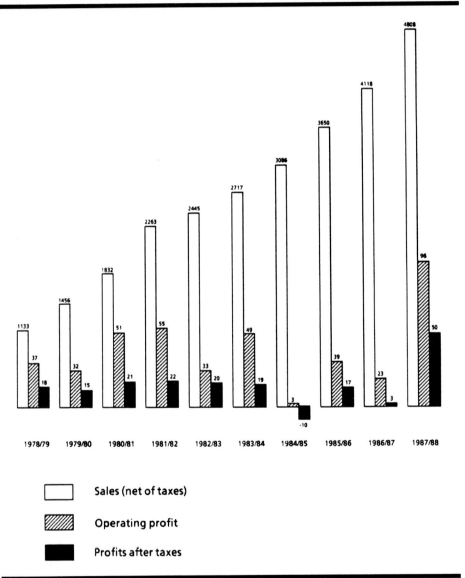

Source: Company records.

Retail Strategy

Located in the center of large cities, FNAC stores offered a very large assortment of books, records, consumer electronics (e.g., audio and stereo equipment, TVs, VCRs, home computers), and photographic equipment and services (cameras, accessories, movie/video cameras, and film processing). FNAC customers could choose from among the best products on the market and find the latest technological innovations. The largest FNAC store in Paris offered more than 130,000 different books, 100,000 records and cassettes, and about 25,000 other items (in consumer electronics and photography), all at discount prices. FNAC published 14 reports each year based on in-house research tests that compared the prices and features of the products it stocked.

FNAC stores were known for their distinctive ambience. The quality of displays, signs, and lighting made the sales floor, in the words of one manager, an "area of pleasure and freedom." FNAC also offered a number of services, many of which such as the sale of tickets for concerts and shows, insurance against camera theft, and FNAC charge cards, represented additional sources of income.

Culture

FNAC built a strong reputation for its stores as leisure and cultural centers. The stores attracted 17 million visitors per year. The FNAC Foundation, established in 1986, organized and supported cultural activities such as the "New Literature Award," the "Tour de France" of short films, and the creation of a contemporary opera. Sponsorship of cultural events represented about 20% of FNAC's communications budget, equivalent to FNAC's media advertising expenditures.

Consumerism

Support of consumer interests was a continuing objective. FNAC pressed the French government to lower the value-added tax (VAT) on records and stereo equipment[2] and to end price controls on books.[3]

---

[2]In France, until 1988, records and stereo equipment were considered luxury goods and were subject to the highest VAT rate of 33.3%. FNAC, in fact, sold these products at 18.6% VAT and paid the difference.

[3]The Lang law, named for the socialist government's minister of culture, imposed fixed retail sales prices on books. This price was determined by the publisher, and the retailer could lower the price only up to 5%. The law protected small independent bookstores that could not compete against the major discount stores. FNAC opposed this law as protectionist and against consumers' interests.

These actions received considerable press coverage, which further enhanced FNAC's image and differentiated it from competitors.

Salespeople also played an important role in the FNAC concept. They were selected for their enthusiasm for the products they sold and their ability to inform and advise customers. Their independence from manufacturers (there were no manufacturer-paid product demonstrators working in FNAC stores) enabled them to give consumers objective advice.

FNAC's principal customers were managers, intellectuals, artists, and other professionals — in other words, the heaviest consumers of leisure and cultural products (*Exhibits 11.2* and *11.3*). These customers demand a high quality of service. They did not come to FNAC only to buy, but also to browse and learn about new products and services (*Exhibit 11.4*). In 1988, a study conducted in France revealed substantial cross-buying, especially for books and records, which were the stores' most important product categories (*Exhibit 11.5*).

From the time it was established, FNAC offered customers a 100 FF membership, renewable every three years. Members received a 3% discount, invitations to cultural events, and credit assistance. They also received the free monthly magazine *Contact*, which carried information on cultural activities and on FNAC's consumer protection efforts. In 1988, there were 400,000 members, who accounted for a fourth of FNAC's retail sales.

FNAC STORES

The Product Lines

FNAC's market penetration and performance (in terms of sales per square meter and profit contribution) varied by product line.

Books. With more than 8.3% of the market in 1988, FNAC was the premier bookstore chain in France. Although more than 400 suppliers were listed, FNAC did most of its business with only 12 of them. The performance of this department was modest in comparison with that of the other product lines: 74,000 FF in annual sales per square meter (*Exhibit 11.6*).

Records. FNAC held over 25% of the total record market in 1988, including 40% of the compact disk and 21% of the tape markets. The depth of assortment, efficiency of the sales staff, cultural image, and aggressive prices on new products were its main advantages. However, there

EXHIBIT 11.2 Comparison of FNAC customer base with Paris population by socioeconomic category of head of household

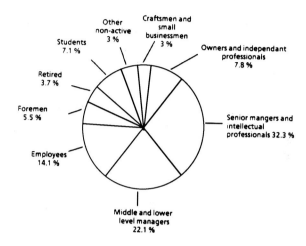

Fnac Customers

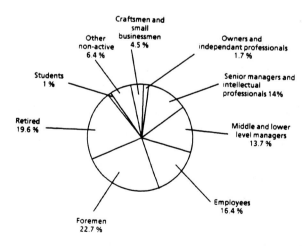

Paris Population

EXHIBIT 11.3 Index of consumption of leisure and cultural products by socioeconomic category of head of household

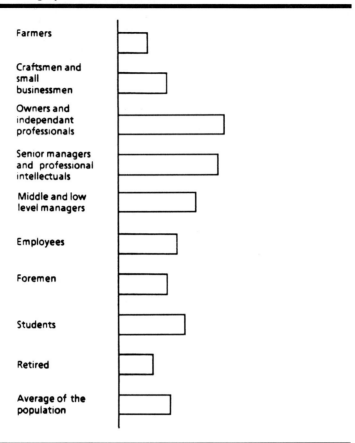

Source: Survey on family budgets, INSEE, 1985.

EXHIBIT 11.4 Customer reasons for going to FNAC

Reasons	Regular customers[a]	Occasional customers[b]
Buy books and records	83%	74%
Obtain information on new products	53	35
Obtain information on products they will buy later	34	33
Wander about	33	33
Purchase HI-FIs	31	30
See an exhibit	14%	9%

Source: Survey GESD 1985.
[a]Customers who come at least once a month.
[b]Customers who come several times every year.

EXHIBIT 11.5 Cross-purchases by FNAC customers

	Purchasers of:										
Have also bought:	Books	Records, tapes	Cameras	Radios, tape recorders	Car radios	TVs	Video-tape recorders	HI-FIs	Home computers	Calculators	Films and film development
Books	100%	70%	73%	61%	52%	60%	73%	63%	71%	68%	74%
Records, tapes	78	100	73	74	69	56	83	85	67	77	74
Cameras	21	19	100	23	26	29	20	23	16	20	40
Radios, tape recorders	7	7	9	100	13	16	16	9	17	14	7
Car radios	2	2	3	4	100	9	4	3	5	3	3
TVs	3	2	5	6	13	100	10	6	12	6	4
Video-tape recorders	4	4	4	8	7	12	100	5	7	6	4
HI-FIs	11	13	14	14	19	24	15	100	18	17	13
Home computers	8	7	7	18	18	31	15	13	100	15	8
Calculators	8	8	8	14	9	14	11	11	14	100	10
Films and film development	22%	20%	42%	20%	33%	24%	21%	22%	19%	26%	100%
No. of respondents:	1164	1301	331	128	36	52	65	202	138	129	344

Source: Publicis Conseil survey conducted with 1750 FNAC customers, 1988.

EXHIBIT 11.6 Performance of the different product lines, 1988

Product	Sales (%)	Surface (%)	Sales/m² (1000 FF)	Contribution (%)[a]
Books	22.0	37.5	74	14.4
Records	27.3	25.0	136	11.7
Photography	14.7	10.0	185	10.3
Sound	36.0	27.5	164	11.8

Source: Company records.
[a] as % of product line turnover.

EXHIBIT 11.7 Position of FNAC by product-market

Product category	Market size (billions of FF)	Market growth	Margin	Critical success factors External	Internal	Competitive position of FNAC
Books	12	+0%	38%	Price Choice	Logistics	Average
Records	3.2	+4%	28%	Price Choice Proximity	Purchases Logistics	Strong
TV Video	16.8	+6,8%	20%	Proximity Price Service	Purchases Costs	Poor
Audio	8.8	+4,8%	28%	Proximity Price Advice	Purchases Costs	Poor
Hi-fi				Price Image	Purchases Costs	Average to strong
Home computers	2.7	+0%	22%	Advice Service Price	Purchases	Average to strong
Photography	4.4	+3%	20%	Advice Price	Purchases Costs	Strong
Film development	3.0	+5%	43%	Proximity Quality Price	Purchases Costs	Strong
Travel	14	+2%	9%	Proximity	Costs	Poor

Source: Company records.

were a few weak points such as long lines at cash registers and congestion in the stores. FNAC listed 168 suppliers but did more than four-fifths of its business with only 10 of them. Sales were satisfactory (17,000 FF per square meter), but the profit margin was lower than on other product lines.

Photographic Equipment and Services. FNAC was the leader in France with 20% of the equipment market, 6% of the film market, and about 4% of the film development market. The establishment of conveniently located FNAC Service boutiques was motivated by FNAC's objective to control 10% of the film development market by 1992. Excluding FNAC Service outlets, this department earned 185,000 FF in annual sales per square meter, and profit margins were high (*Exhibit 11.6*).

Consumer Electronics. FNAC market penetration varied by product. FNAC led in the home computer (11%) and camcorder markets (8%), and was second in the audio market with 6.5%. However, its position was very weak in TVs (1.5%) and VCRs (3.5%). Seventy suppliers were listed, but three accounted for nearly two-thirds of the business. In this highly competitive market, FNAC generated average annual sales per square meter of 164,000 FF (*Exhibit 11.6*).

The internal and external reasons for success varied according to the markets. FNAC's competitive position was strong in records and photography, fair in books and stereo equipment, and weak in other consumer electronics equipment (*Exhibit 11.7*).

Stores

In April 1989, FNAC had 24 stores in France, three of which were in Paris, and four stores in Belgium, one of which was in Brussels (*Exhibits 11.8* and *11.9*). Although the Paris stores represented 50% of revenues, those in the French provinces were contributing an increasing percentage of group revenues (*Exhibit 11.10*). However, the Belgian operation's contribution to sales was weak, and it was running at a loss.

The operating performance of individual stores varied widely. There was a clear distinction between stores in Paris and those in the provinces and, among the latter, between those located in large cities and those located in smaller towns (*Exhibit 11.11*).

The three flagship stores in Paris, each with sales areas over 2,000 square meters, generated more than 230,000 FF in annual sales per square meter, twice the chain's average yield. Except in eastern Paris, opportunities for adding new stores were thought to be limited if can-

EXHIBIT 11.8 Location of FNAC stores

Source: Company records.

nibalization of the existing stores' sales was to be avoided. However, as many as ten new stores could be opened in the large shopping malls on the outskirts of Paris. Strong results obtained in one store located in a Paris suburban mall highlighted the opportunity for new "four product line" stores in shopping malls.

The provincial stores located in university cities with more than 400,000 population generated annual sales per square meter between 100,000 FF and 140,000 FF.

Stores whose annual sales per square meter were below 100,000 FF

EXHIBIT 11.9 Location of FNAC stores as of March 1, 1989

Store	Opening date	Population of the urban center
Paris Etoile	05/69	
Paris Forum	09/79	8,700,000
Paris Montparnasse	03/74	
Annecy	09/81	110,000
Belfort	12/75	106,000
Bordeaux	10/85	640,000
Caen	10/88	180,000
Clermont-Ferrand	09/80	256,000
Colmar	11/81	110,000
Dijon	10/84	216,000
Grenoble	09/85	392,000
Lille	09/79	935,000
Lyon	06/85	1,221,000
Marseille	09/77	1,110,000
Metz	11/76	186,000
Montpellier	10/86	221,000
Mulhouse	09/73	220,000
Nice	04/82	450,000
Orléans	09/85	220,000
Rennes	02/86	234,000
Rouen	11/84	380,000
Strasbourg	04/78	373,000
Toulouse	04/80	541,000
Parly 2	03/88	≈500,000
Anvers	10/87	400,000
Bruxelles	10/81	1,100,000
Gand	04/86	400,000
Liège	04/87	500,000

Source: Company records.

were located either in smaller cities (with fewer than 200,000 inhabitants), in larger cities (such as Bordeaux and Strasbourg) where competition was particularly tough, or nearby larger cities with FNAC stores that competed for their consumers' patronage (e.g., the Orleans store was only a ninety-minute drive from Paris).

EXHIBIT 11.10 FNAC sales growth in total and by location of units

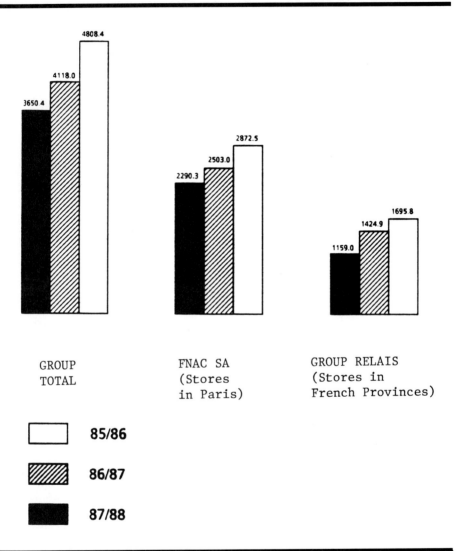

GROUP
TOTAL

FNAC SA
(Stores
in Paris)

GROUP RELAIS
(Stores in
French Provinces)

85/86

86/87

87/88

Source: Company records.

EXHIBIT 11.11 Comparative profitability of the stores, 1988

Location	Turnover m² (FF)	Selling surface (m²)
Paris Forum	230,000	2000
Paris Etoile		
Paris	to	to
Montparnasse	250,000	3700
–Lyon	110,000	750
–Lille		
–Toulouse		
–Marseille	to	to
–Nice		
–Clermont-Ferrand	140,000	1900
–Grenoble	75,000	800
–Rouen		
–Metz		
–Montpellier		
–Bordeaux	to	to
–Dijon		
–Annecy		
–Strasbourg	100,000	1600
–Mulhouse	40,000	500
–Orléans		
–Rennes	to	to
–Belfort		
–Colmar	70,000	1200
Moyenne	125,000	1800

Source: Company records.

In France, there were 13 metropolitan areas with more than 200,000 inhabitants where FNAC was not represented. Seven had considerable potential, while the remaining six were either too close to cities with a FNAC or lacked sufficient per capita buying power.

FNAC executives had believed that a store's selling area had to be in proportion to the buying power of its trading area. The poor results of the smaller units led FNAC to conclude that only cities with more than 200,000 inhabitants could yield satisfactory results. However, the impressive results of a 1,500-square-meter store which opened in late 1988 in Caen, a city with a population of 180,000, suggested that FNAC could open in ten other cities.

Organization

FNAC had traditionally been run on a decentralized basis. Each store placed its own orders and negotiated directly with the suppliers approved by Paris headquarters. Except for the stores in Paris which received their stock from a central warehouse, there was no physical distribution center; goods were delivered directly by the suppliers.

From 1987 to 1989, the role played by headquarters product managers was enhanced. They participated in developing the store marketing policy, particularly in the selection of product mixes, pricing, and promotion. Although the individual stores were in charge of all orders and payments, the product managers negotiated sales conditions with suppliers and pushed for central purchasing. The product managers for photographic equipment and consumer electronics regularly placed joint orders for all the stores, particularly for consumable products (e.g., small accessories, films, blank tapes) and small consumer electronics items (e.g., calculators).

The new approach aimed to reduce the number of suppliers and proliferation of stockkeeping units while still providing a broad assortment of products. Stores were expected to respect the results of the in-house product tests and give preference to those items with better quality-price ratios.

In 1987, to benefit from discounts on prerecorded video tapes, FNAC set up a joint-purchasing arrangement with one of the leading food retailing groups in France. Other European retailers also contacted FNAC regarding the possibility of establishing joint ventures. All these prospective partners employed centralized purchasing and inventory control, yet their sales per square meter were much lower than FNAC's. FNAC was wary of any joint ventures that could compromise its decentralized style of management and limit its ability to adapt to local market needs.

FNAC'S COMPETITORS

Several types of retailers, the majority of them French, competed with FNAC.

Hypermarkets

The amazing growth of hypermarkets in France (from 1963, when the first Carrefour store was established) represented one of the most important phenomena in the history of French retailing since the founding of large department stores in the second half of the 19th century. Hypermarkets were large stores of at least 2,500 square meters where a wide assortment of food and nonfood products was offered at discount prices. The first Carrefour hypermarket was opened in 1963, and by 1988, there were 700 hypermarkets in France, with aggregate market shares of 24.8% in food products and 12.8% in nonfood products.

Hypermarkets were a major threat to FNAC, not so much because of their breadth of assortment, which was not comparable to FNAC's, but because of their very aggressive pricing policies. However, the Lang law (which standardized retail prices on books) prevented hypermarkets from pursuing their normal deep discount strategy in this line of business.

Hypermarket customers read less than FNAC's. They were particularly responsive to promotions and concentrated their purchases on best sellers and books related to TV films or movies rather than on the classics. The average hypermarket offered an assortment of 10,000 books and generated 1% of its total sales from this department.

In FNAC's other product lines (records, VCRs, stereo equipment), the hypermarkets' share of sales was steadily increasing (*Exhibit 11.12*). Hypermarkets held 45% of the audio cassette market, 40% of the video cassette market, 20% of the film, and 25% of the camera markets. Certain chains such as Carrefour imported large quantities of products (e.g., color TVs and compact disk players) directly from Southeast Asia, which they backed with strong advertising and sold at prices lower than those of their competitors.

Specialty Chains

Darty. As France's leading retailer of white and brown[4] goods, Darty had more than 100 stores and over 6 billion FF in sales in 1988. The stores, with an average size of 1,000 square meters, offered a broad and deep selection of household appliances, VCRs, stereo equipment, and accessories. Darty had a solid reputation backed by strong advertising and a "price-choice-service" policy that guaranteed the consumer superiority on any of these criteria. Darty stores were very different from FNAC's. They were showrooms, and customers were supplied from a central warehouse used jointly with other stores. Sales personnel, who

---

[4]White goods included household appliances such as washing machines, refrigerators, and dishwashers; brown goods included stereo equipment, televisions, and video cassette recorders.

EXHIBIT 11.12 Market shares of different classes of trade in seven product categories

Product category	Specialty stores	Traditional stores	Hypermarkets	Department stores	Direct mail
TV					
1986	24%	55%	17%	3%	1%
1987	26	53	18	2	1
1988	27	51	18	2	2
1989	29	49	19	1	2
Video					
1986	35	44	15	4	2
1987	37	42	16	3	2
1988	39	39	17	2	3
1989	40	40	17	1	2
HI-FI					
1986	41	37	15	3	4
1987	40	38	15	3	4
1988	41	38	16	2	3
1989	41	38	16	2	3
Audio					
1986	26	33	32	2	7
1987	27	33	32	2	6
1988	29	32	31	1	7
1989	31	31	30	1	7
Photography					
1986	18	61	16	2	3
1987	18	60	17	2	3
1988	17	62	18	1	2
1989	19%	59%	18%	1%	3%

Product category	FNAC	Traditional book stores	Inter-mediaries	Direct mail	Clubs	Hyper-markets	Department stores	Others
Books								
1986	6%	48%	6%	9%	10%	16%	3%	2%
1987	7	46	6	9	10	18	3	1
1988	8	44	6	9	11	19	2	1
1989	8%	43%	5%	9%	11%	21%	2%	1%

Product category	FNAC	Nuggets[a]	Hyper-markets	Direct mail and clubs	Department stores	Virgin[a]	Small record stores
Records							
1986	22%	3%	18%	3%	3%	—	51%
1987	24	3	19	3	3	—	48
1988	26	4	19	3	2	—	46
1989	26%	4%	20%	4%	2%	4%	40%

Source: GFK and professional trade associations.

[a]Chain of record stores.

were paid commissions on profit margins, pushed products more aggressively to their customers. Finally, Darty conducted no comparative testing of products.

Darty planned to double its network of stores over the next five years. Despite failing in an effort to establish profitable stores in Spain in 1983, Darty management continued to pursue its ambitions for European expansion by buying Vanderborre, one of the leading home appliance chains in Belgium.

Connexion. Connexion was a chain of around 100 franchised and company-owned stores specializing in brown goods. Their stores, with an average area of 400 square meters, offered a wide assortment of medium- and high-quality products. Connexion was strong in the stereo equipment and audio markets, but weak in TVs, tape recorders, and home computers (*Exhibit 11.13*).

Nasa. Set up in the late 1970s by Darty's former R&D manager, Nasa grew rapidly to 150 stores in less than 5 years. Averaging 400 square meters and located mainly in city centers, the stores specialized in consumer electronics. Despite good sales of home computers, Nasa was not able to establish a strong reputation for consumer electronics in general. Following financial difficulties, the group was bought by a British company, Granada, in 1986.

Boulanger/Auchan. Auchan, France's second-largest chain of hypermarkets after Carrefour, diversified its operations through Boulanger, a subsidiary which specialized in white and brown goods at discount

EXHIBIT 11.13 Market shares of the main consumer electronics retailers, 1987

Retailers	TV	VCR	Home computers	HI-FI	Audio
Darty	10%	7%	IN[a]	8%	10%
Conforama	7%	6%	3%	IN	IN
Auchan-Boulanger	4%	4%	2%	5%	7%
Connexion	IN	IN	IN	8%	5%
Nasa	IN	IN	4%	IN	IN
FNAC	2%	3%	4%	8%	5%

Source: Company records.
[a]IN: insignificant.

prices. In 1988, the group had 40 hypermarkets and about 30 Boulanger stores. Despite selling a full range of consumer electronics, Auchan/ Boulanger had a significant market share only in stereo and audio equipment (*Exhibit 11.13*).

Independent Groups

Independent groups included small businesses that grouped together to enjoy economies of scale in procurement and advertising. The two main groups in France were Phox (150 stores) and Camara (150 stores), which were both very strong in photography.

Direct Mail

Direct mail was not as highly developed in France (2% of retail sales) as in other European countries, particularly West Germany. However, book clubs were prominent. France Loisir, for example, which controlled more than 10% of the retail book market, sold through direct mail and through 180 stores.

FNAC DIVERSIFICATION

To balance the group's operations FNAC pursued a four-part diversification strategy into proximity stores, sports equipment stores, travel stores, and international (Belgium) markets. The four-part diversification had many strong points: a common focus on cultural products, allocation of fixed overhead across a broader sales base, and the exploitation of bulk purchasing. However, duplicating the FNAC concept in other product-markets proved difficult, and FNAC had to face many competitors in each sector. The results were uneven.

Proximity Store Diversification

FNAC launched two networks of small "proximity stores" in the late 1970s: 68 FNAC Service shops which specialized in film, blank tapes, and film development; and 7 FNAC Autoradio shops which sold and installed car radios, car telephones, and alarms. These two chains were very profitable, especially FNAC Service shops, which accounted for 3.4% of group sales and more than 11% of operating profits (*Exhibit 11.6*). By 1992, FNAC Service was expected to have 200 stores located in the Paris metropolitan area as well as in the outskirts of other large urban centers. FNAC Autoradio, however, was limited in coverage to Paris and other locations in France where FNAC was already present.

Sports Equipment Diversification

As early as 1966, FNAC had opened a 300-square-meter store where sporting items and accessories were sold. However, FNAC never made a profit on this operation. When Philippe Mondan became managing director, he decided to sell FNAC Sport. FNAC found that its comparative product tests, though useful for photographic and audio equipment, were difficult to apply to sports items such as tennis rackets and skis, and even more difficult to apply to sports apparel and shoes, which represented 60% of the sales. In this highly competitive market, into which hypermarkets had successfully diversified, FNAC was not able to position itself clearly and found difficulty in competing profitably with price discounters. In addition, FNAC did not understand how to market fashion-intensive merchandise and how to run end-of-season sales. Darty, which had also tried to diversify into sports items, encountered the same difficulties and also sold out.

Travel Diversification

FNAC Voyage offered an original formula of travel services and package tours built around various cultural themes. However, FNAC Voyage was not profitable, and only three stores sold FNAC's travel services. Concentration in the travel services market was increasing rapidly, and the leading French company ranked only 13th in Europe. FNAC had to decide whether to associate itself with a strong partner or to leave the market.

International Diversification

In 1981, FNAC opened stores in Belgium, whose cultural heritage was similar to that of France. With four stores in Belgium by 1988, FNAC was the market leader in books (8%) and records (14%). FNAC secured concessions from Dutch publishers to improve the distribution of books at discount prices. However, FNAC was weak in photography and audio equipment, where it had to compete with discounters. Makro, a subsidiary of the German Metro retail group, had 15% of the stereo equipment and 13% of the photography market, whereas FNAC's shares were only 3% and 4%, respectively.

FNAC also encountered management problems. Its marketing and procurement expertise had not been sufficiently instilled in the staff of the Belgian branches. Although FNAC tried to relocate its retail concept in Belgium, opportunities for joint purchases to serve both French and

Belgian stores were limited. For example, Amstrad led the French home computer market, whereas Casio led in Belgium. In addition, France had adopted the Secam system for TVs and VCRs, whereas other European countries had chosen the incompatible Pal system.

THE EUROPEAN MARKET FOR LEISURE AND CULTURAL PRODUCTS

Despite national variations in the household penetration of TVs and stereo equipment, due partly to the economic gap between northern and southern Europe and different cultural preferences, competition in all the product-markets, except books, in which FNAC competed was becoming increasingly international.

The Consumer Electronics Market

The European market for consumer electronics represented 25% of the world market, compared with 32.5% for the United States and 17.1% for Japan. Steady growth in market penetration of color TVs, VCRs and personal computers was evident in all three markets (*Exhibit 11.14*). However, between 1986 and 1992, the world consumer electronics market was expected to register only 5% annual growth. This weak growth was due to the relatively high rate of household penetration of electronic goods already achieved and the maturity of product life-cycles (*Exhibit 11.15*). Household penetration in France lagged behind the United Kingdom and West Germany; hence, its market growth rate was expected to be higher (*Exhibit 11.16*). Consumer electronics was the fastest-growing category of leisure and cultural products in France. But, though leisure and cultural product consumption grew from 5.4% of household income in 1959 to 6.3% in 1985, France still lagged behind the Netherlands (9.3%), West Germany (7.7%), and Italy (7.5%). However, France (after Italy) was the country with the largest number of distribution points for consumer electronics in Europe, reflecting not only a growing market but also a more fragmented retail structure (*Exhibit 11.17*).

The Book Market

Since 1980, unit book sales had been declining in Europe. This trend was particularly evident in fiction. The share of the total publishing market accounted for by books was also falling. France ranked second in Europe, after the United Kingdom, in per capita consumption of books.

The French publishing market was increasingly concentrated. Two

EXHIBIT 11.14 Consumer electronics: World market (in millions of units)

Product	EC		United States		Japan		Rest of the World	
	1981	1986	1981	1986	1981	1986	1981	1986
Color TVs	9,660	14,250	11,380	18,530	6,565	8,270	9,200	13,685
VCRs	2,515	6,535	1,330	12,005	1,550	4,850	1,800	7,795
Home sound systems	8,235	6,315	5,410	4,715	2,410	2,120	5,350	4,385
Compact disk players	—	1,635	—	2,675	—	1,940	—	2,085
Portable sound equipment	36,915	35,630	63,110	67,635	12,360	11,225	37,460	38,165
Camcorders	—	435	—	1,170	—	650	—	750
Digital audio tapes	—	—	—	—	—	—	—	—
Home computers	400	2,475	500	4,500	200	800	365	2,590

Source: DAFSA Survey (1988).

EXHIBIT 11.15 Household penetration of television in European countries, 1985

Country	Number of households (millions)	Number of TV sets (millions)	Television penetration (%)
Austria	2.750	2.570	93.5
Belgium	3.700	3.600	97.3
Denmark	2.200	1.900	86.4
Spain	15.200	9.900	65.1
Finland	1.800	1.700	94.4
France	19.700	16.300	82.7
Greece	4.000	2.600	65.0
Ireland	0.930	0.900	96.8
Iceland	0.053	0.047	88.7
Italy	18.500	18.100	97.8
Luxembourg	0.126	0.122	96.8
Norway	1.700	1.600	94.1
Netherlands	5.300	4.900	92.5
Portugal	3.000	2.900	96.7
West Germany	25.400	24.800	97.6
United Kingdom	22.400	21.300	95.1
Sweden	4.300	3.600	83.7
Switzerland	2.500	2.380	95.2

Source: National Statistics, INA.

large groups, Hachette and Presses de la Cité, controlled 50% of total sales. France Loisir, a subsidiary of Presses de la Cité (which owned 50% of its capital) owned the leading book club and had a 10% market share in France. (Book clubs were much more popular in northern than southern Europe as indicated in *Exhibit 11.18.*) Through retail price controls the Lang law had the effect of protecting publishers against further increases in the power of the discount book retailers.

The Record Market

In 1985, the world market was valued at 106 billion FF. West Germany, the United Kingdom, and France ranked third, fourth, and sixth in consumption, far behind the United States, which accounted for 30% of

EXHIBIT 11.16 Sales, growth, and profitability of leisure and cultural products in six European markets, 1987

Country	Sales (billions of FF)	Average profit margin (%)	Yearly growth rate[a] (%)	Type of retailing	Growth of retailing
West Germany	104	20–25%	2–3%	Very fragmented in spite of the establishment of chains Closed markets due to centralization	Multiplication of specialized subsidiaries owned by large groups
France	59	30	5–6	Leading traditional sector	Currently concentrating
United Kingdom	54	20–25	2–3	Very organized and concentrated	Increased concentration
Italy	32	30–40	3–4	Very fragmented	Very slow growth
Spain	27	25–30	3–4	Very fragmented	Slow growth
Belgium	8	20–25%	2–3%	Organized and highly competitive	Well-established distribution structure

Source: Company records.
[a]Expected average for 1988–1992.

EXHIBIT 11.17 Number of distribution points in European countries for brown goods, 1986

Country	Distribution points
West Germany	12,000
United Kingdom	7,500
France	15,000
Italy	19,000
Spain	13,000
Netherlands	3,750
Belgium	4,700
Sweden	2,000
Portugal	4,000
Austria	3,000
Switzerland	1,750
Denmark	800
Finland	1,500
Norway	1,000
Ireland	800
Total	89,800

Source: EEC/Mackintosh.

EXHIBIT 11.18 Book clubs in Europe, 1987

Country	Number of members (millions)	Percentage of the population reached
West Germany	6.0	10%
France	5.0	9
United Kingdom	2.4	4
Italy	1.8	3
Netherlands	1.5	10
Switzerland	1.5	23
Spain	1.2	3
Austria	1.1	14
Belgium	0.8	8
Portugal	0.4	4%

Source: P. Cahart, "Le livre francais-a-t-il un avenir?" *Documentation Francaise*, 1988.

total sales. At the end of the 1970s, the world record industry had to contend with increased manufacturing costs due to the oil crisis, declining spending on leisure products due to economic recession, and a contraction in the number of 15- to 24-year-olds, the principal buying group. In Europe, France was least affected by this demographic trend. Other factors specific to France, such as bootlegging, the lack of well-known music groups, and a high value-added tax of 33% also contributed to the declining growth of the record market.

With the advent of compact disks, the market recovered. In Europe, sales of CD players rose dramatically from 150,000 in 1983 to 3,000,000 units in 1987, which resulted in a concomitant increase in sales of compact disks, especially in France (*Exhibit 11.19*). The 15- to 24-year-olds were the heaviest per capita music consumers, although the majority of purchases were made by those over 35 (*Exhibit 11.20*). The aging of the European population presented a long-term problem for record manufacturers who would have to adjust the mix of music genres represented in their product lines accordingly.

From 1984 to 1989, specialty record retailers gradually lost share to larger stores selling a broader variety of merchandise. These new chains included FNAC and Virgin in France; World of Music (WOM) and Saturn in West Germany; Virgin, HMV, and Woolworth in the United Kingdom (*Exhibit 11.21*).

In France, two recent developments favored the record market: the lowering of VAT from 33.3% to 18.6%, and the opportunity to run tele-

EXHIBIT 11.19 Growth trends in the French record market

Quantities in units	1986	1987	Growth (%)
45 speed single	49,746,000	45,711,000	− 8.10
45 speed extended play	1,508,000	1,192,000	− 20.95
45 speed / 30	3,312,000	2,550,000	− 23.00
33 speed / 25	3,000	4,000	+ 25.00
33 speed / 30	26,820,000	20,401,000	− 23.90
Compact disks	6,225,000	12,474,000	+ 100.40
percent in classical music	46.7	37.1	+ 5.80
Tapes	20,906,000	22,127,000	
percent in double length	11.7	11.0	

Source: Syndicat des éditions phonographiques.

EXHIBIT 11.20 Percentages of population and of purchases by age group for three European countries, 1985

Age	United Kingdom		West Germany		France	
	Population	Purchases	Population	Purchases	Population	Purchases
8–14	13%	13%	9%	8%	12%	5%
15–25	15	27	17	23	17	27
26–35	17	20	14	21	19	24
Over 35	55%	40%	54%	50%	54%	44%

Source: EAP, European Research Project.

EXHIBIT 11.21 Percentages of 1986 sales by distribution channel in three European countries

	United Kingdom	West Germany	France
Specialized record stores of:	37.0	44.0	40.0
FNAC	—	—	22.0
WOM	—	8.5	—
Our Price	6.5	—	—
HMV	6.0	—	—
Virgin	3.0	—	—
Large stores and stores of:	41.0	45.0	
Woolworth	14.0	—	—
W.H. Smith	12.0	—	—
Boots	7.4	—	—
Record clubs/Direct mail	5.0	8.0	7.0
Book stores	5.0	0.5	3.5
Other	12.0	2.5	9.5

Sources: BPI, Phono Press, articles and interviews.

vision advertising, which had previously been off-limits to the music industry. These two developments were thought to be of most benefit to the discounters.

The Photography Market

The photography market (cameras and accessories) was growing rapidly in most of Europe. In France, 2,270,000 cameras were sold in 1986, 28% more than in 1985. This strong increase was due to the advent of easy-to-use compact cameras; technical advances such as automatic loading, integrated flash, and automatic focus; and declining production costs leading to lower retail prices which facilitated more intensive distribution.

Increasing camera sales fueled increased demand for accessories such as spare lenses and film as well as film development (*Exhibit 11.22*). The profitability of French photographic retailers and importers also grew. Of 2.3 billion FF worth of French photographic equipment imports, Japan accounted for 45%, with an even higher percentage among 35mm cameras (*Exhibit 11.23*). Among the leading manufacturers in the global photography market, two companies were American; two, Japanese; and only one, European (*Exhibit 11.24*).

EXHIBIT 11.22 Size and growth of the French market for photographic equipment and film, 1986

Equipment and accessories	Market in millions of items	Growth in %
24 × 36 Format of:	1,178	+24
nonreflex	845	+31
reflex	333	+ 8
110 + Format Disk cameras	626	− 5
Film development and automatic pictures	245	+48
Supplementary lenses for reflex	170	+13
Slide projectors	110	− 5
Electronic flashes	346	− 2

Source: SIPEC.

EXHIBIT 11.23 Sources of photographic material imported into France

Country	Market share of imports	
	In %	Millions of FF
Japan	45	1,025.10
West Germany	21	478.38
United States	11	250.58
United Kingdom	4	91.12
Italy	4	91.12
Taiwan	3	68.34
Misc.	12	273.36
Total	100	2,278.00

Source: Syndicat des industries photo/cinéma.

EXHIBIT 11.24 World sales of main photographic equipment manufacturers

Manufacturers	Sales (billions of FF)
Eastman Kodak (United States)	79.8
FUJI Photo Film (Japan)	31.8
AGFA (West Germany)	22.0
Konica (Japan)	16.1
Polaroid (United States)	10.6

Source: *L'Expansion*, November 1988.

THREATS AND OPPORTUNITIES IN 1992

There was no directive proposed as part of the 1992 market integration program that directly affected the retailing sector. However, industry analysts expected that the removal of border controls and customs delays would encourage more cross-border shopping by consumers as well as reduce cross-border distribution costs by about 5%. If deliveries involving cross-border shipments became more predictable, manufacturers and distributors would also be able to operate with lower inventories. In addition, analysts believed that store operating hours would lengthen; that direct marketing across national boundaries would increase; and that national controls on the size, type, and ownership of retail stores would eventually be harmonized.

The EC market integration in 1992 was also expected to accelerate the internationalization of retailing and intensify competition on a national and international scale. Retailers would have to defend their positions against new as well as current competitors. Many would also seek outlets in foreign markets to achieve growth through leveraging their retail positioning concepts, to hedge investment risks, and to retaliate against foreign competitors invading their home markets.

Several experts predicted that the internationalization of retailing would accelerate the growth of the biggest companies: large diversified groups and specialized chain stores. Diversified German, British, and Dutch retail groups with strong capital positions would acquire successful companies and open new stores. Specialized chain stores would identify market niches and then extend the same approach to other European countries to achieve the scale economies in purchasing and brand name development that would both exploit and maintain their competitive advantages. The increasing similarity in attitudes and preferences among young consumers in the EC and the success of chains such as Benetton encouraged some FNAC executives in the belief that FNAC could become a Pan-European retailer, in three of its four core product categories, books being the exception.

Intensifying competition promised further industry consolidation, especially in countries with fragmented retail markets. Some observers saw French retailing as strong and believed that 1992 would bring more opportunities than risks. Others, including FNAC executives, expected increased competition from foreign companies such as Virgin, Hyper Market, Interdiscount, and Dixons. European governments were thought unlikely to try to protect their domestically based retailers against foreign competitors because such an approach would mean higher retail prices and provoke consumer opposition.

The New Entrants

Given the relatively strong growth and margins to be earned in France in record, photography, and consumer electronics retailing, France attracted the interest of many European retail groups whose distribution concepts and marketing approaches were sometimes similar to those of the French leaders, but whose prices were often more aggressive (*Exhibit 11.25*). Their interest in France was strong because growth in their own markets had slowed and, consequently, margins were tighter. Among the new entrants into France were the following:

Virgin. Established in 1970 by Richard Branson, the British group had operations in 23 countries, mostly in Europe and in English-speaking countries (United States, Canada, Australia, and New Zealand). Its operations included:

- Music editing and production, which was its core business (Virgin was the sixth-largest music producer and distributor in the world).
- Advertising, with Virgin Television (production and postproduction), Virgin Vision (editing and distribution of video films), and Virgin Broadcasting (with a participation in European Television).
- Retailing, with 10 "megastores," large discount stores specializing in the distribution of records, tapes, and other music-related items.

EXHIBIT 11.25 Size, gross margin, and expected growth of leisure and cultural product-markets through 1992

Sector	Size 1987 (billion of FF)	Gross margin (%)	Growth, 1987–1992 (%)
Travel	14	10–12	1
TV-video	16.8	20–24	7
Photo and film	4.4	20–24	3
Home computer	2.7	18–22	0
Audio	8.8	25–30	4
Records	3.2	26–30	25
Car radios	3	30–35	8
Books	17	32–38	0
Film development and services	3.5	40–50	2

Source: Company records.

- Other leisure activities, including hotels, restaurants, travel agencies, and even an airline (Virgin Atlantic).

Established in 1980, the French Virgin subsidiary held 6% to 7% of the market for record editing and production by 1989. The first Virgin megastore opened on the Champs Elysees in November 1988, amid substantial publicity and advertising. Its total area was 3,000 square meters, half of which was the sales floor. It offered a very wide range of records, tapes, videos, and stereos in a striking decor. There were 100,000 music-related items, and all record companies were represented. As in Virgin's British megastores, the sales area included an open space where artists could sign their records. Although its prices were similar to FNAC's, Virgin ran an aggressive promotion policy and permitted customers to listen privately to both new and rare albums. Service quality was also exceptional; salespeople were young, efficient, and knowledgeable. Moreover, the store remained open until midnight, even on Sundays, whereas FNAC was only open from Monday to Saturday until 7 P.M.

Virgin achieved its first-year sales goal of 300 million FF or 5% of the French record market with only one store. Virgin planned to open a bookstore and boutiques (selling T-shirts, jeans, watches, and other small items) in its Paris megastore and to expand its operations to include a cafeteria, travel agency, and discotheque. The store in Paris was to be the flagship store in a nationwide chain. Virgin presented its store as a mecca of music and cultural diversity.

Some executives believed that Virgin would be followed into France by two other leading record retailers: Tower Records of the United States and HMV, a subsidiary of the British group Thorn-EMI.

Hyper Market. A subsidiary of the West German retailer Kaufhof, Hyper Market was about to open its first electrical home appliance and record store in Strasbourg, France, to be followed by two more stores on the outskirts of Paris. Its after-sales service was poor, and consumers paid for repairs. With limited sales staff, Hyper Market's in-store service was poor, but the labor savings allowed Hyper Market to offer very aggressive prices.

Interdiscount. This Swiss company bought a chain of small stores in West Germany (average size of 200 square meters) which specialized in cameras. Interdiscount widened its range of products to include camcorders, home VCRs, and TV sets. Since early 1988, Interdiscount had been opening a new chain of stores in the German market at a rate of one store per week. France was the next target, with the first stores scheduled to be opened in early 1990. Interdiscount offered low prices on certain key items, but made a profit thanks to astute management of its product mix and to high margins on the sale of consumable products (such as film development).

Dixons. The leader of the British photography (30%) and the brown goods (20%) markets, Dixons was searching for retail locations in the French market to develop a distribution concept similar to that of Interdiscount. Unlike the latter, however, Dixons developed its own brands, which accounted for about 40% of its TV and video sales in the United Kingdom.

STRATEGIC ISSUES FOR 1992

With 1992 approaching, FNAC executives were considering the following questions: Would FNAC have to direct all its energies to defending itself against new entrants on the home front, or should FNAC consider further expansion in other countries? Should FNAC still focus on the four-product-line stores in order to expand, or should the company experiment with other retail concepts? FNAC executives pondered five diversification opportunities:

"Satellite Stores." A market test in Annecy showed that four-product-line stores of less than 700 square meters could be run profitably in cities with a population between 80,000 and 120,000. These stores could rely on larger FNAC stores nearby for their management, logistics, and purchasing.

Record Stores. After considering alternative responses to Virgin's launch in France, FNAC decided to open 2,500-square-meter stores which would carry only records and software products.

Consumer Electronics Stores. FNAC considered opening a chain of 100 stores specializing in consumer electronics, with an average selling area of between 300 and 400 square meters. The investment could be shared with other European partners. FNAC would contribute its brand image and marketing techniques, while its partners would bring their chain-store management expertise and incremental bargaining power with suppliers. FNAC also considered another alternative: an approach toward consumer electronic stores that would counter the Hyper Market challenge. However, FNAC executives recognized that they lacked expertise in this retail format, and that a new brand name would have to be adopted to prevent consumer confusion and a negative impact on the FNAC image.

Stores with a Selection of Books and Records. Some FNAC executives were championing a chain of proximity stores that would carry books and records. These stores could be tied into book clubs which would attract additional customers to one brand franchise.

Addition of Other Product Lines. FNAC was also considering adding new product lines such as musical instruments and/or extending FNAC travel services to all of its stores.

Philippe Mondan thought that FNAC should internationalize to defend its national position. But, before establishing stores in other countries, it was necessary to improve the results in Belgium. Mondan was convinced that the FNAC concept was transferable. However, he was uncertain whether it was preferable to open very large stores in a few main cities or smarter to develop a more balanced national network of stores.

New retail concepts were perhaps necessary for FNAC to grow. Mondan wondered whether FNAC should create single-product stores or whether this would compromise FNAC's identity and culture by distorting the original four-product-line store concept. Mondan knew quick decisions on strategy were needed, and that good store locations were becoming less easy to find and more costly as a result. He wondered, however, how much risk FNAC could afford to take.

EDITORS' COMMENTARY

As noted in the FNAC case, none of the proposals in the 1992 EC market integration program deals directly with retailing. Nevertheless, FNAC executives anticipate changes in competition, both in France and in other EC countries. As a leading French retailer of photographic equipment, records and tapes, books, and consumer electronic equipment, FNAC must consider both how to defend its home market position and how (if at all) to expand into other countries.

FNAC's history is unusual. Founded by "former Trotskyites" in the 1950s, the company was originally a consumer cooperative. While it has evolved into a conventional corporation, FNAC's approach still places heavy emphasis on consumer information and assistance, as well as sponsorship of cultural activities. Other noteworthy elements of FNAC's strategy include:

- Diversification: from its original base in photographic products, FNAC gradually broadened its product lines to include books, recorded music, sporting goods, and (on a smaller scale) photofinishing and travel services.
- Very large stores, located in downtown areas, that require large trading area population bases.
- Highly decentralized management, with each store having considerable latitude in selecting products. Merchandise is also shipped directly from suppliers to the stores.

On the international front, FNAC had opened four stores in Belgium. Because this division of the company was not yet profitable, management was rightly concerned about the company's ability to operate outside of France.

In mid-1989, FNAC management was especially concerned about the recent entry into France of Virgin, a British operator of "megastores" in the recorded music business. In addition, two specialized photographic chains (one Swiss, one British) were expected to open or acquire stores in France, while a German company was about to open a home appliance and record "hypermarket" in Strasbourg.

The most important problem for FNAC management to resolve is that of reassessing the viability of its basic strategy in France. The combination of product lines that the company offers is an unusual one; in most countries each of FNAC's four primary product lines is typically handled by different specialty stores. In the United States, for example, the leading sellers of photographic equipment are local or regional specialty chains like 47th Street Photo in New York City; national chains such as B. Dalton dominate book retailing; and a separate group of specialists handle recorded music (including U.K.-based Tower Records). Will similar single-category specialists (home-grown or foreign) grow in importance in France? Do they enjoy inherent advantages over a "multiline specialist" like FNAC? Will the integration of the EC market further enhance the advantages of more specialized stores via increased cross-border shopping and/or opportunities to utilize more efficient, centralized EC-wide logistics and information systems? FNAC should, we believe, study these issues carefully before embarking on any new ventures outside of France.

CHAPTER *12*

Pan-European Marketing

Volvo Trucks Europe and the Truck Market

EDITORS' INTRODUCTION

Volvo management is concerned that the company is not adequately coordinating its marketing programs across the EC. Currently, almost all sales to end users are through two-step distribution, involving a national importer and dealer. Prices on vehicles, parts, and service are set in each market according to local competitive conditions and, therefore, vary widely throughout the EC. Service contracts on vehicles bought in one country are not necessarily honored by Volvo dealers in other countries. Advertising and promotion are only coordinated to the extent of incorporating standard presentations of the company name and logo. In addition, production planning at European headquarters depends on the sales forecasts developed by each national importer. These often prove inaccurate, significantly adding to production costs.

Volvo management has established a task force to explore how to satisfy the needs of the growing number of international fleet customers who want consistent service throughout Europe and the ability to negotiate a single price for all their European truck purchases. Volvo has also set up a steering committee of national importers and headquarters staff and is planning training programs to enable both groups to discuss how to achieve more marketing coordination.

There are three key questions facing management. First, to what extent should Volvo strive for more marketing coordination throughout the EC? Second, on which elements of the marketing mix is increased coordination especially required? Third, if Volvo continues to use national importers, how can management sell the concept of increased coordination and less local autonomy to its importers and dealers?

Volvo Trucks Europe

Jean-Jacques Lambin and Tammy Bunn Hiller

In early May 1989, Ulf Selvin, Vice President of Marketing, Sales, and Service for Volvo Truck Corporation, Europe Division (VTC Europe), was deep in thought. European Community (EC) directives aimed at creating a single internal EC market by the end of 1992 were reshaping the truck market in Europe. Truck buyers' sales support and service needs and demands were changing and becoming more Pan-European. Competition was growing fiercer and increasingly Pan-European as well.

VTC Europe had historically operated as a multi-domestic marketer, with each national importer management team responsible for the marketing, sales, and service of Volvo trucks within its country. Recently, however, programs had been initiated at both headquarters and importer level which were aimed at moving VTC Europe toward Pan-European marketing. As Selvin reviewed the progress of these programs, he deliberated over whether or not VTC Europe should attempt to become a "Euro-marketer" and, if so, what the appropriate mix was between Pan-European, regional, and national marketing of Volvo trucks in Europe. If he and his management team decided to move VTC Europe from multi-domestic to Pan-European marketing, they would have to identify the critical steps which the company would need to take in order to make such a transition successful, including the implementation implications for VTC Europe's marketing strategy, marketing organization structure, marketing information systems, and human resource development policies.

BACKGROUND

Volvo Truck Corporation (VTC) was a wholly owned subsidiary of AB Volvo (Volvo). Headquartered in Göteborg, Sweden, Volvo was the largest industrial group in the Nordic region. Established in 1927 as an automobile manufacturer, the company gradually expanded its production to include trucks, buses, an extensive range of automotive components, and marine, aircraft, aerospace, and industrial engines. Beginning in the late 1970s, Volvo diversified into the food industry, finance, and oil, fruit and chemicals trade in order to increase the group's opportunities for growth and profitability and to counteract economic fluctuations. Volvo's structure and organization was characterized by decentralization and delegation of responsibility. Its myriad operations were united by the shared values of quality, service, ethical performance, and concern for people and the environment. The group's products were marketed around the world, with almost 90% of sales occurring outside Sweden in 1988. Volvo's sales and net income totaled Swedish kronor (SEK) 96,639 million and SEK 4,953 million, respectively, in 1988, up from 1987 levels of SEK 92,520 million and SEK 4,636 million, respectively.

The first Volvo truck was manufactured in 1928. It was an immediate success and was met with high demand. Volvo's truck production expanded rapidly in the 1930s and 1940s. The profits from truck building financed the company's total operations for most of its first twenty years. It was not until the late 1940s that Volvo's automobile production became more than marginally viable. By the late 1960s, however, this situation had reversed. Despite market leadership in Sweden and the rest of Scandinavia, Volvo's truck operations had become unprofitable due to heavy competition in new export markets, combined with problems with state-of-the-art truck models which were placing severe stresses on Volvo's design and service departments. The truck business had become a drag on the company's automobile operations. Management contemplated divesting Volvo's truck operations, but decided instead to form a separate truck division (VTC).

The creation of VTC marked the beginning of major investment in and continued expansion and profitability of Volvo's truck operations. During the 1970s and 1980s, VTC replaced its entire product line with new models and intensified its marketing efforts in international markets. Between 1979 and 1986, VTC became the first truck manufacturer to win the coveted "Truck of the Year" award three times. In 1981, VTC acquired the truck assets of the White Motor Company in the United States and formed the Volvo White Truck Corporation. In 1987, White Volvo joined with General Motors' heavy truck division to form a joint venture, the Volvo GM Heavy Truck Corporation, with Volvo as the majority shareholder with responsibility for management.

VTC's truck production grew dramatically between 1970 and 1980, from 16,300 to 30,200 trucks. By 1988, production had doubled to 60,500 units. During the 1980s, VTC's share of the world market for trucks in the heavy class — gross vehicle weight (GVW) of greater than 16 tons — doubled to 11%, and VTC became the world's second-largest producer of heavy trucks. In both 1987 and 1988, demand for Volvo trucks exceeded VTC's production capacity.

In 1988, VTC sold (delivered) 59,500 trucks worldwide. *Exhibit 12.1* shows the breakout of VTC's 1987 and 1988 unit sales (deliveries) by market area. The two largest markets were Western Europe and North America, which accounted for 52% and 36% of sales, respectively. Almost 90% of unit sales were in the heavy class. VTC earned SEK 2,645 million on sales of SEK 22,762 million in 1988, which represented 34% of Volvo's 1988 operating income, up from 14% in 1986. *Exhibit 12.2* contains graphs of VTC's sales, operating income, return on capital, and capital expenditure and development costs for the years 1984 through 1988.

VTC's organization chart is shown in *Exhibit 12.3*. Separate divisions were responsible for the manufacture and marketing of trucks in Europe, overseas, the United States, and Brazil. Trucks were produced in ten Volvo-owned assembly plants. Of the 60,500 trucks manufactured by VTC in 1988, 20,000 were produced in the United States, 17,200 in Belgium, 14,400 in Sweden, 3,700 in Scotland, 3,200 in Brazil, 1,500 in

EXHIBIT 12.1 Sales (deliveries) of Volvo trucks by market area and size

	Number of trucks delivered	
Market area	1987	1989
Europe	29,300	31,600
North America	13,200	21,500
White Autocar/WHITEGMC	11,100	9,800[a]
Volvo	2,100	1,700
Latin America	3,300	3,300
Middle East	500	700
Australia	400	800
Other Markets	1,000	1,600
Total	47,700	59,500
of which <16 tons GVW	6,500	6,500
of which >16 tons GVW	41,200	53,000

[a]Includes GM's product line

EXHIBIT 12.2 VTC financial trends, 1984–1988

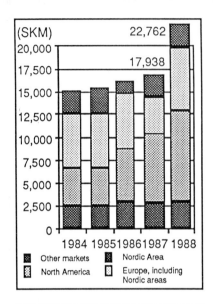

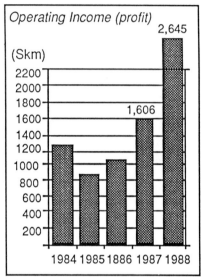

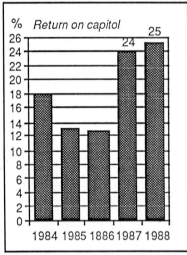

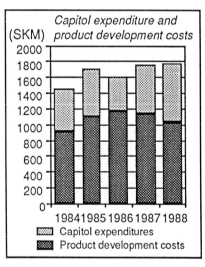

EXHIBIT 12.3 VTC organization chart

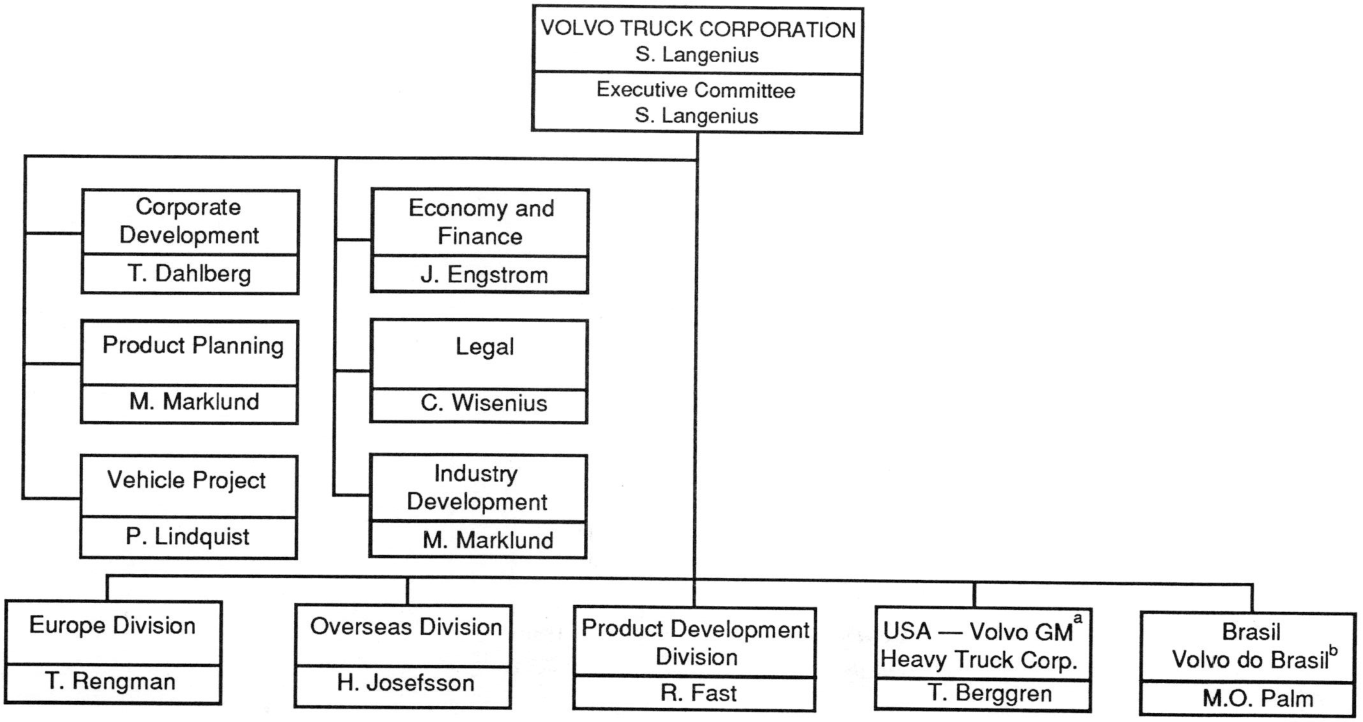

VOLVO TRUCK CORPORATION
S. Langenius

Executive Committee
S. Langenius

Corporate Development
T. Dahlberg

Product Planning
M. Marklund

Vehicle Project
P. Lindquist

Economy and Finance
J. Engstrom

Legal
C. Wisenius

Industry Development
M. Marklund

Europe Division
T. Rengman

Overseas Division
H. Josefsson

Product Development Division
R. Fast

USA — Volvo GM[a] Heavy Truck Corp.
T. Berggren

Brasil Volvo do Brasil[b]
M.O. Palm

353

Australia, and 500 in Peru. VTC's trucks were sold through a network of 850 dealers operating with 1200 service workshops in over 100 countries.

The product development division was responsible for the design and development of global truck concepts and components. It had development departments in Sweden, the United States, Belgium, the United Kingdom, Brazil, and Australia. About 6% of turnover was invested in product development annually.

VTC EUROPE

VTC Europe was responsible for the production and marketing of Volvo trucks in Europe. The Western European market for heavy trucks grew 13% in 1988, to 175,000 vehicles, based on new truck registration statistics. Despite full capacity utilization of its plants, VTC Europe was unable to keep pace with the market growth. Its share of the Western European heavy truck market declined from 14.3% to 14%. The Western European medium truck market (10–16 tons GVW) grew by 4.5% in 1988, to 42,000 vehicles. Volvo's share of this market declined from 10.6% to 9.0%. *Exhibit 12.4* shows a comparison of new Volvo truck registrations and market shares by European country for 1987 and 1988.

Early 1989 registration figures indicated that Volvo was regaining lost share in Europe in both the heavy and medium truck markets, as shown in *Exhibit 12.5*. VTC Europe began 1989 with a large delivery backlog. The division dramatically improved its delivery precision between January and March 1989, moving from 56% to 80% of trucks being delivered within one week of scheduled delivery. However, delivery precision varied widely by country. As of March 1989, it ranged from 54% in Spain to 94% in Austria and Finland.

Distribution System

Two layers in the distribution system separated Volvo truck factories from Volvo truck customers. Each country's distribution network was headed by an importer that was responsible for marketing, sales, and service of Volvo trucks, parts distribution, and the creation and maintenance of a dealer network within its country. Of VTC Europe's 15 importer organizations, only four — Austria, Spain, Portugal, and Greece — were independent importers. The other 11 were Volvo-owned. Importers purchased trucks from VTC Europe's corporate headquarters and sold them to the Volvo truck dealers within their countries, who in turn sold them to Volvo truck customers. VTC's European dealer

EXHIBIT 12.4 VTC Europe sales (registrations) and market share by country, 1987 and 1988

Market	GVW Class[b]	Number of new Volvo trucks registered[a]		Market share (%)	
		1987	1988	1987	1988
Great Britain	>10 tons	5,720	6,610	15.5%	15.4%
France	> 9 tons	4,340	4,580	10.9	10.3
Sweden	>10 tons	2,970	3,030	50.9	53.7
Netherlands	>10 tons	2,140	2,070	17.7	16.4
Italy[c]	> 9 tons	1,490	1,780	6.5	6.8
Spain	>10 tons	1,010	1,700	6.5	8.4
Belgium	>10 tons	1,600	1,600	21.6	20.1
Portugal	>10 tons	1,020	1,280	29.9	27.1
Denmark	>10 tons	1,310	1,130	29.8	33.0
Finland	>10 tons	1,060	1,120	32.2	32.4
West Germany	>10 tons	950	1,030	3.0	3.2
Norway	>10 tons	1,280	800	40.6%	37.5%

[a]According to official registration statistics.
[b]Countries differ as to how they group their registration statistics by weight.
[c]Preliminary information.

network included approximately 400 dealers and about 800 service points. Almost all dealers were independent, although a few were Volvo-owned. All dealers were dedicated — that is, they sold only Volvo brand trucks.

The normal distribution network was rarely circumvented. Almost all sales were conducted through a dealer. VTC Europe headquarters sold directly to end customers only when selling to the governments of state-controlled countries like the Soviet Union. Similarly, importers by-passed their dealers infrequently. For example, the only customer to whom Belgium's importer made direct sales was the Belgian army.

As a matter of course, importer organizations were headed and staffed by local nationals, although in a few cases, a Swedish manager had headed an importer temporarily, during the transition from independent to Volvo-owned importership. Historically, importer managers

EXHIBIT 12.5 Total market new truck registrations and Volvo share by country

Market	For year ending month[a]	Total market registrations (>16 tons)	Volvo market share (>16 tons)	Total market registrations (10–16 tons)	Volvo market share (10–16 tons)
Sweden	3/89	5,541	51.5%	938	74.1%
Denmark	2/89	2,317	34.7	1,379	42.6
Finland	2/89	3,827	30.3	609	34.3
Norway	3/89	1,064	45.1	203	51.9
Great Britain	2/89	39,637	19.6	5,942	8.8
Ireland	1/89	1,782	14.2	672	1.4
Germany	2/89	28,157	4.2	5,593	2.4
Europe I	2/89[b]	83,962	18.1	14,851	14.8
France	3/89	35,921	11.3	8,371	7.3
Belgium	3/89	7,838	21.7	1,568	19.4
Luxembourg	12/88	385	31.9	86	19.8
Netherlands	1/89	9,419	16.0	1,489	22.0
Italy	2/89	27,198	7.5	13,328	2.0
Austria	2/89	3,751	14.5	1,072	7.8
Switzerland	12/88	3,349	15.4	476	19.7
Portugal	2/89	3,752	37.3	1,758	5.4
Spain	3/89	19,227	9.7	2,959	7.5
Greece	12/88	88	28.4	76	36.8
Israel	3/89	764	45.5	284	35.2
Europe II	2/89[b]	111,537	12.4	29,150	7.4
Europe Total (excl. Israel)	2/89[b]	195,263	14.4%	44,288	9.6%

[a]The most current registration information available was used for each market.
[b]Markets with late information on registrations were estimated as of 2/89 for Europe I, Europe II, and Europe Total.

were never transferred to work in the Swedish headquarters or in the importer organizations of other countries.

As one VTC Europe manager stated: "Importers are responsible for their country — period." Each importer's management was evaluated and rewarded on the sales volume, market share, and profit earned within its country. Importers negotiated transfer prices for the trucks they purchased from VTC Europe headquarters. These transfer prices varied from country to country. Importers had the responsibility to set the prices at which they sold trucks to their dealers. Prices to dealers and, consequently, prices to truck-buying customers, varied considerably by country, depending on local competitive pressures. For example, Belgium had no national truck producer. Consequently, the Belgian importer priced Volvo's trucks significantly higher than did the French importer, which faced fierce competition from a local manufacturer.

Marketing Communications

Prior to 1987, importers had complete control of the design and execution of marketing communications programs employed within their countries. In early 1987, Roger Johansson, marketing support manager for VTC Europe, developed a corporate communication platform. His objective was two-fold. First, he hoped to encourage consistency in the visual presentation and underlying message of sales promotion and advertising materials across Europe, so as to enhance the total impact on customers of Volvo truck communications. Second, he aimed to improve the efficiency and cost effectiveness of production of advertising and sales support materials. According to the communication platform, sales promotion and advertising activities were to be divided among all levels of the marketing organization — headquarters, importers, and dealers — based on which level was best suited for a given activity.

The platform was designed to remain in effect through 1989. Every three years a new communication platform was to be introduced. The platform did not dictate the actual content of messages which importers and dealers could use in their communications. Instead, it encouraged creativity in designing messages which took account of local circumstances, as long as the thinking behind the messages was consistent throughout Europe. Consistency was also encouraged by a visual identity program which strictly specified the logotypes, emblems, symbols, colors, typefaces, and layouts that were authorized for use throughout the marketing organization. Responsibility for complying with the precepts of the communications platform and visual identity program rested with the management of each importer organization.

Personal selling occurred almost solely at the dealer level. Each importer ran its own training programs for its dealer's salespeople. In addition, a state-of-the-art training facility in Göteborg was used to train both importer and dealer management whenever a new Volvo truck product was introduced. Importers and dealers were taught the features of the new truck, how those features translated into benefits for the potential buyers, and how to determine the bottom-line impact which the new truck would have on the potential buyer's profit-and-loss statement.

Service

In addition to selling trucks, Volvo dealers maintained and repaired them. Each dealer was responsible for designing its local service system to suit its customers' needs. Each importer was responsible for coordinating service on a national level and ensuring consistency in dealer service offerings throughout its country. Volvo's service philosophy was based on the principle of preventive maintenance. Volvo dealers offered their customers service agreements with fixed prices for maintenance service and repair. Trucks that operated internationally could participate in Volvo Action Service Europe, which provided 24-hour assistance throughout Europe in the event of a breakdown. Volvo offered a DKV/ Volvo credit card to its customers, which could be used at most Volvo workshops in Western Europe and at thousands of gas and service stations.

Volvo's service systems were not consistent across Europe. Service agreements made with a dealer in one country were not automatically valid at service centers in another country. Even when they were honored, prices for the same service or part often differed dramatically across countries, as did parts availability. Opening hours of service centers varied within and across countries, and the work habits and quality of mechanics differed significantly from country to country. According to importer management in Belgium, few Volvo truck owners used the DKV/Volvo credit card when traveling internationally. A customer explained why: "We do not use the DKV card anymore, except for fuel. Outside Belgium, we do not have the same discount; sometimes we find a difference of up to 22% in exchange rate and sometimes the card is simply not accepted." According to Jean de Ruyter, after market manager of Volvo's Belgian importer, repairs made outside of a Volvo truck owner's home country typically resulted in a communication nightmare involving discussions among the customer, the repairing dealer, the importer, the customer's local dealer, and the importer in the customer's home country.

Market Segmentation

Historically, VTC Europe had segmented its market solely on the basis of GVW. It divided the European truck market into three segments: heavy trucks (>16 tons GVW), medium trucks (7–16 tons GVW), and light trucks (<7 tons GVW). Volvo did not produce trucks for the light truck market. Medium duty trucks were further split into a 10–16 ton market, where Volvo has a truck range across Euopre, and into a 7–10 ton market, where Volvo sold a model on selected markets. Therefore, marketing management ignored this segment and concentrated on the other two, emphasizing the heavy truck segment in which Volvo had achieved the bulk of its success concentrating on tractors for international transport.

Marketing Information Systems

VTC Europe did not have a standardized method of forecasting sales across Europe. Each importer developed its annual sales forecast using its own forecasting technique. The importers' forecasts were sent to VTC Europe's marketing planning and logistics department, which used them as a starting point for making a total forecast. Forecasts were used to plan production and for long-term capacity planning. In both 1987 and 1988, several importers underestimated annual sales by as much as 25%, leading VTC Europe to underestimate its total sales substantially.

VTC Europe's marketing planning and logistics department conducted market research and market analysis. Market research included both Europe-wide surveys and individual country surveys. Much of it was qualitative research intended to reveal how Volvo was performing relative to competitors. Results were shared with importer marketing managers. The department regularly tracked new truck registration statistics to try to discern market trends. It bought competitive production figures in order to learn the kinds of trucks which Volvo's competitors were building. The department also tracked Volvo's production, delivery precision, turnover rate, and market share by country.

In addition to research conducted by headquarters, importers commissioned marketing research in their own countries as needed. Most importer-initiated market research was conducted on a project-by-project basis, rather than on a recurrent basis. There was no standardized method of gathering data across countries.

THE EUROPEAN TRUCK MARKET

Between 1970 and 1988, truck sales made by Western European manufacturers grew at a compound annual rate of almost 1%. During that time, however, there were two exaggerated cycles. Sales boomed in the 1970s, peaking at 422,000 trucks (3.5 tons GVW and larger) in 1979. In the early 1980s, depression in Western Europe combined with collapse in demand from Middle East and African export markets. Sales bottomed out at 333,000 vehicles in 1984. Between 1984 and 1988, the Western European truck industry made a strong recovery. In 1988, sales reached 485,000 trucks. As *Exhibit 12.6* shows, market growth was propelled by expansion in the heavy (>16 tons GVW) and light (3.5–7.5 tons GVW) truck segments. Medium truck sales (7.5–16 tons GVW) appeared to be in long-term decline. In 1988, approximately 310,000 new trucks (3.5 tons GVW and larger) were registered in Western Europe.

In 1950, there were 55 independent truck manufacturers, in Western Europe. In 1989, there were 11. During the 1980s, several structural changes occurred in the European truck market. The most significant ones took place in the United Kingdom. Since the 1930s, both Ford and General Motors had based their European truck manufacturing in the United Kingdom. In 1986, Ford entered into a strategic alliance with Iveco, the truck subsidiary of Italy's Fiat, which led to the formation of Iveco-Ford. Ford ceded management control of both its U.K. operations and marketing to Iveco. A few months later, General Motors (Bedford-brand trucks) withdrew completely from truck manufacture in Europe after failed attempts to buy Enasa, MAN, and Leyland Trucks. The state-owned Leyland Trucks was losing more than $1 million per week, when,

EXHIBIT 12.6 Western European truck manufacturers' sales by truck size

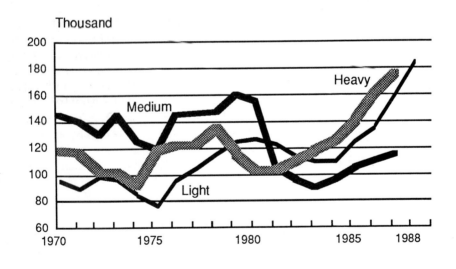

Source: *Financial Times*, May 3, 1989.
Note: heavy = >16 tons GVW; medium = 7.5–16 tons GVW; light = 3.5–7.5 tons GVW.

in 1987, the UK government wrote off Leyland's substantial debts in order to facilitate its merger with the Dutch truck maker, DAF. DAF received 60% of the equity of the merged company and effective control. The Rover Group received the remaining 40% equity stake.

In continental Europe, structural changes were less dramatic. West Germany's Daimler-Benz, the market leader in Western Europe truck sales, reduced production capacity in the early 1980s. The other West German truck manufacturer, MAN, had been heavily reliant on Middle East markets. The 1983 cancellation of a half-completed contract with Iraq left MAN financially crippled in the early 1980s. MAN's management fought off a take-over attempt by General Motors, completely re-organized the company, concentrated on building up market presence in Western Europe, and regained profitability. In 1984, Iveco closed its unprofitable Unic truck plant in France, making RVI, the truck subsidiary of Renault, the sole truck producer in France. During the 1980s, RVI underwent a severe rationalization program. By 1987, it was profitable for the first time since its formation in the mid-1970s. Enasa, Spain's only independent truck producer, entered into a joint venture with DAF for the development of a modern truck cab range which was introduced in 1987. Both of Sweden's truck manufacturers, Volvo and Saab-Scania, survived the recession in very good shape without restructuring in Europe.

There was no common classification of trucks throughout Western Europe. Although the definition of the truck market varied by country, each country maintained new truck registration statistics, which industry members used to calculate market shares. In 1988, the top five truck manufacturers accounted for almost 75% of total Western European truck sales (>3.5 tons GVW). Daimler-Benz (23.7%) was the market leader, followed by Iveco (20.6%), RVI (11.4%), DAF (9.4%), and Volvo (9.0%). In the two segments in which Volvo competed, heavy trucks and medium trucks (10–16 tons GVW only), Volvo was number two and number four in the Western European market, respectively, as shown in *Exhibit 12.7*. In 1988, the market leaders by individual country were as follows: DAF (Leyland) in the United Kingdom, Daimler-Benz in West Germany, RVI in France, Iveco in Italy, Enasa in Spain, DAF in the Netherlands, Volvo and Daimler-Benz in Belgium, and Volvo in Sweden, Denmark, Finland, and Norway.

Impact of 1992 on the European Truck Industry

The expression "1992" was shorthand for a campaign to turn the twelve EC member countries into one barrier-free internal market by the end of 1992. The community's goal was to create a market of 322 million

EXHIBIT 12.7 Western European truck market shares by manufacturer based on new truck registrations

Manufacturer	Market share (>16 tons GVW)		Market share (10–16 tons GVW)	
	1987	1988	1987	1988
Volvo	14.3%	14.0%	10.6%	9.0%
Daimler-Benz	20.1	18.9	23.9	23.7
Iveco	12.8	13.6	24.9	27.6
RVI	11.9	12.3	14.3	16.3
DAF	10.8	11.6	8.0	8.7
Scania	12.4	11.0	1.3	.8
MAN	8.5	8.3	6.2	5.0
Pegaso	4.2	4.7	1.7	.6
ERF	1.6	2.1	0	0
WRIGT	1.7	2.0	1.0	1.0
EBRO	0	0	2.0	2.7
Other	1.7%	1.5%	6.1%	4.6%

people in which the free movement of goods, services, people and capital was ensured. Among the 286 legislative reforms designed to fulfill this objective were ones aimed at liberalizing road haulage in the EC. Already, transport delays at customs posts had been shortened by the January 1, 1988 introduction of a "Single Administrative Document," which replaced the plethora of individual country documents previously required for inter-EC border crossings. Historically, inter-EC transport was strictly limited by a system of quotas which restricted the number of trips that haulers of one country could make into other EC countries in a given year. In June of 1987, the EC member nations agreed to increase these quotas by 40% per year in 1988 and 1989 and to abolish all road transport quotas to EC and non-EC destinations by January 1, 1993. As a result of these two measures, industry analysts expected a 30%–50% increase in inter-EC trade by the year 2000.

The European Commission supported unrestricted cabotage—that is, the freedom for a trucker registered in one EC country to collect and deliver loads between two points inside a second EC country. EC member states had not reached agreement on allowing unrestricted cabotage, but the Commission was pushing for agreement and implementation by the end of 1992. In 1989, restrictions on cabotage were partially responsible for 35% of all trucks on EC roads traveling empty. Unrestricted cabotage would give trucks more flexibility to contract short hauls on their return trips, which would enable them to avoid returning from a long trip with an empty truck.

Trucking companies had already begun to vie for position in the EC's post-1992 transport market. Industry analysts expected concentration in the road haulage industry via mergers, acquisitions, and strategic alliances, particularly among fleets specializing in international traffic. Many observers believed that medium-sized fleets would be squeezed out in favor of small specialized haulers and large efficient international haulers. Most believed that the scramble for business would result in a major shake-up of the EC transport industry, after which there would likely be fewer total competitors and, perhaps, a smaller total market for heavy trucks.

The implications for European truck manufacturers were several. Inter-European transporters had already begun to demand that truck producers supply consistent systems of service and sales support across Europe. As 1992 approached, pressures to harmonize both truck and parts prices throughout Europe would probably increase, as large fleet owners attempted to negotiate Europe-wide prices. In addition, "artificial" differences in truck product standards — that is, unique product standards which were designed solely to protect national markets — would likely disappear over time. Eventually, new trucks might be built to "Euro-specifications," in contrast with the existing situation in which "every European country had two unique possessions—a national anthem and a brake system standard." As large trucking companies became increasingly international, the loyalty of their truck buyers to locally produced vehicles would likely wane. Competition between truck producers was expected to intensify as was concentration within the industry.

VTC EUROPE'S MOVES TOWARD PAN-EUROPEAN MARKETING

Market Segmentation and Sales Forecasting

In 1984, VTC Europe took over its previously independent Belgian importer. Throughout the early 1980s, VTC had experienced heavy price competition and low profitability in Belgium. In order to develop a sound marketing strategy designed to increase the profitability of VTC's Belgian operation, while at the same time satisfying its customers, André Durieux, then marketing manager of VTC Belgium, commissioned an outside consultant, Professor Robert Peeters of the Université Catholique de Louvain, to perform a brand image study in the Belgian truck market. Peeters designed and executed a quantitative survey of a representative sample of truck owners in Belgium.

The first objective of the study was to conceive a truck market segmentation scheme which would help Belgian management decide the right customer groups to target in order to increase the profitability of its sales. The study also aimed to discover the criteria which were determinant to truck owners when choosing a make of truck and, for each criterion, the position which Volvo and each of its competitors held in owners' minds. A third goal of the study was to determine the marketing mix through which VTC Belgium could send the right message to its target segments in the ways which would best reach them and influence them to buy Volvo trucks.

One of the outcomes of this research was the development of a truck industry segmentation scheme which Belgian management used in reshaping its marketing strategy. In 1987, Pol Jacobs, VTC Belgium's current marketing and business development manager, commissioned a follow-up study in order to assess the impact of Volvo's post-1984 marketing efforts on brand image in Belgium and to reveal any changes which had occurred in the makeup of the market by segment. Comparing the results of the second survey with those of the first showed that the pattern of Volvo's penetration of different market segments in Belgium had changed significantly between 1984 and 1987. Between 1984 and 1989, VTC Belgium improved its profitability almost ten-fold. Jacobs was convinced that use of Peeters' segmentation scheme as a starting point from which to design Volvo's marketing strategy for Belgium had contributed to VTC Belgium's success.

Peeters and Jacobs had also worked together to develop an econometric forecasting model, the intent of which was to improve the accuracy of Belgium's short-term (<2 years) sales forecasts. In 1989, the model was being tested in both Belgium and the United Kingdom. Ulf Norman, VTC Europe's manager of marketing planning and logistics, was supportive of expanding the model's use throughout Europe if it proved successful and reliable in the United Kingdom and Belgium.

Volvo Euro Truck Dealer and Eurofleet Task Forces

In late 1988, Selvin organized the "Volvo Euro Truck Dealer" (VETD) project. Its steering committee was made up of two VTC Europe headquarters service managers and five importer after sales and service managers (from Belgium, France, Italy, the Netherlands, and the United

Kingdom). Chaired by John de Ruyter, the steering committee was charged with establishing the project's objectives, coordinating the working process of the project among VTC, Volvo Parts Corporation (VPC), Volvo Dealer Facilities (VDF), and the importers; organizing and providing education for the importers; advising VTC and VPC in policy matters relating to the project; allocating specific tasks to work groups; and motivating all parties involved to take an active part in the project.

By the end of March 1989, the VETD steering committee had established the project's objectives and the procedures which were to be followed at importer level in order to realize those objectives. The fundamental objective of the VETD project was to create a common Volvo truck environment at all Volvo dealers in the EC (Switzerland and Austria were included in the project although they were not EC members). The desired Volvo environment was translated into specific "Euro Dealer Standards" which applied to the external, internal, and service environments of all Volvo dealers. The importers were charged with evaluating their existing dealerships, establishing an action plan for each dealer, and following up to ensure that the plans were correctly executed.

Both the objectives and the importer working procedures were presented to VTC Europe's importer truck division managers in April 1989. Each manager was directed to appoint within his organization a VETD staff which included one specialist who would be responsible for the project. The next step would be taken in June, when the importer's newly appointed VETD specialists were scheduled to be trained.

Around the time that the VETD project was initiated, Selvin created a "Eurofleet" task force composed of the truck division managers of each of VTC Europe's six largest importers and a headquarters liaison. The purpose of the task force was for the importers to work together to satisfy the needs of VTC's international fleet customers. Through May 1989, the Eurofleet task force had operated unsystematically, attending to each issue individually as it arose.

Pan-European Management Training

Selvin had identified 200 VTC importer and headquarter managers throughout Europe whom he targeted to attend a three-day training seminar at the Lovanium International Management Center in Belgium. The purpose of the seminar was for the managers to think through, and discuss together, the changes that were occurring in the European truck industry due to 1992 and the impact of those changes on VTC's business. Managers were to be trained in groups of approximately 35. The groups were to be cross-sectional, made up of managers from different countries and different functional areas in order to foster the interchange of ideas and cooperation throughout the organization. The first seminar had been conducted in March 1989. The second one was scheduled for June 1989.

THE FUTURE OF PAN-EUROPEAN MARKETING IN VTC EUROPE

Selvin strongly believed that, in order to be successfully implemented, any attempts to move VTC Europe toward Pan-European marketing would require the full support of both headquarters and importer management. Importer managers would not likely support a Pan-European strategy which conflicted with their local interests or was perceived as being dictated from Sweden. Therefore, Selvin was convinced that it was crucial to involve managers from throughout the organization in the development and implementation of any future steps toward Pan-European marketing.

EDITORS' COMMENTARY

The 1992 market integration program promises to have a substantial impact on the transportation industry. The streamlining of various procedures at border crossings and the introduction of a single administrative document for use by road haulers throughout the EC will reduce the time long-haul trucks spend waiting to cross intra-EC frontiers. Together with the removal of restrictions of cabotage, these reforms should significantly increase the efficiency of road haulage in Europe.

These changes will not necessarily advantage truck manufacturers and their parts suppliers. If the existing stock of trucks can be used more efficiently, there may be less demand for new trucks unless manufacturers can, through product design and technical innovations, accelerate the repeat purchase cycle. On the other hand, if the removal of barriers to internal trade such as customs formalities increases overall demand for goods within the EC, any slack capacity in road haulage may be absorbed by increased demand.

Market integration should result in significant restructuring in the fragmented road haulage industry. Through acquisitions, mergers, and alliances, the emergence of Pan-European truck companies and road haulage networks seems likely. Haulers in high-cost and highly fragmented markets like West Germany seem especially vulnerable. Dutch companies, on the other hand, which average 14 trucks each and account for 72% of German-Dutch traffic, are much more efficient.

Increasingly, truck manufacturers will have to develop marketing programs for two different customer segments — the fast-growing international haulage company interested in standard product design, pricing, and service arrangements throughout Europe, and the traditional small national haulage company. The more rapid the growth of the first segment, the more imperative it is that Volvo move toward more Pan-European marketing coordination.

Volvo's long-term commitment to marketing trucks in the EC requires not only that it adjust its marketing approach but also that it try to enhance its market share position in the face of increasingly powerful customers and competitors. As a highly profitable truck manufacturer headquartered outside the EC but heavily dependent on the EC market for sales, Volvo is therefore searching for acquisitions within the EC. The company is also aiming to acquire or network with EC parts suppliers to improve the local EC content of its vehicles.

PART 3

Conclusion

CHAPTER 13

Opportunity to the East

Just as U.S. executives were developing an understanding of the impact of the European Community's 1992 market integration program, extraordinary political and economic reforms swept Eastern Europe, focusing their attention on a new 430 million person market. By one estimate, the East bloc accounted for 17.4% of world gross national product in 1989. Hungary, Czechoslovakia, and East Germany alone have a combined GNP greater than that of China. With wage rates much lower than those in Spain, Portugal, and Greece, Eastern Europe represents an important, new, low-cost manufacturing opportunity.

Some companies are ahead of the game. In 1990, PepsiCo will sell over 100 million cases bottled at 60 East European plants while Procter & Gamble will sell as much Crest toothpaste in Russia as in Canada.[1] Other companies see vast opportunities; a Xerox executive, noting that there are only 60,000 photocopiers in the USSR, argued that a Western country of equivalent size would have 5 million installed.[2]

Whether they are already doing business in Eastern Europe or not, most U.S. companies see a large opportunity. Sixty-eight percent of executives responding to a recent *Fortune* survey believe their companies will conduct more business with Russia as buyers or sellers in the next two years. Sixty-seven percent see Eastern Europe as a major new market comparable in importance to Western Europe within 20 years.[3]

Note: The authors gratefully acknowledge the assistance in preparing this chapter provided by Associate Professor Erich Joachimsthaler and Thomas Kollomeier, doctoral candidate, IESE, Barcelona, Spain, Jose Luis Nueno, doctoral candidate at Harvard Business School, and Aimee Stern, research assistant at Harvard Business School.

[1]Patricia Winters and Scott Hume, "Pepsi, Coke: Art of Deal-Making," *Advertising Age*, February 19, 1990, p. 45.

[2]Margie Lindsay, "The Missing Photocopiers," *Financial Times*, December 8, 1989, p. 19.

[3]Mark Alpert, "Wary Hope on Eastern Europe," *Fortune*, January 29, 1990, pp. 125–126.

Such enthusiasm may reflect undue optimism. Since no country has hitherto made the transformation from a socialist system to a market-based economy, the pace of change — both in terms of legislation and public acceptance of a capitalist culture — is hard to predict.[4] Eastern Europe's attractiveness versus other investment opportunities around the world should not be exaggerated. In addition, the magnitude of the opportunity will vary widely by product market and by country, and exploiting it will require an unusual mix of managerial skills.

We begin this chapter by addressing the impact of East European events on the EC's 1992 market integration program. Next, we present an overview of each East European country, drawing contrasts that illustrate their differential attractiveness as investment opportunities and potential markets. We then identify the types of goods and services for which East European demand will be particularly strong in the next five years. We assess different approaches to participation in East European markets, from exports to countertrade to joint ventures. We offer tactical advice drawn from interviews with ten U.S. executives responsible for business development in Eastern Europe. We then discuss "first mover" advantages and the ways in which companies are reconfiguring their organizations to attack the East European opportunity. Finally, we emphasize how important it is that Western business take a leadership role in investing in the reconstruction and economic development of Eastern Europe.

EASTERN EUROPE AND THE 1992 PROGRAM

Will recent events in Eastern Europe and the question of German re-unification distract Western European leaders and the EC bureaucracy from the perhaps more mundane task of formulating and implementing the details of the 1992 market integration program? We do not think so. First, increasing the competitiveness of the EC in world markets — the principal benefit expected from the integration program — remains as important an objective now as it was the day before the Berlin Wall was breached. Second, the EC officials formulating the directives of the 1992 program are well established and already enjoying considerable

---

[4]Stephen Fider, "A New Marshall Plan for Eastern Europe," *Financial Times,* December 8, 1989, p. 20.

momentum. The process should continue unabated. Third, far from detracting from the 1992 program, events in Eastern Europe are focusing further attention on Europe as an investment opportunity.

One Germany

German reunification was considered to be 20 years away as recently as November 1989. East German politicians were not keen, West German businesses found it convenient to exploit low-cost skilled labor in an independent East Germany, and the East German populace was sure to settle down once its curiosity about the West was satisfied by a day trip to West Berlin.

However, many East Germans determined to achieve the prosperity of their West German counterparts as soon as possible. In February 1990, 2,500 East Germans — many of them the best, brightest, and youngest — were still emigrating each day to the West, straining West German hospitality and debilitating the East German economy through loss of key personnel. At the same time, Chancellor Kohl realized that he could find a place in history as the architect of German reunification. Opposition to a united Germany, based on memories of the Third Reich, was less than expected, particularly from Moscow; respect for the principle of self-determination, decades of German disarmament, West German recognition of existing borders with Poland, and a new generation of Germans who appeared to identify themselves strongly with Europe as a whole minimized the external opposition to reunification.

A reunited Germany, with a population of 80 million and a gross national product over $1 trillion, promised to be the dominant economic force in the EC. At the same time, West Germany was already established as Europe's economic powerhouse, accounting for half of all EC exports in 1989. In competing with North America and the Pacific Rim, the entire EC could expect to benefit from an economically stronger Germany. However, EC politicians were concerned that a reunified Germany would "tilt east." This trend seemed unlikely since, in 1988, only 1.4% of West German exports went to East Germany and only 5.6% to the entire East bloc; West German exports to the rest of the EC were 13 times this level.[5] Nevertheless, EC politicians, supported by Washington, were determined to ensure that a reunified Germany would be in-

---

[5]Martin Wolf, "Still Firmly in the Bosom of the West," *Financial Times*, November 30, 1989.

tegrated in the EC and remain a member of NATO. Such concern gave further impetus to EC economic and political integration and the completion of the 1992 program. At the same time, the swift progress toward reunification reduced the likelihood that it would distract from the 1992 integration program. A strong joint communique stressing that this should not be allowed to happen was issued by Chancellor Kohl of West Germany and President Mitterrand of France in April 1990.

Expanded Membership

Most of the 12 EC members favored expansion in EC membership as an aid — albeit marginal — to diluting the potential dominance of a reunified Germany. Austria, Norway, Malta, and Turkey had all expressed interest in EC membership. Austria, in particular, as a service industry bridge from Western to Eastern Europe, promised to become an even more attractive candidate for early membership.[6] Many considered it essential that the market integration program be completed promptly so that attention could turn to broadening the membership of the Community.

German reunification and the de facto admission of East Germany to the EC seemed likely to prompt interest among other East European countries in EC membership or, at least in the short term, in an associate relationship approximating that enjoyed by the European Free Trade Association countries. An associate relationship would give them preferential tariff treatment and the opportunity to participate in EC research and development and other initiatives. While such an arrangement would result in more cheap East European exports to the EC in competition with EC manufactures, the fact was that such products already found their way in through East Germany.

The prospect of German reunification also focused attention on the free movement of labor within the EC and presented a further obstacle to the development of a common EC social charter. It seemed unlikely that West Germany would permit the free immigration of Greeks into Germany if free movement of East German labor throughout the EC were still restricted. If border controls between EC member countries were abolished, as proposed under the 1992 market integration program, such free movement of labor would be perfectly possible. The

---

[6]Philip Revzin, "Fast-Changing House of Europe Defies Single Blueprint," *Wall Street Journal,* February 22, 1990, p. A10.

prospect of a destabilizing influx of workers seeking higher wages in Western Europe made highly improbable the early admission of other East bloc countries to the EC.

Winners and Losers

Events in Eastern Europe clearly benefited some EC members more than others. With or without reunification, West Germany would benefit from its head start over other EC countries in joint ventures, not only with East Germany (thanks to a common language and the desire of West German businessmen born in the East to invest "back home") but with other East bloc countries. Once included in the EC through reunification, East Germany would become an obvious distribution conduit both for EC exports to other East European countries and for imports from Eastern Europe into the EC. A low-cost manufacturing plant located in East Germany could potentially export to both COMECON and the rest of the EC.

On the other hand, Spain, Portugal, and Greece would be disadvantaged. Manufacturing investments chasing low-cost semi-skilled and skilled labor would more likely consider the East European option. In December 1989, for example, Mitsubishi put a new Spanish plant on hold pending consideration of alternative East European sites.[7] Such decisions promised to reinforce the gap between the richer and the poorer EC member countries and stimulate further demands from the poorer EC members for transitional protection against full market integration.

Investment in Eastern Europe was thought likely to increase overall European capacity in many industries, such as automobiles. The Japanese planned to use East European plants to build quality products at low cost and to increase their penetration of Western Europe as well as serve the emerging demand in the East. These two effects in combination promised to place more competitive pressure on West European manufacturers in certain sectors but also to stimulate further healthy improvements in the competitiveness of West European manufacturing.

Overall, Eastern Europe seemed likely to siphon off some investment in the 1990s — particularly West German capital — that would otherwise have been placed in EC member countries. In addition, further delay in achieving European monetary union seemed likely as the

---

[7]*The Economist*, "European Community: Eyes East," January 6, 1990, p. 50.

Bundesbank focused on merging the ostmark with the deutschmark, with its attendant risks of short-term inflation and higher interest rates.[8] Payback to the West German economy on its probable heavy East German investments was not expected for ten years. The short-term drag on the West German economy caused by East German investment offered the other major EC countries an opportunity to catch up.

DESIGNING A BUSINESS STRATEGY FOR EASTERN EUROPE

Eastern Europe represents both a marketing and a low-cost manufacturing opportunity. In the short term, the East European countries need to obtain industrial technology and know-how to upgrade their manufacturing facilities. In turn, Western companies will be further encouraged to invest in low-cost manufacturing in the East. Later, with economic development, the products being made in Eastern Europe for export will also become affordable in the countries that make them, and the market for consumer products in particular will boom.

Companies considering investment in Eastern Europe must address five principal questions:

1. In which country or countries should a company participate, and in what sequence should it enter them?
2. What products or services should be (a) manufactured and/or (b) marketed in these countries?
3. What form should the company's participation take in each product market?
4. Should the company enter now or "wait and see"?
5. How should the company organize to address East European markets?

Which Countries?

A key question facing Western companies is to assess which country or countries to do business with and in what sequence to proceed. The countries of Eastern Europe differ radically in market size, cultural traditions, quality of infrastructure, pace of economic reform, and political

---

[8]John Templeman and Gail E. Schares, "One Germany, But at What Price?" *Business Week*, February 26, 1990, pp. 54–55.

stability. *Exhibit 13.1* contrasts these countries on the basis of demographic and macroeconomic measures. Clearly, there are wide variations, for example, in GNP per capita and in the debt service load.[9, 10] Note that GNP estimates vary widely due to inaccurate government statistics, sometimes inflated for propaganda purposes, sometimes deflated to qualify a country for preferential tariffs and international loans.[11] For example, the estimates for Poland's and the USSR's GNP per capita are probably too high relative to the others. *Exhibits 13.2* and *13.3* demonstrate the substantial trade links among the COMECON countries and highlight the varying importance of different economic sectors in each country. We will now provide a brief profile of each country.

Hungary. Hitherto, Hungary has been the East European country most favorably disposed to Western investment. It has permitted majority ownership of joint ventures since 1985, and the prospect of 100% foreign ownership in 1989 caused the number of joint ventures to double to over 600.[12] Foreign investors can repatriate hard currency profits equivalent to the amount invested. As a result, many U.S. companies — Rockport Shoes, for example — have coventured manufacturing operations there. Hungarian exports to the West were a substantial 20% of total exports in 1988. Familiarity with Western business practices is greater than that in other East European countries. An embryo capital market exists. Western financeers and the National Bank of Hungary recently set up the First Hungary Fund, which plans to raise and invest $50 million in Hungarian companies. Major accounting firms, even advertising agencies, are established in Hungary, and a broad range of consumer goods is available.

Hungary's major problems are its alarming $17.3 billion foreign debt and 16% inflation rate. Seventy-seven percent of foreign export earnings were absorbed by debt service in 1989. At the same time, it must be noted that this debt-funded development has put Hungary in the vanguard of East European economic reform. Other drawbacks include opposition from the Workers' Councils to government plans to privatize one third of state enterprise and the fact that Hungary cannot provide easy access to the Soviet market. Nevertheless, U.S. companies unfa-

[9]Stephen Fider, "Much More Than Money Required," *Financial Times*, January 24, 1990, p. 7.

[10]*USA Today*, "East Bloc Business," March 19, 1990, p. 6B.

[11]*The Economist*, "Grossly Deceptive Product," March 10, 1990, p. 71.

[12]*The Economist*, "Testing the Water," October 21, 1989, pp. 78–79.

EXHIBIT 13.1 Macroeconomic indicators of East European countries: 1988

	Hungary	CSSR	Poland	GDR	Bulgaria	Romania	Yugoslavia	USSR
Area (000 km²)	93	128	313	108	111	237	256	22,400
Population (million)	11	16	38	17	9	23	23	287
GNP (billion $)	92	158	276	209	68	126	*	2,500
GNP per capita ($)	8,360	9,000	7,260	12,600	7,550	5,470	*	8,700
Net growth 1989 (%)	0–1	1–2	–2– +3	0–1	5.5	*	–1.7	1–2
Estimated inflation (%)	18.0	2.2	900	0.8	*	2.2	346	8.4
Black market over official exchange rate	1.25×	6×	6×	14×	*	*	*	25×
Imports ($ billion)	8.0	8.8	0.8	*	16.1	8.7	13.2	106.8
Exports ($ billion)	8.6	9.0	0.9	*	16.7	11.5	12.6	110.2
Trade surplus/deficit ($ billion)	0.6	0.2	0.1	0.3	0.6	2.8	–0.6	3.4
Gross debt ($ billion)	19.0	5.7	39.2	20.1	6.9	2.9	19.8	38.0
Net debt ($ billion)	10.4	3.7	38.6	6.8	5.8	2.2	17.7	23.7
Gross debt/GNP (%)	67.9	4.7	56.8	10.3	6.7	3.2	*	2.8

Sources: General source: Bundesstelle fur Aussenhandelsinformation, Bonn. National Westminster Bank, London. Zu den Ost-Wahrungen gibt es keine Brucke, *Das Handelsblatt*, November 22, 1989. Commerzbank, Frankfurt. *USA Today*, "East Bloc Business," March 19, 1990.
*Not available.

EXHIBIT 13.2 East European trade patterns, 1988: Percentages of total export and import

With \ From	Hungary		CSSR		Poland		GDR**		Bulgaria		Romania		Yugoslavia		USSR	
	Exp.	Imp.	Exp.	Imp.	Exp.	Imp.	Exp.	Imp.	Exp.	Imp.	Exp.	Imp.	Exp.	Imp.	Exp.	Imp.
COMECON	44.6	—	75.5	76.5	40.7	—	69.0	*	80.9	*	40.8	*	*	*	58.3	61.2
Hungary	—	—	5.5	5.5	—	—	5.2	*	2.1	1.9	—	—	—	—	6.7	7.6
CSSR	5.4	5.1	—	—	6.0	6.4	8.1	*	4.6	5.4	4.0	6.3	4.2	—	9.5	10.5
Poland	3.3	4.1	10.3	10.6	—	—	6.1	*	4.1	4.9	4.8	6.7	3.9	—	9.4	10.9
GDR	5.3	6.4	8.8	10.6	4.4	5.0	—	—	5.2	5.8	—	—	—	—	10.7	10.7
Bulgaria	—	—	3.5	3.2	—	—	*	*	—	—	—	—	—	—	9.1	10.6
Romania	—	—	2.0	2.4	—	—	*	*	2.1	2.1	—	—	—	—	3.5	3.7
Yugoslavia	—	—	—	—	2.7	3.3	*	*	—	—	—	—	—	—	—	—
USSR	27.6	25.0	43.1	40.1	24.5	23.3	38.0	*	62.8	53.7	24.2	25.9	18.7	13.3	—	—
EEC	*	*	10.1	9.6	*	*	*	*	4.6	9.7	*	*	36.7	38.8	15.1	11.5
FRG	11.0	13.9	4.6	4.6	13.1	13.3	16.9	*	—	3.0	6.3	3.8	11.3	17.2	3.8	5.5
Italy	4.2	3.1	—	—	—	3.3	1.0	*	—	—	7.0	—	15.0	10.4	2.5	2.1
U.K.	1.9	1.8	—	—	5.0	4.2	1.0	*	—	—	—	—	—	—	2.7	1.0
Austria	5.7	7.2	—	—	3.1	4.4	1.0	*	—	—	—	—	3.4	4.6	0.6	1.0
U.S.	—	—	—	—	2.6	—	0.4	*	—	—	6.2	—	5.8	5.5	0.5	2.7
Japan	—	—	—	—	—	—	0.5	*	—	—	—	—	—	—	1.8	3.0

Sources: Bundestelle fur Aussenhandelsinformation, Bonn. Gesamtdeutsches Institut, Koln.

*Not available.

**Data for trade with Western countries from 1987.

EXHIBIT 13.3 East European trade by industrial sector, 1988: Percentages of each country's total exports and imports

Sector	Hungary		CSSR		Poland		GDR		Bulgaria		Romania		Yugoslavia		USSR	
	Exp.	Imp.	Exp.	Imp.	Exp.	Imp.	Exp.	Imp.	Exp.	Imp.	Exp.	Imp.	Exp.	Imp.	Exp.	Imp.
Machinery	26.9	16.8	67.7	41.7	39.1	35.7	4.2	—	58.7	39.8	24.9	24.1	1.7	—	15.5	41.4
Chemicals	—	—	4.6	4.3	10.9	15.9	—	—	4.0	5.0	8.8	5.0	—	6.8	3.4	5.3
Energy	12.4	13.1	8.0	38.9	10.2	14.8	13.6	—	8.2	40.7	23.2	53.5	—	13.4	46.5	—
Industrial goods	16.0	11.7	13.0	6.5	6.6	5.6	—	—	11.0	3.0	12.1	4.1	3.4	4.1	—	13.0
Raw materials and parts	34.0	50.8	—	—	10.1	8.2	32.4	—	—	—	—	—	1.7	—	8.5	8.1
Food and agricultural goods	20.7	7.6	—	4.4	11.9	8.9	10.9	—	11.2	—	7.7	4.0	—	—	—	16.1

Sources: Bundesstelle fur Aussenhandelsinformation, Bonn. Gesamtdeutsches Institut, Koln.
Notes: Raw materials and parts are included in energy for CSSR, Bulgaria, and Romania. Chemicals and industrial goods are included in raw materials for GDR. Data for the GDR are from 1987 and only for trade with West Germany. Import data for GDR not available.

miliar with doing business in Eastern Europe will find Hungary a particularly easy country in which to get started. Like Poland, Hungary has been granted a $1 billion stabilization package by the EC. Further aid will depend partly on the level of political stability provided by the governing coalition that emerged from the March elections in which 52 parties competed.

Czechoslovakia. The CSSR is moving rapidly on economic reforms. Its free market oriented finance minister has embraced currency convertibility, drastically devalued the Czech currency, initiated restructuring of the inefficient banking system, proposed leaving COMECON, cut state subsidies by 15%, and proposed 100% foreign ownership of business enterprises. Inflation is low, and debt service payments on a modest $6 billion eat up only 16% of foreign earnings, allowing the CSSR continued access to market loans at good rates. However, hard currency repatriation is likely to be limited to a share of hard currency earnings, and foreign currency accounts must be maintained at the central bank. Nevertheless, with a well-trained work force, convenient borders with West Germany and Austria, strong manufacturing and democratic traditions from the 1930s, and an industry specialization in machinery, the CSSR should attract substantial foreign investment. Based on the successful U.S. visit of playwright-president Vaclav Havel, the U.S. government seems likely to focus a disproportionate share of its economic support for Eastern Europe on the CSSR. The pace of economic reform has been slower than expected, pending the results of June elections, but a smooth transition to a democracy with cohesive leadership seems likely.

East Germany. With reunification and therefore inclusion in the EC or, at least, some form of transitional economic association imminent, the GDR seems likely to receive the swiftest infusion of substantial Western capital. However, foreigners cannot at present own real estate. Since the West German government and business will invest heavily in improving manufacturing capabilities, the infrastructure, and the environment, the GDR could progress more rapidly than other East European countries. Thus, it could emerge as a natural beachhead for companies wishing to sell into Eastern Europe as well as into the EC from a single low-cost manufacturing plant, particularly considering that 70% of its exports have traditionally gone to other COMECON countries. The GDR has modest foreign debt and inflation, and the government has ended food subsidies. However, the GDR has lost 3.5% of its work force — many of them highly skilled — to emigration in 1989, with a corresponding reduction in GNP. Elections in March brought to power a center-right co-alition interested in reunification and further economic reform.

Poland. In 1989, Poland's inflation rate exceeded 1,000 percent. Servicing the $40 billion foreign debt absorbed 47% of foreign currency earnings. Not surprisingly, hard currency accounts in Polish banks are not allowed. Being union-led, Solidarity has implemented an economic retrenchment program that includes cutbacks in government subsidies to state enterprises and progress toward full currency convertibility. These and other measures precipitated a 35% slump in real income in January 1990. The consequent fall in demand almost brought the economy to a standstill; many companies were unable to pay their suppliers because customers canceled orders, and they were reluctant to drop their prices to improve the export competitiveness of their manufactures. However, because of its courage in being the first to challenge Moscow's authority and because of the political influence of sizable Polish immigrant populations in key Western countries, including the United States, outright aid to Poland is likely to be substantial, along with rescheduling or forgiveness of trade credits and debt-equity swaps.

In the short run, Poland appears to be a less attractive opportunity for foreign investment than Hungary or Czechoslovakia. Whatever legislation on hard currency repatriation of profits may emerge from the May elections, there is simply little available. Under the terms of a recent agreement, West German investors will not be able to repatriate profits until 1993 and then only in limited amounts.

Bulgaria. With $9 billion in foreign debt, Bulgaria's debt service ratio is 30%. Its economic growth rate, if government statistics are correct, has averaged 5.5% per annum over the last ten years, albeit on a small industrial base. This is the highest growth rate of the East European countries. Bulgaria is heavily dependent on foreign trade, with export and import transactions equivalent to 42% of GNP. However, over 80% of Bulgaria's trade is with other COMECON countries, and its progress on economic reforms, such as foreign majority ownership of joint ventures, is lagging. Although elections are scheduled for May, opposition parties are still dominated by the entrenched communists.

Romania. Thanks to oil exports, Romania has only $1.9 billion of foreign debt and debt service consumes only 17% of foreign earnings. Romania can therefore access market capital at good rates, now that foreign borrowing is again permitted. However, the Ceaucescu regime depleted the intelligentsia, the infrastructure is in poor condition, and sustained progress toward political and economic reform is uncertain. Historical ties suggest that France will spearhead investment activity in Romania. Elections are set for May 20, but the opposition groups challenging former communists in the Salvation Front are fragmented and poorly organized.

USSR. With 287 million people, the Soviet Union is potentially the third largest national consumer market in the world. However, the population is very heterogeneous in its tastes, a reflection of cultural and ethnic diversity. Per capita income is lower than in East Germany and Czechoslovakia.

Long lines for poor-quality consumer products reflect the use of obsolete process technology, the long-standing direction of technological investment to the military, and the policy of exporting the best of its manufactures to generate foreign currency. Partly as a result, the Soviets are able to pay one third of their trade debts in dollars. West German companies investing in the USSR can now repatriate their profits with only a three-month delay. Due to the cost of the Chernobyl disaster, declining oil export prices and output below expectations, COCOM restrictions on Western exports to the USSR, and the cost of servicing a heavy foreign debt of $38 billion, economic growth is limited. At the same time, *perestroika* and *glasnost* are causing Soviet citizens to demand better and more consistently available consumer goods, so less of the USSR's production will be available to export. Progress toward a more market-driven economy is painfully slow, thanks to bureaucratic impediments and a deeply divided populace. Government sales of gold reserves and other commodities will be needed to facilitate the transition. Today, doing business in the USSR seems especially complex, but, if Gorbachev succeeds in revitalizing the economy, the business opportunity in Moscow and Kiev alone will be equivalent in magnitude to that of some of the other smaller East European countries.

Exhibit 13.4 provides a checklist of some of the criteria a Western company might use to decide in which country, or countries, to invest time and effort.[13] At present, Hungary has accommodated itself most to the needs of Western business and is benefiting from being positioned as the gateway to other East European markets. Competition for limited Western capital has sparked a possibly unproductive race to see which

---

[13]*The Economist*, "Eastern Europe's Economies: What Is to Be Done?" January 13, 1990, pp. 21–26.

EXHIBIT 13.4 Checklist of country selection criteria

Overall economic and political conditions
- What is the foreign debt service expense as a percentage of hard currency foreign exchange earnings?
- What is the inflation rate? If hyperinflation exists, are appropriate fiscal and monetary policies being implemented to bring it under control?
- How substantial are raw material reserves that can be converted to hard currency?
- Are state subsidies, cheap credits, and tax concessions for state enterprises being phased out?
- Does the government intend to sell stakes in state enterprises to foreign investors?
- Is there an emerging capital market based on real interest rates?
- How likely is continued progress toward a stable democracy and a free market economy?
- What progress is being made toward developing a code of company law?

Climate for foreign investment
- What percentage ownership may foreign companies have in joint ventures? Is government approval required?
- Is private ownership of property recognized?
- Can foreign investors own real estate?
- Can an initial capital investment by a foreign company be held in hard currency?
- Can a foreign investor sell its stake in a joint venture?
- Can hard currency be used to pay for imported raw materials and/or to repatriate profits?
- What is the tax rate on business enterprise profits?

Market attractiveness
- What is the sales potential in this country?
- Do the country's geographical location and political relations permit it to serve as a gateway to other East European markets?
- How well developed are the necessary managerial and technical skills?
- How skilled is the labor pool? What are labor costs?
- Can continued supply of the raw materials required for production be assured?
- What is the quality of the transportation and telecommunications infrastructure?
- Will Western executives accept being located in the country?
- To what degree have government officials developed a familiarity with Western business practices?

East European country can implement most quickly the most generous, market-oriented reforms and has prompted Vaclav Havel to propose that Hungary and Poland join with Czechoslovakia in a cooperative approach. This pact began to crumble after Havel's February 1990 visit to the United States, which was viewed as a public relations triumph for Czechoslovakia. Some Hungarians began to view the pact as a Czech effort to catch up with Hungary in perceived attractiveness as a place to invest capital.

Which Products?

In which product categories will the greatest business opportunities be available? The immediate need will be for industrial products and business services critical to economic development and the upgrading of existing manufacturing plants. These product categories include computers and telecommunications, machine tools, electronic process controls, packaging and processing equipment to manufacture consumer goods, and environmental pollution control equipment, especially in countries where the controlling political parties embrace a "green" philosophy. Chemicals, pharmaceuticals, and medical equipment, along with agricultural machinery, construction equipment, and project management assistance, also will be in demand.

Opportunities in some industrial product markets may be limited by the fact that technologies have evolved differently in East and West. For example, East German printing machinery, dominant in COMECON, is so different and switching costs so high that the market for Western-made equipment will develop only slowly.[14]

Consumer goods will be increasingly in demand, but the ability of East European consumers to buy them will be limited in the short term. More and more East bloc citizens are visiting the West. Others are familiar with the Western goods in hard currency shops. Many are keen to buy whatever Western goods they can before their savings are devalued by the phasing in of realistic exchange rates. They are unlikely to tolerate an end to egalitarian wages and guaranteed jobs in favor of a market economy unless the shelves are stocked. Current shortages will have to be corrected; for example, USSR plants produce only 60% of the razors needed by Soviet men. Processed foods, toiletries, and health care products will be especially in demand; governments will try to provide them to motivate the work forces to raise productivity. An improvement in the quality and availability of automobiles may be especially valued by male voters. However, a sustained boom in demand for consumer goods can emerge only after restructuring of the industrial sector and the growth of East bloc exports that will earn foreign currency.

Travel-related services to enhance the attractiveness of an East bloc country as a travel destination will be helpful in attracting foreign currency. Everything from new passenger aircraft for state airlines to hotels, car rental services, and better-quality taxis will be needed to support a tourism industry. Already, considerable enthusiasm for tours

---

[14]*The Economist*, "Busting Open Eastern Europe," December 16, 1989, p. 68.

to Prague and Budapest is evident among American travelers, as occurred a few years ago when China was opened to tourism. Visitors will
increasingly be able to make purchases with major credit cards; American Express has established offices in all the East European capitals.

How to Participate?

There are two main approaches to participation: contractual arrangements that are either short term (exporting) or long term (licensing), and
direct investment through joint ventures and acquisitions. In addition
to the standard exposure risk versus control trade-offs involved in these
decisions, companies must assess the importance to attach to repatriating profits and, if necessary, plan how to do so.

Exporting. The two principal obstacles to exporting have been barriers
to payment in hard currency and restrictions on advanced technology
exports from West to East by COCOM (Coordinating Committee for
Multilateral Export Controls), a 40-year-old trade association of 17 Western countries. It appears that direct exporting will be easier in the 1990s
as COCOM restrictions are eased in the face of a diminished security
threat from the East and greatly increased numbers of applications from
companies for COCOM export approvals.[15]

For unique high-technology products essential to economic development, direct payment in foreign currency is increasingly likely. For
example, Digital Equipment Corp., excluded by COCOM restrictions
from selling most of its product line to Eastern Europe for eight years,
will soon be shipping state-of-the-art minicomputers to Hungary and
will be paid in hard currency.[16] Companies selling products not important enough to warrant immediate full payment in hard currency are
increasingly turning to leasing options whereby the buyer pays for the
production equipment in hard currency installments earned from exports of manufactures made using the equipment.[17] Export credit guarantees can be used to cover the risk. Eximbank, for example, has $10
billion in annual export credit guarantee authority, while the Overseas

---

[15]William Dawkins, "COCOM Takes a Hard Route to a Softer Line," *Financial Times*, February 14, 1990, p. 5.

[16]Alan Cane, "DEC Secures First Base in Eastern Europe," *Financial Times*, February 13, 1990.

[17]Margie Lindsay, "Two Way Access from Vienna," *Financial Times*, December 8, 1989, p. 18.

Private Investment Corporation has available $8 billion in political risk insurance and has also established a $100 million Eastern Europe Growth Fund.

Licensing. Long-term contractual arrangements such as licensing agreements and R&D alliances are often attractive to small- and medium-sized firms lacking the experience, capital, and confidence to risk direct investment. For example, Epson of Japan has licensed East Germany's VEB Robotron to manufacture computers and printers for distribution throughout Eastern Europe. The problem with such arrangements is the licensor's potential lack of control over both manufacturing quality and distribution. Gillette, for example, has found that products manufactured under license in the USSR "leak" into Western Europe at much lower prices, disaffecting trade channels and Gillette country managers in the affected markets.[18]

Joint Ventures. East European governments are increasingly interested in attracting hard currency investment through joint ventures. Such ventures typically involve the transfer of Western managerial and technical know-how to leverage Eastern Europe's abundant raw materials and cheap, skilled labor to quickly catch up to Western quality and productivity levels. In turn, improved quality and productivity will enable the East European countries to satisfy domestic demand and to increase exports that will earn hard currency to pay off their foreign debt.

Some 3,345 joint venture agreements between COMECON countries plus Yugoslavia and Western companies were in place at the end of 1989.[19] There are four reasons for the recent increase in joint venture activity:

- Competition among East European countries for Western investment is precipitating, in most cases, a progressive loosening of foreign investment controls, as indicated in *Exhibit 13.5.*
- Similar competition is evident among Western companies seeking first mover advantages. A joint venture by one company in an industry such as automobiles can precipitate a scramble for similar deals by its global competitors; Suzuki, Ford, and General Motors,

[18]David Buchan, "Groping for a New Strategy," *Financial Times,* December 8, 1989, p. 19.

[19]Anthony McDermott, "Joint Ventures with East Europe Pass 3,300 in 1989," *Financial Times,* January 19, 1990.

EXHIBIT 13.5 Foreign direct investment regulations in East European Countries

Country	Date of regulation	Limits on foreign ownership
Hungary	1972	49%
	1985	majority allowed
	1989	100% (government approval)
CSSR	1987	45%
	1989	99%
Poland	1976	49%
	1986	majority allowed
	1989	100%
GDR	1990	49%
		51% (small businesses)
Bulgaria	—	fully restricted
		majority promised
Romania	1972	49%
Yugoslavia	1967	49%
	1984	no limits
USSR	1987	49%
	1989	99%

for example, all announced joint ventures in Hungary within two months of each other.[20]

- As joint venture regulations become more favorable, companies currently exporting on a transaction-by-transaction basis or licensing the manufacture of their products will seek to upgrade their involvement to joint venture status. Over time, with progress toward free market economies, the joint ventures should be superseded in turn by wholly owned subsidiaries. Hungary, Poland, and East Germany have announced plans to privatize selected state-owned enterprises. While the precise level of foreign equity participation has not been determined, ASEA Brown Boveri has taken majority control of Zemtech, the Polish turbine and generator manufacturer, in order to assure its continued status as low-cost producer in Europe. Carl de Benedetti recently set up the first Western-owned holding company

[20]Kevin Done, "A Fast Autobahn to Unity," *Financial Times,* March 13, 1990, p. 21.

in Hungary to raise funds to buy controlling stakes in state-owned companies. East European governments are trying to avoid selling these interests at fire-sale prices despite their urgent need for hard currency.

There are two caveats regarding joint ventures. First, it is necessary to look beyond the permissible foreign ownership percentages listed in Exhibit 13.5. For example, an East German joint venture regulation issued in January 1990 allows foreign majority stakes but only for specified nonstrategic industries and in small- to medium-sized companies. Similarly, the proposed Czechoslovakian foreign ownership statute includes a stiff 40% tax on profits and does not provide for hard currency profit repatriation.[21]

A second concern is that bureaucratic delays in reviewing joint venture applications now represent a serious bottleneck. In addition, the success rate is likely to be modest. In the USSR, for example, of the more than 1,000 joint ventures registered, only 40 are in operation. Unofficially, 14 of these ventures are in liquidation due mainly to the reluctance of Western partners to invest as much as Soviet government officials expected. Because of the lower level of capital investment, joint ventures in service industries are easier to establish than those in manufacturing. Fifty of 79 ventures registered with the Finnish–Soviet Joint Venture Partners Association are in services.[22]

Successful joint ventures are likely to be those that make strategic sense for both partners. An outstanding example is General Electric's recent $150 million acquisition of a 50% stake in Tungsram, a Hungarian light bulb manufacturer. Since Tungsram already exported 20% of its production, its managers were used to dealing with Western business executives. GE now helps manage a major supplier of the private label light bulbs that have for years competed with its own branded line in the United States and can use Tungsram as a low-cost source of light bulbs with which to compete against Philips in the European market.

In-Bond Assembly Plants. Although none exist at present, in-bond assembly plants may be developed in the future along the borders of Eastern and Western countries. Numerous plants of this type operate on the U.S.–Mexico border by means of an in-bond assembly plant agreement

---

[21]Charles Leadbeater, "Pitfalls and Promise for Investors in the East," *Financial Times,* January 1, 1990, p. 28.

[22]Peter Montagnon, "Finnish Companies Unravel the Soviet Labyrinth," *Financial Times,* September 29, 1980, p. 15.

that permits the temporary import of machinery and equipment. Accounts can be maintained in hard currency. Proximity to the border permits close supervision by company managers who typically live on the other side of the border from the plant. In many casaes, a twin plant in the developed country makes the components that are assembled by low-cost labor in the developing country.

Countertrade. Investment in Eastern Europe has been minimized by the inability of Western firms to repatriate profits in hard currency and thereby cover the costs of imported raw materials for manufacturing joint ventures and pay the salaries of headquarters executives assigned to oversee them. Some companies like McDonald's of Canada, having already invested $50 million enroute to opening 20 ruble-only stores in Russia, are clearly taking a long-term perspective and intend to reinvest their profits in local advertising and market development.[23, 24] Other companies have turned to countertrade, whereby profits are extracted in the form of East European–made goods. For example:

- To develop the East European market, PepsiCo has taken Stolichnaya vodka as payment for the concentrate it ships to its Russian plants while, in Poland, the company accepts furniture that is later installed in Pizza Hut restaurants in the United States.
- Fleet Street Ltd. of New York uses a direct offset or buy-back approach, shipping raw materials to the USSR, then shipping manufactured coats back to the United States. The objective in this case is to take advantage of low manufacturing costs rather than develop the local market for a brand name.
- Fiat takes profits from its Soviet manufacturing joint ventures in the form of its own production. Fiat is permitted to export one third of the output.

There are several problems with countertrade. First, goods available for countertrade are often those that cannot be sold in the West on their own merits. Many of the best countertrade opportunities have already been taken up or are in the hands of established countertrade brokers. Ideally, companies should accept in countertrade goods they can use in their own businesses and whose quality they are therefore better able to

[23]Scott Hume, "How Big Mac Made it to Moscow," *Advertising Age,* January 22, 1990, pp. 16, 51.
[24]Quentin Peel and Mark Nicholson, "Mac Attack in Pushkin Square," *Financial Times,* January 31, 1990.

assess. Tambrands, for example, is taking profits in cotton from its Soviet joint venture to make and market sanitary napkins.[25, 26] Second, the ability of a Western company to expand its business in Eastern Europe can be limited by the level and quality of output of the countertraded products and/or by their marketability in the West. To do business in Bulgaria, PepsiCo has had to invest time and energy in developing a U.S. market for Bulgarian wine. Coca-Cola's East European sales lag PepsiCo's partly because its countertrade items are Soviet Lada cars sold in the United Kingdom, and apple juice concentrate. A third problem is the cash flow delay pending resale of the countertraded products. Although countertrade is sufficiently well developed that receivables can often be factored, the cash flow uncertainties discourage participation by smaller companies.

For three reasons, it is unlikely that countertrade will expand as East European markets open up. First, countertrade involving indirect offsets of unrelated products requires central government dictate as to whom factory managers should sell their goods. With looser central controls, factory managers will aim to export their own goods to earn hard currency for their own enterprises. Soviet furriers, for example, are refusing further cooperation in countertrade. Second, much countertrade involves commodities whose world prices have been depressed since the early 1980s. These prices seem unlikely to rebound in the short term so that the foreign currency earnings from this source will remain fairly stable. Third, there will be less need for countertrade as East European countries move toward full currency convertibility and permit repatriation of profits earned by foreign investors.

Company Size and Participation Strategy

Because most East European enterprises are large and state-owned, large companies or consortia make better matches for joint ventures, especially those already established in Europe and employing personnel with relevant language skills and prior joint venture experience. Companies with previous East bloc experience are also at an advantage; Honeywell, for example, had a Moscow office in 1974 that was closed as COCOM restrictions tightened, but that experience helped Honey-

---

[25]David Lanchner, "The Rush to Russia," *Adweek's Marketing Week,* February 20, 1989, pp. 24–32.

[26]Lee Smith, "Can You Make Money in Russia?" *Fortune,* January 1, 1990, pp. 103–107.

well negotiate a joint venture with the Soviets in 1988.[27] *Exhibit 13.6* lists the major East–West joint ventures as of 1990.

Four other important factors explain why large multinational companies have been the first to exploit business opportunities in Eastern Europe:

- The difficulty of extracting foreign currency and arranging countertrade deals requires a sophistication most small companies do not enjoy and are reluctant to invest in.
- Building business relationships with East bloc countries requires considerable time. McDonald's of Canada invested $50 million and 14 years of negotiating effort before opening its first restaurant in Pushkin Square. Tambrands was in negotiation on its joint venture since the early 1980s.
- Large companies can decide to expand in Eastern Europe without concern for repatriating profits in the near term. McDonald's, for example, will build 20 ruble-only restaurants in the USSR and reinvest its ruble profits in further advertising market development.[28]
- Large multinationals can take advantage of bilateral trade agreements between other countries (such as India and Turkey) and East European nations and withdraw profits in their currencies.

To spread the financial risk of joint ventures, a trend is evolving toward industry consortia whereby large companies in a particular industry and from a single Western country pool their investments. Such consortia are often able, through experience and size, to access the highest level government officials, obtain faster approvals for their ventures, and make mutually beneficial countertrade arrangements. The American Trade Consortium (Johnson & Johnson, Chevron, RJR Nabisco, and others) and the American Medical Consortium (Colgate-Palmolive, Abbott Labs., Baxter Healthcare, and others) are two such examples.

As the East European countries move toward market economies and begin to permit repatriation of profits in foreign currency, the attractiveness of the business opportunity to small- and medium-sized firms will grow. The East Europeans will benefit, in turn, from the consequent increase in Western companies competing for their business.

---

[27]Tim Dickson, "Honeywell Sets Sights on Soviet Venture," *Financial Times*, March 5, 1990, p. 5.

[28]Laura Bird, "For U.S. Marketers, the Russian Front Is No Bowl of 'Vishnyas,'" *Adweek's Marketing Week*, March 5, 1990, p. 4.

EXHIBIT 13.6 Principal East–West joint ventures: 1990

Western partners	Country	Eastern partners	Country
Electronics			
Pilz	West Germany	VEB Robotron	GDR
Hoesch	West Germany	VEB Robotron	GDR
Akai Electric	Japan	Electron	Bulgaria
Thomson	France	Orbita	USSR
General Electric	United States	Tungsram	Hungary
Automobiles			
Fiat	Italy	Elaz	USSR
Volkswagen	West Germany	VEB 1FA	GDR
Suzuki	Japan	Konsortium Autokonszern	Hungary
Food			
PepsiCo	United States		USSR
Coca-Cola	United States		USSR
McDonald's	Canada		USSR
Archer Daniels Midland	United States	Pettina	USSR/Finland
Pharmaceuticals			
Hoechst	West Germany		GDR
Bayer	West Germany		GDR
Petrochemicals			
Combustion Engineering	United States	Tobolsk Petrochemical Company	USSR
Travel-related services			
Club Med	France	Intourist	USSR
Holiday Corp.	United States	Lot	Poland
Kepinski	West Germany	VEB Interhotel	GDR
Marriott	United States		Poland
Financial services			
Dresdner Bank	West Germany		GDR
Fuji	Japan	Magyar Hitel Bank	Hungary
Allianz AG	West Germany	Hungaria Biztosito	Hungary

There are entrepreneurial opportunities for Western distributors to seek out customers for the best East bloc products. For example, a single trading company in Washington now represents a consortium of 3,000 small Hungarian companies seeking U.S. sales. The many expatriates of East European countries living in the West will be well placed to trade with the East European entrepreneurs, who will doubtless increase in number as restrictions on private enterprise are lifted.[29] The United States is particularly attractive as potentially the largest single export market for East European goods. Facilitating exports will generate the hard currency the East European countries need to permit U.S. companies to export goods there.

Other opportunities for small industrial businesses lie in the licensing and commercialization of East European inventions. About one third of the world's Ph.D.-level scientists and engineers reside in Eastern Europe.[30] Some 6,000 research institutes exist in the USSR alone. Recently, for example, the Weir Group of Scotland licensed technology from Litostroj, a world leader in water turbines for hydroelectric power generation.[31]

Timing

First mover advantages will accrue to Western firms that take an early and serious stance on investing in Eastern Europe. In the short term, procurement decisions will still be concentrated in the hands of government officials who will often prefer to allocate their contracts to a single known supplier in each product market. Developing relationships, cultivating goodwill, learning the nuances of the negotiating process, and investing for the long term now when foreign currency is so short and immediate profits modest — all may yield dividends later. Because learning how to do business in these countries will take time, gaining experience and contacts today will bear fruit when the business opportunities become sizable. Consumer marketers will benefit from the development of early brand recognition when few brands are competing for consumer attention; brand loyalties developed now will be valuable later when prosperity encourages the entry of competitive brands. Industrial marketers entering Eastern Europe now will give themselves the necessary time to develop a customer service network to back up their products once installed. This is one reason why Fanuc, the Japanese numerical controls manufacturer, and Mitsui, the Japanese trading house, have joined forces to take a 50% stake in Stanko-Fanuc Service

---

[29]John W. Kiser III, *Communist Entrepreneurs* (London: Franklin Watts, 1990).

[30]Thomas A. Stewart, "How to Manage in the New Era," *Fortune,* January 15, 1990, pp. 58–72.

[31]Nick Garnett and Peter Marsh, "Investing in the Revolution," *Financial Times,* January 15, 1990.

Ltd., a Moscow-based machine tool service firm. The joint venture will facilitate increased Fanuc exports to the USSR, where the machines will be serviced by the new company.

IMPLEMENTING THE STRATEGY

Once a company has determined which countries it plans to enter, the products it will launch in each market, and the timing of entry, it must confront the challenges of implementation. We interviewed ten executives responsible for business development in Eastern Europe to understand better the tactical issues and common pitfalls encountered by firms penetrating this market. We now report our findings in four sections dealing with securing the initial sale, negotiating the joint venture, marketing, and organizing.

Securing the Initial Sale

The first challenge is typically to ensure that a company's name and reputation as well as its product line and benefits are known to government procurement agents. Attendance at international trade fairs and advertising in industry trade journals can establish such awareness.

Any inquiries should be thoroughly attended to since they are more likely than in the West to be followed by a bid request. Most often, the initial bid request is for a small order. Before placing large orders, risk-averse procurement officers with minimal hard currency tend to test the product and the firm's ability to deliver as promised.[32]

When submitting a proposal, it is often tempting to quote a penetration price, especially if sales to Eastern Europe are viewed merely as "plus business." However, underpricing may result in diversion of the product back to higher-priced Western markets, especially in the case of low-bulk-to-value items. Low initial prices can also set a precedent for subsequent, larger-scale sales. In the proposal, it is important to specify product costs separately from the costs for installation and other follow-on services so that delays in commissioning plants in which the equipment is to be used cannot stall payment. The prices quoted should also

---

[32]Charles Batchelor, "No Block to Trade with East Europe," *Financial Times*, January 23, 1990.

make account of the long lag time that often occurs between proposal submission and placement of the final order. In the event of such a delay, it is important to ship the originally specified model even if it has since been superseded by a new version.

When a firm order is placed, it is advisable to request a deposit and the balance at time of final shipment. On subsequent orders, it is not appropriate to offer price discounts because they often imply to procurement officers that they overpaid on the initial order. Finally, components should be prepared for substantial variations in order size and frequency; attempting to forecast sales appears to be futile.

Negotiating the Joint Venture

All the executives interviewed recommended participating only in majority-owned joint ventures. Securing appointments with East bloc officials to discuss joint ventures is not difficult. The challenge, as one executive put it, "is determining which of the many groups of government officials who will want to negotiate actually have the power to transfer money to your company's bank account." For this reason, and to speed up project approval, working with influential locals as advisers or joint venture partners is recommended, even in countries where 100% foreign ownership is now permitted. Gaining an endorsement from the quasi-official Soviet Women's and Children's Organization, for example, helped Tambrands close its Femtech joint venture with the Ukraine health ministry.

Government officials often extend the negotiating process as a means of securing as much technical information as possible free of charge. In addition, the officials involved in the negotiation often change as the process advances. It is important to avoid making any concession with a view to securing a quid pro quo at the next negotiating session; a new group of negotiators will plead ignorance of earlier discussions. Patience is essential to the eventual conclusion of an agreement.

In the absence of company and contract law in East European countries, it is essential to document all details of any negotiation. In addition, Western companies should plan on drawing up documents in English for the East bloc negotiators to sign rather than relying on them to follow up on commitments made in negotiating sessions. ABB's Combustion Engineering subsidiary even contributed to writing some of the initial Soviet joint venture laws.

Where possible, companies should acquire existing manufacturing facilities and rebuild them to state-of-the-art standards to avoid bureaucratic delays in the approval of new building projects. If consistent quality of output cannot be assured, building from scratch may be necessary; McDonald's invested $40 million in a new food processing facility to assure the highest standards of quality control. If possible, plants should be located near major cities with adequate communications and transportation; Tambrands' Femtech joint venture operation in the Ukraine has only one telephone for a staff of 70.

Companies must check in advance on the consistent availability of quality raw materials. RJR Nabisco has not been able to establish cookie plants in the USSR in the absence of an assured supply of sugar.[33] Where raw materials are available, it is useful to try to secure a contractual agreement on the price of raw material inputs. Interestingly, as Ben & Jerry's discovered in planning an ice cream parlor in Moscow, the lowest prices on some essential commodities such as milk may be in the retail store rather than at the source of supply.

Companies must not underestimate the cost of management and worker retraining. Managerial and technical skills cannot be taken for granted. The production emphasis in Eastern Europe has been consistently on quantity rather than quality, managers are better at coping with shortages than boosting customer demand, and management–labor relationships differ greatly from those common in the West.

Marketing

Consumer products will require minimal adaptation for sales in East European markets. East European consumers are unlikely to accept models that are obsolete in the West, although financial constraints will favor sales of good-quality mass market products rather than premium priced entries. Industrial marketers will need to balance more carefully the purchaser's desire to buy only state-of-the-art products against the level of technical sophistication that can be accommodated. With this caveat, marketers should not assume that buyers can afford only the less-expensive products in the line and shy away from trying to create customer demand and preference for higher margin products.

Western brand names should be retained. Many East bloc consumers are familiar with them, view them (correctly) as being of higher quality than domestic manufactures, and often see their purchase and use as making a political statement. Likewise, Western packaging graph-

---

[33]Stephen J. Simurda, "Opening in the East," *Adweek's Marketing Week,* November 20, 1989, pp. 2–4.

ics should also be retained, but the brand name and usage instructions should be in the local language as well as English. This customization may also discourage cross-border product diversion in items that are being offered initially in Eastern Europe at penetration prices to build brand awareness and loyalty.

The distribution infrastructure in Eastern Europe is weak, so that in most countries initial sales of Western consumer products will be restricted to the major cities. Retail stores are typically unattractive but receptive to simple point-of-sale merchandising aids. Given the difficulties of distributing products intensively and the pent-up demand for any Western consumer goods, the use of mass media advertising is inefficient and unnecessary. In addition, television is not seen as an especially trustworthy medium by many citizens. Advertising regulations impose further constraints; in Hungary products must be available before they can be advertised, and in Czechoslovakia advertising messages are allowed to focus only on specific product features. Consumer goods companies should, however, look closely at sponsorships of sporting events, such as the World Cup Soccer Championships; East European television coverage will include advertising for the first time in 1990.

Consumer goods companies can usefully distribute free product samples at trade fairs. Colgate-Palmolive has found Moscow consumers willing to queue for hours to obtain them, so handbills with information on product usage and the rest of the Colgate line are handed to the waiting crowds. Small and large industrial companies can also reach a broad East European audience by exhibiting their products at the international trade fairs held each year in Leipzig, Budapest, and other East bloc industrial centers. Xerox spends 40% of its East European communications budget on trade shows. In addition, advertising in the industry trade journals can be productive; although dull, they are widely and thoroughly read.[34]

Finally, Western companies must remember that market research is unfamiliar. The closest thing to a market survey that many East Europeans have experienced is a government interrogation. Preliminary consumer research can sometimes usefully be conducted among the relevant ethnic immigrant populations in the United States.[35]

---

[34]Brian Barr, "Breaking into the Bloc," *Business Traveler*, December 1987, pp. 23–27.

[35]Mark Landler, "Mad Ave Takes the Perestroika Challenge," *Business Week*, March 5, 1990, p. 68.

Organizing

Depending on their level of interest and commitment, U.S. companies are organizing their East European marketing efforts in different ways. One option is a group at European headquarters. Digital Equipment Corp., for example, houses its East European sales and marketing staff at European headquarters in Paris. This approach ensures that the East European strategy is integrated in the company's West European strategy, recently revamped to address the emergence of the integrated market in 1992. One problem with this approach is that, in the short term, senior Pan-European management may give the East European business opportunity insufficient attention because of its modest size.

A second approach is to assign the East European opportunity to an international business development group. Colgate-Palmolive's group, based at U.S. headquarters in New York, has like others valuable depth of experience in negotiating joint ventures, strategic alliances, and licensing arrangements around the world. In addition, such a group will be able to champion the East European opportunity as an important priority.

It is, however, worth noting that some of the best-known U.S. company joint ventures in Eastern Europe were not initiated from corporate headquarters partly because of strained U.S.–Soviet relations in the early 1980s. For example, McDonald's Canadian unit and Tambrands' U.K. subsidiary identified the opportunities and led the negotiations for their joint ventures.

A third, widely used, approach is to attach a sales office for Eastern Europe to the Austrian or Swiss country subsidiary. Austria is well placed geographically to act as a financial services bridgehead into Eastern Europe. In addition, bank credits for trade with Eastern Europe are readily available from Austria since such trade accounts for 9% and 7% of total Austrian imports and exports, respectively, much higher than the corresponding EC averages. Gillette sells into Hungary from its Austrian subsidiary. PepsiCo houses in Vienna its quality control engineers who travel to inspect its East European plants, thereby circumventing the difficulty of enticing executives to live in poorly developed East bloc countries. However, the opportunistic Austrian sales office is an increasingly inadequate approach for companies wishing to penetrate Eastern Europe. Competition is prompting companies to establish representative offices in East European capitals to project a visible presence and long-term commitment and to garner goodwill. Honeywell, for example, with 1989 sales of $50 million in Eastern Europe, has opened offices in Warsaw, Prague, and Bratislava, supplementing its existing joint venture operations in Russia, Bulgaria, and East Germany. Greater decentralization of decision-making authority in procurement is also requiring a stronger local presence; for this reason, ICI has recently had to set up an office in Kiev to supplement its Moscow office.

In many companies, including Colgate-Palmolive, the East German market is addressed as a special case outside the international business development group by the West German country subsidiary. With reunification imminent, this approach seems appropriate.

In addition to assessing the merits of alternative organization approaches, U.S. companies planning on business in Eastern Europe should check whether they are already employing personnel with relevant language skills and ethnic backgrounds who can be appropriately reassigned. The importance of these assets cannot be underestimated, as there is a shortage of qualified interpreters. The fact that the leader of U.S. West's negotiating team was born in Hungary doubtless helped the company to win a contract to establish a cellular phone system in that country. Interestingly, managers with West European experience are not necessarily always well equipped to handle business with the East. Managers who have worked in the unpredictable, bureaucratic, high-inflation environments of Latin America are often more likely to have the appropriate "street smarts" and resourcefulness.

SEIZING THE OPPORTUNITY

Increased East–West Trade

In 1960, COMECON accounted for 3.7% of both EC exports and imports but, by 1988, the figures were 3.6% and 3.0%, respectively. A similar trend was evident for U.S.–COMECON trade. This decrease in trade was due to the increasing technological gap between East and West, bureaucratic red-tape, progressive obsolescence of manufacturing process technology resulting in an inability to supply manufactured goods that were salable in the West, COCOM restrictions, and the price depression of the raw materials used in countertrade.

Given the low trade base, the need for East European countries to restructure, and the consequent redirection of resources from military expenditures, a significant increase in East–West trade seems certain. However, trade *among* the COMECON countries will still predominate in the short term.[36] There are five reasons for this. First, the quality of

---

[36]Tim Carrington, "East Bloc to Transform COMECON, Retain Economic Ties to Moscow," *Wall Street Journal*, January 10, 1990, p. A8.

many East European goods is so low that they will be able to find markets only in other East bloc countries. Second, Hungary, Poland, and other countries have ruble surpluses with the USSR that can be balanced only through continued trade. Third, COMECON trade relationships are based largely on long-term agreements of up to 20 years. Fourth, certain industrial technologies (such as printing) have evolved differently within the East bloc such that only East European firms can provide the appropriate maintenance, spare parts, and upgrades. Fifth, hard currency convertibility will devalue existing consumer savings, while the phasing out of state subsidies will result in price increases for domestically produced goods. There will be an acute shortage of hard currency with which to buy Western goods pending economic restructuring.

The USSR's Ryzhkov plan of December 1989 suggested that COMECON members begin trading at world market prices by 1991. This proposal was motivated by the fact that the Soviets pay higher than real market prices for the goods they import from Hungary, Poland, and Czechoslovakia in return for Soviet oil. The Soviet proposal, if implemented, would accelerate the demise of COMECON because COMECON members will wish to limit the hard currency allocated to purchases within COMECON.

Western companies involved in joint ventures should monitor COMECON developments closely. A rapid disintegration of COMECON will jeopardize the East European exports of some state-run industrial enterprises with which partnership agreements have been signed.

Role of American Business

In some West European capitals, a European version of the Monroe Doctrine is evident. The East European problem (and opportunity) is viewed primarily as Western Europe's business. The U.S. government, facing a severe budget deficit, has gladly ceded leadership to Brussels on the economic rehabilitation of Eastern Europe and seems content to focus on Czechoslovakia and Poland as its pet projects. The U.S. government is taking a cautious approach to participation in the proposed European Bank for Reconstruction and Development, fearing that it will lend to and thereby prop up state-run enterprises; the United States wishes to focus its aid on developing the private sector.

Nevertheless, there are important geopolitical and competitive reasons why American capital must participate significantly and broadly in the East European development effort:

- The permanent eradication of communism in Western Europe requires the emergence of viable alternative market-based economies. This can occur only with an infusion of risk capital.
- The United States is lagging the EC in opening up trade with Eastern Europe. The EC has trade agreements with Hungary, Poland, and the USSR to reduce or phase out quotas on their exports to the EC. By contrast, not until December 1989 did the United States grant the USSR most favored nation trading status.
- East European government officials do not wish the foreign capital investments in their countries to be solely West European, even though they may see themselves as Europeans and aspire to eventual EC membership. In particular, the Poles and Czechs wish to avoid being dominated by West German capital. They are seeking a balanced infusion of capital from multiple sources, including the United States. Though the East bloc accounted for only 0.3% of Japanese world trade in 1989, Japanese companies are rapidly buying their way into Eastern Europe on the coattails of substantial government aid. Japan was second only to West Germany in economic assistance to the East bloc in 1989; the United States ranked ninth. Japan has an ongoing border dispute with the USSR, but the ten major Japanese trading houses have small offices in every East bloc country.[37] Despite strained diplomatic relations, South Korean companies have also been aggressively scouting joint venture manufacturing opportunities in Eastern Europe.

There is no doubt that U.S. business will be playing "catch up" in Eastern Europe. For example, only 30 out of 650 international business partnerships in Hungary involve U.S. companies. On the bright side, U.S. trade with Eastern Europe increased from $2.5 billion in 1987 to $6.5 billion in 1989. U.S. business is justifiably excited by the magnitude of the investment and trade opportunity. While caution is in order, it is essential that U.S. business not concede this promising new market to Western European and Asian competition.

---

[37] *The Economist*, "Window Shopping," February 17, 1990, pp. 97–98.

CHAPTER 14

An Action Agenda for Managers

Historians of future generations will, we believe, recognize 1992 as an important date in European economic development. With the benefit of hindsight, the main effects of market integration will no doubt be clear: lower costs of doing business, enhanced efficiency, and a higher rate of economic growth. The connections between these effects and the changes that are currently under way may seem straightforward. But for present-day managers who will, in the final analysis, make the benefits of 1992 come to pass, life is not so simple. Harmonizing product standards, for example, may make it easier for a company like Chloride Lighting to expand its operations throughout Europe. But how should the executives responsible for Chloride Lighting respond to this change? Should they make acquisitions, form joint ventures, rationalize manufacturing, or devise new systems of distribution?

The case studies presented in Chapters 4–12 make it abundantly clear that the process of market integration is creating important new opportunities and threats for companies both within and outside the EC. To take advantage of the opportunities and defend against the threats, managers must reconsider their strategies and, eventually, take actions. Passively waiting to "see what happens" is not, we believe, an adequate response.

How should managers go about responding to the changes associated with the 1992 program? We suggest that managers take the following steps:

- Assess the likely effects of the 1992 reforms on their specific industries.
- Make sure that their companies' interests are adequately represented as new standards and regulations are developed in Brussels and, later, in individual national capitals.
- Consider, or reconsider, the strategic options open to their firms in light of the anticipated effects of market integration.
- Explore possible changes in marketing programs and marketing organization that will be needed to carry out a chosen strategy.

403

Each of these "action agenda" topics is discussed in the sections that follow.

ASSESS THE LIKELY EFFECTS OF 1992 REFORMS

As we have suggested in Chapter 3, the structures of some industries will be more affected than those of others by the 1992 reforms. For example, the EC is keen to improve its global competitiveness in telecommunications and other high-technology areas in which it suffered a net trade deficit of $10 billion in 1988; harmonization of standards and the opening of government contracts to competitive bidding are especially likely in such industries. On the other hand, industries such as airframe manufacture which have already become global in scope will be little affected by 1992. Also affected to a lesser degree will be industries like textiles, where national differences in products and marketing practices stem largely from variations in consumer needs and climate, rather than from the existence of trade barriers. These differences will presumably persist after 1992. *Exhibit 14.1* presents a checklist of criteria that permit

EXHIBIT 14.1 Criteria for assessing the industry impact of 1992

Industries that will be *most* affected by 1992 are those which are:
- Open to exploitation of incremental scale economies
- Subject to excess capacity
- Dependent on high research and development investment
- Responsive to large-scale advertising and promotion
- Vulnerable to strong competition from North America and Asia
- Currently impeded by significant intra-EC trade barriers
- Subject to cross-border price differences
- Affected by EC directives already passed or proposed
- Aware of the need for change

Industries that will be *least* affected by 1992 are those which are:
- Already global in competitive scope *or*
- Subject to strong national consumer preferences
- Not much constrained by existing intra-EC trade barriers
- So politically sensitive (e.g., pharmaceuticals) that removal of barriers may be hard to implement
- Protected by national regulations that are not affected by the 1992 reforms

managers to assess the degree to which their industries will be affected by market integration.

Managers should try to assess the likely future structures of their industries in the post-1992 EC marketplace. Will the industry become much more concentrated? What will be the key requirements for survival as a major player: low production costs, efficient logistics or information systems, large-scale marketing, critical mass in R&D, or some combination of these? What minimum market share will be required for profitability in the future? Will viable market niches for smaller, specialized competitors emerge and, if so, what will these niches be?

To assess likely changes in their industries, many managers will require substantially more and better *information* about their (actual or potential) customers and competitors in the EC. This point is illustrated by several of the case studies:

- Chloride Lighting (Chapter 7), like many other companies that have focused on a single national market, had very little information about prospective EC competitors, buying practices, or methods of distribution.
- Biokit (Chapter 6) and David Del Curto S. A. (Chapter 10) relied on agents or large OEM customers to handle their sales and distribution in major EC countries. This approach can be very efficient, but both companies were effectively insulated from contact with or knowledge about end users and competitive developments.

Large multinationals that actively participate in the EC countries are, of course, typically well informed about their markets. But smaller companies, or those that are primarily oriented to a single country, must find ways to become more fully informed. Much of the needed information can be obtained from public sources, including the European Commission's new network of 1992 information offices, and also from syndicated market studies and trade journals. Some kinds of information, however, can only be secured through special studies.

ADEQUATE REPRESENTATION OF COMPANY INTERESTS

The process of establishing product standards, commercial regulations, and other 1992 reforms has been under way since 1985. As of mid-1989, roughly half of the 279 White Paper proposals had been approved or had at least reached the stage of a "common position" among the

European Council.[1] Even after the Council has finished its work, the 1992 reforms must be incorporated into national laws in the various EC countries and then put into practice. Thus, even after 1992, the legislative and administrative agency rule-making process will continue.

Managers should take steps to see that their companies' interests are represented in both the EC and national rule-making processes and in the subsequent enforcement procedures. For many, this will require new or expanded lobbying efforts or legal representation. Smaller companies will rely primarily on their industry associations for representation; many large companies have already begun aggressive lobbying programs in Brussels.[2]

CONSIDER OR RECONSIDER STRATEGIC OPTIONS

Among multinational firms that are well established in the EC, the need to reconsider basic business strategies in light of 1992 seems to be generally recognized. This is reflected in the stepped-up pace of mergers and acquisitions since 1985, as well as in the programs that are under way in many large firms for rationalizing their production and logistics systems. Managers of other companies, too, should reconsider their strategies for competing in the EC marketplace, including those companies — like Chloride Lighting — that only export to EC customers on a small scale. The danger for these kinds of firms is that more aggressive competitors will make pre-emptive moves to tie up distribution channels or otherwise gain important "first-mover" advantages in the post-1992 marketplace.

The strategic options that are reasonable for a company depend, naturally, on its current position in the EC market. In *Exhibit 14.2* we outline the most likely alternatives for four types of companies: those based within the EC that already operate in most countries; those with a single-country focus within the EC; non-EC companies with a strong position in the EC; and non-EC companies with relatively weak market positions.

U.S. multinationals like Ford and IBM have long histories of manufacturing and marketing in the EC and are seen by many Europeans

---

[1]*The Economist*, July 8, 1989, p. 11.

[2]Michael Bartholomew and Brooks Tigner, "Lobbying Brussels to Get What You Need for 1992," *Wall Street Journal/Europe*, January 31, 1989, p. 7.

as local companies or at least as good European corporate citizens. In preparing for the post-1992 market, they may enjoy an advantage over many EC companies of having long viewed Europe — perhaps mistakenly — as a single market. The Japanese, on the other hand, have invested less heavily in Europe. As illustrated by the Nissan case study (Chapter 9), Japanese automobile and financial services companies in particular are now scrambling to establish a more convincing insider status before 1992. Meanwhile, the objective of many European multinationals is to achieve a more balanced European sales mix rather than have a dominant share in their home markets and smaller shares in the other EC countries.

For many smaller companies like Chloride Lighting (Chapter 7), Biokit (Chapter 6), and Nokia-Mobira Oy (Chapter 5), the immediate concern is that of achieving a sufficient scale of operations in the EC — either through mergers or strategic partnerships — to survive in the more competitive environment that is expected in the 1990s and beyond. Others, like FNAC (Chapter 11), are responding to 1992 by exploring the potential for exporting their innovative retail concepts to other countries just as, at the same time, they are having to defend their domestic market shares against new foreign competition.

EXPLORE NEEDED CHANGES IN MARKETING

For many firms, the post-1992 EC environment will dictate changes in competitive strategies. These strategic changes, in turn, will often require new functional strategies for manufacturing or operations, such as relocation or consolidation; for information systems; and for other functions. Here, we are concerned with the kinds of modifications that may be appropriate for companies' marketing programs and organization structures. Developing the right marketing policies — especially those dealing with product lines, pricing, distribution, and marketing communications — will be critical to a firm's success in the next decade. In many cases, changes in organization structure will also be vital, either for purposes of developing adequate strategic focus or for achieving lower costs.

To determine the kinds of changes that are most likely to take place in marketing as a result of the 1992 reforms, we conducted an informal survey among prospective and actual participants in two Harvard Business School executive programs during June 1989. We obtained 160 usable responses from these executives, all of whom had five years or

EXHIBIT 14.2 1992 Strategic planning matrix

Headquarters location	Current position	Alternative strategies	Comments
EC Companies	Single-country focus	■ Consolidate domestic market position through mergers, acquisitions, alliances. ■ Identify local market niches and tailor products/services to local needs. ■ Sell out to an expanding Pan-European company. ■ Become a Pan-European company by identifying a specialized customer segment with common needs throughout Europe. ■ Become an OEM supplier in multiple markets to Pan-European companies.	■ Vulnerable to larger European competitors. ■ Vulnerable to lower-priced standard Euro-products.
	Pan-European	■ Fill in gaps in European product/market portfolios (via acquisitions, alliances) to create a more strategically balanced Pan-European company. ■ Develop European plan in context of global strategy.	■ Sales of many so-called Pan-European companies are today weighted heavily toward the headquarters country market. ■ Avoid European-myopia as markets become more global.

Non-EC Companies		
Weak EC representation	■ Consolidate domestic market position. ■ Establish alliances with EC firms (especially for mutual distribution of products). ■ Sell out to EC firm expanding overseas. ■ Establish initial or additional offices and manufacturing plants within EC before 1992. Acquire or invest if large company; joint venture if small company.	■ Stronger European competitors will attempt further penetration of non-EC markets. ■ Easier to penetrate multiple EC countries with trade barriers removed. ■ EC protectionism, local contender and reciprocity requirements may impede exports into EC after 1992.
Strong EC representation	■ Fill in gaps in European product/market portfolios to become even more strategically balanced.	■ Already see EC as one market — need to consolidate further as EC companies develop same perception.

more of experience in marketing and/or general management. Two-thirds of the respondents worked for companies based in the United States, and one-fifth worked for EC-based companies. The remainder of the respondents worked for organizations headquartered elsewhere in the world. While the sample of respondents was not randomly drawn, we believe that the results are nevertheless indicative of the kinds of changes that experienced managers expect during the next few years.

We supplied the respondents to our survey with a list of possible changes in the EC marketplace and asked them to rate each item on a 5-point scale ranging from "very unlikely" at one end to "certain" at the other. Combining the two highest points on this response scale, we can compare the percentages of the sample that viewed each possible change as being "likely" — that is, rated it either "4" or "5" in terms of likelihood. Thus, for example, the percentages of respondents who thought that "a few leading competitors will control a bigger share of the EC market" were as follows: U.S.-based, 63%; EC-based, 77; total sample, 67. Similarly, the percentages rating it likely that "There will be more cross-border mergers and acquisitions" were: U.S.-based, 75%; EC-based, 93%; total sample, 80%. The respondents to our survey, in other words, agreed strongly with our assessment (outlined in Chapter 3) that industry concentration in the EC will increase, and that this will take place in part through mergers and acquisitions.

A combination of increased industry concentration, harmonization of product and service standards, and other changes that are going on in the EC can be expected to lead to significant changes in marketing programs. What changes are most likely? The opinions of our survey respondents regarding product policies and pricing are summarized in *Exhibit 14.3*. Here we show, as before, the percentages of the respondents who rated each possible change as "likely" or "certain."

Among the changes seen as most likely are growth in standardized "Euro-products" and equalization of prices among EC markets. A majority of the respondents also expect that the variety of products and services available to EC customers will increase and that new products will grow in importance. On the other hand, fewer than half predict increases in R&D spending or reductions in average EC price levels. Both of these outcomes are stated goals of the 1992 reforms; the implication of the survey results is that these goals may be hard ones to achieve.

Prospective changes in distribution methods, selling, advertising, and sales promotion are listed in *Exhibit 14.4*. As the exhibit shows,

Index

EXHIBIT 14.3 Managers' assessments of prospective changes in product policy and development and pricing in the EC marketplace

Possible changes	% Rating likely		
	U.S.-based	EC-based	Total sample
Product policy & development:			
Standardized Euro-products will increase in importance	62%	60%	60%
Product line variation will be reduced (for a given supplier)	37	33	34
On average, product variety available to customers will increase	63	54	55
New products will increase (as a % of sales)	50	53	52
R&D spending will increase (as a % of sales)	43	34	39
Pricing:			
Prices will tend to equalize among EC countries	57	61	60
Average EC prices will decrease	40	36	37
"Grey marketing" will increase	40	21	27
Marketers will increase the use of deals as a means of varying prices	53%	69%	61%

nearly three-quarters of the EC-based respondents to our survey expect lower distribution costs, increased cross-border purchasing, and growth in Pan-European distributors and retailers in the post-1992 era. Interestingly, only a slight majority expect significant growth in Pan-European advertising media or campaigns, and only a third anticipate rising advertising-to-sales ratios.

Finally, the views of our survey respondents on possible changes in marketing organization are displayed in *Exhibit 14.5*. As expected, the overwhelming majority anticipate a greater role for Pan-European product line managers and for regional headquarters groups. A clear implication of these shifts, if they come to pass, is a reduction in the autonomy of individual country organizations.

EXHIBIT 14.4 Managers' assessments of prospective changes in distribution, advertising, and sales promotion in the EC marketplace

Prospective changes	% Rating likely		
	U.S.-based	EC-based	Total sample
Distribution:			
Fewer distribution centers will be needed to serve the EC.	59%	73%	63%
Costs of transport and warehousing will be reduced.	57	73	60
Cross-border cooperative buying by dealers and distributors will increase.	61	73	64
Pan-European retailers and distributors will become more common.	59	73	64
Direct marketing will grow.	50	53	51
Advertising and sales promotion:			
Pan-European advertising media will grow in importance.	58	57	56
Standardized European advertising campaigns will become more widespread.	53	57	54
Advertising expenditures (as a % of sales) will increase.	46	33	42
Sales promotion costs (as a % of sales) will increase.	53%	47%	49%

EXHIBIT 14.5 Managers' assessments of prospective changes in marketing organization in the EC

Prospective changes	% Rating likely		
	U.S.-based	EC-based	Total sample
Pan-European product line managers will play a more important role	77%	80%	78%
European regional headquarters will play a more important role	74	76	75
Managers will more frequently work in several EC countries during their careers	81	77	80

CONCLUDING COMMENTS

The prospect of a unified EC market has already stimulated changes in companies' competitive strategies, most visibly mergers and acquisitions. Many other companies are still in [the process] of discussing and exploring the strategic opportunities [and problems] posed by the 1992 reforms.

As we have noted in Chapter 2, most of the changes incl[uded in the] 1992 program will not in themselves lead to increased co[mpetition or] enhanced efficiency. Instead, the changes (once adopted) w[ill fa]*cilitate*, or *stimulate* new strategies for firms that compete in [the mar]ketplace. To some extent, managers are changing (or will ch[ange their] strategies simply because the publicity surrounding 1992 h[as created a] "climate" of change. On the other hand, some of the goals [of the 1992] program may not be achieved, or only partially achieved, be[cause man]agers do not view them as necessary or desirable. In other [words, the] actual effects of market integration will depend on manag[ers' percep]tions of the changing environment as well as the "economi[c logic" that] was employed by the architects of the 1992 program. If this [logic is] correct, the management opinions summarized in Exhibit[s 14.4] and 14.5 provide valuable clues regarding likely directions [of market] change in the years ahead.

According to an old adage, in times of change there are [three kinds] of managers:

- Those who make things happen;
- Those who adapt to what has happened; and
- Those who wonder what *did* happen.

As companies respond to the challenges of 1992, we expe[ct all] three kinds of management behavior. We expect the bigges[t winners] in this process to be those who make things happen — bu[t only after] careful study and thought.